A HISTORY OF THE
ULSTER UNIONIST PARTY

Published in our
centenary year
~ 2004 ~
MANCHESTER
UNIVERSITY
PRESS

MANCHESTER STUDIES IN MODERN HISTORY
General editor Jeremy Black

ALREADY PUBLISHED

British foreign policy, 1919–39
Paul W. Doerr

Poverty and welfare in England, 1700–1850
Steven King

Making sense of the Industrial Revolution
Steven King and Geoffrey Timmins

British fascism, 1918–39
Thomas Linehan

Origins of the Second World War
Victor Rothwell

A HISTORY OF THE ULSTER UNIONIST PARTY

PROTEST, PRAGMATISM AND PESSIMISM

Graham Walker

MANCHESTER
UNIVERSITY PRESS
Manchester and New York

distributed exclusively in the USA by Palgrave

Published by Manchester University Press
Oxford Road, Manchester M13 9NR, UK
and Room 400, 175 Fifth Avenue, New York, NY 10010, USA
www.manchesteruniversitypress.co.uk

Distributed exclusively in the USA by
Palgrave, 175 Fifth Avenue, New York,
NY 10010, USA

Distributed exclusively in Canada by
UBC Press, University of British Columbia, 2029 West Mall,
Vancouver, BC, Canada V6T 1Z2

British Library Cataloguing-in-Publication Data
A catalogue record for this book is available from the British Library

Library of Congress Cataloging-in-Publication Data applied for

ISBN 0 7190 6108 3 *hardback*
ISBN 0 7190 6109 1 *paperback*

First published 2004

13 12 11 10 09 08 07 06 05 04   10 9 8 7 6 5 4 3 2 1

Printed in Great Britain
by Bell & Bain Ltd, Glasgow

For Alexander

CONTENTS

PREFACE

This is a study of a political party that grew out of the particular circumstances surrounding 'the Irish question' in the late nineteenth and early twentieth centuries. It is about a party that came to represent – and pursue – the political project of a community arguably best described as either an ethno-religious or an ethno-national entity. The 'ethnic' designation would appear at any rate indispensable, given the capacity of the group in question, the Ulster Protestants, to meet the relevant criteria.[1] Put starkly, this community can be viewed as having developed, since at least the mid-nineteenth century, a distinctive social profile and a consciousness of a common history and culture drawing heavily on religious variables.

A historical appreciation of the Ulster Unionist Party must take account of the interaction between political processes and ideology on the one hand, and questions centring on community identity and cohesion on the other. This study will endeavour to demonstrate awareness of the relationship of the Ulster Unionist political movement to its constituency: it will acknowledge the constraints that this relationship imposed and the parameters that it established within which political behaviour has to be assessed and political successes and failures evaluated. However, it will also be concerned with questions pertaining to the transcendence of such boundaries and the consequent political results. An analysis of the Ulster Unionist Party thus involves investigation into the ways in which a community's perception of itself, its past and its future finds political expression over time.

As the book goes to press, the results of the election for the Northern Ireland Assembly of 26 November 2003 have tilted the balance within Ulster Unionism away from the party which forms the subject of this study. Nevertheless, its leader, David Trimble, has vowed that it will resume its position as the main voice of Unionism in the near future. His leadership position is precarious as he struggles to frustrate the ambitions of internal challengers and to lead Unionism out of the 'dreamland' which he believes many within this community inhabit (Ulster Television interview, 28 November). This book thus seeks to provide an informed historical and contemporary evaluation of the Ulster Unionist Party at a crucial juncture for this organisation and for Northern Ireland as a political unit.

Note

1 By relevant criteria I am following those set down by A. D. Smith in his *National identity* (London, Penguin, 1991), p. 21; see also A. D. Smith and J. Hutchinson (eds), *Ethnicity* (Oxford, Oxford University Press, 1996), Introduction. Smith lists the following: collective name; myth of common descent; sense of shared history; shared culture; relationship to territory; sense of social identification.

  See also discussion in M. Poole, 'In search of ethnicity in Ireland', in B. Graham (ed.), *In search of Ireland* (London, Routledge, 1997); D. Officer, 'Raising the Ulsterman: blood and battlefields in the creation of an ethno-religious subject', Ph.D. Thesis, Queen's University of Belfast, 1997, ch. 2; S. Bruce, *Conservative Protestant politics* (Oxford, Oxford University Press, 1998), chs 2 and 3.

ACKNOWLEDGEMENTS

The research for this book was greatly assisted by an award from the Arts and Humanities Research Board, and the costs of preparing the manuscript for publication were met in part by a grant from the Publications Fund of the Queen's University of Belfast. My sincere thanks to Michelle McComb for her professionalism.

I am grateful to the officers of the Ulster Unionist Council for permission to see sections of the organisation's vast archive.

My 'handlers' at Manchester University Press, Jonathan Bevan and Alison Welsby, were models of patience and cooperation, and I am grateful to the press's anonymous reader for the advice tendered.

I am indebted to Ian S. Wood, a friend who selflessly passed on copious material and provided stimulating conversation on Northern Ireland politics. Likewise, I am grateful to John Erskine for his perennially wise musings on history and politics, and his constant encouragement. I was given valuable help by Christopher Farrington and Steven King in the preparation of the appendices, and both shared their thoughts and insights on the subject generously. I was fortunate also to be able to discuss matters at various junctures with Gordon Lucy, Richard English, Paul Bew, Henry Patterson, Jeff Dudgeon, David Officer, Alan Bairner, Esmond Birnie and Ashton Hanna.

Above all I thank Elda and Alexander for tholing day by day the whole excessively protracted exercise.

ABBREVIATIONS

AOH	Ancient Order of Hibernians
APL	Anti-Partition League
BIC	British–Irish Council
CDU	Campaign for Democracy in Ulster
CSJ	Campaign for Social Justice
DUP	Democratic Unionist Party
EEC	European Economic Community
ICTU	Irish Congress of Trade Unions
IIRC	Inter-Irish Relations Committee
INLA	Irish National Liberation Army
IOO	Independent Orange Order
IRA	Irish Republican Army
IRB	Irish Republican Brotherhood
LAW	Loyalist Association of Workers
NICRA	Northern Ireland Civil Rights Association
NIHT	Northern Ireland Housing Trust
NILP	Northern Ireland Labour Party
NUM	New Ulster Movement
PIRA	Provisional Irish Republican Army
PUP	Progressive Unionist Party
RUC	Royal Ulster Constabulary
SDLP	Social Democratic and Labour Party
UDA	Ulster Defence Association
UDP	Ulster Democratic Party
UKUP	United Kingdom Unionist Party
UPA	Ulster Protestant Action
UPL	Ulster Protestant League
UPNI	Unionist Party of Northern Ireland
UPVDA	Ulster Protestant Voters' Defence Association

Abbreviations

USC	Ulster Special Constabulary
UUC	Ulster Unionist Council
UULA	Ulster Unionist Labour Association
UUP	Ulster Unionist Party
UUUC	United Ulster Unionist Council
UUUM	United Ulster Unionist Movement
UVF	Ulster Volunteer Force
UWC	Ulster Workers' Council
VUPP	Vanguard Unionist Progressive Party

CHAPTER ONE

ORIGINS: IRISH HOME RULE AND THE POLITICAL BIRTH OF PROTESTANT ULSTER, 1885–1905

We, the loyal minority, ask for no favours or privileges which we do not wish to share with all our fellow-countrymen of all shades of religious faith and political creed. All we ask for is that we may be permitted to live, as we have lived, under the protection of the British Throne, and as part of this great Empire. (Rev. James Cregan, quoted in G. Lucy, ed., *The Great Convention*, Lurgan, Ulster Society, 1995, p. 29)

The political organisation of Ulster Unionism was the offspring of the broader Irish Unionist movement which emerged to oppose the Nationalist cause of Irish Home Rule.[1] This movement was mobilised on an all-Ireland basis with the single purpose of thwarting a measure of legislative Home Rule for the whole of Ireland and preserving intact the legislative union with Great Britain, in existence since 1800. Irish Unionism campaigned first against the Gladstone Liberal government's Irish Home Rule Bill of 1886, defeated in the House of Commons, and then against the same governing party and Premier's next attempt in 1893, this time overthrown by the House of Lords. The Unionist aim was to preserve the unity and centralist coherence of the United Kingdom state: at one level a civic objective which implied support for the concept of equal citizenship for all.

However, conditions for the launch of Ulster Unionism extended well beyond formal politics and the bounds of a civic United Kingdom nationalism. Account must be taken of the salience of distinctively *Ulster* characteristics. There was, for example, the popularisation from the mid-nineteenth century of an Ulster 'persona' or 'type' befitting the turbulent history of a frontier people in the place apart that was Ulster within the island of Ireland.[2] The most obvious social and cultural feature of the north-east of the island

1

was the concentration of Protestants since the settlements of the seventeenth century, and the religious complexion of the area came to be associated with its industrialisation in the early to mid nineteenth century. In this era Belfast and the Lagan Valley region grew into an economic conurbation resembling Glasgow and Clydeside and Liverpool and Merseyside. To the dynamism of the linen industry was added the imperious prestige of iron, steel, shipbuilding and engineering. 'Ulster', resonantly if glibly, became a by-word for progress, and the uneven development of capitalism on the island of Ireland became a substantial force for political and cultural division.[3]

Protestantism in Ulster, in contrast to the rest of Ireland, possessed a multi-denominational character. In this regard the impact of the Presbyterians has to be stressed: economically through their relative dominance of manufacturing and commerce, and socially and culturally through their theological – and largely Calvinist – *Weltanschauung*.[4] Protestantism's strength in Ulster logically provided the soil for the Orange Order to flourish. This oath-bound society, although linked most strongly to the Episcopalian Church of Ireland and with its headquarters in Dublin, became a popular focus of Ulster Protestant solidarity during the nineteenth century.[5] From its origins during the revolutionary upheavals at the end of the eighteenth century, Orangeism had posed as an ethno-cultural movement in defence of 'the Protestant Constitution',[6] and made a marked impact on the politics of the North long before the Home Rule dramas. The Order was cross-class in its appeal, and its sizeable labouring element was able to exert political leverage through it after the franchise reforms of 1884–85.[7]

The significance of Orange populism is a reminder that religious sectarianism had long been a feature of Ulster politics, and that, predating Home Rule, there had developed a bi-polar struggle between an ultramontanist Catholicism (associated with Irish Nationalist sentiment) on the one hand and evangelical Protestantism (fuelled by seismic events such as the Revival of 1859) on the other.[8] Evangelical Protestantism, in the manner of Orangeism, was important also as a solvent of Protestant fractures, and instrumental in the construction of a collective identity.

Sectarian dichotomies were expressed physically in the residential segregation of working-class Protestants and Catholics in Belfast, and in the many rural communities throughout the Province that were virtually ethnic-exclusive.[9] Religious and cultural differences were magnified as social and economic ones diminished – the hallmark, in the view of one astute commentator, of a 'frontier society' disputed by rival ethnic blocs.[10] Nevertheless, it should not be forgotten, particularly for the purpose of assessing political developments, that the respective Protestant and Catholic blocs were potentially fissiparous, especially around matters of social class. In relation to the Protestants, class divisions often shadowed denominational ones: landlords were overwhelmingly Church of Ireland, and urban businessmen and tenant farmers were largely Presbyterian. Internal tensions were a feature of both Unionism and Nationalism in Ireland. Both movements had in common the fact that they were coalitions of different interests and the subject of competing agendas.

The theme of identity has already been introduced, and its importance as a primary context for the development of Ulster Unionist politics affirmed. It is necessary to explore it further before paying more detailed attention to political events.

Identity questions surrounding Ulster Protestants in the era spanning the Home Rule controversies, from the first bill of 1886 through to the partition of the island of Ireland in 1920, have attracted much scholarly debate and speculation. The contributions of Peter Gibbon and David Miller are cardinal reference points for the more recent contentions of historians such as James Loughlin and Alvin Jackson.[11] Gibbon's Marxist approach to the subject of Ulster Unionism's emergence involves the urban Ulster bourgeoisie assuming leadership of the political movement by the time of the second Home Rule Bill, and shaping it into a form of nationalism, replete with claims of self-determination and cultural distinctiveness. Miller's take on Ulster Unionist distinctiveness, by contrast, is to perceive this community as holding a pre-modern 'contractarian' political outlook rather than any kind of modern concept of national self-determination. Miller pursues the theme of 'conditional loyalty' on the part of Ulster Unionists, arguing that their loyalty to Britain turned on the willingness of the government to uphold their citizenship rights. Primary loyalty, according to Miller, was thus not invested in the state, but in the British crown, and Ulster Unionists' sense of Britishness was more oriented towards Empire.

Out of both Gibbon's and Miller's work emerge themes and ideas inseparable from any evaluation of Ulster Unionist political history: the question of whether Ulster Unionism was a form of nationalism;

the suggestiveness of the concept of contractarianism in relation to Ulster Unionist political theory and practice; the identity puzzle that 'Britishness' has over time represented; the significance of aspects of British identity to Ulster Unionism such as the crown and the Empire. All of these issues echo through the history of the Ulster Unionist Party and invite contextual evaluation.

Loughlin's studies of Ulster Unionism in relation to British national identity have discounted the salience of Ulster nationalism while highlighting the development of the stereotype of the 'Ulsterman' which built on theories of racial categorisation current in Victorian times. The 'Ulsterman' was thus presented as the honest, resolute and resourceful (Protestant) citizen in contradistinction to the disloyal, feckless and treacherous Nationalist (Catholic) Celt. For Loughlin, however, the British national loyalty of Ulster Unionists was unequivocal. He attacks the notion of Ulster 'exceptionalism' at the heart of Miller's thesis, arguing that contractarian ideas permeated other aspects of the makeup of the UK, particularly Scotland's conception of the Union, and that Ulster Unionist Empire enthusiasms were a logical extension of pride in British nationality and not some form of substitute for it. However, notwithstanding his salutary points about the problems of relating Ulster Unionism to arbitrary definitions of British identity, Loughlin's later works deal in precisely the reductionist readings of Britishness he had warned against.[12] Moreover, valuable as Loughlin's observations are on the development of an 'Ulsterman' stereotype, he overstates the degree to which it encompassed baleful representations of rural and agrarian qualities.[13]

Jackson's dissections of Ulster Unionist political organisation point to a more fluid and complex context to which identity matters related. Jackson never loses sight of Unionism's character as a collection of disparate groups and interests and its overriding objective of constructing and maintaining unity to defeat Home Rule. This necessitated a degree of vagueness and equivocation on matters of identity and communal self-definition. Jackson argues, contrary to Gibbon, that there was no middle-class takeover of Ulster Unionism until the early twentieth century, and that an alliance between the landed interest and the urban bourgeoisie (and the Anglicans and Presbyterians accordingly) was crucial to the formative period of Ulster Unionism's political development. Such an alliance served to preserve Unionism's all-Ireland character through the duration of the first and second Home Rule episodes, and a sense of Irish identity – an Irishness felt to be totally compatible with British allegiance and loyalty – was also a significant strand in the Unionist tapestry. Jackson is sceptical about Loughlin's association of Ulster Unionists with an exalted British nationalism, querying the meaningfulness of the latter concept as employed by Loughlin; and Jackson seeks to correct Loughlin's depiction of an overriding British and imperial outlook with a demonstration of how preoccupied Ulster Unionist politicians were instead with fundamentally local Ulster issues. In addition, Jackson takes issue with Loughlin's (and indeed Miller's) dismissal of the idea of Ulster nationalism. Using the criteria set out by Anthony D. Smith,[14] he concludes that the Ulster Unionists could theoretically – and potentially – be regarded as a nation and not merely a British region, although in practice an Ulster nationalism did not develop largely on account of Unionists being inhibited from employing explicitly the language and the idiom of their opponents. Jackson stresses that it made more political sense for Unionists to gear themselves to the negative end of defeating Irish Nationalism, rather than risk divisions in essaying a more positive and affirmative creed.

This scholarly debate stands as a warning against too sweeping generalisations about the nature of Ulster Unionism's politics and identity in the era of its birth. Unionism is in a way prudently viewed as a reaction to a political agenda set by others, and it contrasted with its rival Irish Nationalist movement in terms of romantic rhetoric and visionary zeal. Nevertheless, there were also similarities between the two movements, and Ulster Unionism counted for more than political expediency from its beginnings. In its 'Ulster' manifestation Unionism bore Irish Nationalism's hallmarks of class alliances, religiosity, the politics of populist defiance, the resort to myth-making, and a clamorous appeal to history. And as Unionism became progressively 'Ulsterised', the conflict with Nationalism grew more intractable.

As McBride has observed in his judicious overview of Ulster Unionism's position within modern British and Irish history, Ulster Protestants in the period of the Irish Home Rule bills held, to varying degrees depending on different contexts, British, Irish and Ulster allegiances.[15] It might be said that attachments to the Union, the Empire and the British crown were paramount, but this permits no easy conclusions about British national identity, and an Irish identification was often proclaimed proudly. However, the Nationalist appropriation of Irishness in the political struggles of the era and the association of Irish identity with Catholicism and Gaelic culture increasingly called into question the compatibility of Britishness and Irishness, and made life difficult for those who only felt secure in their Irishness when it was complemented with Britishness. This reflected the fear that Home Rule would ultimately break, or at least impair, the British link.

It was against such a background that the cultivation of a distinctive Ulster identity was driven as a cultural project to serve political ends. The raw materials for this enterprise were in existence long before in the form of 'historical narratives and folktales, poems and songs, customs and rituals'.[16] From the mid-nineteenth century there is striking evidence of a concern to remobilise the past, to capture – in the manner of Sir Walter Scott in Scotland – the living traces of the past believed to have survived in language, dialect and folklore. Just as such activities fuelled the development of an Irish Nationalist consciousness in general, and the Gaelic Revival in particular, the same kind of efforts in the Ulster context proved useful to the countervailing force of Unionism.[17]

Such antiquarianism, though, came merely to accentuate a distinctiveness primarily defined around religion. A binary opposition between 'Protestant Ulster' and 'Catholic Ireland' deepened against the background of the waning intra-Protestant conflict, particularly after the disestablishment of the Church of Ireland in 1869, and the intensifying pan-Protestant rivalry with Catholicism. In this connection the role of the Presbyterians was crucial: their grievances regarding Anglicanism shrank beside the prospect of Catholic Church supremacy in Ireland, a prospect which chilled the radical and liberal congregations of the Presbyterian community as much as the conservative, and which resulted in the bulk of Presbyterian Liberals joining with the Conservatives to oppose Gladstone's bill in 1886. Around the Presbyterian community, moreover, hung the mythology of the 'Ulster-Scots' as a pioneering people who had endured a history of sacrifice and struggle in Ulster and among whose number were those who emigrated to America to make their political and cultural and economic mark in the eighteenth century. In the wake of the Irish Home Rule Bill question's political eruption in 1886 a steady stream of literary texts was produced extolling the special virtues of the Ulster-Scots people; this effort made the 'Ulster-Scot' label in practice interchangeable with that of 'Ulsterman' and helped to embroider the stereotype, in some ways racial, of a uniquely self-willed, self-reliant and indomitable people steeled by a covenanting Calvinist heritage, and not to be bent to the political designs of Catholic Ireland.[18] The latter's historical narrative was thus countered by one in which the same dramatic themes of sacrifice, suffering and resistance were trailed, and Ulster Unionism's ideological repertoire in many respects took on the complexion of contemporaneous nationalism in Ireland and elsewhere.

Ulster Protestants in effect came to feel that their protestations of loyalty to the Union, as Irishmen, were not enough in the political battle against Irish Nationalism. To the civic strain of argument against any change to their British citizenship was added the decidedly ethnic one of an Ulster Protestant distinctiveness with its own right of self-determination, albeit to be held in reserve. Notwithstanding a reluctance to admit to the strength of Irish Nationalist feeling which was unwilling to be incorporated in the manner of the other identities in the UK at the time, there developed a conscious effort to sharpen an Ulster Protestant ethnic profile as a means of countering the political dangers perceived to lie in the Nationalist project. Ulster Unionists appeared to see no inconsistency in dabbling in the ethno-nationalism of 'Ulsterness' while denying the validity of Irish Nationalist claims and invoking notions of the 'higher wisdom' of Britishness.[19]

However, questions of British identity were not straightforward. Ulster Unionist attempts to convince opinion in Britain that they should not be regarded as 'less than British' were made against a background of competing ideas and definitions of Britishness. From the outset Ulster Unionism related ambiguously to concepts of civic British identity which were pluralist and inclusive. Such secular readings of Britishness were offered by Unionists, and the scholarly contributions of Arthur Aughey in recent years have sought to position Unionism as essentially a political doctrine concerned with rights of citizenship within the state.[20] Unionism, Aughey contends, should not be assessed on the same conceptual ground as Nationalism. Unionist politics, for Aughey, have been imbued by rational liberal precepts rather than primordial ethnic passions, and his thesis serves as a reminder that Unionism did not necessarily play on the idea of ethnic difference and was often concerned to couch its opposition to Irish Nationalism in the corresponding civic terms of the day.

Nevertheless, this was only one of its appeals and one mode of argument. The political scientist Jennifer Todd has written of two predominant traditions in Unionist political thought: the 'Ulster

Loyalist' and the 'British Unionist'.[21] Aughey's conception of Unionism promotes the latter, but passes over the practical inter-weaving of rational political discourse with ethno-religious or ethno-nationalist myth-making. From the Home Rule crises of the late nineteenth century onwards Ulster Unionism always oscillated between the universal and the particular, the civic and the ethnic. The cultivation of an Ulster identity might even be regarded as another variant of an ethnic form of Britishness which had at its core the concept of a Protestant crown and constitution and an essentially Protestant 'civilising' Empire.[22]

What is less debatable is that Ulster Unionist opposition to Home Rule highlighted the ambiguities and uncertainties of Britishness.[23] Indeed, the Irish Home Rule issue triggered not only a further twist to the 'Irish question' in political debate but also the 'British Isles question'. Discussion of Ireland's future developed into speculation about possible federal or quasi-federal constitutional arrangements for the UK as a whole; even the idea of imperial fed-eration gained currency.[24] Irish Home Rule provided the pretext for facile notions of the UK as a 'unitary' state to be challenged and alternative decentralist visions to be promoted and discussed. This was a theme which would survive the demise of Irish Home Rule as an issue and continue to be germane to the fortunes of Ulster Union-ism.

In Ulster Unionist history the date 1886 exercises a gravitational pull. The coming together in this year of Conservatives and Liberal Unionists in opposition to Home Rule provided the foundations for what became, almost twenty years later, a formally distinct political organisation.

For some twenty years before this the Liberal–Conservative trial of political strength in Ulster had been absorbing.[25] The Conserva-tives, especially before the introduction of the secret ballot, were electorally the more powerful, but the Liberals were able to make headway around the emotive question of land reform. In the 1870s, in the absence of a strong Home Rule organisation in the North, the Liberals built up considerable support among tenant farmers, both Presbyterian and Roman Catholic, on the platform of tenant rights. In the 1880 election the party won half of Ulster's rural seats, al-though the shine was somewhat taken off the achievement by the Liberals' continuing failure to loosen the Tories' urban strangle-hold. Gladstonian Liberalism held a strong appeal, on the grounds of its assaults on privilege, to the radical strand in Ulster Presbyterianism; but even beyond these circles there was a general feeling among Presbyterians that they did not receive a fair deal in terms of public offices and representation.

However, Presbyterian resentments softened to a significant degree with Church of Ireland disestablishment in 1869, and such reforms confirmed Liberal Presbyterians in their belief that the Gladstonian approach would in short time eradicate the religious and economic inequalities which constituted the 'Irish question' and leave the country contented and prosperous within the Union. The popularity of the tenant rights agitation in fact led the Ulster Conservatives to indicate compliance with the principle of reform when Gladstone introduced his Land Act of 1881.[26]

By then the political waters had been muddied by the impact of the movement for Home Rule led astutely by Charles Stewart Parnell, and the violent upheavals wreaked by the Land League which originated in the West of Ireland. Parnell's leadership transformed the Irish Party at Westminster literally into a show-stopping phenomenon: 'Home Rule' ceased to be the polite aspiration given expression since 1870 by the gentlemanly Isaac Butt and instead assumed the righteous demand of a nation seeking just treatment. The Land League's uprising against an iniquitous system of land ownership was largely fuelled by a similar sense of wider Nationalist grievances. When he took over the leadership of the Irish Parliamentary Party in 1880, Parnell in effect presided over a mass movement in the country encompassing the land agitation, the Catholic Church's agenda, and the revolutionary spirit of the Fenian Brotherhood. Nationalist-Catholic-Ireland was on the march, led by the Protestant Parnell.

Home Rule and Land League activity in Ulster in the early 1880s prompted a response by the Orange Order, and sectarian passions once more flared. Parnellism conjured in Protestant eyes the spectre of O'Connell's mobilisation of the Catholic masses earlier in the century. Then, as now, constitutional concerns and atavistic fears cut across issues of fair treatment. Parnell's linkage of the land question, with its potential for non-sectarian political campaigning, to Home Rule undermined the Ulster Liberal position, although the franchise reforms of 1884, creating as they did an expanded Catholic electorate, may have been the crucial determinant of the Nationalist political impact in Ulster prior to the curtain being raised on Home Rule by Gladstone. Certainly, there was an established trend

of Catholic defections from the Liberals before Gladstone's conver-
sion.[27] The Conservatives, meanwhile, turned franchise extensions
to their advantage through their influence with Orangeism, and
demonstrated their capacity for Parnellite machine politics among
the Protestant electorate. In the early 1880s organisations such as
the Ulster Constitutional Club were set up and would later prove to
be 'organisational pivots' for Ulster Unionism.[28] The 1885 election
resulted in humiliation for the Liberals, in no small measure aided
by Parnell's call on Nationalists to vote tactically for the Conservatives in some seats. A Conservative–Home Rule adversarial pattern
emerged, to be confirmed the following year when, following
Gladstone's raising of the Home Rule standard, Ulster returned 15
Conservatives, 2 Liberal Unionists and 16 Nationalists.[29] Parnell,
by 1885, was the sole Protestant left in the Irish Parliamentary
Party, whose candidates were often selected by the Catholic clergy.[30]
Tory flexibility on land reform reflected the perceived need for
cross-class Protestant unity, although even after 1886 Protestant
tenant farmer groups were active and land issues continued to be a
source of tension between Tories and those former Gladstonian
Liberals who became 'Liberal Unionists' in response to Home Rule.

The latter chose their Unionist future at a meeting in Belfast in
March 1886, and they formed a clear majority of Liberals. A new
Ulster Liberal Unionist Association was established, and its first
President, the prominent Presbyterian layman and Belfast provision
merchant Thomas Sinclair, eloquently conveyed his colleagues'
sense of betrayal over Gladstone's decision to hitch his programme
of 'remedial legislation' to the 'vexed question of Home Rule'.[31]
Businessmen like Sinclair immediately took up the theme of Home
Rule resulting in economic ruin for the industrious, thrifty North,
and the involvement of this business class was to be a crucial component in the development of the anti-Home Rule campaigns and of
Unionism as a political movement.[32] A small group of Liberal Presbyterians remained loyal to Gladstone, and were to be repeatedly
invoked in pro-Home Rule propaganda for years to come.[33] The
Liberal Unionists for their part were vital to the formation of a mass
Unionist response to Parnell and Gladstone. Their adherence to the
anti-Home Rule political front ensured the alliance of the Church of
Ireland landed interest with the Ulster Presbyterian middle class,
and the financial clout of both.[34]

The Ulster Tories were able to enlist the demagogic support of Sir
Randolph Churchill, whose visit to Belfast in February 1886 swiftly

entered Unionist folklore. The Tories also had a strong base among the professional classes, especially lawyers, whose political skills had been well honed in successive election contests. However, the Liberal Unionists brought Presbyterian dissenting energies and popular tenant farmer backing if carefully handled. Their social reformism, as Jackson points out, balanced the raw sectarian Orangeism of the Unionist alliance;[35] and they could call on the backing of the formidable radical figure of Joseph Chamberlain who had broken with Gladstone over Home Rule. Although numerically the junior partner in the alliance, the Liberal Unionists strove effectively to ensure that they were not swallowed up by their Tory and Orange allies.[36] Social radicalism, however, has to be set against a tradition of Irish Whiggery in which, for example, the emerging Irish Unionist leader and landowner Colonel Edward Saunderson was immersed.[37] The course of Irish – and Ulster – Unionism through the first Home Rule Bill episode and beyond was decisively steered by the comparatively modest figure of Saunderson rather than the maverick political heavyweights who revelled in the theatre provided by the anti-Home Rule cause.

The all-Ireland opposition to Home Rule was foreshadowed in 1885 by the formation of the Dublin-based Irish Loyalist and Patriotic Union, an Ulster counterpart of which – the Ulster Loyalist Anti-Repeal Union – appeared the following year. At Westminster the Irish Loyalists pursued a path of parliamentary independence, and took on the appearance of a separate 'Ulster Party' after the December 1885 election at which all but two were returned from the North.[38] However, when Gladstone's bill was introduced in April 1886 the objective of these Irish members was its total defeat: while the issue of the Ulster Protestant community's position was raised in debate on the measure, Irish Unionists were in no way prepared to reach a compromise over Ulster which would allow Home Rule to pass for the rest of Ireland.[39] At the time of the first Home Rule Bill the great majority of Irish Unionist MPs were from the landed class, and the landlord influence – pervasive as it was in the whole of Ireland – continued to tell politically deep into the 1890s.[40]

Unionists thus denied the right of any part of Ireland to Home Rule. The tendency of intellectual argument against Home Rule provided by such figures as the English constitutional lawyer A. V. Dicey was towards the notion of the organic development of the United Kingdom into a 'syncretic state'.[41] Home Rule was viewed as in itself a retrograde concept, at variance with the Whiggish progress of the UK, and potentially destructive of the sovereignty of the Westminster parliament. To such arguments skilful debaters among the Ulster Liberal Unionists like Sinclair added warnings about the dire consequences of Home Rule for the manufacturing and business prosperity of the North-East and the alleged intentions of the Catholic Church to use Home Rule to maximise its power and influence in areas such as education.[42]

Gladstone's measure met a fusillade of parliamentary criticisms – weaknesses on issues such as the question of Irish representation at Westminster after Home Rule and the financial basis of the devolution scheme proposed were ruthlessly exposed[43] – and the defectors from his own side (the Whiggish wing along with the Chamberlainite radicals) ensured its defeat in the House of Commons in June 1886, to great Unionist rejoicing. An election victory for the Conservatives – or 'Unionists' – duly followed.

Though relieved, Irish Unionists remained wary. The popular strength of 'Parnellism' continued to set the tone of Irish political life, and it seemed more than likely that, if returned to power, Gladstone would be obliged to attempt Home Rule all over again. The Irish Unionist MPs at Westminster, under the leadership of Saunderson, conducted an intense parliamentary campaign against Irish Nationalism and supported, with some misgivings on the part of landowners like Saunderson, the Irish chief secretaryship of Arthur Balfour between 1887 and 1891.[44] The Balfour dispensation combined coercive and conciliatory measures, the effects of the latter being far-reaching in terms of state-aided land purchase. Such reforming legislation was acknowledged by Saunderson as necessary for the maintenance of the Unionist alliance in the absence of an immediate Home Rule threat. Unionists were also happy to look on as Parnell was deposed as leader of the Irish Parliamentary Party in 1890 amidst scandal, and 'Parnellite' and 'anti-Parnellite' factions assumed a bitter enmity. In 1891 'the Uncrowned King of Ireland' died, and with him a messianic cult which had chilled his Irish Unionist adversaries. On the other hand there was no noticeable modification in the Unionist perception of Irish Nationalism as a tyrannical dispensation in-waiting, a movement bent on curtailing the benefits of the Union and the British connection, and the rights and liberties of Irish Protestants. Home Rule was always viewed as the route to such a fate, and Irish Unionists could not be persuaded that any legislative safeguards or checks would prove effective.[45]

Unionist unity in anticipation of another Home Rule threat was put yet more securely in place with a carefully stage-managed show of strength and resolve in Belfast in June 1892. The 'Ulster Convention', as it was called, brought together Unionists of all classes, denominations and political leanings.[46] It sought to answer Gladstonian Liberal and Irish Nationalist accusations that Unionism was the creed of a narrow landed elite clinging on to privileges and duping Orange workers with sectarian appeals. Some speeches were notably conciliatory towards Catholics, and the use of 'Erin go Bragh' as one slogan on the Convention Pavilion indicated an enduring pride in Irish identity. Conscious of Presbyterian Liberal opinion in Scotland, and Nonconformist Protestant radicalism in England, Thomas Sinclair used his speech to cite the record of Liberal Unionists like himself struggling alongside Catholics in the past for justice and equality. Sinclair's contribution, however, was also notable for the pledge of Unionist civil disobedience and passive resistance in the event of a Dublin parliament being imposed on them.[47] This was in effect the extent of the threats of resistance uttered by Unionists, notwithstanding darker hints of force, but it would probably have been counterproductive in relation to British opinion to appear to threaten violence openly. Out of the Convention there developed an Ulster Convention League, followed in 1893 by the Unionist Clubs movement and the Ulster Defence Union.[48]

It is plausible to view the Convention as a key moment in the 'Ulsterisation' of the anti-Home Rule campaign, an event which helped sharpen the consciousness of difference on the part of Ulster Protestants and awareness of their 'front-line' position in relation to the central question of Ireland's future direction. However, it arguably represented the ripening of such a collective sense of identity rather than its birth; and it was not the occasion on which the urban bourgeoisie took custody of the Unionist political project.[49] While it was an event geared to Unionist consensus, there was nonetheless a distinct Presbyterian and Liberal Unionist flavour to it, and it was a significant precedent for future Ulster initiatives.[50]

The general election of 1892 brought the Liberals back to office with Irish Nationalist help, but the position of the Irish Unionists was strengthened: 23 seats were won, 19 of them in Ulster. One of the Dublin University seats was won by a young Liberal Unionist lawyer by the name of Edward Carson. Another Dublin constituency was captured by a Roman Catholic Liberal Unionist, an indication of the greater equanimity towards religion among Southern Unionists in contrast to their Northern colleagues. Gladstone's overall majority was only 40 but he pressed on with another Home Rule measure. His bill, introduced in February 1893, differed in several respects from the first,[51] but failed to provide convincing answers to such problems as future Irish representation and voting rights at Westminster. No special provision was made for Ulster. As in 1886 Unionists set their sights on the bill's total defeat, an eventuality secured this time by the House of Lords' right of veto. Unionists, as previously, argued that rejection of Home Rule was essential to harmony in Ireland as a whole, but there was more debating capital made this time out of the prospect of the coercion of the coherent Protestant Unionist community in Ulster. Such were the themes of, for example, Arthur Balfour and Lord Salisbury's orations in Ireland at the time of the second Home Rule Bill.[52] Ulster in a sense now defined the terms of the Home Rule debate, notwithstanding Gladstonian Liberal and Irish Nationalist dismissals of what were claimed to be its special features.

Concomitantly, it was Ulster which witnessed the most intense and enthusiastic demonstrations against the bill, protest meetings sometimes organised by Unionist women's groups, another feature of the broader-based and more democratic Ulster mobilisation.[53] In addition, a vigorous extra-parliamentary propaganda campaign in Britain was undertaken and financed by Unionist businessmen, and a Belfast Chamber of Commerce deputation was granted an audience with Gladstone himself.[54] The Prime Minister's brusque response to their entreaties was probably less important than the publicity garnered. The defeat of the bill sparked spectacular rejoicing among Ulster Protestants, which led in some places to violent clashes with Nationalists. The populism, acerbity and volatility which Ulster Unionism had come distinctively to represent widened the gulf between Northern and Southern Unionism, and strained relations with British Unionist politicians, notwithstanding the willingness of the latter to help inflame passions at times of crisis such as 1886 and 1893.

Gladstone retired after his Home Rule failure and a short lame duck Liberal administration under Lord Rosebery followed. A general election in 1895 brought Salisbury's Conservatives/Unionists to power and for the next decade there were to be notable reforms passed in a bid to resolve the Irish problem without calling into question the Union. This was the era of the secretaryships of Gerald

Balfour and George Wyndham, a time of 'Constructive Unionism' which brought a substantial extension of state-aided land purchase, local government reorganisation, agricultural development and technical education.[55] It was an era which also posed dilemmas for Irish Unionists in their desire to maintain unity in the absence for the moment of constitutional alarms.

Land reform was the most piquant case in point. The measures were designed to benefit the tenant farmers and they signalled the decline of landlordism in Ireland. Perhaps the key legislation in this respect, coming on top of several Liberal and Tory government measures since the 1880s, was the Wyndham Land Act of 1903, which went a substantial way towards the creation of a farmer proprietorship in Ireland. However, loss of landlord standing and influence, given this class's importance to the movement, posed a threat to the overall influence wielded by Unionism. On the other hand, for Unionism to throw its weight behind landlord resistance to reform would have been to threaten grassroots revolt among tenant farmers in Ulster.[56] As it was, Colonel Saunderson's truculent defence of his class at Westminster provoked the Ulster Liberal Unionist MP for South Tyrone and land reformer T. W. Russell to put himself at the head of the farmer agitation.[57] More moderate Liberal Unionists like Sinclair saw the dangers of splits in the Unionist alliance, and were anxious to keep landlord influence alive and well while proceeding gradually with reforms.[58]

Along with land purchase, local government reforms had been the main item in the Liberal Unionist prescription for Ireland's ills, and here too Salisbury's government delivered with the Act of 1898 which democratised local councils. In practice, however, this meant the immediate transfer of power to Nationalists in many areas, and Unionists – Conservative and Liberal – duly fretted about the possibility that the reform could lead to abuse of Unionist rights. Nevertheless, it was felt that by giving Irishmen the same control over local affairs as Englishmen and Scotsmen the cause of Home Rule would come to be viewed as superfluous.[59]

'Constructive Unionism' was also a label given to the work of Sir Horace Plunkett, a Liberal Unionist MP for South Dublin between 1892 and 1900 who championed rural cooperatives among other progressive ventures. The Ulster Liberal Unionists Thomas Sinclair and linen baron Thomas Andrews joined Plunkett's 'Recess Committee' on agriculture and technical education along with Parnellite Nationalists.[60] The work of the Committee was criticised by Saunderson, who, along with the Conservative Irish Unionist members, viewed Plunkett's activities in general with grave suspicion. As his biographer has argued, Saunderson's opposition to the forms of Liberal Unionism represented by both Russell and Plunkett left him by 1900 'merely the captain of a Conservative fragment of Unionism'.[61]

In the early years of the new century Saunderson's weaknesses were exposed by the continuing threat to Unionist unity posed by Russell's land campaign and an outbreak of urban Protestant working-class disaffection led by a hitherto obscure shipyard worker. The former wreaked the greater electoral havoc, 'Russellite' candidates standing successfully in by-elections in 1902 and 1903. Their platform was the demand that landlords be compelled to sell up and facilitate the wholesale transfer of land to the tenant farmers. The Wyndham Act of 1903 stopped short of this, but its far-reaching provisions satisfied the bulk of the constituency on which Russell had launched his ambitions. Despite further electoral successes, Russellism in effect had peaked by 1903. The episode was nonetheless an indication of the fragility of the Unionist class alliance and to a degree a reminder of the continuing salience of Presbyterian/Episcopalian tensions. Indeed, in 1898 a Presbyterian Voters' Unionist Association had been set up to express Presbyterian grievances over perceived discrimination in the matter of public appointments.[62]

Saunderson's leadership was also challenged from an urban working-class and extremist direction in the figure of Thomas Sloan. Sloan was an Orangeman and a member of the Belfast Protestant Association, founded in the 1890s to counter the efforts being made by the Independent Labour Party to propagate socialism.[63] Sloan's dizzyingly rapid ascent to political prominence began with a public denunciation of Saunderson for being insufficiently anti-Catholic at the Orange Order demonstration of 12 July 1902, and continued with his successful stance as an Independent against the official Unionist at a by-election in South Belfast later in the year. The seat had been that of the legendary William Johnston of Ballykilbeg, who had similarly challenged the Orange and Tory ruling cliques back in 1868.[64] There was thus a strain of independent Protestant populism to draw upon, and Sloan's credentials in this regard were confirmed by his dismissal from the Orange Order and the subsequent formation in 1903 of an Independent Orange Order (IOO) on the part of those who followed him out in sympathy.

Although Sloan was for a short time mollified by the Unionists, and taken under their wing at Westminster, the IOO represented an independent base with the potential to channel class resentments against the Unionist machine. The IOO in fact was steered in this direction by a journalist, Lindsay Crawford, who drew up a policy document for the new movement in 1905. 'The Magheramorne Manifesto' denounced the landlord and capitalist leadership of Unionism and prospected new political vistas involving Protestant and Catholic cooperation in pursuit of a progressive social programme. This was too radical for Sloan, and he continued to mine the seam of Orange populism in order to hold on to his seat at the general election at the end of 1905. The IOO's impact waned after this amidst sharp ideological conflicts.[65] However, its emergence – and short-lived successes in the manner of 'Russellism' at the expense of the Unionists – constituted another factor prompting a reorganisation of the Unionist political movement which was to have lasting impact.

In September 1904 proposals for a limited scheme of devolution for Ireland were published. They represented appreciably less in terms of autonomy from a Nationalist point of view than Home Rule, but still caused great alarm among Unionists. The proposals were not to form the basis of any legislation, yet they did act as the final spur to younger middle-class Ulster Unionist politicians to refashion their movement. What emerged in March 1905 was the Ulster Unionist Council (UUC), a central, coordinating organisation, confirmation of 'a tendency towards a new and localized form of political activity'.[66] Politically, and in the context of social, cultural and economic characteristics by now well-established, Ulster Unionism came of age.

Notes

1 The literature on Irish Home Rule is extensive – see A. O'Day, *Irish Home Rule 1867–1921* (Manchester, Manchester University Press, 1998) for a recent comprehensive treatment which includes a useful bibliographical essay. For Unionism the works of Patrick Buckland are still an indispensable guide – see his *Irish Unionism*, 2 vols (Dublin, Gill and Macmillan, 1972–73).
2 See J. Bardon, *A history of Ulster* (Belfast, Blackstaff Press, 1992); J. Loughlin, *Gladstone, Home Rule and the Ulster question 1882–93* (Dublin, Gill and Macmillan, 1986); F. Wright, *Two lands on one*

17

soil: *Ulster politics before Home Rule* (Dublin, Gill and Macmillan, 1996); D. Fitzpatrick, *The two Irelands* (Oxford, Oxford University Press, 1998), pp. 220–1.

3   See P. Gibbon, *The origins of Ulster Unionism* (Manchester, Manchester University Press, 1975); H. Patterson, *Class conflict and sectarianism* (Belfast, Blackstaff Press, 1980).

4   The best short works on Ulster Presbyterians are R. F. G. Holmes, *Our Irish Presbyterian heritage* (Belfast, Presbyterian Church of Ireland, 1985); R. F. G. Holmes, *The Presbyterian Church in Ireland: a popular history* (Dublin, Columba Press, 2000). See also P. Brooke, *Ulster Presbyterianism: the historical perspective, 1610–1970* (Dublin, Gill and Macmillan, 1987); D. H. Akenson, *God's peoples* (New York, Cornell, 1992); S. Bruce, *Conservative Protestant politics* (Oxford, Oxford University Press, 1998), ch. 2.

5   But see comments below (pp. 8–9) on Presbyterian politics.

6   For a recent treatment of the Orange Order both in historical and contemporary contexts see R. Dudley Edwards, *The faithful tribe* (London, Harper Collins, 1999); see also H. Kearney, 'Contested ideas of nationhood 1800–1995', *Irish Review*, 20 (Winter/Spring 1997), pp. 1–22.

7   See B. Walker, 'The 1885 and 1886 general elections: a milestone in Irish history', in P. Collins (ed.), *Nationalism and Unionism: conflict in Ireland* (Belfast, Institute of Irish Studies, 1994).

8   See D. Hempton, *Religion and political culture in Britain and Ireland* (Cambridge, Cambridge University Press, 1996), chs 4 and 5; D. Hempton and M. Hill, *Evangelical Protestantism in Ulster society* (London, Routledge, 1992); D. G. Boyce, *Nineteenth-century Ireland* (Dublin, Gill and Macmillan, 1990), chs 5–7.

9   See the insightful discussion in A. T. Q. Stewart, *The narrow ground* (London, Faber, 1977).

10 See Wright, *Two lands*, passim; also F. Wright, *Northern Ireland: a comparative analysis* (Dublin, Gill and Macmillan, 1987). See discussion of Wright's work in S. Howe, *Ireland and empire* (Oxford, Oxford University Press, 2000), pp. 210–16.

11 Gibbon, *Origins*; D. Miller, *Queen's rebels* (Dublin, Gill and Macmillan, 1978); Loughlin, *Gladstone*; A. Jackson, *The Ulster Party* (Oxford, Oxford University Press, 1989).

12 See J. Loughlin, '"Imagining Ulster": the North of Ireland and British national identity, 1880–1921', in S. J. Connolly (ed.), *Kingdoms united? Great Britain and Ireland since 1500: integration and diversity* (Dublin, Four Courts Press, 1999); J. Loughlin, *Ulster Unionism and British national identity since 1885* (London, Pinter Press, 1995).

13 Loughlin, '"Imagining Ulster"'.

14 See Jackson, *Ulster Party*, pp. 11–12; A. D. Smith, *Theories of*

nationalism (London, Duckworth, 1983). See also note to Preface.

15 I. McBride, 'Ulster and the British problem', in R. English and G. Walker (eds), *Unionism in modern Ireland* (Basingstoke, Macmillan, 1996).

16 I. McBride, *The Siege of Derry in Ulster Protestant mythology* (Dublin, Four Courts Press, 1997), p. 80.

17 See D. Officer and G. Walker, 'Protestant Ulster: ethno-history, memory and contemporary prospects', *National Identities*, 2:3 (2000), pp. 293–307.

18 Ibid. Examples of such literary texts include: J. Harrison, *The Scot in Ulster* (1888); J. Heron, *The Ulster Scot* (1900); C. Hanna, *The Scotch-Irish* (1902); J. B. Woodburn, *The Ulster Scot* (1914).

19 See G. Walker, 'Thomas Sinclair: Presbyterian Liberal Unionist', in English and Walker (eds), *Unionism*.

20 See especially A. Aughey, *Under siege: Ulster Unionism and the Anglo-Irish Agreement* (Belfast, Blackstaff Press, 1989).

21 J. Todd, 'Two traditions in Unionist political culture', *Irish Political Studies*, 2 (1987), pp. 1–26.

22 See Kearney, 'Contested ideas'; T. Hennessey, 'Ulster Unionist territorial and national identities 1886–1893: province, island, kingdom and empire', *Irish Political Studies*, 8 (1993), pp. 21–36. See the analyses of Unionism in relation to identity questions in Howe, *Ireland and empire*, especially ch. 10.

23 See McBride, 'Ulster and the British problem'; Officer and Walker, 'Protestant Ulster'.

24 See J. Kendle, *Ireland and the federal solution: the debate over the United Kingdom constitution, 1870–1921* (Kingston and Montreal, Queen's University Press, 1989); A. J. Ward, *The Irish constitutional tradition* (Dublin, Irish Academic Press, 1994), ch. 4; G. Walker, *Intimate strangers: political and cultural interaction between Scotland and Ulster in modern times* (Edinburgh, John Donald, 1995), ch. 2.

25 See B. M. Walker, *Ulster politics: the formative years 1868–1886* (Belfast, Ulster Historical Foundation, 1989).

26 G. Greenlee, 'Land, religion and community: the Liberal Party in Ulster, 1868–1885', in E. Biagini (ed.), *Citizenship and community* (Cambridge, Cambridge University Press, 1996).

27 Ibid.; also P. Bew and F. Wright, 'The agrarian opposition in Ulster politics', in S. Clark and J. S. Donnelly Jnr (eds), *Irish peasants* (Manchester, Manchester University Press, 1983); O'Day, *Irish Home Rule*, p. 93.

28 A. Jackson, *Ireland 1798–1998* (Oxford, Blackwell Press, 1999), p. 218.

29 Walker, 'The 1885 and 1886 general elections'.

30 O'Day, *Irish Home Rule*, p. 106.

31 See Walker, 'Thomas Sinclair'.

32 See P. Ollerenshaw, 'Businessmen and the development of Ulster Unionism, 1886–1921', *Journal of Imperial and Commonwealth History*, 28:1 (2000), pp. 35–64.

33 See R. B. McMinn, *Against the tide: J. B. Armour, Irish Presbyterian Minister and Home Ruler* (Belfast, Public Record Office, 1985).

34 Jackson, *Ireland*, p. 215.

35 Ibid., p. 218.

36 See Walker, 'Thomas Sinclair'.

37 A. Jackson, *Colonel Edward Saunderson: land and loyalty in Victorian Ireland* (Oxford, Oxford University Press, 1995), chs 3 and 4.

38 See Jackson, *Ulster Party*.

39 O'Day, *Irish Home Rule*, pp. 113–14.

40 Jackson, *Ireland*, p. 225.

41 O'Day, *Irish Home Rule*, p. 129.

42 Walker, 'Thomas Sinclair'.

43 See O'Day, *Irish Home Rule*, chs 4 and 5; Ward, *Irish constitutional tradition*, ch. 4; Walker, *Intimate strangers*, ch. 2.

44 For which see C. Shannon, *Arthur J. Balfour and Ireland 1874–1922* (Washington DC, Catholic University of America Press, 1988); A. Gailey, *Ireland and the death of kindness: the experience of constructive Unionism, 1890–1905* (Cork, Cork University Press, 1987).

45 See comments of Ulster Liberal Unionist T. W. Russell quoted in O'Day, *Irish Home Rule*, p. 156. See discussion below (pp. 30–1) on the third Home Rule Bill.

46 See G. Lucy, *The great convention* (Lurgan, Ulster Society, 1995); Gibbon, *Origins*, pp. 132–8; Buckland, *Irish Unionism*, vol. II.

47 Walker, 'Thomas Sinclair'.

48 See Ollerenshaw, 'Businessmen', regarding the influence of Ulster businessmen on these bodies and the extent to which their activities represented moves towards 'democratization'.

49 See Jackson's comments on Gibbon in *Ulster Party*, pp. 5–6.

50 See comments of W. C. Trimble quoted in Lucy, *Great convention*, p. 26; also Walker, 'Thomas Sinclair'; T. McKnight, *Ulster as it is*, Vol. II (London, Macmillan, 1896), ch. 15.

51 See O'Day, *Irish Home Rule*, pp. 161–2.

52 See quotes in Lucy, *Great convention*, pp. 53–4.

53 See D. Urquhart, *Women in Ulster politics* (Dublin, Irish Academic Press, 2000), ch. 2.

54 Ollerenshaw, 'Businessmen'; Walker, 'Thomas Sinclair'.

55 See Gailey, *Ireland*.

56 See D. Burnett, 'The modernisation of Unionism, 1892–1914?', in English and Walker (eds), *Unionism*.

57 See Jackson, *Saunderson*, ch. 9. Russell was born in Scotland, and had impeccable Presbyterian Liberal credentials.

58 Walker, 'Thomas Sinclair'; Burnett, 'Modernisation'.
59 See Sinclair speech in *Ulster Echo*, 5 October 1900.
60 So called because it sat during parliamentary recesses.
61 Jackson, *Saunderson*, p. 126.
62 See R. McMinn, 'Presbyterianism and politics in Ulster, 1871–1906', *Studia Hibernica*, 21 (1981), pp. 127–46.
63 See Patterson, *Class conflict*.
64 For a discussion of the Johnston affair in the context of class tensions within Ulster Unionism see F. Wright, 'Protestant ideology and politics in Ulster', *European Journal of Sociology*, 14 (1973), pp. 213–80.
65 See Patterson, *Class conflict*; A. Morgan, *Labour and partition* (London, Pluto Press, 1991), ch. 3.
66 Jackson, *Saunderson*, p. 156. See also J. F. Harbinson, *The Ulster Unionist Party 1882–1973* (Belfast, Blackstaff Press, 1973), ch. 4.

CHAPTER TWO

CONFRONTATIONS: 'CARRY ON CARSON', 1905–1920

Let me impress upon the people of Great Britain that Ulster opposition to Home Rule is no party matter. It is an uprising of a people against tyranny and coercion; against condemnation to servitude; against deprivation of the right of citizens to an effective voice in the government of the country. (The Marquis of Londonderry, in S. Rosenbaum, ed., *Against Home Rule*, London, Frederick Warne, 1912, p. 164)

The initiative for the formation of the Ulster Unionist Council was taken by some Ulster MPs clearly perturbed at the extent to which Unionism was suffering from organisational decay, and beset by threats from within in the shape of Russellism and the Independent Orange Order, as well as from Nationalism. To all this was added the perceived treacherous plot concocted over devolution by the British government administration in Dublin Castle.[1]

The Ulster MPs forcing events were William Moore, Charles Craig and J. B. Lonsdale, the Honorary Secretary of the party. They represented a new radicalism, impatient with the leadership of Saunderson and decidedly focused on Northern Unionist priorities such as combating electoral threats. Moore and Craig were instrumental in setting up a meeting of Ulster Unionist MPs in December 1904 at which a resolution calling for an Ulster Council to be formed was adopted. The inaugural meeting of the UUC duly took place on 3 March 1905.

The organisational structure of the new body reflected a desire to bring constituency associations into closer involvement with the party and its MPs. Half of the membership of two hundred was to be drawn from constituencies, and a further fifty from the Orange Order. The latter institution was thus recognised for its mobilising abilities and its history of political service to the Conservatives. By placing it so prominently within the engine room of Unionism, the party officers and MPs were empowering an organisation in crisis and sending a message to defectors and would-be defectors; moreover, they were signalling their willingness formally to embrace religious sectarianism and the militant ethnic politics which accompanied it. It was to prove a historic and fateful decision, especially in the light of Jackson's observation that the UUC can be viewed as a 'prototype' for the Unionist parliament in the North which came into being in 1921.[2]

The practical management of the UUC was undertaken by members of a Standing Committee and the organisation's permanent staff. The Standing Committee represented the Conservative and Liberal Unionist strands of Ulster Unionism, and the manufacturing and commercial as well as landed economic interests; Labour interests would be included later. E. M. Archdale, a prominent Fermanagh landowner, was elected Chairman and would become Northern Ireland's first Minister of Agriculture. Richard Dawson-Bates, a Belfast solicitor, was made Secretary, and would become Northern Ireland's first Minister of Home Affairs. The Belfast Unionist press hailed the new initiative, one commentator remarking that 'Tory, Liberal Unionist and Orangeman spoke with one mind'.[3]

The tenor of the press reaction, however, reflected overwhelmingly the Unionist sense of anxiety which had promoted the UUC's formation, and central to this were the religious fears which were to be so strongly foregrounded in the coming crisis over another Home Rule Bill. The Presbyterian *Witness* paper labelled the architect of the 1904 devolution proposal, Irish Under-Secretary Sir Anthony MacDonnell, 'a bigoted Roman Catholic' and an 'enemy' of the Union, proof as they saw it of traitors operating at the heart of government where 'the priests are masters'.[4] A *Belfast Weekly News* editorial alleged that MacDonnell had negotiated secretly for the establishment of a Catholic university,[5] while a columnist asserted that 'the policy of the Catholic Association' was being 'quietly and constantly pushed everywhere'.[6] Against a background of Unionist divisions over socio-economic issues and intra-Protestant squabbling, the devolution proposals provided a pretext for Ulster Unionist revivalism, all the more useful for the Catholic MacDonnell's involvement as a fillip to a pan-Protestant sense of persecution. The Orange Order's incorporation into the new Ulster Unionist political machine has to be viewed in this context.

The MacDonnell devolution affair ended the political career of the Irish Chief Secretary, George Wyndham, who resigned a matter of days after the UUC came into being. The proposals were then buried. Nevertheless, Irish Unionist sensitivities were not easily soothed, and the episode reinforced a tendency towards self-reliance among the Ulster part of the movement. Relations with British Unionists – by now preoccupied with their own divisions – were substantially damaged; if the Ulster Unionists could not count on the support of a British Conservative and Unionist government then they would have to look to their own resources and – it was implied – their own ways and means. While Wyndham's scalp was welcome, and the succession to his post of Walter Long reassuring, Ulster Unionists continued to regard Conservative Prime Minister Arthur Balfour with deep suspicion.[7] Long's popularity ensured his selection as Irish Unionist leader after the death of Saunderson in October 1906, and he sought to strengthen the somewhat attenuated bonds between Northern and Southern Unionism. For all his personal standing and influence his efforts met limited success;[8] the drive towards concentration of Ulster's resources in the constitutional struggle was well under way. Long's election as Chairman of the UUC in January 1907 put him at the head of a body with its own democratic – and sectarian – momentum.[9]

The ascent to power at Westminster in January 1906 of the Liberals paved the way the following year for a similar devolution scheme to that of 1904. Unionist panic was forestalled by Nationalist hostility to the plans, which were quietly dropped. The Liberals too had other priorities, and enjoyed a massive majority in the Commons.

The importance of the constituency association, reflected in the structure of the UUC, is hard to exaggerate. Jackson has identified its three functions as supervising and financing the registration of voters; selecting parliamentary candidates for the constituency; and working for their election.[10] Of these, the first took up most of the party workers' energies; elections were in effect won in the revision courts which ruled on the composition of the register. Much depended on the capacity of the local association to gather the required information on the constituency to ensure that party supporters were registered and opponents not entitled to vote were denied. In Irish constituencies a rough but generally reliable guide to voting intentions was that of religion. As the Secretary of the

North Tyrone Unionist Constituency, William Wilson, wrote to UUC Secretary Dawson-Bates in November 1910: 'I quite agree with you that in Irish constituencies the whole fight is at the Revision, not at the Election. Of course this is different in England, but as everyone knows in this country it is a mere matter of religion.'[11]

The Unionist perception of the political struggle in most Northern constituencies was that of Unionist Party workers versus the Catholic priests. Advising against contesting the East Donegal seat, the local Unionist constituency secretary wrote to Dawson-Bates to say that 'the other side are well organised and the show is run by the priests'.[12] Priestly involvement was accompanied, in Unionist eyes, by the machinations of the exclusively Catholic secret society, the Ancient Order of Hibernians (AOH), whose mass membership was largely concentrated in Ulster and whose influence on the Irish Parliamentary Party grew significantly in the early years of the century.[13] The AOH became in many ways the principal Unionist bogey in the period up until the First World War, a society which they viewed as the tool of a power-grasping Catholic Church; such images became a trademark of Unionist anti-Home Rule literature and speeches.[14] Again, the increase in Orange Order numbers and political clout has to be set beside Catholic Church involvement in Nationalist politics, the rise of the AOH, and the darkening Protestant prophecies regarding the intentions of both.

The vast majority of Ulster Protestants – and certainly of Ulster Protestant Unionists – saw in Catholic claims a hidden agenda of Catholic supremacy. Protestants found it difficult to take Catholic demands for equality at face value. This was vividly illustrated in relation to the controversy over the establishment of a Catholic university, an issue which climaxed in 1908 when the Liberal government legislated for a new national university in Ireland with state funding.[15] The new university became *de facto* a Catholic institution, which, from a Catholic viewpoint, merely redressed an imbalance dating back many years during which Trinity College Dublin was an Anglican institution and Queen's College in Belfast in practice a Presbyterian one, while the other higher education institutions on the island did not reflect a Catholic ethos. For Ulster Protestants, however, the university issue symbolised the Catholic Church's drive for dominance. Back in 1905 the Presbyterian *Witness* had editorialised as follows:

Protestants are willing to work and live and be educated with
Roman Catholics; but the bishops and priests demand separation,
isolation, exclusiveness. Who are the bigots we would ask? Protestants are content with equality; Romanists demand supremacy.[16]

Thomas Sinclair, the leading Liberal Unionist and founding
member of the UUC Standing Committee, responded to the 1908
Act by recalling the stance of Young Irelander Thomas Davis
against denominational education, and pointed to the reform of
Trinity College and the non-sectarian constitution of the Queen's
Colleges of Belfast, Cork and Galway:

> The failure of a reformed Trinity College and of the Queen's Univer-
> sity to satisfy the rulers of the Roman Catholic Church results from
> the refusal of the hierarchy either to accept the principle of religious
> equality or to surrender their claim to control the government and
> the administration of the University and its Colleges.

Sinclair went on to allege that the Catholic Church refused to accept
that the secular and the religious could be separated.[17]

The issue of education, indeed, might be regarded as crucial to
the failure, since the 1870s, of most Liberal Presbyterian and
Catholic efforts to form a purposeful political alliance,[18] and ultimately to the hardening of Liberal Presbyterian attitudes to the constitutional question. The University Bill controversy joined the
illiberal Orange Order and the Liberal Unionist Presbyterians in a
harmonious denunciation of Catholic designs, and the atmosphere
was further embittered by the Catholic Church's announcement,
also in 1908, of the *Ne Temere* decree. The latter stipulated that
'mixed marriages' (that is of a Catholic with a non-Catholic partner) were only valid if conducted under the rites of the Catholic
Church, and that the children of such unions had to be brought up
in the Catholic faith. Just as the education debate had aroused Presbyterian fears in particular, so too did *Ne Temere* bear more heavily
down upon Presbyterians, who carried with them the folk memory
of having their marriages declared invalid under the old Anglican
ascendancy. *Ne Temere* became a significant factor in the marshal-
ling of Unionist opposition to the next Home Rule Bill, and in the
construction of Unionist arguments and propaganda by Presbyterian ministers and clergymen. More broadly, such episodes as the
university controversy and *Ne Temere* had the effect of further
sectarianising, and indeed 'Ulsterising', the ongoing Unionist–Nationalist political struggle.

The formation of the UUC gave impetus to constituency organisation, although the problems which had dogged the local workers in the 1890s and early 1900s[19] lingered in some areas. Thus Dawson-Bates found himself harangued by Wilson of North Tyrone over a shortage of funds to undertake the revision work in that constituency.[20] Much hard slog fell on the shoulders of a handful of people, and the selection – and behaviour – of candidates could produce quite fractious disagreement.[21] On the other hand there was evidence of Unionists working more effectively: in South Down the Honorary Secretary's report of 15 October 1910 commented on 'the excellent way in which our men answered the summons to attend [the revision courts] to substantiate their claims, or refute objections: this point alone is a clear indication of greater enthusiasm among the Unionists than heretofore'.[22]

If the level of Unionist enthusiasm and political acumen was uneven throughout Ulster, there seems little doubt that a localisation process took place in the Edwardian era with significant consequences for North–South Unionist relations and for future anti-Home Rule campaigning. The role of Belfast became ever more pre-eminent, and the character of Unionism shaped more decidedly by the urban manufacturers, merchants and lawyers.[23] By the time the Liberal government in London had opted to confront the House of Lords over its power of veto, used in 1909 to torpedo the Chancellor Lloyd George's 'People's Budget', Ulster Unionists had largely dealt with their internal divisions and restored their morale. If indeed they were also spoiling for a fight, this is precisely what came to them by way of the Liberals / House of Lords drama. Pledging to curb the Lords' veto, the Liberals went to the polls in January 1910 seeking a mandate to do so. The result was inconclusive but the Liberals remained in office and were able to count on the support of the Irish Nationalists: the latter, of course, would step up their demand for another Home Rule measure, and Unionists in Britain and Ireland now had to contemplate the possible loss of their line of defence in the upper house.

The Irish Unionists, all but two of whose parliamentary representatives came from Ulster seats after the election, 'brooded'[24] over the recrudescence of Home Rule under new leadership. With Long returned for a London seat, the irascible member for Dublin University, Edward Carson, was approached to succeed him. Carson, an eminent barrister with alternative political opportunities potentially available to him, made the sacrificial gesture required to bind him to a cause instead of a career.[25] There was certainly no denying Carson's determination to fight Home Rule, and as a Southern Irishman he devoutly desired its defeat for the whole country. However, his elevation to the leadership followed a period in which Unionist reorganisation in Ulster had highlighted the particular depth of Northern feeling. Between Carson's assumption of the leadership in February 1910 and his top billing at mass Ulster demonstrations the following year, the Dubliner was moulded, quite wittingly, into an honorary 'Ulsterman', predestined to save 'his' people from the bondage of Dublin rule. Moulder-in-chief was James Craig, Ulster MP, stockbroker and millionaire – inheritor of a profitable family whiskey business – whose marketing and public relations skills in the political arena were far ahead of their time. It was Craig, authentic unshowy Presbyterian Ulsterman, who directed the 'King Carson' spectacle for the next decade, but whose achievements were most singular in the orchestration of the dramatic Ulster Loyalist campaign of protest in the period leading up to the First World War.[26] Carson the outsider contrived to bring unity to Ulster Unionists and gain the absolute trust of his highly querulous and motley following; as Gailey has remarked, he seemed to relish 'the new political theatre of democracy'.[27] What resulted was the blending of a messianic cult around Carson with a communal sense of purpose and resolve carrying its own dynamic.

When the outcome of a second general election in 1910, held in December, virtually replicated the verdict of the first, the Liberal government proceeded to legislate for reform of the House of Lords. The government introduced its Parliament Bill in February 1911, and after a protracted and bitter parliamentary struggle, enough peers accepted their fate to permit the bill to become law in August. The power of the Lords to veto legislation was removed; henceforth the upper chamber could only delay the passage of legislation it disliked. The implications for Irish Home Rule were now clear, although in neither election in 1910 had a commitment been significantly trailed by the Liberals. Moreover, it appeared that there was a genuine possibility of the Irish issue being resolved in the context of 'all round' Home Rule for the whole UK, a quasi-federal proposal popularised from 1910 by such figures as the Scottish Conservative Frederick Scott Oliver. Support for such a project crossed party lines, but Irish Nationalists were impatient and the Liberal government's Irish Chief Secretary, Augustine Birrell, sympathised with their demand that priority be given to the Irish case. There was no enthusiasm among Irish Unionists for a 'federal' solution either, and the Tory party leader Arthur Balfour was resolute in his adoption of the A. V. Dicey defence of the constitutional status quo. Nevertheless, the idea had resurfaced and it would always hang in the air when radical constitutional changes were debated.[28]

The Conservative Party, outraged at the humbling of the Lords and anxious to heal its own rifts over the issue of tariff reform, accused the Liberals of corrupt bargaining with the Irish Nationalists to subvert the venerable British constitution. The Liberals, it was claimed, had not received a proper mandate either for the reform of the Lords or for Home Rule. When the Liberals signalled their intention to bring in another Irish Home Rule Bill, the Conservatives pledged total opposition. A clue as to how far they might be prepared to take their stance was provided by the choice of leader to succeed Balfour in November 1911: Andrew Bonar Law. Law was the Presbyterian Scottish son of an Ulster Presbyterian minister and his family connections with the Province profoundly shaped his sympathies with the Ulster Unionist cause.[29] It appears that Law only accepted the Tory leadership when he had ascertained from Carson that the latter did not desire it.[30] Certainly, a formidable alliance between the two men was put in place in time for the campaign against the Liberals' third attempt at Irish Home Rule.

In Ulster itself, preparations were well developed. Jackson notes that confidential schemes for the arming and drilling of Orangemen had been drawn up prior to the second 1910 election,[31] while in September 1911 a 'Commission of Five' was appointed 'to frame and submit a Constitution for a Provisional Government of Ulster', to come into operation on the day of the passage of any Home Rule Bill and 'to remain in force until Ulster shall again resume unimpaired her citizenship in the United Kingdom'.[32] Mention was duly made about having regard to 'the interests of the Loyalists in other parts of Ireland',[33] but this was in spirit a unilateral kind of move by Ulster Unionists. The Commission was made up entirely of local men including James Craig and Thomas Sinclair. The Parliament Act of 1911 which blunted the powers of the Lords cleared the way for a showdown over Home Rule. Yet the militant disposition and extra-parliamentary direction of Ulster Unionism pre-dated the climax of the constitutional controversy at Westminster; an apocalyptic mood had never been difficult to conjure among the people with whom Carson had entered into a 'compact'.[34]

The Liberals introduced the Home Rule Bill on 11 April 1912.[35] Notwithstanding lengthy deliberations on the part of a cabinet committee over the 'federal' idea, the measure was eminently Gladstonian: it provided only for an Irish parliament with legislative powers in respect of most domestic affairs. It resembled Gladstone's second bill in retaining Irish representation at Westminster, although much reduced; and it made no provision for special treatment for Ulster. The notion of Ulster exclusion, or temporary exclusion, had been mooted, but Nationalist antipathy to any carve-up of the country was total. Much thought had gone into the financial clauses of the bill, which again were Gladstonian in kind, but they pleased neither side in the Irish conflict: Nationalists took the view that the control of the Treasury in London would be too tight, while Unionists chafed at their economic subjection to a Dublin parliament.

The Liberals remained true to their Gladstonian inheritance but at the cost of unleashing ferocious Unionist protests and a political crisis which was to threaten to spill over into civil war. Jalland, to cite the most notable of critical historians, squarely blames Asquith and his government for not addressing the Ulster question effectively, and adopting a perilous 'wait and see' approach.[36] An amendment was duly tabled by a Liberal back-bencher, Thomas Agar-Robartes, proposing the exclusion of a four-county 'Ulster': Antrim, Down, Londonderry, Armagh. Unionists were placed in a quandary, but decided to support the amendment, perhaps in the spirit of a wrecking tactic, but more probably as an affirmation of their argument regarding the right of 'Ulster' to self-determination.[37] The amendment was rejected and the bill eventually passed on its third reading by a majority of 110. Allowing for the delay in passing through the reformed House of Lords, Home Rule for all Ireland looked set to become law in 1914. The government in effect trusted to the ultimate compliance of Ulster.

Unionist opposition to Home Rule rehearsed arguments and themes from the previous crises. However, there were new twists. As the Home Rule question centred increasingly on Ulster, the religious issue assumed even greater proportions than before. Safeguards against religious privileges were written into the bill but they were contemptuously dismissed as futile by Ulster Protestants. The controversial *Ne Temere* decree was seen to have a practical impact in Belfast in 1910 when a Presbyterian wife was deserted by her Catholic husband and their child was taken away to be baptised and raised Catholic. The 'McCann case' sparked a torrent of Protestant outrage, and reconfirmed Unionists in their view of the Catholic influence in any future Dublin parliament.[38] As Thomas Sinclair put it at the time of the McCann case:

> Subject as they themselves are to Vatican control, no restriction of the powers of a Dublin parliament would be permitted which would limit the Church in its use of the Ne Temere decree. Rather would she insist that the substance of that decree be enacted in an Irish Parliamentary Statute.[39]

In 1911 the Catholic Church issued another decree, *Motu Proprio*, which seemed to Protestants to be an attempt to secure the immunity of the Catholic clergy from the process of civil or criminal law. Protestants could not envisage a Catholic-dominated Irish legislature challenging the Church's objectives, regardless of so-called safeguards. The common stereotype entertained by Protestant society about Catholics – and perhaps Catholic politicians especially – was that of priestly dupes.

By the time of the third Home Rule Bill Protestants also had had time to reflect on the impact of the local government reform of 1898. Thus they made much of the pitifully small number of Protestant representatives on county councils, and they alleged discrimination in the matter of local government appointments and patronage.[40] Again, there was an assumption that Protestant marginalisation begun at the parish council level would be taken to new lengths by a Dublin parliament.

Then, as the Unionist reaction to the Home Rule Bill was raging, a party of Presbyterian Sunday School children was attacked at Castledawson in County Londonderry by a gang of AOH members. Some of the children and women in the party suffered injuries and the incident triggered Protestant anger which resulted the following month in the expulsion of large numbers of Catholic workers from the Belfast shipyards. Deteriorating community relations were not helped by political myopia on both sides: Unionists exploited Castledawson in a manner which appeared to give licence to retaliation, while Nationalists made light of the affair and more generally were prone to ridicule Protestant religious fears over matters like *Ne Temere*.[41] Notwithstanding the degree of dialogue which did exist between mainstream Unionism and Nationalism in this period, and the relative absence of serious violence,[42] there was no significant attempt made to bridge the gap in respective community perceptions over the religious issue in particular. Moreover, Protestants and Catholics in Ulster each accused the other of using secret societies to further sectarian agendas: the Orange Order and the AOH especially. Castledawson merely underlined the central role of the AOH in Ulster Protestant demonology, and the fact that the society's figurehead in Ulster was Joseph Devlin, Nationalist MP for West Belfast, was considered ample proof of the anti-Protestant character of the Home Rule project.[43]

Ulster Catholics regarded the Unionist case against Home Rule to be motivated by simple bigotry. Some historians have agreed,[44] and others have gone as far as to label this perceived bigotry as 'racism'.[45] The prominence of the Orange Order and its brand of populism in the Unionist campaign provides grounds for such charges, but not enough attention has been paid to the significance of the AOH in the period from around 1905 to 1915 when it increased its membership to 125,000[46] and formed an organisational network for the Home Rule Party along with the more impressively all-Ireland mass movement the United Irish League. Racist labels have been too loosely applied to what was in essence a question of cultural assumptions determined by religious identity.[47]

Charges of racism tend also to focus on the cultivation of an Ulster identity in the course of the Home Rule dramas, culminating in the 1912–14 years. Central to this was the celebration of the 'Ulster-Scot' concept: the moulding of a singularly redoubtable people out of a blend of Scottish and Ulster influences. In the late nineteenth and early twentieth centuries there was something of an 'Ulster-Scot' industry in historical and polemical volumes produced with the intention of promoting a distinctively ethnic strand to the anti-Home Rule case.[48] It was an effort largely undertaken by Presbyterian ministers and historians who either explicitly or implicitly identified 'Protestant Ulster' with Presbyterianism,[49] and who either wrote in the vein of racial typecasting prevalent in the era or explicitly rejected racial categorisation as inappropriate.[50]

Two points might be made about this. First, the 'Ulster-Scot' enterprise represented a 'Presbyterianisation' of the Ulster Unionist anti-Home Rule campaign, notwithstanding the actual heterogeneous denominational character of Protestant Ulster and the powerful non-Presbyterian figures in the van of the movement. Second, it was

indicative of Ulster Unionism meeting the challenge of Irish Nationalism on its own myth-making, ethnic exclusivist and perhaps
racialist ground. It represented an attempt to controvert the unitary
vision and narrative of Irish Nationalism to which Protestant Ulster
was at best marginal and at worst invisible, and within which that
people's emotional British identity and allegiance could not be
admitted. Ulster Unionism, through the cultivation of the notion of
a distinct Ulster Protestant 'people', 'society', or indeed 'nation',
attempted to legitimise its demands in similar ways to Irish Nationalism, and nationalist movements elsewhere. As previously
observed, Ulster Protestants in effect felt that their protestations of
loyalty to the Union, as Irishmen, were not enough in the political
battle against Irish Nationalism. To the civic strain of argument
against any change to their British citizenship, and the pragmatic
economic case against a Dublin parliament with financial powers,
was added the decidedly ethnic one of an Ulster Protestant distinctiveness with its own rights of self-determination. These varieties of
argument were featured in the landmark statement *Against Home
Rule* produced in response to Asquith's bill in 1912.[51]

Thus the 'Ulster-Scot' volumes took on the character of classic
'Whig' histories of the kind produced by nationalists elsewhere at
this time.[52] The Reverend J. B. Woodburn's *The Ulster Scot: his history and religion* might be considered the apogee of this genre. It
was a book rapturously received by the Unionist press in Ulster and
perceived as a timely propaganda weapon which would explain the
Ulstermen and their stand to British audiences.[53] Such concerns mirrored the priority the Unionist movement placed on arguing its case
in Britain and winning over the Scottish Presbyterian and English
Nonconformist Liberals.[54] Support from the former was especially
desired, in accordance with the Ulster-Scottish sentiment in circula-
tion, but there was always a tinge of disappointment over the
limited results attained. As a *Witness* editorial plaintively put it:

> We would ask our Scottish Presbyterian friends to remember that the
> majority of us are Scots in tradition, feeling and love of liberty, and if
> we did not feel that our liberties were at stake we would not make
> the protests we do or undertake the serious risks which our strong
> determination and united action involve.[55]

This kind of appeal from Ulster Presbyterians to their Scottish counterparts was much heard throughout the era of all three Irish Home
Rule Bills, but it was a more central feature of Ulster Unionist

propaganda during the crisis of 1912–14.

And there were those Scots, beyond the circles of church ministers and Orange Order leaders, who did respond supportively. Thus the novelist, son of the Free Church manse, and Conservative MP John Buchan, in a speech in Innerleithen in Peeblesshire in 1912, referred to Ulstermen as 'a race composed of men of our own blood and our own creed', before proceeding to argue: 'If Home Rule Ireland is a nation, how on earth can you deny the name to the Ulster Protestants? Indeed, they have a far higher title to it. They are one blood and one creed; they have such a history behind them as any nation might be proud of.'[56] Buchan's tribute, along with the famous encomium of the Presbyterian former Liberal Prime Minister Lord Rosebery which adorned the title page of Woodburn's book,[57] was exactly the kind of pay-off the publicists of the 'Ulsterman' and 'Ulster-Scot' narratives sought, and it was illustrative of the degree to which the case against Irish Home Rule had come to be argued in a similar nationalist idiom as that of its opponents, with historicist justifications and a cultural gloss of a peculiarly Presbyterian and Scottish kind.

The Scottish Presbyterian dimension to the Ulster Protestant story lent itself far more readily to the political defiance required to defeat Home Rule, and indeed also to the rebellious posturing against the British government. It provided the stuff of ethnonationalism to rival its Irish Catholic counterpart. At a Presbyterian anti-Home Rule convention in Belfast in 1912 a delegate, the educationalist and leading Presbyterian layman T. G. Houston, proclaimed that Ulster's stand had been misunderstood in Britain, that it was not a manifestation of the 'jingo spirit' but of the 'martyr spirit'.[58] In his pamphlet *Ulster's appeal* (1913), Houston summed up very well the prevailing Presbyterian self-image of the time as 'the backbone of Ulster', before referring to their forefathers who 'signed another covenant at the time of the persecution in Scotland'.[59] The Solemn League and Covenant of 1912 – to which Houston compared the Scottish model – was indeed the prime example of a process in which the anti-Home Rule struggle was identified with the language and symbolism of a Presbyterian, and Scottish, heritage.

The Covenant[60] was a statement of intent, in suitably biblical language, to resist Home Rule and defend 'for ourselves and our children our cherished position of equal citizenship in the United Kingdom'. On 28 September 1912 Carson led a signing ceremony in Belfast involving many thousands of Ulster men and women. All in all some 450,000 signed the document. The 'Ulster Day' signings – conducted in an atmosphere of solemn communal resolve and religious reverence – constituted probably the most impressive of the many expertly stage-managed Ulster anti-Home Rule demonstrations, and the message of defiance was certainly conveyed to Britain.

If this Ulster anti-Home Rule campaign could be said to have had a soundtrack – and it was certainly a cinematic phenomenon – then it was the battle hymns which expressed, in the words of the novelist George Birmingham, 'majestic confidence in an eternal righteousness'.[61] 'O God our help in ages past' rang out at Loyalist gatherings throughout the Province, and provided much sport for Irish Nationalist and English Liberal satirists; however, George Bernard Shaw made the more percipient observation that when Ulster Protestants sang it they were in earnest.[62] This implacability bred a similar 'exaltation of spirit' to that discerned soon after in Irish Nationalist extremists by the Liberal Chief Secretary Augustine Birrell.[63]

The Covenant demonstrated the radical populism defining Ulster Unionism, the notion of 'the Sovereign People'[64] which arguably derived in large part from a history of grievance felt in particular by Presbyterians. Ian McBride has identified this in relation to the Siege of Derry commemorations;[65] it might be said that it was also instrumental in the making of the 'Ulsterman' and the shaping of an ethnic consciousness around notions of contracts and rights, and entitlements to separate treatment. Donald Akenson's study of the Ulster-Scots has illuminated such themes in the course of advancing the thesis that Ulster-Scots Presbyterians derived their world-view from the Old Testament scriptures. Akenson also perceives a process of 'Presbyterianisation' of the wider Protestant community during the Home Rule era, culminating in a form of 'cultural hegemony'.[66] It might be added that this reached its height in the 1912–14 period when Presbyterian 'ethno-history' and Scottish aspects of Ulster's makeup were pressed tellingly into service for Ulster Unionism. This involved obscuring other aspects of Ulster identity which did not fit the needs of the time, and 'ironing out' the complexities of the past – in the manner of Irish and other nationalists – to the end of constructing a coherent and serviceable narrative, a 'myth of common descent' and 'sense of shared history'. Presbyterian historians were doing what the scholar John

Hutchinson has pointed to in relation to cultural nationalist intellectuals and their influence: they were providing a map of collective identity at a time of crisis which helped to mobilise a larger social constituency.[67]

Moreover, it was a remarkable feature of 'the Ulster crisis' that the outsider figure of Carson, instinctively agnostic regarding the concept of 'two nations' in Ireland, should enter into a contract with his followers to supply political leadership within the terms of the peculiarly Ulster rhetoric which had been cultivated and popularised; as Gailey has observed, Carson translated 'the myth of "the Honest Ulsterman" into the language of the English Yeoman', while himself holding to an idealised picture of the Ulsterman as pure and uncorrupted.[68]

Implicit in the text of the Covenant was the belief that all methods, including force, would be justified in pursuit of the defeat of Home Rule. In July 1912, indeed, Bonar Law had declared that he could imagine 'no length of resistance to which Ulster can go' in which he would not be prepared to support them. Although it is doubtful how far Law spoke for his party, the speech was a significant morale boost for Ulster Unionists. The UUC, the organisational hub of the campaign, duly devised an 'Ulster provisional government' in September 1912 to assume control of the Province when Home Rule became law. Ulster businessmen underwrote the planned rebellion with financial guarantees.[69] In January 1913 the UUC paved the way for the formation of a body to be known as the Ulster Volunteer Force (UVF),[70] to be comprised of the many who had been secretly drilling and training along with new volunteers. The UVF rank and file included small farmers, labourers, factory workers and artisans, and soon military expertise was provided by former British Army officers such as Commander General Richardson. It is widely agreed by historians that the establishment of the UVF represented an attempt by the leadership to impose discipline among their impassioned followers and avoid outbreaks of sectarian violence such as the shipyard expulsions of the previous year. Carson, though, was lyrical in his recognition of how much his less-well-off followers were prepared to sacrifice. In true Liberal Unionist paternalist fashion he wrote of 'the wage earners of our democracy' setting an example to those in better circumstances.[71] In the climate of militancy which prevailed, the UUC had to prioritise the prevention of any splintering likely to weaken the anti-Home Rule cam-

paign and the effective coordination of resistance. The political
unity achieved by the UUC gave credence in turn to the threat of
Loyalist violence.

Arming the UVF proceeded apace in 1913, a precedent quickly
imitated by an outfit named the 'National Volunteers' in the South.
Ironically, the UVF had revived the dormant physical force tradition
of Irish Nationalism. Against this background of emerging private
armies the government moved to prohibit the importation of arms
into Ireland, and to identify efforts to reach agreement with the con-
tending parties. An amendment was introduced in parliament to the
Home Rule Bill in March 1914 proposing that each of the Ulster
counties vote on the issue of Home Rule, those voting against being
permitted exclusion from the scheme for a limited period of six
years. Carson angrily rejected this as 'a sentence of death with a stay
of execution'. A further blow to the government resulted from its
attempts to secure the situation militarily in Ulster. Rumours of
troop movements provoked an incident at the Army Headquarters
at the Curragh in the South of Ireland when a number of officers
made clear their opposition to any attempt at coercion of Ulster.
The affair badly damaged the government's credibility while stok-
ing up alarm in Ulster about possible coercion being used. It also
inflamed the parliamentary battle, with the government now
labouring under the knowledge that it could not with any certainty
count on the army in any eventual confrontation with Ulster.

In April 1914 the situation took a still more ominous turn when
the UVF carried out a highly successful gun-running operation in
which 20,000 German rifles and a stock of ammunition were
landed at Larne and distributed throughout the Province within
hours.[72] In July it was the turn of the National Volunteers to bring
arms into Dublin, an ensuing riot claiming the lives of three people
shot by troops. In desperation the government convened a conference, held at Buckingham Palace, but intense deliberation yielded
no breakthrough over the vexed issue of special provision for Ulster.
Nonetheless, Carson seems by this time to have settled on the exclusion of a six-county Ulster comprising Antrim, Down, Armagh,
Derry, Fermanagh and Tyrone.[73]

The deadlock threatened to bring the government to its knees,
when the situation was entirely altered by the outbreak of war in
Europe in August 1914. The Home Rule crisis was postponed: the
Act was placed on the statute book in September but further legislation suspended its operation until the end of the war, and until an

additional measure could be implemented to resolve the Ulster problem.

The Great War created a new context within which the Irish problem could be prospected, both by the political players and by highly politicised outsiders. The new context brought new opportunities, although these may have been obvious to some more than others. Certainly, John Redmond, leader of the Irish Party, saw the opportunity to display to the British government, to British public opinion, and to the Unionist opponents of Home Rule that Irish constitutional nationalism could be trusted in times of crisis, that Home Rule would in no way prove to be harmful to British interests.[74] Redmond also placed much hope in the spectacle of Irish Catholic Nationalist and Ulster Protestant Unionist fighting together in a common cause; hence his pledge, along with that of Carson in relation to the UVF, that his National Volunteers would be ready to defend Ireland. Redmond indeed desired the formation of a Nationalist and Catholic 'Irish Brigade' to mirror the 36th (Ulster) Division which was speedily created out of the UVF volunteers,[75] and eventually something akin to such a division was duly contrived. Redmond's, however, was always a precarious balancing act: gestures of trustworthiness to the British patriotic gallery ran the risk of stretching Irish Nationalist sentiment too far; after all, the Home Rule demand arose out of, and was sustained by, perceptions of British misgovernment and repression. Thus Redmond's unconditional pledge to send Volunteers to fight wherever needed, made at Woodenbridge, County Wicklow in September 1914, was too much for a section of Nationalist Ireland, among whom numbered a small minority of the Volunteers themselves. These malcontents split from the movement, took on the name of the 'Irish Volunteers' and declared allegiance to Ireland alone. The Woodenbridge speech is widely regarded by historians as a crucial turning point in Irish developments within the catalytic phenomenon which was the Great War itself.[76] It is likely that Redmond's offer was made in the confident expectation that the British government's gesture of placing Home Rule on the statute book had softened Irish opinion, and it has to be admitted that his party suffered no short-term electoral backlash. Nevertheless, in striking a raw nerve, Redmond contributed to a mood of growing restlessness; it was not long before recruitment figures in Nationalist Ireland began to fall sharply.[77]

For Carson the political pay-off for patriotic gestures probably appeared less clear. It was, of course, appreciated that the UVF was ready to fight the German enemy, but it was also expected in a way that Redmond's gesture was not. Carson made it clear that Ulster would have no truck with the 'England's difficulty, Ireland's opportunity' idea. Moreover, in becoming part of the British armed forces, the UVF sacrificed its threat of rebellion. Against this, by May 1915, there was the broadening of the Westminster government by Asquith to include prominent Unionists, including Carson himself as Attorney General. Redmond too was offered a post, but refused. Nationalist Ireland was outraged by the inclusion of the man who had threatened to have his private army fight the forces of the crown only months before; Nationalists rehearsed bitter denunciations of the lack of good faith exercised by the British. Redmond's refusal may have been wise in such circumstances but, equally, it did not serve him as well at home as he might have hoped; he was by now too close to the British government in any case.

The Easter Rising of 1916 in Dublin blew apart Redmond's vision of a peaceful process towards Home Rule. It was undertaken, in the absence of the German help sought, by a collection of radical Nationalists and Republicans drawn from the Irish Volunteers, the Irish Citizen Army (led by the socialist James Connolly), and the Irish Republican Brotherhood (IRB), whose Fenian philosophy it epitomised. Along with Connolly, Patrick Pearse provided military leadership. Pearse, in his published writings prior to the Rising, had repudiated the constitutional nationalist tradition of which Redmond's party was the latest exponent, and proclaimed separatism as the 'National' position.[78] The British suppression of the Rising, in particular the execution of fifteen of the leaders including Pearse and Connolly, hardened Irish public opinion and yielded the political advantage to the Sinn Fein party which stood as the alternative to Redmond's. For Sinn Fein, Home Rule was a discredited cause, and the Easter rebellion a cathartic moment of idealism to be brought to fruition through the securing of Ireland's freedom.

For the British government, from which Carson had resigned back in October 1915, the Rising was merely the pretext for the renewal of efforts to resolve the Home Rule imbroglio. Lloyd George, the minister charged with the task, focused on the question of the nature of exclusion for a six-county Ulster: would it be temporary or permanent?[79] Redmond was still reluctant to accept any notion of partition, but appears to have been prepared to shift on the understanding that exclusion would be temporary. Carson, on the other hand, interpreted exclusion as being permanent and took the still risky step of seeking the endorsement of the Ulster Unionist Council in June 1916. This was forthcoming, albeit with much agonising over the potential sacrifice of fellow Unionists in the other Ulster counties.[80] The government eventually decided on 27 July not to proceed, wary of Redmond's delicate position and the opposition of Southern Unionists. Nonetheless, another marker regarding partition and the form it was likely to take was laid down.

As these negotiations took place, the Ulster Division was suffering catastrophic losses at the Battle of the Somme in northern France. On 1 July the Division had launched an attack on enemy trenches: initial success was bought at the price of leaving men exposed to counterattack, which duly came later in the day with devastating consequences. At least 5,000 men of the Ulster Division were killed or wounded or imprisoned. The significance went far beyond a military setback; the Ulster Division had come to represent the collective identity of Protestant Ulster, to stand for a people as no other division did in the Great War. Such losses were viewed as sacrificial vindications of a people's cause. The Somme made horrifically real the mythology surrounding the Ulstermen which had been promoted in the ethno-historical propaganda of the Unionist campaign against Home Rule and Irish Nationalism. This campaign was indeed about the 'martyr spirit' identified by the Presbyterian schoolmaster T. G. Houston; the Somme delivered the martyrs in reality and in turn created an obligation on future generations to be as unyielding in their fidelity to the cause and true to the memory of the fallen.[81] The Nationalist martyrs of Easter 1916 had been joined by their Unionist counterparts on the Somme. A war memorial to the Ulster Division was quickly completed, and henceforth the commemoration of the Somme became an integral part of the Ulster Unionist ceremonial calendar: an affirmation of loyalty to the British link and of Ulster's Protestant heritage.[82] Another effusion of popular history soon celebrated Ulster's distinguished contribution to the war and her transcendent loyalism.[83]

Blood sacrifices were not likely to improve the chances of political compromise over the Irish question, but this is more easily appreciated with hindsight. The search for a political breakthrough continued, under the direction of a new coalition government led by Lloyd George from December 1916, which included both Carson and Bonar Law. Thus the Unionist influence on governmental circles again increased. The government set up an Irish Convention which deliberated from May 1917 through to April the following year.[84] No agreement was reached, and the refusal of the Ulster Unionist delegates to yield on the principle of exclusion was widely viewed as the main reason for failure.[85] These delegates stood firm in the face of much pressure from the press, government circles and august figures such as the Convention Chairman Horace Plunkett. They were led by the Scottish-born businessman Hugh Barrie, and included the President of the Belfast Chamber of Commerce Hugh Pollock and Sir George Clark of the Workman Clark Shipbuilding firm. An Advisory Committee featured linen magnates J. M. Andrews and J. Milne Barbour. Priority early on was given to securing labour and trade union representation on this Advisory Committee,[86] a foreshadowing of the formation of the Ulster Unionist Labour Association (UULA) and its incorporation into the UUC. By September 1917 the Moderator of the General Assembly of the Presbyterian Church had been made a delegate.[87] The Convention, therefore, witnessed an Ulster Unionist phalanx characterised by a strong Presbyterian and Ulster-Scot flavour, and an accommodation of the different interests involved in an industrial capitalist economy. Such features meant that the Ulster Unionists coexisted with their Southern counterparts very uneasily from the start, and when the latter moved in the direction of compromise with the Nationalists, estrangement was assured.

The Convention for a time raised hopes and did bring certain parties closer; it also raised again the possibility of a way out of the impasse being found through a federal or 'federal devolution' route.[88] However, of more lasting significance was the continuing unbending stance of the Ulster Unionists on the question of rule from Dublin, a position undoubtedly adopted more rigidly in view of developments in the South of Ireland in the aftermath of the Easter Rising and the rise of Sinn Fein. The latter party declined to attend the Convention, and it is unlikely that it would have accepted any Home Rule proposal to emerge from it. Sinn Fein was pursuing complete independence, a state of affairs which Ulster Unionists considered testimony to their long-held belief in the essential separatist intentions of Irish Nationalists of whatever hue.[89] As Southern Unionists sought to cut a deal with moderate Nationalism in the light of the new Sinn Fein separatist threat, Ulster Unionists justified their self-preservationist and exclusive outlook on the same grounds. The only respite from the embattled mood among Ulster

Unionists came with their tribute to John Redmond following his death in March 1918.[90] Redmond, mercifully, was not to live to see the decimation of his party at the hands of Sinn Fein at the general election following the end of the war in November 1918.

Unionist campaigns against Home Rule had always sought to demonstrate, for the consumption of British audiences, the cross-class nature of the movement. The third Home Rule Bill episode reflected the increasing profile of a Labour component: a greater readiness on the part especially of those in the Belfast working class who were Unionist on constitutional matters to raise their voices against what they viewed as misrepresentation by other Labour spokesmen.[91] By the time of the Irish Convention sittings, as has been noted, the UUC was engaged purposefully in building Labour representation into the overall Unionist machine.

Records of the Trade Unionist Watch Committee, which was to mutate into the Ulster Unionist Labour Association[92] by June 1918, date from October 1917, and reveal a group of industrial workers presided over by the paternalist employer figure of John Millar Andrews. The group was concerned with the Representation of the People Act, by which many thousands of working men, and women over 30, were to be enfranchised.[93] The UUC was thus alert to the need to ensure that as many Protestant working-class voters as possible resisted the lure of Labour politics and socialist alternatives and reinforced the ethnic bloc in defence of the constitutional position. To this end it was decided to provide for 'Unionist Labour' candidates in a certain number of seats, as well as Unionist Labour representation on the UUC.[94]

Carson was particularly favourable to this project. He recognised the challenges which the post-war era posed for Unionism, against a background of turbulence in Ireland as a whole. In April 1919 he wrote to the UUC Secretary Dawson-Bates:

> I should like to draw the earnest attention of the whole Province to the necessity of placing our organisation on a thoroughly democratic basis. It is essential that in the future we should avoid all friction amongst those who deem the maintenance of the Union as of permanent importance for the prosperity and happiness of the Province. Complete unity can only be secured by taking care that all classes and all views are thoroughly represented in our local organisation and that opportunities are taken to keep in touch with the feelings and requirements of the people. The outcome of the war must lead to

a great progression of democratic force and ideals and this we must encourage and make effective by a complete understanding of the wants of the people. It is by unity alone that we can expect to maintain our position in the councils of the state and enforce our policy of obtaining for Ulster all that is thought essential for the democracies of Great Britain.

Carson went on to observe that the 'general unrest' worldwide, by which he meant events in Russia and workers' agitation in several countries, could be taken advantage of by their 'separatist opponents', and he called for a renewal of Unionist propaganda activities:

We must recollect that after nearly five years a great deal of our Educational work has been forgotten and with a new and enlarged Electorate and a new Parliament the work must now be restarted and continued if our case is to be properly understood.

He concluded with reference to 'the serious condition of affairs existing in the South and West of Ireland', and urged the necessity of being prepared for 'all eventualities':

I have myself but little trust in politicians or political parties in relation to Ireland, and I say once more as I said at Craigavon when I was elected leader of loyal Ulster that in the last resort it will be found that we must rely upon ourselves. This I believe we are prepared to do.[95]

As the rest of the UK, and elsewhere, witnessed the sharpening of class divisions, with class warriors among employers and workers alike, the case of Ulster Unionism stood in apparent contrast. Businessmen like Andrews were clearly regarded with the greatest affection by trade unionists, while there was little indulgence in trade union – or worker – bashing on the part of Ulster employers. It has to be remembered, of course, that Ulster Unionism as a political party spoke only for a portion of the working class, and indeed the Protestant working class: in 1919 a strike by predominantly Protestant (and on the constitutional issue Unionist) engineers caused consternation in Unionist Party ranks – the strike was not supported by the UULA.[96] The Belfast Labour Party, largely made up of older Independent Labour Party (ILP) members in the city, served warning to the Unionists that they could not count on a blanket Protestant working-class vote when it won 12 seats in the local elections of 1920.[97] Such events prompted the Unionists to link

'Bolshevism' more and more with 'disloyalty' on the 'national question', a political stroke which could be pulled successfully in Ulster
alone of the 'democracies of Great Britain'. Moreover, the Unionists
proved adept at directing the discontent of unemployed ex-servicemen to sectarian ends in 1920–22, and the Orange Order expanded
significantly its proletarian flank.[98]

Nevertheless, the development of the UULA in the immediate
post-war years was perhaps the most remarkable feature of Ulster
Unionist re-grouping,[99] and it held portents for the party's future.
Three UULA candidates were put up and elected in the general election of 1918, all for Belfast seats, and on the basis of a commitment
to vote with the party only on 'questions affecting the Union'.[100]
This might have led to intra-party squabbles had any of the UULA
MPs been as troublesome as, for example, Thomas Sloan had contrived to be in the Edwardian years. However, they were quiescent
and somewhat overawed by Westminster, and never likely to challenge the leadership at home.[101] The UULA meetings certainly discussed social issues such as housing, and passed resolutions about
fair rents,[102] but in general they avoided any stance likely to be controversial or divisive to the wider Unionist movement. Later, in the
context of the Northern Ireland parliament, it was to be left to
populist Unionists outside of the Ulster Unionist Party, along with
Labour representatives, to express with a real sense of urgency the
social and economic concerns of the Protestant working class.

The outcome of the 1918 election saw a batch of Unionists, 23 out
of 26 from Ulster, face the overnight political Leviathan of Sinn
Fein. The Irish Party's meagre return of 6 seats in effect discounted
it from the next phase in the political saga of 'resolving the Irish
question'. The government, a continuation of Lloyd George's coalition with increased Conservative representation, sought to press on
with the task of constitutional engineering, notwithstanding Sinn
Fein's defiant creation of its own parliament in Dublin and its
refusal to sit at Westminster.

Thus, in October 1919, a cabinet committee was set up under the
chairmanship of Walter Long and a report issued by it the following
month. This was in essence another Home Rule scheme, hardly
likely to tempt Sinn Fein, or the republican militants of the Irish
Republican Army (IRA) who had taken to guerrilla violence to end
British rule in Ireland.

Yet it was an interestingly different Home Rule scheme from its predecessors. It envisaged two devolved administrations and parliaments in Ireland: one for a six-county North and the other for the rest of the island. Both were initially to have limited powers, with control of the major fiscal powers remaining with London. In addition, there was to be a Council of Ireland, a forum in which both parliaments, North and South, could join forces to work on issues of mutual concern. The Council has been viewed as a cosmetic gesture, but it is more plausible to argue, given the efforts made to keep avenues to unity open, that the Long Committee sincerely believed that it would play a unifying role in time.[103] Indeed, the Committee's intentions were non-partitionist: if they had not been then it would have been simpler to exclude Ulster from Home Rule altogether and continue to govern it as an 'undifferentiated part' of the UK.[104] Instead, the scheme involved what was viewed as a dynamic towards unity: it was probable, for example, that if North and South drew together and acted as one then more powers, including taxation, would be devolved. All of this, moreover, was consistent with a 'federal' line of thought which had come to be adopted by Long himself: Ireland (in the shape of one parliament or two) might simply be the first to receive the devolutionary powers later to be distributed throughout the UK, leaving Westminster to deal with matters such as Empire and foreign policy. Gradually, it could be said, the 'federal' idea had been brought to bear on policy-making, and the arguments – long rehearsed and fitfully entertained even by Carson himself – that it might reconcile the different aspirations of the two parts of Ireland commensurate with British coherence and security were accepted at government level.[105]

Further evidence of the Long Committee's proclivity towards eventual Irish unity (albeit still within the UK) can be discerned in the wishes of most of its members (Balfour being an important exception) for nine-county Ulster exclusion rather than six.[106] Such was the evenness of the religious and therefore Unionist/Nationalist balance in the nine-county unit that the motivation to work the Council as a mechanism for achieving unity would certainly have been powerful. James Craig, at the forefront of developments as Ulster Unionist spokesman and conscience, clearly recognised as much, and pressed – ultimately successfully – for the six-county option.

Thus the Government of Ireland Bill which emerged early in 1920 delivered, ironically, Home Rule to those who had threatened civil war to avoid the all-Ireland form of it. The UUC approved the bill in May 1920, although there were 80 dissenters out of 390 who could not stomach the sacrifice of the other three counties of the Province, and the residue of bitter feeling was to linger well into the future. The problem of defining 'Ulster' had been crudely, but necessarily, resolved on the lines predictable since 1914. As Mansergh points out, once the notion of subordinate parliamentary institutions was settled upon as the most appropriate device to protect the interests of the Protestant population of the North-East, then it was unrealistic to think of a four-county unit having the population and the resources to sustain them, or a nine-county option proving to be stable given the population balance. Those framing the Act thought in terms of a balance of sacrifices:

> If for the majority this meant the abandonment of the idea of national unity, and if for the minority it meant the abandonment of their objection to self-government, or Home Rule, these were the sacrifices consistent with the application to majority and minority alike of the fashionable Wilsonian principle of self-determination.[107]

It needs to be reiterated, however, that those responsible for drawing up the Act envisaged the application of the self-determination principle as a means to the end of fashioning a later unity, and that the fundamental compromise enshrined in the Act would induce a spirit of compromise to produce more harmonious relationships in the future. The Government of Ireland Act was an imaginative and admirably open-ended piece of legislation.

Nevertheless, it did not meet the harsh realities of the time. It was rejected, predictably, by the ascendant Sinn Fein, and this and the strife-torn condition of the South of the country in 1920–21 meant that the Act could not be implemented there. From July 1921 the British government negotiated with the leaders of Sinn Fein to produce another outcome: the Treaty of December 1921 conferring Dominion status on Ireland with an opt-out for six-county Ulster, which was duly availed of. The government had indeed made renewed efforts to bring Ulster into all-Ireland structures. The Government of Ireland Act was thus only partially put into practice: the six-county unit of 'Northern Ireland' was brought into being with elections in May 1921, and the formal opening of the parliament in Belfast was performed by the King the following month. This was in no small measure due to the eagerness of the pragmatist Craig – who succeeded Carson as Ulster Unionist leader in February 1921 – to have the new administrative arrangements and institutions functioning as quickly as possible and owed nothing to a foot-dragging British government;[108] Craig saw the political value in Northern Ireland establishing itself while the rest of Ireland was in turmoil. From the middle of 1921 further efforts to grapple with the Irish problem would have to take account of the material reality which was the Unionist-controlled government of Northern Ireland.

Ulster Unionism killed off Irish Unionism in order to preserve itself.[109] Within the terms of its experience, its prejudices and its fears, and within the context created by the Government of Ireland Act, it identified preservation with control of its affairs. It found infinitely preferable the option of separation from an increasingly separatist Nationalism, than forming part of an all-Ireland Home Rule arrangement in which it felt it would be progressively marginalized by that restless Nationalist force. Unionism prioritised its own security, which in practice meant that of the Protestant community whose political project it functioned as to a considerable extent. Protestant Ulster rather revelled in the notion of being an ethnic frontier of the UK, notwithstanding the edginess which that position entailed. It had always upheld the Union, and the Union remained after 1921, if in an altered state.

Unionists had argued, to some ultimate, if qualified effect, that they should not be the price of the Irish Nationalist desire – alone of the peoples of the UK – to disrupt the constitutional arrangement then in being. They had also contended that the whole political unit of the UK should decide on the matter, given the way that any change to these arrangements would in some way affect all.[110] Unionists believed their own rhetoric implicitly: loyalty should be rewarded not travestied by treachery. By the time the Government of Ireland Act and the Anglo-Irish Treaty emerged to shape a new era in Irish history, the Unionists could point to their sacrifices in wartime for Britain. As far as they were concerned they had proved themselves: their loyalty had been demonstrated in the ultimate terms. As an exasperated Carson declaimed at a 12 July rally in 1919: 'For God's sake cease threatening us! For God's sake recognise that we are one with you! For God's sake admit that we have done our share and our duty in the war. Treat us as good citizens.'[111]

It was the Unionists' authentic determination to be British citizens which preserved them from what they fixatedly regarded as the assured misery of all-Ireland polity. Equally, it was their continuing Achilles' heel that their appeals to the British state were not heard with the sympathy to which they felt entitled. Demands for equal treatment within the UK jostled with a 'special people' mentality.[112] It is worth noting that Carson's civic-sounding plea for citizenship rights was made in the decidedly ethnic and tribalist setting of an Orange demonstration. The more Ulster Protestants felt let down by, or unable to trust, British governments and British opinion, the more an 'ourselves alone' and particularist outlook intensified throughout the community and its politics.

It might be added that Irish Nationalists, along with their disinclination to take the Ulster Unionist case seriously, never properly appreciated the peculiarly difficult political problem faced by British governments in forcing a section of British citizens out of the set of arrangements with which they felt content, and into another which they regarded with dread.[113] Any such action by a British government would have raised all sorts of questions about the nature of UK membership and citizenship, and would have had possible knock-on effects. Such was the ambiguous nature of the unwritten British constitution which nonetheless commanded such emotional allegiance from so many.

Notes

1 See A. Jackson, *The Ulster Party* (Oxford, Oxford University Press, 1989), pp. 235–40 and ch. 6; P. Buckland, *Ulster Unionism and the origin of Northern Ireland 1886 to 1920* (Dublin, Gill and Macmillan, 1973), chs 1 and 2; R. McNeill, *Ulster's stand for union* (London, John Murray, 1922), ch. 3; G. Lucy, 'The formation of the Ulster Unionist Council', *New Ulster*, November 1995.
2 Jackson, *Ulster Party*, p. 231.
3 *Belfast Weekly News*, 9 March 1905, 'Ulster Scot Junior' column.
4 *Witness*, 3 March 1905.
5 *Belfast Weekly News*, 9 March 1905.
6 Ibid., 'Ulster Scot' column.
7 J. Kendle, *Ireland and the federal solution* (Kingston and Montreal, McGill Press, 1989), ch. 2; also Long to Dawson-Bates, 27 November 1907, Ulster Unionist Council (UUC) Papers, Public Record Office of Northern Ireland (PRONI), D1327/23/1A.
8 UUC Papers, D1327/23/1A, letters from Long to Dawson-Bates, 30 November 1907 and 4 December 1907.
9 Kendle, *Ireland*, ch. 2; Jackson, *Ulster Party*, pp. 276–81.
10 Jackson, *Ulster Party*, p. 200.
11 UUC Papers, D1327/23/1A, Wilson to Dawson-Bates, 9 November 1910.

12 Ibid., W. H. Boyd to Dawson-Bates, 21 December 1909; see also Wilson to Dawson-Bates, 6 October 1911.

13 See D. Fitzpatrick, *The two Irelands 1912–1939* (Oxford, Oxford University Press, 1998), p. 14; P. Bew, *Ideology and the Irish question* (Oxford, Oxford University Press, 1994) refers to the AOH as boasting a membership of 125,000 by 1914 (p. 75).

14 See, for example, A. W. Samuels, *Home Rule: what is it?* (Dublin and London, 1911).

15 See S. Paseta, 'The Catholic hierarchy and the Irish university question, 1880–1908', *History*, 85:278 (2000), pp. 268–84; Jackson, *Ulster Party*, pp. 176–92.

16 *Witness*, 10 March 1905.

17 Ibid., 1 May 1908.

18 Note must be taken of the Presbyterian Home Rulers mentioned in the previous chapter, and the willingness of the 'Russellites' to cooperate with Irish Nationalists on the land issue.

19 See Jackson, *Ulster Party*, pp. 198–211 for an account of problems in the associations during the late 1890s and early 1900s.

20 UUC Papers, D1327/23/1A, Wilson to Dawson-Bates, 5 November 1910.

21 Jackson, *Ulster Party*, pp. 211–22.

22 UUC Papers, D1327/23/1A, report by Frank Hall, 15 October 1910. Frank Hall was to be a central figure in the Ulster Volunteer Force (UVF). Unionists alleged unfairness in the distribution of seats, that it much more often took fewer votes to elect Nationalists.

23 Jackson, *Ulster Party*, pp. 235–42.

24 G. Dangerfield, *The strange death of Liberal England* (New York, Capricorn Books, 1961), p. 81. Dangerfield's is the classic account of the various political dramas of this period, including Home Rule; it is decidedly out of sympathy with the Ulster Unionists.

25 A recent biographical treatment of Carson, Alvin Jackson's *Sir Edward Carson* (Dublin, Historical Association of Ireland, 1993), is the best starting point for an exploration of the Carson historiography.

26 See A. Jackson, 'Unionist myths 1912–1985', *Past and Present*, 136 (1992), pp. 164–85; A. Gailey, 'King Carson: an essay on the invention of leadership', *Irish Historical Studies*, 30:117 (1996), pp. 66–87; McNeill, *Ulster's stand for union*; P. Buckland, *James Craig* (Dublin, Gill and Macmillan, 1980).

27 Gailey, 'King Carson'.

28 See Kendle, *Ireland*; J. Kendle, *Federal Britain* (London, Routledge, 1997); G. Walker, *Intimate strangers: political and cultural interaction between Scotland and Ulster in modern times* (Edinburgh, John Donald, 1995), ch. 2; A. O'Day, *Irish Home Rule 1867–1921* (Manchester, Manchester University Press, 1998), ch. 9.

29 See A. Jackson, 'Andrew Bonar Law', in R. Eccleshall and G. Walker (eds), *A biographical dictionary of British Prime Ministers* (London, Routledge, 1998).

30 McNeill, *Ulster's stand for union*, p. 60.

31 Jackson, *Ulster Party*, p. 314.

32 McNeill, *Ulster's stand for union*, p. 53.

33 Ibid.

34 See Carson speech at Craigavon, 23 September 1911, quoted in McNeill, *Ulster's stand for union*, p. 49; for a critique of McNeill's hypothesis regarding Ulster militancy see Jackson, *Ulster Party*, ch. 7.

35 For a clear outline of the bill and insightful discussion see O'Day, *Irish Home Rule*, ch. 9.

36 P. Jalland, *The Liberals and Ireland* (Brighton, Harvester Press, 1980).

37 See McNeill, *Ulster's stand for union*, pp. 93–7.

38 UUC Papers, D1327/18/1A, 'File re mixed marriages'.

39 Quoted in G. Walker, 'Thomas Sinclair: Presbyterian Liberal Unionist', in R. English and G. Walker (eds), *Unionism in modern Ireland* (Basingstoke, Macmillan, 1996).

40 See P. Bew, *John Redmond* (Dublin, Historical Association of Ireland, 1996), p. 30.

41 See file on 'Castledawson', UUC Papers, D1327/18/1A; Bew, *John Redmond*, pp. 32–3; Bew, *Ideology*, ch. 3.

42 See Bew, *Ideology*, passim.

43 See examples from Unionist propaganda cited in Walker, *Intimate strangers*, ch. 2.

44 For example, Dangerfield, *Strange death*.

45 J. J. Lee, *Ireland 1912–85* (Cambridge, Cambridge University Press, 1989), ch. 1.

46 Bew, *Ideology*, p. 75.

47 For discussion of this issue see D. Hempton and M. Hill, *Evangelical Protestantism in Ulster society* (London, Routledge, 1992), ch. 9; D. Hempton, *Religion and political culture in Britain and Ireland* (Cambridge, Cambridge University Press, 1996), ch. 5.

48 For example, J. Harrison, *The Scot in Ulster* (1888); W. T. Latimer, *The Ulster Scot: his faith and fortune* (1899); J. Heron, *The Ulster Scot* (1900); C. Hanna, *The Scotch-Irish* (1902); J. B. Woodburn, *The Ulster Scot: his history and religion* (1914).

49 See, for example, Latimer, *The Ulster Scot*, and Woodburn, *The Ulster Scot*.

50 See Heron, *The Ulster Scot* for the former, and Woodburn, *The Ulster Scot* for the latter.

51 S. Rosenbaum (ed.), *Against Home Rule* (London, Frederick Warne, 1912).

52 See C. Calhoun, *Nationalism* (Buckingham, Open University Press, 1997), ch. 2.
53 See review in *Witness*, 29 May 1914.
54 See Buckland, *Ulster Unionism*, ch. 4.
55 *Witness*, 29 May 1914.
56 J. Buchan, *What Home Rule means* (1912).
57 'I love highlanders and I love lowlanders, but when I come to the branch of our race which has been grafted on to the Ulster stem I take off my hat with veneration and awe. They are, I believe, without exception the toughest, the most dominant, the most irresistible race that exists in the universe at this moment.'
58 See Walker, *Intimate strangers*, p. 42; on Ulster-Scot Presbyterians and martyrdom see D. H. Akenson, *God's peoples* (New York, Cornell University Press, 1992), pp. 140–3.
59 See G. Walker, 'The Irish Presbyterian anti-Home Rule convention of 1912', *Studies*, 86:341 (1997), pp. 71–7.
60 For which see Jackson, 'Unionist myths'; McNeill, *Ulster's stand for union*, ch. 10; Bew, *Ideology*, ch. 3; G. Lucy (ed.), *The Ulster Covenant* (Belfast, Ulster Society, 1989).
61 G. A. Birmingham, *The red hand of Ulster* (London, John Murray, 1919 edn), pp. 178–9. Birmingham was the pseudonym of Rev. J. O. Hannay, a pro-Home Rule Anglican.
62 Quoted in A. T. Q. Stewart, *The Ulster crisis* (London, Faber, 1967), pp. 42–3.
63 See R. F. Foster, *Modern Ireland 1600–1972* (London, Penguin, 1989), p. 476, and p. 470 on Frederick Crawford, who organised the Larne gun-running.
64 See A. Aughey, 'The character of Ulster Unionism', in P. Shirlow and M. McGovern (eds), *Who are 'the people'? Unionism, Protestantism and Loyalism in Northern Ireland* (London, Pluto, 1997).
65 I. McBride, *The Siege of Derry in Ulster Protestant mythology* (Dublin, Four Courts Press, 1997).
66 Akenson, *God's peoples*, chs 4 and 6; Bew, *Ideology*, p. 48 on the views of James Bryce.
67 J. Hutchinson, 'Ethnicity and modern nations', *Ethnic and Racial Studies*, 23:4 (2000), p. 655; also D. McCrone, *The sociology of Nationalism* (London, Routledge, 1998), ch. 3.
68 Gailey, 'King Carson'.
69 See UUC Papers, D1327//2/14. The Businessman's Executive Committee included J. M. Andrews and J. Milne Barbour, linen merchants, and George Clark, shipbuilding magnate. See P. Ollerenshaw, 'Businessmen and the development of Ulster Unionism, 1886–1921', *Journal of Imperial and Commonwealth History*, 28:1 (2000), pp. 35–64.
70 Stewart, *Ulster crisis*; D. Fitzpatrick, *The two Irelands* (Oxford,

Oxford University Press, 1998), pp. 44–51.

71 UUC Papers, D1327/2/14, letter dated 10 March 1914.

72 See Stewart, *Ulster crisis*; Jackson, 'Unionist myths'.

73 For Carson and partition and six-county exclusion see discussion in Bew, *Ideology*, ch. 5.

74 Bew, *John Redmond*, p. 38.

75 K. Jeffery, *Ireland and the Great War* (Cambridge, Cambridge University Press, 2000), p. 39.

76 See, for example, Foster, *Modern Ireland*, pp. 471–6.

77 Jeffery, *Ireland*, pp. 6–7.

78 See essays in P. H. Pearse, *The murder machine and other essays* (Cork, Mercier Press, 1976). See, by contrast, discussion of Joseph Devlin's speech in Bew, *Ideology*, p. 128.

79 See N. Mansergh, *Nationalism and independence* (Cork, Cork University Press, 1997), ch. 5.

80 See account in McNeill, *Ulster's stand for union*, ch. 21; also correspondence on the issue of a six- or nine-county Ulster between J. St Loe Strachey (editor of *The Spectator*) and Robert Lynn (leading Ulster Unionist and editor of *Northern Whig*), PRONI, D3480/59/8.

81 See D. Officer and G. Walker, 'Protestant Ulster: ethno-history, memory and contemporary prospects', *National Identities*, 2:3 (2000), pp. 293–307; also P. Orr, *The road to the Somme* (Belfast, Blackstaff Press, 1987).

82 Jeffery, *Ireland*, pp. 131–3.

83 For example, Lord Ernest Hamilton, *The soul of Ulster* (1917); R. Collis, *The history of Ulster* (1919–20); H. S. Morrison, *Modern Ulster* (1920); McNeill, *Ulster's stand for union* (1922); C. Falls, *The history of the 36th (Ulster) Division* (1922); J. Logan, *Ulster in the x-rays* (1923). See also the UUC pamphlets c. 1918–21 in UUC Papers, D1327/20/4/142, for example *Ulster and the war*.

84 The standard work is R. B. McDowell, *The Irish Convention 1917–18* (London, Routledge and Kegan Paul, 1970). See also O'Day, *Irish Home Rule*, ch. 10.

85 UUC Papers, D1327/2/17, minute books of meetings of Ulster Unionist delegates, the Advisory Committee, and Ulster Unionist MPs.

86 UUC Papers, D1327/2/17, 21 July and 7 August 1917.

87 Ibid., 18 September 1917.

88 See Kendle, *Ireland*, p. 196; PRONI, MIC.127/24, Adam Duffin to Lord Londonderry, 16 November 1917. Duffin was a Liberal Unionist and emphatically against compromise in the Irish Convention.

89 See McNeill, *Ulster's stand for union*, passim.

90 UUC Papers, D1327/2/17, 6 March 1918.

91 See A. Morgan, *Labour and partition* (London, Pluto, 1991), pp. 215–17.

92 The best accounts of the UULA are to be found in Morgan, *Labour*

and partition, ch. 10; and H. Patterson, *Class conflict and sectarianism* (Belfast, Blackstaff Press, 1980).

93 UUC Papers, D1327/11/4/1, 26 October 1917 and 8 November 1917.

94 UUC Papers, D1327/2/18, 'Papers of Central Council'.

95 UUC Papers, D1327/18/19, Carson to Dawson-Bates, 21 April 1919.

96 UUC Papers, D1327/11/4/1, 1 March 1919. The strike was mentioned at the monthly meeting but discussion was postponed. There is no record of it taking place later.

97 Morgan, *Labour and partition*, chs 11 and 12.

98 Ibid., chs 11–13; P. Bew et al., *Northern Ireland 1921–94* (London, Serif, 1995), pp. 25–7.

99 For which see UUC Papers, D1327/18/6, Dawson-Bates correspondence regarding new associations and composition of the UUC.

100 UUC Papers, D1327/11/4/1, 8 November 1917.

101 See Morgan, *Labour and partition*, ch. 10.

102 UUC Papers, D1327/11/4/1, 29 June 1918; 1 March 1919; 8 November 1919.

103 See J. Kendle, *Walter Long, Ireland and the union 1905–1920* (Dublin, Irish Academic Press, 1992); O'Day, *Irish Home Rule*, pp. 294–9.

104 Mansergh, *Nationalism*, ch. 2.

105 Kendle, *Federal Britain*, pp. 76–7; Walker, *Intimate strangers*, ch. 2.

106 O'Day, *Irish Home Rule*, pp. 295–6; Mansergh, *Nationalism*, ch. 5; Kendle, *Walter Long*, ch. 6.

107 Mansergh, *Nationalism*, ch. 2; the principles in question were those of US President Woodrow Wilson, himself of Ulster descent.

108 O'Day, *Irish Home Rule*, p. 303. Craig was also willing to work the Council of Ireland – see D. Kennedy, *The widening gulf* (Belfast, Blackstaff Press, 1988), pp. 60–3.

109 A. Jackson, *Ireland 1798–1998* (Oxford, Blackwell, 1999), p. 243.

110 See McNeill, *Ulster's stand for union*, p. 15.

111 *Belfast Newsletter*, 14 July 1919.

112 See Morrison, *Modern Ulster*, p. 75 on 'the grit and business capacity' of the Ulster-Scots making Unionist Ulster the place it was. Morrison was a pupil of T. G. Houston, 'the most influential and proficuous character-builder among the Irish schoolmasters of his time'.

113 Mansergh, *Nationalism*, ch. 2, Lloyd George quotation (pp. 16–17).

CHAPTER THREE

DEVOLVED AND DOMINANT: CRAIG'S PARTY, 1920–1940

A Rome-fearing, priest-puppeting, shilly-shally, namby-pamby pro-Roman Catholic administration, always on the lookout for doing the Pope a good turn. (Alexander Ratcliffe, leader of the Scottish Protestant League, on the Ulster Unionist government, 1933)

Two days before the Ulster Unionist Council met finally to decide on acceptance of devolved government for a six-county 'Ulster', a Unionist Party member from County Tyrone wrote to James Craig. He informed Craig of his long experience on behalf of the party in revision work and of 'tactics adopted by the Nationalists'. His blunt assessment was that a nine-county unit would mean a Nationalist majority in five years. He wrote of Nationalist political efforts:

> This work has commenced already ... there are funds provided in different centres for the purchase by Nationalists of properties in or about the several towns in Ulster, and even already, Nationalists from the Midlands, South and West are being drafted in to such an alarming extent that even with the six counties alone, we would have to be constantly on the watch.

Of Unionist political capabilities he glumly concluded:

> It is asked by some of our people what is to prevent us doing the same, but I know from bitter experience that we cannot do so. We have not the power of the Church behind us to force our people to come, and as you know, the other side have a hundred to every one of ours in the South and the West on whom to operate.[1]

This letter is indicative of the kind of factors which weighed on the minds of the Unionist Council delegates as they voted to consign their colleagues from Cavan, Donegal and Monaghan to a Southern dispensation, a decision which generated much bitterness among those cast aside[2] and transferred the burden of survival fears onto those Unionists, in places like County Tyrone, who now assumed the border positions. The reasoning of the letter is likely to have chimed with the outlook of Craig personally, given the way he had been instrumental in directing the framers of the Government of Ireland Act towards the six-county option.[3] Craig's correspondent, moreover, was providing an insight into the Unionist mentality which would shape so tellingly the new 'Northern Ireland': he accurately delineated the baleful perception of Nationalists as a cohesive, purposeful and cunning 'bloc' directed by an all-powerful Church and pursuing insatiably the goal of Unionist obliteration. Unionists in a sense never became truly partitionist in their thinking: they were always mindful of the 'hinterland factor', their minority status in the island of Ireland, and of the perennial threat posed by Nationalist numbers in Ireland as a whole. It was an outlook which regarded any softening of Unionist postures or tendency towards accommodation as potentially fatal. Unionist inflexibility – from which much of the character to be assumed by the new Northern Ireland state derived[4] – was itself the product of exaggerated fears of the other side's unity of resources and objectives, and a pessimistic appraisal of its own collective strength and political stamina.

Yet the establishment of government and state structures[5] in Northern Ireland witnessed an impressive display of Unionist unity, and comparative disarray among their opponents. Once they had agreed to accept the provisions of the Government of Ireland Act – and the six-county unit in which Protestants would outnumber Catholics two to one – the Unionists moved swiftly to make the Northern administration a reality, while Nationalists and Republicans decried the partition of the country and trusted to an alternative political solution. The IRA, at war with the British troops and auxiliaries ('Black and Tans') in the South, also carried out operations in the North in 1920, prompting the formation of the Ulster Special Constabulary (USC) as a defence force.[6] As with the UVF in 1913–14, the 'Specials' constituted a means of control for the Unionist leadership over their militant followers; indeed, many former UVF men were enlisted. Craig and Carson were deeply perturbed about their followers' habit of taking the law into their own hands in reprisal for IRA attacks.[7] Loyalist mobs hounded Catholics in

Belfast and Lisburn in the summer of 1920, and thousands of Catholic workers – and Protestants deemed 'disloyal' – were forcibly ejected from the shipyards in the same period. The 'Specials' were viewed as vital to the prevention of a state of anarchy, but their ultra-loyalist character from the start alienated Catholics, for whom they were simply hooligans in uniform.[8] They also became widely recognised as a major source of patronage (jobs, albeit mostly part-time, for Protestants) and central to the 'pork barrel' politics of successive Unionist governments.[9]

Craig wanted to get on with the job of state-building without interference from the British government. He was relieved by the appointment to the position of Lord Lieutenant of Lord Edmund Talbot: 'I have been in fear and trembling that one of the Southern Peers would be jockeyed in, and a Roman Catholic at that, in which case we would never have been left alone', he wrote to fellow Unionist and *Northern Whig* editor Robert Lynn in April 1921.[10] Since the Lord Lieutenant's role was nominally to oversee fair play to religious minorities, Craig's comments in retrospect take on an ominous aspect. Being 'left alone' came to mean being unhindered in the execution of a discriminatory form of government. This was evident in security matters – the Special Powers Act passed in 1922 was exercised disproportionately against the minority – and in the re-drawing of local government ward boundaries to contrive Unionist majorities wherever possible in the politically sensitive border counties and, most infamously, in the city of Londonderry. Control of local authorities meant control of housing provision and allocation of jobs in services, as well as considerable influence in education. In the years to come Catholic grievances accumulated around the question of discrimination on the part of Unionist local authorities in relation to these issues.[11] The first Unionist government led by Craig not only provided for the gerrymandering of local government boundaries, but also legislated to scrap the proportional representation electoral system stipulated by the Government of Ireland Act, and replaced it with the 'first past the post' system in use in Britain for all elections. The British government's displeasure stopped short of intervention when Craig threatened to call an election on the issue in the summer of 1922.[12] Combined with a declaration by the Speaker of the House of Commons in March 1922 that Northern Ireland business would not be discussed at Westminster, this set a crucial precedent and signalled to the Unionists that they would be likely to be 'left alone'.

The feelings of dread entertained by the Catholic and Nationalist minority over their future in the new state were to be amply borne out, but their abstentionist and non-cooperative approach in the early days was crucial in determining the extent of Unionist partiality. Nationalists declined to take their seats in the new Northern parliament until 1925, Nationalist-controlled local authorities refused to recognise or cooperate with the state, and Catholic Church spokesmen turned down invitations to be involved in the construction of the new services in areas such as education and policing. The minority found it impossible to think practically, certain individuals aside. They seemed traumatised by the prospect – as they saw it – of a sudden halt being brought to years of steady progress, of a slow but sure march to a Nationalist 'destiny' as conceived and experienced within the context of the whole island. For Nationalists in Ireland as a whole history was perceived as flowing towards them: hence the Northern Nationalists' incredulity and outrage regarding what looked to them like a reversal of the process.[13]

The first Northern Ireland parliamentary election, conducted under proportional representation on an 89 per cent turnout, saw 40 Unionists returned, the remaining 12 seats being evenly shared by Nationalists (the old Irish Parliamentary Party led in the North by Joseph Devlin) and Republicans who had formed a pact. It was a resounding vote of confidence for Craig, notwithstanding the warnings he had received in the run-up to the polls from his confidant Herbert Dixon (later to be the party Chief Whip) about the parlous state of party organisation and electoral machinery.[14] The election was fought against a background of violence and intimidation, the communal divide merely accentuated by the outcome. Despite a degree of acrimony over the selection of candidates for certain seats,[15] the Unionists held together in the manner of their pre-war Home Rule struggle: class, denominational and regional divides were transcended. The UULA had five of its members returned, including its figurehead John M. Andrews, who was to become the first Minister of Labour. The Orange Order's role in Unionist Party election work and selection of candidates had been written into the revised set of rules for associations prior to the election.[16] Craig's assumption of the role of 'tribal chief' was convincing enough to prevent Unionists becoming over wistful about Carson. Nevertheless, Craig was anxious, prior to the election, that the latter should delay the announcement of his move to the House of Lords; from the time of Carson's relinquishing of the party leadership Ulster Protestants had been reassured by the prospect of a united Unionist effort in the Belfast and London Houses of Commons led respectively by Craig and Carson. 'Somehow the feeling', wrote Craig to Carson, 'that you are a reality or even a shadow in the background creates a feeling of security among the timid and promotes caution on the part of some of those who might feel inclined to break away from the official party.'[17]

The devolved parliament of Northern Ireland was closely based on the Westminster model and comprised a House of Commons and a Senate. The former, however, was to be the effective legislative body with an executive comprising a Prime Minister and six ministers to carry out the business of government.[18] The devolved parliament was given power over a wide range of 'transferred' areas of competence including education, agriculture, planning, local government, law and order, health and social services, the appointment of magistrates and judges, and some minor taxation. Matters of so-called imperial or national concern, such as defence, foreign affairs and major taxation, were reserved to Westminster.

Given the fate of the Government of Ireland Act in respect of the South of Ireland, Northern Ireland took on its own the role of a constitutional experiment within the context of the United Kingdom. Northern Ireland's parliament was strictly subordinate to that of Westminster: sovereignty was not divided, as it would have been in a proper federal relationship. On the other hand, as has been observed, a decision was taken at Westminster not to discuss any business pertaining to Northern Ireland since the Province now had its own devolved legislature and executive. Northern Ireland was thus virtually removed from British politics, consistent with the wishes of those responsible for the 1920 Act who had had in mind such a design for all Irish affairs, and none of the political parties which existed throughout England, Wales and Scotland organised or stood for election in the new Northern Ireland state. Northern Ireland retained representation at Westminster: it elected 12 MPs to the House of Commons, and these MPs were permitted to discuss and vote on business which affected England, Scotland and Wales.[19]

The situation was thus anomalous and there was a great deal of confusion about Northern Ireland's status, and for precisely what Belfast and London were respectively responsible. Indeed, within government circles there appeared differences of opinion between ministers who viewed Northern Ireland as being in a federal type of relationship with Britain and those who stressed the Province's sub-ordinate position.[20] In an address entitled 'Ulster's contribution to the Empire', published as a leaflet by the UUC, Northern Ireland's first Minister of Education, Lord Londonderry, remarked: 'As a measure of Federation within the United Kingdom, Ulster has a Parliament of her own which is competent to deal with her purely local problems'.[21]

Such constitutional ruminations took place only after a fraught beginning for the new government and parliament, opened by King George V in June 1921. For the first few months of its term the government had scant powers to wield: the London government under Lloyd George delayed the transfer of services while it negotiated with the leaders of Sinn Fein in the wake of the truce established in July. Ulster Unionist pressure – in effect Craig's personal lobbying in establishment circles with which he had become familiar – brought about the transfer of some powers in November, but it was not until February 1922 that the government was finally able to run its own show in proper accordance with the Government of Ireland Act. British government reluctance to consolidate Northern Ireland has been attributed to its desire to reach accommodation with Sinn Fein, and certainly Craig and the Ulster Unionists were put under intense 'moral' pressure to accept an all-Ireland form of government.[22] Their implacable hostility to the idea resulted in the 'opt-out' clause of the Anglo-Irish Treaty of December 1921, but the price for this was another aspect to the agreement: a Boundary Commission to determine the final nature of the border between North and South. Sinn Fein signatories to the agreement invested much hope in this clause regarding future Irish unity, and there was a corresponding level of anxiety in the Unionist camp that what they had believed was a 'final settlement'[23] – the Government of Ireland Act – had been revised such as to put at risk their future as a distinct entity.

Unionist grassroots opinion – restless and querulous in the light of the delay in the transfer of powers – imposed enormous pressure on Craig to yield 'not an inch'.[24] Even Craig's necessary diplomacy with the British government alarmed his followers: one such, the Presbyterian minister R. C. Marshall, wrote to Robert Lynn, whom he obviously regarded as a more trustworthy custodian of the Unionist cause, to complain of Craig's 'nebulous verbosity' on the issue of the boundary and to warn of a party split unless there was 'straight dealing'. 'Lloyd George tactics', Marshall went on, 'are no use, and the Northern Government rests in the last resort on the *ordinary* voter who just understands one or two things well and whose opinions are rooted in a manner altogether different from the ever-changing views of the English elector.'[25]

Boundary Commission fears among Unionists and an IRA onslaught on the fledgling state – with the connivance of Michael Collins and other Republican leaders in the South – ratcheted up the inter-communal violence and murder rate in the North in the first half of 1922 to unprecedented levels. In a way it was to prove a watershed. With the outbreak of the Civil War in the South (over the question of acceptance of the Treaty of December 1921) IRA energies were diverted and the North subsided into an uneasy peace. Nonetheless, ethnic antagonisms had deepened beyond the capacity of any government to heal by reforming and reconstructive action, far less the embattled Unionist administration so tightly bound to the narrow outlook and absolutist demands of its supporters. Back in January 1921 Craig had appealed to Sir Hamer Greenwood, the British government's Irish Chief Secretary, to acquiesce in the wishes of 'the people in the North' to 'speed up their disconnection from Dublin end', and argued that the easier it was made for them in this respect the easier it would be 'to promote harmonious relations at a later date'.[26]

Craig knew the limits of his people's patience and of their trust in the British government: he was to regard with profound dismay the building of uncertainty and nervous apprehension about the future which accompanied the delay in transfer of services, perceived British government treachery in dealings with Sinn Fein, and continuing violence. The intentions he seems to have possessed personally – and which marked his first cabinet in general – towards providing for meaningful participation by the minority in the state fell victim to developments from mid-1921 until mid-1922. In August 1921, the Northern cabinet dealt brusquely with an objection concerning an appointment at the Ministry of Agriculture of a Roman Catholic. It was stated that the government 'intended to enrol members of all creeds in their staff provided their loyalty was unquestioned' and it was hoped Southern Ireland would be equally broad-minded.[27] It was not long, however, before ministers took such objections more seriously, and indeed pandered to those individuals and groups who habitually made them.[28] Soon the early appointments of the Catholic Unionist Sir Denis Henry to the position of Lord Chief Justice, and the civil servant Bonaparte Wyse to that of Permanent Secretary at the Ministry of Education, became the exceptions that proved the rule. Early efforts to encourage Catholics to take up their quota of places in the reformed police force – the Royal Ulster Constabulary (RUC) – were in effect abandoned. Border Unionist fears – and perceptions of British government intentions to create Nationalist-controlled councils before the advent of the Northern Ireland government[29] – resulted in the gerrymandering referred to above with Nationalist protestations given short shrift. Attempts were made by Craig and Collins (head of the provisional government in the South) to stabilise the situation in the first half of 1922: Collins ended the 'Belfast Boycott' which had been pursued by the South in response to the expulsion of Catholic workers in 1920, while Craig ensured that one-third of an Unemployment Relief grant went to Catholics in Belfast,[30] and tried, with limited success, to get Catholic workers reinstated in the shipyards. However, atrocities committed by the IRA and by Loyalists, combined with polarised views of the purpose of the Boundary Commission, ensured the collapse of these pacts. Throughout, the provisional government in the South impeded the Northern Ireland government in its efforts to get the business of government and state provision of services off the ground.[31]

Ulster Unionist detestation of the Boundary Commission clause of the 1921 Treaty led to a severe strain in relations with British Conservatives who, in coalition with the Lloyd George Liberals, had permitted it. Even the break-up of the coalition and the ascent to the premiership of old ally Bonar Law in 1922 did not remove the difficulties: Bonar Law's first priority was the unity of his own party rather than Ulster's gripes about the treaty.[32] Any moves to bring Irish matters to the centre of British politics once again would have been deeply unpopular in terms of both the political parties themselves and public opinion in Britain.

In 1923 Bonar Law gave way to Stanley Baldwin, who was similarly determined not to let Irish affairs rend his party. Ulster Unionists were unhappy with the lack of Conservative action, but this paled beside the shock of Labour taking power – albeit as a minority government – after the Tory setback at the general election of 1923. Labour made life difficult for the Unionists by withholding funding for the USC and appointing a representative for Northern Ireland – in the light of Unionist refusal to cooperate – to allow the work of the Boundary Commission to proceed. The representative was a former editor of the *Northern Whig*, J. R. Fisher. As Carson fulminated in the House of Lords about Ulstermen being 'sacrificed on the altar of British politics', Craig demanded that the Tories attempt to prevent the passage of Labour's bill on the Boundary Commission's establishment. Craig was unmoved by Baldwin's dilemma, leading the Northern Ireland Minister of Education, Lord Londonderry, to acknowledge privately that 'our people are very headstrong, and can only think for themselves. They cannot take the long view of British politics which might be that an election on this point would not serve the interests of the Conservative party.'[33]

In the event the Labour government soon fell and the Conservatives were again returned. Craig struck up a good working relationship with former foe Winston Churchill,[34] now in the Conservative Party and in the government as Home Secretary. The Boundary Commission proceeded to complete its report recommending only minor changes to the border,[35] but the resulting political backlash in the Irish Free State led to the report being suppressed. An agreement was then signed by Craig, Baldwin and Irish Taoiseach William Cosgrave on 3 December 1925 confirming the existing border. This agreement was then registered at the League of Nations. The Boundary Commission episode, satisfactorily as it turned out for Unionists, nonetheless indicated that the previously close, if at times uneasy, relationship with the Conservatives in Britain was a thing of the pre-war past. Ulster Unionist influence in British political circles was marginalised by the detachment of Irish matters in general, and by a new pattern of post-war party rivalries around class issues. Ulster Unionist MPs at Westminster almost invariably voted with the Conservatives, but they had no significant say in the latter party's affairs, and only contributed substantially to the very occasional debates which involved Ulster either directly or indirectly.[36] Later, in 1929, the Northern Ireland cabinet was to discuss the need for improved communication between the Westminster MPs and the Ulster government.[37]

The boundary issue also revealed the distinctive character of the Ulster Unionists as a political party. Unionists throughout demanded a permanent solution to the Irish question, of which the border dispute was part, and were outraged that the Government of Ireland Act had not in fact constituted that permanent settlement. This was to be a continuous theme in the party's political history during the twentieth century: Unionist anger at the Irish question being revisited and reframed, and their desire for 'permanence' competing with the changing political contexts in London (and

Dublin) and the changing strategies and priorities of governing (and opposition) parties. In this sense the Ulster Unionist Party was not a conventional political party: it was bad at adapting to changed circumstances and seemed to crave a virtually static political arena in which to function. Largely as a result of this approach to government, the political arena of Northern Ireland was to be congenially stagnant for decades, but this only delayed the shock of having to cope once again with the vagaries of British politics when the time eventually came. As Lord Londonderry put it, his party proved incapable of taking 'the long view' and was by nature a short-term 'survivalist' movement primarily geared to ethnic mobilisation around a single objective. Where that objective had been the defeat of Home Rule, after 1921 it became the survival of Northern Ireland as a distinct but loyal part of the United Kingdom.

Yet from the beginning the Unionist government in Northern Ireland was prepared to risk an ambiguous impression being given of its loyalty in order to strengthen its position. This was evident in the fractious delays between Craig's government and British governments over the Local Government Bill of 1922 and the retention and funding of the Special Constabulary.[38] It was also the case in relation to the broader question of the financial basis for devolution in Northern Ireland, although in this instance it might be said that the Northern Ireland government had little choice but to seek a revision of the terms of the Government of Ireland Act.

These terms had been drawn up in anticipation of a very different outcome to the Irish question, as discussed in the previous chapter, and in the middle of a post-war trading boom which benefited the Province's staple heavy industries. This boom gave way to slump, and it became clear, early in the life of Northern Ireland's first parliament, that the revenue resources would not be sufficient to cover expenditure. Northern Ireland controlled only a number of minor taxes, the major ones being reserved to the central Exchequer in London which decided on the Province's share. The 1920 Act also specified the payment to the Treasury of the cost of reserved services and a so-called 'Imperial Contribution' covering Northern Ireland's share of defence costs and such like. The burden of this, combined with the cost of providing for the Province's own needs and services, raised the prospect of the UK's first experiment in devolution foundering on the rock of bankruptcy.[39]

The Northern Ireland Minister of Finance, the widely respected

Hugh Pollock,[40] set out to reduce the 'Imperial Contribution', while the Minister of Labour, John Andrews, with the crucial backing of Craig, pursued indefatigably the objective of maintaining the level of social services such as unemployment benefit, old age pensions, and health insurance in line with Britain. Andrews and Craig were determined that devolution would not mean lower standards of social welfare services for Northern Ireland, and they recognised the potential damage of such a development to the Unionist Party in the form of the disaffection of its working-class supporters.[41] Tough negotiations with the British government resulted in an arbitration process conducted by the Colwyn Committee, out of which the 'Imperial Contribution' was made a final rather than a first charge on the Northern Ireland exchequer in 1925. Parallel with this an unemployment reinsurance agreement was reached which kept the level of social security and welfare benefits on a par with Britain.[42] Pollock's inclination, as a canny Minister of Finance, was not to insist on this latter issue with the greater degree of dependence on the British Treasury which it implied, but Craig and Andrews's 'populist' line won the day. The 'step by step' policy, as it was to be colloquially known, was trumpeted by Craig as evidence of the government getting what was due for its citizens; while an opposing tendency in government, epitomised by Pollock and the Head of the Northern Ireland Civil Service, Wilfrid Spender, adopted the 'anti-populist' view that 'step by step' resulted in an embarrassing 'begging bowl' approach to Westminster and a lack of independence.[43] For ministers like Pollock, Northern Ireland's obligation was to stand on its own feet and treat the relationship with London in a 'federal' spirit. For Craig and Andrews, whose views prevailed, Northern Ireland was obliged to be treated in the manner of other parts of the UK which were economically depressed, and devolution was to be operated in a spirit of 'minimalism' with little divergence from the rest of the UK in most areas of policy. After all, Ulster had never asked for it in the first place. The outcome was a situation in which Northern Ireland received subventions from the British Treasury, and *ad hoc* payments were made periodically to balance the Province's budget.

The extent to which Northern Ireland marched 'step by step' with Britain has been well discussed and detailed.[44] Certainly, the Province lagged notably behind Britain as a whole in terms of housing, health and education provision. However, as one scholar has pointed out, Northern Ireland's performance has often been unfairly judged relative to overall UK figures: taken in comparison with Wales or Scotland, Northern Ireland's position is put into better perspective.[45] In respect of such social benefits as unemployment insurance Northern Ireland kept in line, probably at the cost of reducing its scope for investment and expansion in other areas. However, the maintenance of parity was of enormous political importance to the Unionist Party and government – particularly for Andrews's own leadership role in the UULA[46] – and went far towards keep working-class Unionists away from political alternatives. The Unionist Party indeed combined commitment to British standards of social services with an emphasis on traditional Ulster values of thrift and industriousness: a dual populist appeal to the majority's sensitivities.

Northern Ireland was effectively hamstrung by the lack of financial powers available to it, and would probably have been incapable of developing a regional economic policy even if the Unionist administrations of the inter-war era had not been in thrall to the economic orthodoxy of sound money and non-interventionism. The limited powers the administration did possess were used to shore up the ailing heavy industries such as linen and shipbuilding,[47] but the closure of the Workman and Clark yard in 1935 could not be prevented, and new industries were conspicuous by their absence. Unsurprisingly in view of its industrial and commercial orientation,[48] the government was especially receptive to employers' concerns, yet the agricultural industry was also looked after carefully, and some of the Northern Ireland parliament's more innovative measures concerned farming and food marketing. Some Northern Ireland ministers of the inter-war period had significant business ties which straddled the divides between land and industry, and industry and finance.[49]

The Unionist government might have pressed local authorities to provide better standards in crucial areas such as housing, but such was the reluctance of the government to come into confrontation with its own supporters and fellow party members who controlled most of the councils, that the sectarian agendas of many of the latter were permitted to flourish and the policy of keeping down rates was generally adhered to. As Buckland has observed, the Northern Ireland government was 'uncomfortably sandwiched between the imperial government with its exacting Treasury and congeries of parsimonious local authorities'.[50] The relationships between different layers of government were allowed to grow stale: London was content to turn a blind eye to the Belfast administration (tight control of the budget aside), which in turn permitted the local authorities under it to indulge in partisan and in many cases corrupt conduct. Unionist Party cohesion demanded an indulgent government in Belfast, and Craig, with his informal readiness to respond to favour-seekers, provided it.[51]

If reforming zeal was not a characteristic of the governance of Northern Ireland under devolution, acknowledgement still needs to be made of the first government's initial efforts to create an integral educational system for the Province.[52] The failure of these efforts revealed the intractability of religious issues in Ulster, and the extent to which educational questions were to be troublesome for the Unionist Party in its quest to maintain political and ethnic unity.

The first Minister of Education, Lord Londonderry, was a passionate advocate of integrated schooling, and relished the obligation to overhaul the old system of clerically managed schools in accordance with the Government of Ireland Act's direction about not endowing religiously controlled schools. In September 1921 Londonderry set up a committee, chaired by Robert Lynn, on how best to effect education reform and the transfer of religious schools to the state sector. At once the minister had to confront the problem of Catholic Church non-cooperation. The Catholic Archbishop of Armagh, Cardinal Michael Logue, refused an invitation to supply Catholic representatives to the committee which he viewed as antagonistic to Catholic schools.[53] Londonderry's disappointment was genuine – 'I would do anything to raise this Committee above all political and sectarian prejudices'[54] – although he could be regarded as naïve for believing that the Church would share his vision for a new education system, and for appointing the outspokenly anti-Catholic Lynn in the first place. For the first year of the Northern Ireland parliament around one-third of all Catholic schools refused to recognise the new Ministry of Education, and their teachers continued to draw salaries from Dublin.[55]

The Lynn Committee proceeded to produce a report recommending structural changes and local accountability for state schools and, significantly, the provision of Bible instruction. Londonderry rejected the latter recommendation as unconstitutional and was prepared only to permit religious instruction after school hours with parental consent. The Education Act of 1923 thus bore a secular stamp, although it also abandoned the ideal of community comprehensiveness by providing for different categories of school: those under full state control; those controlled by a so-called 4x2 committee in which the local authority would have two representatives against four clerical ones; and those under full Church (in effect Catholic Church) control. Funding for the latter category was less than the intermediate category, which in turn received less than those under full state control. Nevertheless, Protestants who transferred their schools (the great majority) to the state were to ponder on the new situation in which the Catholic Church (whose schools overwhelmingly stayed independent) received state aid, including the payment of teachers' salaries which was the biggest single cost, while retaining control of their property and educational system. Soon Protestant protests increased as it was perceived that Protestant churches had sacrificed their property and influence in return for a system in which religious instruction could not be guaranteed and there was no Church control over teacher appointments. It was also pointed out that the Catholic Church not only retained control of its schools but also had special provision made at the expense of the state for the training of their teachers in denominational institutions,[56] and had a say in the appointment of state teachers through Nationalist members of local education authorities.[57]

Protestant Church and Orange Order opposition to the bill reached such peaks that the government passed an Amendment Act in March 1925, ahead of the second Northern Ireland parliamentary election, to the dismay of Londonderry, who was to resign his post the following year. Again Unionist unity was deemed paramount; the concession of a firmer undertaking to supply Bible instruction – although still after school hours – and more say for Protestant clerics in the appointment of teachers was intended to prevent any electoral backlash against the ruling Unionist Party.[58] Inevitably, this was viewed by Catholics as further biased legislation on top of the 1923 Act under which they received less state funding than other categories of school. 'We are Protestant people', stated the Presbyterian *Witness* paper, 'we love the Bible. It was their best heritage in the minds and hearts of our fathers and mothers. We believe we owe our best to it in Ulster. We and our children need the Bible more than ever if we are going to be able to solve the social and economic problems of today.'[59] There was no facile means of bridging this gulf in religiously shaped world-views, and of accommodating the stress put by the vocal Protestant lobby and the Catholic Church on the transmission of the respective sets of beliefs and values through schools.

Bible instruction was a Presbyterian cause especially, and Robert Lynn was a Unionist voice with a pronounced Presbyterian inflection. He distrusted the relatively secular and liberal outlook of Lord Londonderry, to whom he wrote in outraged terms after the Education Bill was introduced. Lynn claimed that he had been reluctant to chair the committee, and that no single important recommendation of his committee's report had been adopted. The bill, he averred, reproduced 'every objectionable feature to be found in the Scottish Act', a reference to the 1918 Education Act for Scotland which provided Catholic schools with full state funding. Lynn protested that the Northern Ireland Bill would 'rivet denominationalism more firmly than ever on the necks of the people of Ulster', and he vowed to carry his objections 'into every corner of Northern Ireland'.[60] Londonderry in reply accused Lynn of desiring to 'wreck' the government,[61] although more conciliatory letters from the minister were to follow.[62] Then, in February 1924, Craig wrote to inform Lynn that he had been nominated by Baldwin for a knighthood.[63] Given that Lynn's promise to campaign against the bill was not carried through,[64] there is a strong suggestion here that he was in effect 'bought off'. Nevertheless, Lord Londonderry, in a letter to Lynn in June 1925, referred to Lynn's 'hostility' to Craig, which he alleged was damaging the Unionist Party;[65] and Lynn's capacity for annoying the leadership was to be demonstrated again over the question of representation for North Antrim in 1929.

The episode thus furnishes evidence of severe strains within the Unionist Party over educational questions. The 1925 concession did not in fact satisfy Protestant dissidents, and the issue resurfaced in 1930 when the government again bowed to Protestant Church/ Orange Order pressure to provide for Bible instruction in state schools on demand, and a greater say for the churches on local education authorities. In an attempt at balance, the 1930 Education Act also increased government funding for Catholic schools, a move which persuaded the Catholic Church to drop a challenge to the legality of the Act.[66] The controversy was only damped down in 1930: it was to continue to be a fault-line in the relationship between the Unionist government and its constituency, resurfacing spectacularly in the late 1940s.

The education controversies of the 1920s fuelled activities among certain Presbyterians to alter the shape of the governing Unionist

Party. A 'country Presbyterian Minister' wrote to Lynn in 1928 tracing the perceived ills of the government to 'the time when the "Londonderry" influence was strong in the cabinet', and observing that the Bible instruction issue and the government's refusal to give a grant to the Presbyterian training college in Derry were 'disastrous' developments. On top of this, he went on, the government was also unreceptive to the churches' request for 'a measure of local option giving the right to the people of each community to say whether they desire the liquor trade to continue or not in their midst'. The clergyman referred to the strong criticism of the government voiced at the recent Presbyterian General Assembly, and concluded by calling for a 'grand alternative' leadership comprised of men like Lynn (whom he suggested as Premier), Rowley Elliott, H. S. Morrison, William Grant and Sir Robert Anderson.[67]

Some months earlier a disillusioned Lord Londonderry had also corresponded with Lynn, claiming that Presbyterian ministers were 'not at all popular' and that when opportunities came to keep them off committees they 'were taken with alacrity'. 'I was the only person', Londonderry asserted, 'who even stood up to the Presbyterians and I should have done more in that direction if I had felt that my colleagues would have (I won't say supported me) not worked against me. There is no democratic feeling and very little religion amongst a good many of the well known Churchmen.' Londonderry concluded by saying that politicians in Northern Ireland only gained support by 'coming forward as the champion of some sort of ascendancy'.[68]

These contrasting opinions highlight points of interest. There is, for example, a suggestion that deep-rooted denominational divisions among Ulster Protestants still had some energy even after the establishment of Northern Ireland's 'Protestant' state. Indeed, early in the state's existence, the Unionist parliamentary party was alerted to Presbyterian grievances over the matter of public appointments and honours.[69] In rural County Antrim the strain of Presbyterian agrarian radicalism was apparent in the victory of an 'Unbought Tenants Association' candidate over the official Unionist in the 1925 Northern Ireland general election. Rumblings over the issue persisted into the following election campaign in 1929 when Sir Robert Lynn was at the centre of a major Unionist Party row over the selection of a candidate for the North Antrim seat. Lynn was outraged by what he saw as 'a small landlords clique' trying to foist Colonel Angus MacDonnell on the constituency, and he conveyed to the Unionist Party whip Sir Herbert Dixon the views of his 'Orange brethren' of the area who had taken note of MacDonnell's vote in favour of the 'Anglo-Catholic Prayer Book' at Westminster.[70] Dixon replied to Lynn that the party was trying to persuade Captain Charles Craig to stand in order to avoid a split, and betrayed his annoyance with what he regarded as Lynn's deliberate attempts to embarrass him and the party leadership.[71] Lynn, however, was defiant: referring again to 'a small landlord clique' trying to impose 'their Romanising nominee' on the area, he declared that the 'sturdy independent electors in Antrim' had not yet been reduced to 'the position of the Russians under Bolshevik rule; they are still masters in their own house and able to think and act for themselves'.[72] In the event Lynn was put forward as Unionist candidate, fought a vigorous campaign in which he praised the Wyndham Land Act,[73] and was duly elected. In so doing he had stirred echoes of 'Russellism' with his use of anti-landlord language, and upset the party hierarchy. Significantly, the latter were sufficiently persuaded by his threats and warnings to allow him to stand in order to prevent further internal divisions, perhaps leading to a split. This time 'Russellism' was not allowed to take a more damaging turn.

Another pertinent point which emerges from these developments, therefore, is the level of anxiety at the top of the Unionist Party about the dangers of factions and of splits. Unionist leaders were constantly made aware of the breadth of interests and opinions represented within their movement, and were always attending to the task of maintaining an uneasy unity. The examples of Lynn and of the Presbyterian grievances of the 1920s were managed, and Lynn indeed was to become a more loyal supporter of Craig and the leadership in the 1930s when there were other disaffected voices to be heard.

However, dissent was not always contained within the party, and the threat of Independent Unionists on the outside constituted, in the Unionist Party leaders' own view, the greatest danger to the government's position. Nationalist opposition was taken for granted, and Craig openly declared that he wished to see a 'straight fight' between those in favour of the constitutional position and those against.[74] The Northern Ireland Labour Party (NILP) was a different matter, and will be discussed below (pp. 75–7), but it seems to have aroused less anxiety than the Independents, whose potential for turning Unionist supporters against 'their' government and thus giving an impression of Unionist fragmentation was amply acknowledged. Divisions within Unionism which were allowed to get out of control were regarded as harbingers of a wider sense of demoralisation with all its attendant dangers in a political context defined by 'zero-sum' attitudes: what damages 'us' benefits 'them', in this case the Nationalist opponents of Northern Ireland's existence and of its link to Britain. In as much as the Craig-led Unionist governments practised 'normal' political strategising, it was to the end of halting any drift to the often more extreme Loyalist Independents. The abolition of the proportional representation system for Northern Ireland parliamentary elections in 1929 was directed primarily against the government's Independent Unionist and Labour opponents, and intended to facilitate the straightforward struggle with Nationalists which Craig desired.

In 1925 three Independent Unionists were returned to parliament, including the self-styled champion of the working people of the Shankill Road in Belfast, Tommy Henderson. Henderson's was one of the most colourful political careers in Northern Ireland's history: he represented the Shankill seat at Stormont until 1953, and his populist, combative style on matters like unemployment and workers' welfare drew him close to Labour and even Nationalist members in opposition. However, he essentially campaigned on an exclusively Protestant basis, leading the periodic choruses of criticism from disaffected Protestants about the poor performance of the government or its neglect of the least well-off Loyalists.[75] Representing the adjacent Woodvale seat from 1929 till his death twenty years later, John W. Nixon's career provides further evidence of the depth of Protestant working-class desire for an alternative, though impeccably 'Loyalist', Unionist voice. Nixon, in fact, was a former Unionist Party member who left soon after he had been sacked by the government from the RUC for making sectarian speeches in 1924. Nixon's reputation among Nationalists at the time was infamous: he was widely believed to have led a gang of 'Specials' in the murder of Catholics during the troubles of 1920–22.[76] Correspondingly, he enjoyed folk-hero status among those Protestants who regarded the Specials as having defeated the IRA and saved Northern Ireland, only to have the Unionist government later behave towards them as if they were the state's enemies.[77] Nixon, like Henderson, castigated successive Unionist governments in terms both of social and economic policies, and of letting down the very people to whom he believed the governments owed their power and pomp. These governments in turn attempted to blacken the image of the maverick Independent Unionists by publicising the number of times they had voted in parliament with Labour and, more damningly, the Nationalists.[78]

As well as Henderson and Nixon, the government faced challenges from 'Local Optionists' in 1929, campaigning in effect for prohibition, and the Presbyterian minister's letter to Lynn cited earlier reminds us of the extent to which the temperance cause was very much part of a dissenting Liberal heritage within Unionism which had to be carefully handled.[79] Less manageable was another essentially Presbyterian tendency towards religious fundamentalism which proved to be the soil out of which grew the militant political force of the Ulster Protestant League (UPL) by the early 1930s. The UPL, with which Nixon was closely associated, became a channel for the expression of a range of Protestant grievances: allegations of scarce jobs going to Catholics instead of Protestants; Catholic 'peaceful penetration' into sensitive areas of the state's apparatus such as the police force; permission given for what were seen as displays of Catholic 'triumphalism' such as the Eucharistic Congress (1932) and the Catholic Truth Society Festival (1934); Orange marches banned (if later permitted).

In its earliest days the UPL was almost a kind of 'ginger' group within the Unionist Party: Unionist MPs like Major McCormick patronised it, and meetings were held at the Unionist Party headquarters. However, by the mid-1930s the Unionists had lost influence over the UPL, which regarded the government as weak-kneed and treacherous – or, *pace* the eloquent description of the Scottish Protestant League leader Alexander Ratcliffe (an important inspiration for the Ulster variant), 'a Rome-fearing, priest-puppeting, shilly-shally, namby-pamby pro-Roman Catholic administration, always on the lookout for doing the Pope a good turn'.[80] The activities of the UPL lay behind the severe sectarian violence of the summer of 1935 in Belfast, in which Loyalist mobs fought the police as well as Catholics. These disturbances worried the government, although it might be said that the extremist speeches of certain ministers like Basil Brooke and the Prime Minister himself in previous years[81] had contributed to the worsening climate of communal antagonism. The point of these speeches, however, had been to limit the appeal of groups like the UPL to Unionist voters, and the possible electoral danger to the Unionist Party. As the Education Minister in the early 1930s, Lord Charlemont, reasoned, bearing out the opinion of his predecessor Lord Londonderry: 'unless ... the

Herodianism of the Protestant League can be out-Heroded, I, a supporter of the Government, will lose my seat to a jackanapes, and with it, my chances of preferment'.[82] The electoral threat posed by the extremists was a real one: in 1936 the official Unionists suffered setbacks in local elections in the constituencies in which the riots of the previous year had been most intense.[83] Back in September 1935 Craig (now Lord Craigavon) urged his colleagues to ponder the situation which had arisen in Glasgow in 1933 when Ratcliffe's Protestant League had split the Conservative vote to give Labour control of the council.[84] In Northern Ireland a split Unionist vote in some areas could hand Nationalists control of councils.

The UPL remained a force until the outbreak of the Second World War altered the political context. It continued to be a focus for Protestants with grievances, although it also sought to maintain the fundamentalist Protestant appeal of its origins at the risk of alienating Protestants of a different orientation. 'Is UPL Orangeism too Protestant for Anglo and Roman Catholic Unionists?' asked the UPL newspaper, in a clear jibe against the perceived Londonderry/Charlemont tendency in government.[85]

Within the Orange Order too, as the above indicates, there was discontent with the government over what was regarded as insufficient attention to Protestant interests.[86] Again, the government's approach was one of appeasement – the Order wielded substantial influence in the party and in 1935 a high-ranking civil servant jaundicely remarked that the Orange tail was wagging the government dog[87] – but this did not prevent the Grand Master of Belfast District Lodge threatening to resign from the UUC in 1934 on the grounds that the loyalty of his brethren was being taken too much for granted.[88] The reply from the UUC, in seeking to smooth ruffled feathers, stated: 'The Council [UUC] has since its formation been very closely allied to the Orange Institution, the members of which have given us whole-hearted support and it would be a very serious matter to sever any link in the Loyalist chain'.[89] It was undoubtedly the case that the Unionist Party leadership considered the role of the Order, along with that of the UULA, as especially crucial in steering Protestant workers away from Labour or socialist politics.[90] The extent to which the Order had been built into the Unionist Party structure from the earliest times effectively ensured that it remained ultimately loyal to the government, notwithstanding the participation of some of its members in extremist political groups.

The Unionists, helped by the abolition of proportional representation, saw off the Independent challenges comfortably in the parliamentary elections of 1929 and 1933, and Northern Ireland indeed took on the appearance of a 'Bolshevik' one-party state. This situation, as well as reinforcing Nationalist alienation, produced restlessness of the sort exploited by the UPL, but also, in relation to the 1938 Northern Ireland election, a challenge from a new party, the Progressive Unionist Party. This was led by a former Unionist Westminster MP and UUC Standing Committee member, the wealthy businessman W. J. Stewart. Stewart had something of a history of fall-outs with the party,[91] and his challenge may have been motivated by personal grudges and ambition as much as policy. Nevertheless, in its espousal of an interventionist and 'Keynesian' approach to the economic problems of the time and a demand for a large programme of public works and house-building, Stewart's party attempted to relate Northern Ireland to the wider terms of political debate in Britain and to avoid wallowing in the 'zero-sum' sectarian struggle of the streets. Stewart criticised the government for not obtaining enough help from London to act more positively; in effect, he was saying that the Unionist government did not know how to make devolution work.[92]

In late 1937 and early 1938 the government faced the critiques of Stewart and those of an assortment of Independent Unionists whose complaints ranged from the sectarian agenda of the UPL through to allegations of government 'extravagance'. In the ethnically oriented political world of Northern Ireland classic middle-class or lower-middle-class complaints about the waste of taxpayers' money, officialdom and government 'restrictions' were voiced along with working-class interests in issues such as public works and higher government spending, all under a 'Greater Unionist/Loyalist' banner.[93] These critics were brought together around a shared indictment of the 'patrician' Unionist leadership of the day and a shared sense of betrayal, by an out-of-touch government, of the 'ordinary' Protestants, whether unemployed engineers and fitters or beleaguered small traders.

Stewart might have possessed the leadership abilities to mount a more focused challenge and the wealth to fund a proper party, but defeat at the polls in 1938 seems to have emptied him of the will to carry on. In any case, it is doubtful whether the various Independent groups and maverick individuals could have merged into one party with a positive set of agreed policies as opposed to a rag bag of grievances. In the diversity of Independent Unionist politics there was security for the Unionist Party, although this may not have been obvious in the charged political climate of the inter-war era.

Next to the Independent Unionists, the NILP was the biggest nuisance to the official Unionists. As early as 1923 when the then Belfast Labour Party, represented by Harry Midgley, came very close to defeating Robert Lynn for the Westminster seat of West Belfast,[94] it was clear that the Unionists would have to work hard to ensure the continuance of their cross-class appeal.

One of the main vehicles through which this had been achieved in the critical years 1918–22 was the UULA, but in the more stable conditions of Northern Ireland from 1923 this body appears to have gone into a decline. Certainly, by 1925 it was anxiously canvassing views as to how membership might be boosted.[95] As unemployment took a stronger grip in the late 1920s and early 1930s the UULA pressured the government for more relief schemes and demanded that the Poor Law Guardians increase the rates of payment for the outdoor relief work which was provided.[96] Rates of relief payment in Belfast were the lowest in the UK.[97] The UULA demands were not met, and anger and desperation did in fact lead to unemployment riots in October 1932; uniquely, Protestants and Catholics fought together against the authorities. This caused consternation within government circles and the Guardians were at last forced to cave in to the demands for increases. The government had been anxious for some time about the unemployment situation and the inflexibility of the Poor Law Guardians,[98] but once again reluctance to confront their own supporters in local authorities impeded any pre-emptive action being taken before the trouble erupted. The recrudescence of sectarian street violence in the following years indicated the brittle and ephemeral nature of the working-class alliance between Protestants and Catholics, rather than any refortifying of this particular link in the 'Loyalist chain'; as argued above, discontent remained anti-establishment, if not oriented towards class politics.

The unemployment problems and the disturbances did not in fact greatly benefit the NILP. By the 1930s the party, led by Midgley, was pursuing a strictly 'reformist' course, modelling itself on British Labour and discountenancing any form of direct action. That was left to the Communists, who were behind much of the agitation of 1932. The NILP set its sights on playing the main opposition role in the Northern Ireland parliament which the

Nationalists were reluctant to assume, and, in contrast to both Unionists and Nationalists, it sought to build a cross-community base of support to achieve this. Significantly, it also equivocated on the question of Northern Ireland's constitutional position. In its objective, the NILP was considerably hampered by the success of the Unionists, and the compliance of the Nationalists, in persuading the electorate that the issue of overriding importance at each election was precisely that of the constitution, and the NILP attracted condemnation from both sides for its 'fence-sitting'. Yet this was not the only obstacle the NILP had to surmount.

Besides beating the 'loyalty' drum continuously, the Unionists' approach to devolution under the leadership of Craigavon had the effect of nullifying much of the appeal of a party like the NILP around social and economic policies. When Labour members of parliament, like Midgley after 1933, demanded that the government make more of its powers to solve social and economic ills, the stonewall reply was invariably that these decisions rested with Westminster. Besides ensuring that Northern Ireland remained 'step by step' in respect of social services – and in 1938 a further agreement with the British government reconfirmed this officially – the government claimed that it could do no more than reproduce British measures. Where the NILP's criticisms fastened on to practical details of social and economic matters, it was usually British government policies that were the object of discussion. Thus the NILP's frequent attacks on the limited scope of unemployment insurance and on the means test in the 1930s[99] were really echoes of a critique developed by the British Labour movement of the National Government from 1931. Midgley was reduced to frustrated outbursts in parliament:

> This is a deadly institution ... Every time you come forward with a new idea or try to develop a new problem and inculcate it into the minds of members you are met with the argument, 'it is outside our powers; it is a reserved service; do you expect us to do that on our own when other areas are not prepared to join us?' After you have been here for a while you become obsessed with the feeling that you can perform no useful function.[100]

Such were the political benefits for the Unionists in reducing much of the parliamentary business to an empty ritual.

The Unionist government found the broadsides fired at it in parliament by Midgley and other Labour members of the period such as Jack Beattie irksome rather than politically damaging.[101] In private correspondence with Major Blakiston-Houston, defeated by Midgley for the Belfast seat of Dock in the 1933 election, Craigavon exuded equanimity: 'We will just have to put up with your successor [Midgley] and try to keep him in order. I do not mind quite so much what these sort of people say as the length of time it takes them in the saying, but it cannot be helped.'[102] Midgley lost his seat at the following election in 1938 when he was the victim of a Catholic backlash against his stance on the Spanish Civil War.[103] Indeed, the conservative Catholic Nationalism of Northern Ireland, in so many ways the tribal equivalent of Unionism, was bitterly opposed to what were viewed as attempts by Labour to 'steal' Nationalist votes.[104] Unionists, on the occasions when a Labour challenge looked potentially troublesome, shamelessly leafleted Catholic voters reminding them of the Church's condemnation of socialism. In such ways did the religiosity and tribalism of the Province play straight into their hands.

Craigavon's Unionist regime, which spanned the years from the foundation of Northern Ireland in 1921 to the death of the Prime Minister in 1940, adopted a consistently cautious approach to the operation of devolved government. Devolution was not used, contrary to the commonly perceived dynamics of a delegation of power, in order to diverge significantly from Britain. Craigavon's governments, in fact, attempted as much as possible to affirm the Province's British identity through the constitutional arrangements Unionists had been given. Hence the emphasis on 'step by step' in relation to social services as a means of minimising the disjunctive effects of devolution: the detachment of Northern Ireland politically from Westminster and the British party system. 'Step by step' also made political sense: it took the ground from beneath a party like the NILP and made credible the Unionist pleas for Protestant working-class support. It could also be used by Craigavon to refute – however dubiously – allegations of discrimination against the minority; social welfare benefits were administered impartially between Protestants and Catholics.[105]

In a broad cultural sense, it is arguable that Northern Ireland was not as cut off from inter-war Britain as has been argued.[106] The economic miseries of the period were visited on many regions of Britain which shared with Northern Ireland a dependence on export-based heavy industry, and hunger marches and riots occurred in other parts of the UK at the same time as in Northern Ireland. Even sectarian conflict of an Orange and Green kind was alive and well in the West of Scotland and Merseyside, and, indeed, the populist appeal of Scottish Unionism in the period bore many of the hallmarks of its Ulster counterpart.[107] On top of this the Unionist government made great efforts to mount 'spectaculars' which were designed to promote strong identification with Britain and unity at home of the Protestant Loyalist ethnic 'bloc'. Hence the significance of royal visits and the prominent inclusion of the Protestant churches, schools and other organisations.[108]

Other events combined the promotion of British loyalty with the celebration of local achievement, pride and distinctiveness. Such was the motivation behind the grand royal opening of the parliament building at Stormont in 1932, a towering edifice out of all proportion to the business it was housed to transact.[109] The ceremony for the unveiling of Carson's statue at Stormont, and the 'state' funeral for the deceased leader in Belfast in 1935, served as uncomfortable reminders to Britain of the defiant nature of Ulster's loyalty. Equally, Great War commemorations and memorials served to bring Northern Ireland firmly in line with British practice and experience as the war was being manoeuvred out of the national consciousness in the rest of Ireland; but simultaneously they carried with them in Northern Ireland an edgy impression of a muted British response to the Province's claims to be part of such rituals. Somme commemorations tended to reflect on the part of Ulster Protestants the lack of security in terms of 'national' belonging, as opposed to the strong sense of ethnic self-preservation and survival which was perceived as having been forged through fire. To this interpretation of the sacrifices of the Great War was added the Ulster Protestant version of the years 1920–22 and the survival – again through fire – of 'their' state, with no help from Britain. Identity matters continued to be ambiguous, if often presented by the Unionist Party as its strength.

In terms of propaganda it should be said that the party was more vigorous and attentive than has often been suggested, and within the senior ranks there were prominent journalists and newspaper editors such as Lynn and Thomas Moles.[110] Indeed, the close relationship between the party and the Belfast press, excluding the Nationalist *Irish News*, should be acknowledged as central to the maintenance of a communal self-image, and to the level of awareness of the development of Southern Ireland towards an insular

Catholic state in which Protestant numbers were declining substantially.[111] Craigavon could not have asked for more from his opposite numbers in the South in this respect. Under de Valera especially, from 1932, factors such as legislation reflecting Catholic teaching, the privileging of Gaelic culture and language, economic protectionism, and increasing anti-Britishness all served to make the Unionists' case (to their own supporters mostly) for them, even before de Valera's new constitution of 1937 which proclaimed a Republic in all but name, granted a special recognition to the position of the Catholic Church, and, in an irredentist flourish, laid claim to the territory of Northern Ireland.[112] In Unionist eyes de Valera had torn up the tripartite treaty of 1925 with its apparent guarantees of Northern Ireland's political and territorial integrity.

In the light of this it is hardly surprising that Craigavon felt obliged to call a snap election in February 1938 to provide an answer. An increased Unionist vote duly delivered it. In retrospect, Craigavon was wise to have gone to the polls early in 1938. Later that year he had to look on impotently and grimly as the British government negotiated the return of 'the Treaty ports' in the South to the Irish government.[113] Outraged Unionists considered this further evidence of Britain's proclivity for appeasing her and Ulster's enemies, and the issue of the ports was indeed about to be thrown into sharp relief in terms of questions of national security.

Ordinary Ulster Protestants quite simply continued to see irreducible threats to them in the overwhelmingly Catholic island of Ireland. Moreover, they perceived the threat nearer home in the vigorous Catholic Church sense of mission which enthused its often economically impoverished yet politically defiant flock. That there was no let-up in the 'No Surrender' politics of Unionism was in a sense an inevitable reflection of the continuation of Catholic Nationalist hostility to Northern Ireland. The more the Catholic minority, politically and culturally, was seen to accept the 'disloyal' designation, the more Orange populism made claims on government attention and indulgence. The political culture of Northern Ireland was thus shaped by the extent of alienation engendered.

Given such a context it is difficult to accept Jackson's judgement that the Northern Ireland government's performance under Craigavon in respect of conciliatory strategies compares badly to that of Cosgrave's administration in the South in the 1920s.[114] The comparison, arguably, is not appropriate: Cosgrave's Republican opponents bore little antipathy to independent Irish structures of government as opposed to perceptions of lingering British influence, while the Northern Nationalists were encouraged to believe – by all political parties in the South – that partition, while detestable, would not endure. The scope for conciliation was thus severely circumscribed in Northern Ireland, where ethnic conflict, rather than the albeit deadly family quarrel of the South, was the defining feature. The problem of conciliation, moreover, was compounded by the relative isolation of the Ulster Unionists' position: their British 'hinterland', politically, was not as supportive or tangible as that of the Nationalists' relationship to the South, and the determination to guarantee their own future, evident since at least the beginning of the century, dictated the uncompromising nature of the Unionist approach to government and, indeed, to wider community relations.

'A terrible dilemma occurred', wrote the Ulster novelist Forrest Reid in correspondence about a member of his bridge circle,

> Lord Craigavon's funeral and the wedding of Norman Greaves happened on the same day, almost at the same hour. Picture poor Mrs Joseph, torn between twin yearnings. In the end she elected for the funeral, though it was then too late to get a ticket and she arrived home exhausted.[115]

Reid lived a short distance from the Belmont Presbyterian Church where Craigavon's funeral took place in November 1940. The social routines of this leafier quarter of East Belfast were a world away from the Loyalist working-class clamour of the nearby shipyards; far less did the plight of Catholic Belfast intrude. The impression is of a relatively comfortable middle class either mockingly indifferent (as in Reid's case) to the local political scene, or prepared to put their trust in the avuncular and respectable figure of Ulster's first Prime Minister. The shock to the psyche of 'middle Ulster' of Craigavon's death was profound, coming as it did after the outbreak of another World War. The succession of John M. Andrews, in so many ways Craigavon's trusted lieutenant for twenty years, was a signal that, notwithstanding the extraordinary circumstances brought about by the war, Ulster Unionism was bent on 'business as usual'.

Notes

1 Ulster Unionist Council (UUC) Papers, Public Record Office of Northern Ireland (PRONI) D1327/18/27, Barry Meglaughlin to Craig, 8 March 1920.
2 See material in UUC Papers, D1327/18/27.
3 P. Buckland, *James Craig* (Dublin, Gill and Macmillan, 1980), pp. 41–4.
4 See the general histories by P. Buckland, *A history of Northern Ireland* (Dublin, Gill and Macmillan, 1981); D. Harkness, *Northern Ireland since 1920* (Dublin, Helicon, 1983); T. Hennessey, *A history of Northern Ireland* (Dublin, Gill and Macmillan, 1997). M. Farrell's *Northern Ireland: the Orange state* (London, Pluto Press, 1976) is a sustained assault on Ulster Unionism with a lot of important historical detail, while Tom Wilson's *Ulster: conflict and consent* (Oxford, Blackwell Press, 1989) provides something of a case for the Unionist defence (Wilson was an economic adviser to the O'Neill Unionist government in the 1960s). P. Bew et al., *The state in Northern Ireland* (Manchester, Manchester University Press, 1979), revised as *Northern Ireland 1921–1994* (London, Serif, 1995), and B. O'Leary and J. McGarry, *The politics of antagonism* (London, Athlone Press, 1993) are involved scholarly treatments.
5 For which see P. Buckland, *The factory of grievances* (Dublin, Gill and Macmillan, 1979); B. Follis, *A state under siege: the establishment of Northern Ireland* (Oxford, Oxford University Press, 1995).
6 The USC was divided into three categories: 'A', 'B' and 'C'. Class 'A' were full-time, class 'B' part-time, and class 'C' a reserve force. Classes 'A' and 'C' were stood down in 1925. See M. Farrell, *Arming the Protestants* (London, Pluto Press, 1983); A. Hezlet, *The 'B' Specials* (London, Tom Stacey, 1972).
7 See PRONI, D3480/59/34, letter from Carson to Robert Lynn, 28 August 1920; also Follis, *A state*, pp. 12–13.
8 See PRONI, PM 1/71, correspondence between Wilfrid Spender and Charles Blackmore regarding indiscipline among the Specials; also Farrell, *Arming the Protestants*, passim.
9 See Steve Bruce's points about the Unionist regime in 'Sectarianism in Scotland: a contemporary assessment and explanation', *Scottish Government yearbook* (1988).
10 PRONI, D/3480/59/41.
11 See J. H. Whyte, 'How much discrimination was there under the Unionist regime, 1921–1968?', in T. Gallagher and J. O'Connell (eds), *Contemporary Irish studies* (Manchester, Manchester University Press, 1983).
12 See PRONI, PM 9/3, correspondence between Craig and Wilfrid Spender (First Secretary to the Northern Ireland cabinet).

13 For Northern Nationalists see E. Phoenix, *Northern nationalism* (Belfast, Ulster Historical Foundation, 1994); A. C. Hepburn, *A past apart: studies in the history of Catholic Belfast 1850–1950* (Belfast, Ulster Historical Foundation, 1996); M. Elliott, *The Catholics of Ulster* (London, Penguin, 2001).

14 See correspondence PRONI, PM/1/70.

15 Ibid.

16 UUC Papers, D1327/18/47.

17 Correspondence in PRONI, PM/1/71.

18 From 1921 to 1925 the Ministries of Agriculture and Commerce were the responsibility of one minister.

19 The best one-volume treatment of devolution in the UK is V. Bogdanor, *Devolution in the United Kingdom* (Oxford, Oxford University Press, 1999).

20 See Bew et al., *Northern Ireland*, pp. 60–1 on Hugh Pollock and J. M. Andrews.

21 UUC Papers, D1327/20/4/142.

22 See Follis, *A state*, ch. 4.

23 See PRONI, CAB 4/12/1, letter from Craig to de Valera.

24 See commentary on the Ulster Protestant Voters' Defence Association (UPVDA) of the time in C. Norton, 'Creating jobs, manufacturing unity: Ulster Unionism and mass unemployment, 1922–34', *Contemporary British History*, 15:2 (2001), pp. 1–14.

25 PRONI, D3480/59/43. See D. Kennedy, *The widening gulf* (Belfast, Blackstaff Press, 1988), p. 69 on Unionist press reaction to the 1921 Treaty, and Follis, *A state*, p. 191 on Lynn's remark about attacks on Northern Ireland in 1922 being infused with the 'spirit of 1641' (the date of a massacre of Protestants by Catholics in Ireland).

26 PRONI, PM/1/71, 27 January 1921.

27 PRONI, CAB 4/12/7.

28 See Bew et al., *Northern Ireland*, p. 57.

29 See UUC Papers, D1327/24/1.

30 PRONI, CAB 4/38/15; see discussion in Norton, 'Creating jobs'.

31 Follis, *A state*, pp. 78–9.

32 See PRONI, PM/9/5, Spender to Craig, 12 January 1923, regarding Bonar Law's complaints that Ulster was making life difficult for him.

33 See K. Matthews, 'Stanley Baldwin's "Irish question"', *Historical Journal*, 43:4 (2000), pp. 1027–49.

34 PRONI, D3480/59/56, see Craig to Churchill, 10 December 1924, regarding an invitation to speak in Belfast and 'wipe out the memory' of his previous visit in 1912 when he addressed a Home Rule gathering.

35 See PRONI, D3480/59/58, letters from Fisher to Lynn.

36 For example, the unemployment insurance agreement of 1929: see *Northern Whig*, 27 February 1929 and 2 March 1929; see also

H. Shearman, *Not an inch: a study of Northern Ireland and Lord Craigavon* (London, Faber and Faber, 1942), pp. 175–7.

37 PRONI, CAB 4/242/2.

38 See note 6 above.

39 For fuller discussion see Follis, *A state*, ch. 6; Buckland, *Factory*.

40 For whom see Bew et al., *Northern Ireland*, p. 34.

41 See Craig's comments, *Northern Ireland House of Commons Debates*, XVI, c. 36–7, 18 December 1933.

42 But many of these went with stricter rules on qualification, something that had political fall-out. See Norton, 'Creating jobs'.

43 Bew et al., *Northern Ireland*, ch. 2.

44 See Buckland, *Factory*; D. Birrell and A. Murie, *Policy and government in Northern Ireland* (Dublin, Gill and Macmillan, 1980).

45 D. S. Johnson, 'The Northern Ireland economy, 1914–39', in L. Kennedy and P. Ollershaw (eds), *An economic history of Ulster* (Manchester, Manchester University Press, 1985).

46 See William Grant's comments at UULA meeting, *Northern Whig*, 4 March 1929. Grant himself was later to become a cabinet minister in 1940.

47 See discussion of Loans Guarantee Acts in Norton, 'Creating jobs'.

48 See E. Gordon and R. Trainer, 'Employers and policy making: Scotland and Northern Ireland, c. 1880–1939', in S. J. Connolly et al. (eds), *Conflict, identity and economic development* (Preston, Carnegie Publishing, 1995).

49 Ibid.

50 Buckland, *James Craig*, p. 90.

51 Ibid., ch. 4; Bew et al., *Northern Ireland*, ch. 2; J. Bardon, *A history of Ulster* (Belfast, Blackstaff, 1992), p. 513.

52 For this issue see Buckland, *Factory*, ch. 11; D. H. Akenson, *Education and enmity: the control of schooling in Northern Ireland, 1920–50* (Newton Abbot, David and Charles, 1973); S. Farren, *The politics of Irish education 1920–65* (Belfast, Institute of Irish Studies, 1995); M. McGrath, *The Catholic Church and Catholic schools in Northern Ireland* (Dublin, Irish Academic Press, 1999).

53 PRONI, CAB 4/18/7.

54 PRONI, CAB 4/18/13.

55 See N. Fleming, 'Lord Londonderry and education reform in 1920s Northern Ireland', *History Ireland*, 9:1 (2001), pp. 36–9.

56 See *Witness*, 4 April 1930.

57 Fleming, 'Lord Londonderry'.

58 See J. M. Andrews's quote in P. Buckland, 'A Protestant state: Unionists in government, 1921–39', in D. G. Boyce and A. O'Day (eds), *Defenders of the Union* (London, Routledge, 2001).

59 *Witness*, 13 March 1925.

60 PRONI, D3480/59/44, Lynn to Londonderry, 19 February 1923.

61 Ibid., Lynn to Londonderry, 21 February 1923.
62 See PRONI, D3480/59/45–46.
63 PRONI, D3480/59/51.
64 See *Northern Whig* editorial, 16 June 1923; McGrath, *The Catholic Church*, ch. 12.
65 PRONI, D3480/59/57.
66 Buckland, 'A Protestant state'; see also PRONI, CAB 4/260/18.
67 PRONI, D3480/59/75.
68 PRONI, D3480/59/68.
69 UUC Papers, D1327/22/1, 9 June 1925.
70 PRONI, D3480/59/81.
71 Ibid.
72 Ibid.
73 *Northern Whig*, 16 May 1929.
74 See Buckland, *Factory*, p. 235.
75 See Henderson's mischievous telegram to Craigavon on the former's election for the Shankill in 1933 in PRONI, PM/4/20/1.
76 See Phoenix, *Northern Nationalism*, pp. 195–6; *Irish News*, 4 October 1996.
77 In this respect there was great anger over the disbandment of the 'A' and 'C' category 'Specials'.
78 PRONI, PM 4/20/3.
79 See UUC Papers, D1327/20/4/142, 'True temperance' leaflet.
80 Quoted in G. Walker, '"Protestantism before party!": the Ulster Protestant League in the 1930s', *Historical Journal*, 28:4 (1985), pp. 961–7; see also references to UPL activities and significance in P. Bew et al. (eds), *Passion and prejudice* (Belfast, Institute of Irish Studies, 1993).
81 See Hennessey, *A history*, pp. 61–7, for a contextual discussion of these speeches.
82 Quoted in Bew et al., *Passion*, p. 50.
83 See Walker, '"Protestantism before party!"'
84 See A. C. Hepburn, *The conflict of nationality in modern Ireland* (London, Edward Arnold, 1980), pp. 165–7.
85 Walker, '"Protestantism before party!"'
86 See PRONI, D2222 Box 8, for various reports of Orange Order proceedings, resolutions on 'peaceful penetration' by Catholic Nationalism, and loss of property and territory to Nationalists.
87 Quoted in Bew et al., *Passion*, p. 20.
88 UUC Papers, D1327/18/160, Joseph Davison letter, 26 November 1934.
89 Ibid., reply to Davison, 27 November 1934.
90 See Lord Charlemont's comments in Bew et al., *Passion*, p. 3.
91 See material in PRONI, D3480/59/25 and D3480/59/32.
92 UUC Papers, D1327/20/4/142, see 'Mr Pollock's Striking Review'

for the government's response to Stewart's charges.

93 See also *Belfast Newsletter*, 23 November 1937, on the policy of the Ulster Independent Unionist Party led by Shankill councillor William Wilton. Henderson was associated with it. Strong attacks were made on the government regarding alleged apathy towards the unemployment problem.

94 See G. S. Walker, *The politics of frustration: Harry Midgley and the failure of Labour in Northern Ireland* (Manchester, Manchester University Press, 1985), pp. 29–34.

95 UUC Papers, D1327/11/4/2.

96 Ibid.

97 See P. Bew and C. Norton, 'The Unionist state and the Outdoor Relief Riots of 1932', *Economic and Social Review*, 3 (1979), pp. 255–65.

98 See, for example, PRONI, CAB 4/303/5 and CAB 4/304/2.

99 *Northern Ireland House of Commons Debates*, XVI, c. 1919–20, 29 May 1934.

100 Ibid., c. 1486, 9 May 1934.

101 Although see fears expressed by Charlemont and Spender regarding the appeal of socialism in Bew et al., *Passion*.

102 PRONI, PM 4/20/1.

103 Walker, *Politics of frustration*, ch. 6.

104 See M. Harris, 'Catholicism, Nationalism, and the Labour question in Belfast, 1925–1938', *Bullán*, 3:1 (1997), pp. 15–32.

105 See D. Fitzpatrick, *The two Irelands 1912–1939* (Oxford, Oxford University Press, 1998), pp. 238–9. It should be remembered that there was a distinct paucity of skilled Catholic workers able to qualify for unemployment benefit.

106 See J. Loughlin, *Ulster Unionism and British national identity since 1885* (London, Pinter, 1995).

107 See G. Walker, *Intimate strangers: political and cultural interaction between Scotland and Ulster in modern times* (Edinburgh, John Donald, 1995), ch. 3.

108 G. McIntosh, *The force of culture* (Cork, Cork University Press, 1999).

109 See D. Officer, 'In search of order, permanence and stability: building Stormont, 1921–32', in R. English and G. Walker (eds), *Unionism in modern Ireland* (Basingstoke, Macmillan, 1996).

110 See S. McDougall, 'The projection of Northern Ireland to Great Britain and abroad', in P. Catterall and S. McDougall (eds), *The Northern Ireland question in British politics* (Basingstoke, Macmillan, 1996).

111 See Kennedy, *Widening gulf*, ch. 1; also quote from Archbishop McQuaid (Letters, *Irish Times*, 1 December 1999) in 1932 for an indication of the outlook of the 'official' Catholic South, particularly

the reference to a 'conspiracy' of 'Jews, Freemasons, Protestants and Communists'.

112 Articles 2 and 3 of the Constitution. For commentary see C. O'Halloran, *Partition and the limits of Irish Nationalism* (Dublin, Gill and Macmillan, 1987); J. Bowman, *De Valera and the Ulster question 1917–73* (Oxford, Oxford University Press, 1982).

113 The ports of Lough Swilly, Berehaven and Cobh. This, as Bardon, *A history*, p. 545 points out, demonstrated that the South was 'in practice a sovereign independent state' and made neutrality in a European war 'a practical possibility'.

114 See A. Jackson, *Ireland 1798–1998* (Oxford, Blackwell, 1999), p. 347.

115 PRONI, MIC 45/1, Forrest Reid to Knox Cunningham, 30 November 1940. Cunningham would become a Unionist MP at Westminster after the war.

CHAPTER FOUR

UNION DUES, DIVIDENDS AND DILEMMAS: THE IMPACT OF WAR AND ITS LEGACIES, 1940–1958

In God's name will you go to the country that your affections lie in.
(Eamon de Valera on Ulster Unionists, 1948)

The Ulster Unionist Council report for 1940 had much of significance to put on record. There was, firstly, a tribute to Craigavon: 'a
great Ulsterman, a great Irishman, a great Imperialist' in whom 'Ulster saw an epitome of itself'. Then there was a resolution to refrain
from political activities for the duration of the war. Condemnation
of the neutral position adopted by Eire at the outbreak of war was
coupled with criticism of the return of the 'Treaty ports' to the
South, and implicitly therefore of Craigavon. Finally, a warm welcome was accorded to Andrews, who was perceived to be carrying
on 'the great tradition' of his Liberal Unionist father who had taken
his stance against Gladstone in 1886.[1]

The listless performance of the incapacitated Craigavon during
his last two years did in fact dim his star in the Loyalist firmament,
notwithstanding his embodiment of the Ulster ideal. Sir Wilfrid
Spender, writing in 1941, thought that the issue of the ports would
have been resolved in 'the Empire's interests' had it been left in the
hands of Andrews, and he reflected ruefully that Craigavon had
allowed himself to be persuaded by Chamberlain that the question
of the ports was one in which the Northern Ireland cabinet had no
status.[2] The war[3] then brought further pressure from the British
government on Craigavon to parley with de Valera, against the
background of the latter's criticism of the Northern Ireland government's treatment of the Catholic minority. The Craigavon government's wish to have conscription applied to the Province was
humiliatingly stymied by the representations in London of the
Southern government, and the outrage of Northern Nationalists

was articulated by Catholic clergy such as the fiercely anti-British Cardinal MacRory. The latter's hostility to the Unionists was also made clear by his refusal to cooperate with the government in the war effort. The decision not to extend conscription, first taken by Chamberlain as Prime Minister in 1939, and re-endorsed by Churchill when he took over in May 1940, was in a pragmatic sense wise: as well as the resentment it would have caused among Nationalists, there was the possibility of arms making their way to the IRA, which in 1939 embarked on a bombing campaign in England as it courted assistance from Nazi Germany.[4]

Nevertheless, it reflected badly on the Unionist government that Northern Ireland had to be treated differently from the rest of the UK, and the absence of conscription fuelled the notion that the Province was only 'half-involved' in the war.[5] This impression was given further currency by a relatively sluggish initial recruitment rate, and the failure of the government to secure a due share of contracts for war production and to mobilise labour effectively. In 1940 the Province's unemployment rate still stood at 20 per cent, and thousands of workers were sent to Britain to participate in war work there. In June 1940 the government faced a vote of censure at Stormont, and two junior ministers – one of whom, Edmund Warnock, was to develop into the 'stormy petrel' of the party – resigned.

In the same month, after the fall of France, Northern Ireland's strategic importance to the Allied cause was vividly revealed. With Britain standing alone against Germany and invasion a possibility, the Province's harbour and air facilities were vital for the British convoys bringing in essential supplies via the North-West. Northern Ireland was also to prove an important bridgehead to the Atlantic, and a haven for ships in the 'Battle of the Atlantic'. In the light of the South's neutrality, Northern Ireland's contribution to the war was ultimately to be crucial to the Allies, and to have domestic political ramifications for future generations.

However, in the perilous days of 1940 a fearful people found little sense of leadership from the Northern Ireland government, and it seemed likely for a time that Eire would use – or be persuaded to use – her neutrality as a bargaining counter to end partition and bring about a united Ireland in the face of Unionist demoralisation. Thus the negotiations between the British and Irish governments following the fall of France, which were terminated by de Valera's refusal of the offer of unity in return for Eire's abandonment of neutrality in July 1940. De Valera valued neutrality too highly, and trusted insufficiently in the British government's pledge to coerce the Ulster Unionists. A more ambiguous message from Churchill to de Valera a year later, following the entry into the war of the USA, was also rejected.[6] Unionists, meanwhile, had cause to reflect, not for the first time, that they were considered expendable by a London government. That the issue had arisen, moreover, was directly due to the loss of the Treaty ports which the Northern Unionist government had accepted, in the eyes of its party members and supporters, all too compliantly.

The situation, on Craigavon's death in November 1940, seemed to require a new dispensation with a radical outlook and sense of purpose to match the crisis. Instead, Andrews chose to stand by his colleagues, trusting to war horses such as the septuagenarian Milne-Barbour (who was in effect promoted to Minister of Finance) and Dawson-Bates (Minister of Home Affairs), rather than engage in the wholesale reconstruction of the administration. This, ominously, was against the advice of the new Minister of Commerce, Basil Brooke, whose performance in the war at the Ministry of Agriculture had outshone those of his colleagues and had resulted in increased production. It also dismayed the Svengali figure of Sir Wilfrid Spender, still head of the Civil Service, who was duly impressed by Brooke and came quickly to regard him as leadership material.[7]

Andrews frittered away the personal credit he had accumulated through his family name and his ministerial achievements since 1921. Criticism mounted within the Unionist Party over the failure to put Northern Ireland on a proper war footing, and it was significant that a cabinet which featured several businessmen with local interests, including Andrews himself, should be so apparently reluctant to ensure that local employers prioritised the wider war effort over their narrow economic concerns.[8] State intervention on the scale demanded by the wartime circumstances was plainly a doctrine the Andrews cabinet found difficult to assimilate.

The warning signs came early. In February 1941 the Unionist Party lost Craigavon's North Down Stormont seat to an Independent Unionist candidate, reviving the party's deep-rooted fear of Unionist fragmentation leading to weakness regarding the defence of the constitutional position of Northern Ireland. Then, in April and May 1941, German air raids on Belfast left almost 1,000 dead and whole districts of the north of the city devastated. Thousands were evacuated in the panic-stricken atmosphere, leading to a severe refugee problem in rural areas.[9] The city was woefully unprepared for such attacks, although it has to be said that even the higher expenditure permitted on air raid defence in mainland cities did not prevent similar catastrophes. However, if the Northern Ireland government was not strictly to blame for the lack of protection, its utter failure to respond purposefully to the suffering and to attempt to restore morale left it further exposed to condemnation from all parts of society.[10] Moreover, the impact of the air raids revealed more glaringly the extent of the poverty and the deleterious social conditions which thousands of working-class people of all denominations had to bear. The Moderator of the General Assembly of the Presbyterian Church predicted solemnly that a revolution would ensue if these problems were not tackled.[11]

With the backing of his colleagues Andrews chose, in the aftermath of the blitz of Belfast, to press the conscription issue again.[12] This was hardly calculated to encourage whatever degree of Protestant–Catholic community solidarity had emerged out of shared trauma, and it ran the political risk – duly incurred – of another embarrassing outcome. The British government's negative decision appears this time to have been determined by American representations made out of concern as to how such a measure would be received in the USA, although the Byzantine mind of Sir Wilfrid Spender suspected that some other factor came into play, possibly the influence of 'Rome'.[13] The episode demonstrated that Andrews sought primarily to address his own party difficulties, and to bolster tribal support by pursuing a traditional Loyalist goal, when the tragic circumstances afforded the rare opportunity to effect a measure of cross-community cooperation and a better public mood in the wider interests of the war effort through sympathetic and more generous-spirited direction.[14]

Lack of confidence in the government continued to be reflected in matters such as poor labour relations: strikes, indeed, were to be of an unprecedented number and intensity throughout the course of the war.[15] In May 1941 the British Home Secretary, Herbert Morrison, wrote to Andrews to convey Churchill's concern about under-utilisation of resources.[16] The fall in unemployment, due mainly to Brooke's moderately successful efforts to acquire contracts for war work, was insufficiently dramatic to earn the government any popular gratitude.

By December 1941 the context was still not favourable for an election contest. Nevertheless, a by-election which took place in the solidly Unionist Belfast constituency of Willowfield was not expected to result in anything more than a reduced Unionist winning margin. The contest was a straight fight between the Unionists, represented by Councillor Fred Lavery, and the NILP, represented by its well-known leader Harry Midgley. Even allowing for Midgley's dynamism and his patriotic 'win the war' stance, the NILP victory by 7,209 votes to 2,435 constituted the biggest electoral upset in Northern Ireland's political history. The Unionist press urged the government to regard it as a serious warning, and there was a widespread expectation that the complacency perceived to be rife in government circles would at last be shaken off.[17]

Within the Unionist Party there were calls for urgent reorganisation. The new Secretary of the UUC, William Douglas,[18] wrote to Andrews citing the party's acceptance of the wartime truce and embargo on political activity as resulting in the breakdown of the divisional association machinery. Even the headquarters, he lamented, was not exercising the influence that it should.[19] Back in October 1941 a conference of the Belfast Unionist associations had been held because of Unionists' anxieties over their political opponents allegedly exploiting the 'truce'.[20] Andrews himself, in the wake of Willowfield, confessed to a correspondent that the Unionist associations were not 'the democratic institutions they were intended to be' and that he did not know how to reform them.[21]

At any rate the UUC underwent some changes during the next three years, including alterations to its constitution and more frequent meetings of its Standing Committee and its Business and Propaganda Committees.[22] In 1942 J. O. Bailie,[23] a future stalwart of the party, was appointed as a go-between in relation to headquarters and the divisional associations, and instructions on how to run associations were circulated with an emphasis on recruiting members from the young and from all classes.[24] The highlighting of one division's success in attracting 'factory lassies and mill workers'[25] perhaps indicated the value placed on attracting female members, whose organisational acumen was widely appreciated. Certainly, by 1943 the women's associations were emboldened sufficiently to seek – and receive – representation equal to that granted to divisional associations affiliated to the UUC.[26] The Women's Unionist Council also appeared to be the prime mover in the formation in 1942 of a Junior Unionist Society,[27] the activities of which from this point supplied much critical commentary on the government and encouraged debate about the post-war future.[28]

The reform of the divisional associations clearly required some action from the top of the party, but the evidence suggests that Lord Glentoran, the Chief Whip until March 1942, was reluctant to intervene.[29] Glentoran's response to the Willowfield defeat had been disingenuous,[30] and his patrician attitude was not in sync with the times or the difficulties in which the government and the party found themselves. His relinquishing of the office of Chief Whip and his replacement by Sir Norman Stronge helped open the way for more fluid communications within the party structure, but Andrews's loyalty to old allies was again evident in Glentoran remaining in government as Minister of Agriculture.

Party reorganisation, at least in Belfast, was also made more difficult by an inquiry into the activities of the Unionist-dominated Belfast Corporation in 1941. The findings revealed high levels of corruption and abuses of position, and the government was put in the awkward dilemma of having either to take punitive steps which might alienate its own party members, or to side-step the issue at the risk of further adverse public reaction to it. The 'City Hall' group within the Unionist Party exercised a great deal of influence, and was championed by leading Belfast Orange Order figures such as Joseph Cunningham and Harry Burdge. The government for a time left it to the Council to reform itself, but when it became obvious that no such thing would happen the Minister of Home Affairs, Dawson-Bates, intervened to appoint city administrators to carry out executive functions.[31] A party document dated March 1942 stated baldly that not much in the way of reorganisation of Unionist associations would be achieved without 'better feeling' between the government and the Unionist members of the Belfast Corporation, and that a powerful section of the party was now furious with Dawson-Bates.[32] The latter, for his part, thought that taking any stronger action, such as the dissolution of the Council, would result in Unionists being unable to hold office.[33] It was another illustration of the extent to which the Unionist leadership felt constrained by its followers, and of how priority was invariably given to the containment of divisions within the party.

As ever, the party leadership feared the defection of members and supporters to the Independent strand in Unionism, and – especially since Willowfield – to the NILP. Correspondence concerning the East Down association in early 1942 referred to 'the more or less independent Unionist Party', and to the influence exercised by government critics such as the maverick figure of Warnock. The correspondent also identified the farming community as possessing 'very independent ideas' and being particularly resentful of government 'interference' in the form of inspectors and restrictions.[34] Indeed, the extent to which war conditions had imposed more fetters on people's activities, whether in their social or working lives, caused resentment which was glibly channelled against the Northern Ireland government. Complaints about officialdom were exploited by disaffected Unionist politicians and those who wished to enter public life rapidly and directly. Less instrumentally, there were those who had come to regard the lack of proper opposition to the government in parliament as a major reason for the growing public discontent, and who believed the Unionist Party would become stronger if faced with a responsible and constructive opposition.[35]

From this perspective the election of someone like Midgley – personally 'sound' on the constitutional question – was all to the good, and Midgley's arrival at Stormont was indeed openly welcomed by Warnock and other Unionists. On the other hand, it seemed a possible portent of a dangerous trend away from the Unionist Party on the part of the Protestant working class. As the humiliated Lavery put it in a post-election letter to Andrews:

> A new feature of the election was the large number of the electorate termed Loyalist Labour, including many Unionists and members of the Orange Institution, who supported and voted Labour. The Ulster Unionist Labour Association should consider the reopening of Ballymacarrett branch, Albertbridge Road to counter this danger to the Unionist Party.[36]

But the matter had gone beyond the capacity of any revived UULA organisation to tackle at this time. Public opinion, in Northern Ireland as well as the rest of the UK, had shifted leftwards in the circumstances of a war in which 'fair shares' emerged as a popular theme. In addition, the Northern Ireland government had lost the confidence of its traditional supporters so comprehensively that cosmetic alterations here and there would simply not suffice.

The war news from the Continent improved during 1942, but the Andrews government continued to flounder. Labour disputes and disruption of production reflected the government's lack of effectiveness in dealing with both management and workers in the war industries, and it did not go unnoticed in London.[37] The importation of Southern Irish labour to meet demands particularly of construction work raised the old bogey of Nationalist 'penetration' of the North while thousands were away in Britain in employment. Nothing could be more sensitive for a Unionist government, and the issue indeed exercised the cabinet at the expense of other problems.[38] In fairness to the government it should be said that the jobs concerned often involved security risks at a time when the IRA was conducting operations against the RUC and the Special Constabulary. In April 1942, an IRA gang of six were convicted and sentenced to death for the murder of a policeman, a Roman Catholic, in West Belfast. All but one of the sentences, that of Tom Williams, were commuted, but Williams's hanging further embittered community relations. It also elicited protests from de Valera's government in the South, notwithstanding that government's more draconian action against the IRA, involving several executions, in the same period.

In the summer of 1942 Andrews attempted to turn the tide of popular criticism by declaring the government's intentions to embark on social reconstruction. He had been frustrated by opposition politicians like Midgley making 'extravagant promises' and strengthening the impression of the public that Northern Ireland had more resources and more financial room to move than was the case.[39] He now decided, probably at the urging of colleagues, on a bout of reckless headline-grabbing of his own with promises about slum clearance, new housing and new educational and health schemes.[40] It was an attempt to show that there was life left in the government, that it could act independently, and that it took notice of people's aspirations and of the kind of world sketched out in the Beveridge Report on social welfare reform which made such an impact throughout the UK from the time of its publication in 1942. It also may have been intended as a pre-emptive strike, forcing a commitment from the Treasury by creating a situation in which a refusal would cause political difficulties all round. To a very limited extent, if so designed, the strategy worked, for the British Chancellor of the Exchequer, Sir Kingsley Wood, did entertain the view that there was 'leeway' to be made up regarding the standard of social services in Northern Ireland. However, this was only after an initially hostile response from the Treasury, which feared that the 'parity' principle which had been established in social welfare benefits would be injured.[41]

Andrews's impetuousness appalled the cautious figure of Spender, who now took the view that only Brooke could be relied upon to govern 'responsibly'.[42] The issue, far from renewing confidence in Andrews, discredited him even more, although it is possible, with the benefit of hindsight, to conclude that Andrews had merely 'jumped the gun', that he had anticipated correctly the priorities, preoccupations and conduct of post-war politics, and that his plans were eminently in the interests of a Unionist governing party which had lost support among the working class. The problem was perhaps one of inter-governmental relations deriving from Northern Ireland's devolved status. The Province remained cut off, with no representation in the British cabinet. Whereas Scotland, in the same wartime period, had the redoubtable Tom Johnston as Secretary of State adept at prising substantial benefits such as the electrification of the Highlands from a government anxious not to offend Scottish national sensitivities,[43] Northern Ireland enjoyed little such leverage. Moreover, no proper inter-governmental machinery between London and Belfast existed beyond *ad hoc* meetings, usually in relation to finance.

By the end of 1942 even the ultra-loyal *Belfast Newsletter* was complaining that the government was too old and too 'static',[44] and Warnock was calling for Labour representation in the cabinet.[45] In February 1943 the Westminster seat of West Belfast was lost to Jack Beattie of the NILP, due to the intervention of an Independent Unionist. The Ulster Unionist Council continued to support Andrews,[46] but discontent could not be assuaged in the ranks of the parliamentary party. At a meeting of the latter in January 1943 there were frank denunciations of the government and calls for a 'new team' supported by such as the Attorney-General J. C. MacDermott and junior ministers Brian Maginess and Dehra Parker.[47] Andrews resisted the pressure to make changes and on 28 April rejected the suggestion that he hand over to Brooke after the Estimates were completed in the House of Commons. The proposal that Andrews re-form the government along with Brooke also failed to find agreement, and after some consideration Andrews announced that he would resign.[48] Brooke was installed as Prime Minister a few days later, although there was a suggestion that the Governor had first asked Andrews's old ally Lord Glentoran.[49]

The fall of Andrews was quite long-drawn-out and agonising for the individuals and different sections of the party and government involved.[50] Andrews, of course, was aware of the critical voices around him in the parliamentary party, but he was also receiving comforting counsel from senior party figures such as Glentoran and he retained the confidence of the UUC to the bitter end. He could also be forgiven for believing that stubbornness was a virtue of the highest order in the Unionist codebook, and would ultimately be recognised as such. More seriously, Andrews was simply unlucky: he was Premier during the darkest days of the war,[51] and he was unfairly blamed for matters such as the absence of conscription when the final decision rested in London. On the other hand, Andrews's government never came to terms with the demands of the wartime circumstances, and could not dispel the impression of being out of its depth. Andrews's weak leadership as Prime Minister was replicated as party leader. In the course of his period at the top the party was riven as never before, and morale was at its lowest ebb. Loyalty to old friends did not prove to be in either the government's or the party's interests.

If Andrews's performance is measured by wider and more objective criteria the verdict is also damning. He personally fussed about Catholics in government departments, and missed the chance to soften communal antagonisms in the wake of the blitz. This was a uniquely tragic event the common experience of which could have been built on to the end of a more cooperative war effort. However, Andrews, instead, gratuitously preoccupied himself with the divisive issue of conscription.

As his biographer contends,[52] Brooke probably did not manoeuvre significantly to oust Andrews. By the time matters came to a head in April 1943, Brooke was having to come to terms with the death of his son in action abroad, the first of two sons he was to lose before the war was over. Rather, Andrews had by his own weakness brought about a situation in which people looked for an alternative, and Brooke's performance in government made him the best-qualified candidate. Brooke was younger, and had the air of a winner at a time when many in the Unionist Party, in the light of the wartime by-elections, considered that an unprecedented general election defeat was a possibility.[53]

The urbane and well-connected Brooke did appear to instil more self-belief from the start of his premiership. His military background and family name[54] were used to advantage, and his correspondence reveals many messages of support from senior military figures in both the British and American forces.[55] He also represented to some a different kind of Unionist. The Church of Ireland minister J. G. MacManaway – later to become a Unionist MP – wrote to say that he was thankful that Brooke had been made Prime Minister, going on to observe: 'For some years I had felt that the old Ulster Imperial tradition was being submerged in a purely six-county parochialism, and had lost confidence and enthusiasm for our leadership'.[56] This was more than just a 'country squire' form of Unionism replacing that of the industrial magnate. Whereas the Andrews lineage had commended itself to a section of Unionism on account of its impeccable Ulster credentials, Brooke's was symbolic of a broader Unionist kinship, spanning the border, close to which he resided at Colebrook in County Fermanagh, and networked through the Empire. Some of Brooke's past utterances, most notoriously as Minister of Agriculture in 1933, and much that lay in the future, were evidence of his own affinity with that 'six-county parochialism', but there was nonetheless substance to the notion that Brooke, on becoming Premier, supplied a more cosmopolitan approach in keeping with a time of international reckoning.

Brooke certainly made the kind of changes resisted by Andrews. Only himself and William Grant, the UULA leader, kept their cabinet rank, and the 'old guard' of Milne-Barbour, Dawson-Bates and Lord Glentoran departed with Andrews. Younger junior ministers were promoted: Maynard Sinclair to Finance Minister and William Lowry to Home Affairs. The Reverends Corkey and Moore took Education and Agriculture respectively, while, in his boldest stroke, Brooke appointed Harry Midgley as Minister of Public Security, the first non-Unionist to sit in the government of Northern Ireland. Midgley by now led the Commonwealth Labour Party, which he had set up on leaving the NILP when it became clear that he could not counsel that party to make a firm declaration in support of Northern Ireland's constitutional position.[57] For Brooke Midgley still possessed the requisite Labour qualifications to allow him to claim that his government was broader-based and more representative of society. This undoubtedly was done chiefly to impress the coalition government in London in which Labour ministers were playing such a decisive part. However, it left Nationalists at home distinctly unimpressed, and was described by the NILP's Jack Beattie as the alliance of 'traitors' from one party (UUP) with those of another (NILP).[58] Beattie was playing to the Nationalist gallery, and he was soon to be expelled from the NILP for flouting its neutral position on the constitution in the opposite way from Midgley.

Given Beattie's fervent anti-partitionism, the continuing non-cooperation of Nationalists in the war effort, and the recent deeds of the IRA, it was not feasible for Brooke to have widened his government any further. However dubious the term 'coalition' might have been as a description of the new administration, it was as close to it as could be achieved in the circumstances.

Buoyed by the more optimistic outlook on the war front, Brooke established better working relations with the Civil Service and presided over increased production. He set up a post-war reconstruction committee to ready Northern Ireland for whatever reforms would be initiated at Westminster after the war. A start was made on the acute housing problem with legislation culminating in the creation of the Northern Ireland Housing Trust (NIHT) in February 1945. This measure took large sectors of the housing market into public and out of private hands, and was eminently in keeping with the social and political trends in Britain towards state intervention, public ownership and social planning. As such, it upset right-wing Unionist back-bench opinion. The NIHT came on top of the establishment of a new Ministry of Health and Local Government in June 1944, and the laying of plans for the Northern Ireland equivalent of the Butler Education Act of 1944 in Britain by which secondary school education was made a right for all school children. Brooke, notwithstanding internal party dissent over his being 'too advanced',[59] rapidly re-tuned Ulster Unionism to the 'New Jerusalem' symphony emanating from across the water.

He also displayed prudence in relation to the hot potato of conscription which continued to be demanded by many in his party. In the early days of his premiership he wrote in respect of the matter: 'I don't think it would be right for us to force the issue and embarrass British ministers'.[60] Brooke thus appears to have felt that the way the issue had been forced in the past had only succeeded in causing difficulties for the British government.

On another issue with a great bearing on the sensitivities of the minority in Northern Ireland, Brooke by contrast showed a lack of foresight. This was the question of the assimilation of the parliamentary and local government franchises which it became clear was going to take place in Britain after the war. In August 1944 an official of the Northern Ireland Ministry of Home Affairs wrote to Robert Gransden, the Cabinet Secretary, pointing out that the assimilation procedure might not be acceptable in Northern Ireland from 'the political point of view'. He went on to say that William

Douglas, the UUC Secretary, seemed 'very doubtful'.[61] Douglas, of course, feared the alteration of the local government franchise from the ratepayers system then in operation, which favoured the Unionists and meant their retention of control of certain councils, to that of 'one man, one vote'. The latter system involved the enfranchisement of proportionally more Catholic voters and this held out the threat of Unionist losses at local government level with all that entailed in respect of control over employment, housing allocation and appointments. Clearly, any Unionist Party leader would have faced a severe dilemma, and retaining the old system was the lowest-risk political strategy in the short term. Brooke, however, had the advantage of a favourable context provided by wartime exceptionalism, the fair wind of his ascent to power and his government's impressive performance, and a better relationship with London, in which to take a risk and strike a blow for fairness. By signalling that Northern Ireland would go down the British road in this respect as in others, he might convincingly have been able to give himself the political cover of requiring to be in step. The implications of the question, at any rate, ought to have been grasped: the choice which existed between narrow party advantage in the short run and avoiding the supply of another grievance to the minority with possible long-term political ramifications and the threat of further instability. In the event Brooke decided against assimilation,[62] and after the war the government introduced legislation preserving the old system in accordance with Douglas's advice.

The Brooke wartime government record was also somewhat damaged by continuing industrial unrest. Although there is evidence to suggest more sensitive handling of labour relations at cabinet level,[63] strikes in the aircraft and shipyard industries resulted in the imprisonment of shop stewards and waves of protest. Moreover, the Eire workers and ex-servicemen issue raised cabinet fears of immigrants gravitating 'to the disloyal element in our population'.[64] Education continued to be a stringent test of ministerial abilities, the Reverend Corkey being relieved of his post after a year and replaced by Colonel Hall-Thompson. Corkey's protests about difficulties in achieving a satisfactory form of religious instruction in schools presaged trouble to come.[65]

In April 1945, as Allied victory in Europe beckoned, Maynard Sinclair announced to the cabinet that a comprehensive re-insurance agreement covering the whole field of social security services had been made with the British Treasury.[66] Legislation at

Westminster after the war was duly introduced to implement this arrangement, and in a way served to vindicate the beleaguered Andrews's efforts three years previously. However, this was a solid commitment on which the Unionist Party could base its pledges to take Northern Ireland into the new British welfareist and socially transformed era. Arguably, such pledges were to be crucial to the party's continuing dominance of Northern Ireland politics.

In the Province's general election, held at the end of the war, the Unionist Party won 33 seats, a handsome enough victory. However, this was six fewer than 1938, and the party's vote also fell by 6 per cent. There was a 'labourist upsurge',[67] although not nearly on the scale of that in the British election soon after, at which the Unionist Party held its Ulster seats. The significance of the Northern Ireland election is best illustrated by comparing the total Unionist Party vote – over 178,000 – with that of the combined total of parties and candidates standing on a 'Labour' or 'socialist' platform, including the Communist Party.[68] This came to nearly 126,000, an indication of the radicalising impact of the war and the wide desire for social change. The 'left' in Northern Ireland was of course fragmented, and the constitutional question still bedevilled its largest party, the NILP. Nevertheless, in the context of such a vote at home and the landslide election victory of the British Labour Party, the Ulster Unionist Party was going to have to grapple with political challenges which gave a new twist to its traditional concerns.

Standing as a Nationalist in South Armagh at the Northern Ireland election in 1945, Malachy Conlon issued a remarkable address to the voters. He began piously by referring to the 'duty under God' by which the Irish nation had to lead a 'crusade of mercy and charity', going on to observe the suffering of war-scarred Europe. 'But to the East', he continued in a sharp change of tone, 'is the sneering bulk of communist Russia, where the Jews have marshalled mighty forces to carry on their age old struggle – the destruction of Christianity.' Conlon asserted that the communist blight had spread to England:

> For here surely the seed bed is ready for the vile henchmen of the Communist Jew. The crumbling edifice of Christianity which they have built out of the ruins of the so-called reformation has been deserted for the crystal palaces of vice and pleasure. Standards of purity which we in Ireland hold dear and sacred, are scoffed at in England.

Conlon's stance was 'under the emerald banner which has been raised aloft by the great leader of our race Mr Eamon de Valera', and he declared himself certain 'that I am but one of a bristling mass of Irishmen, Republican and Hibernian alike'. 'At last in this year of 1945', he continued, 'we have come together like children round our mother Ireland to listen to her commands, to defend her rights and if needs be, to shed our blood that her altars and shrines to God and God's Mother may forever remain unsullied.' By way of peroration, and with reference to a Labour opponent depicted as in thrall to Soviet Russia, Conlon stated: 'Ireland stands today where she stood at Limerick. We are marshalled together and we are asked to march. There are two flags in the sand – the Hammer and Sickle of the Communist Jew – and the flag of our own land.'[69]

Conlon was elected, defeating the Labour candidate – in reality a Catholic moderate on social questions who was firmly anti-partitionist – by 6,720 votes to 4,143. In November 1945 at a conference organised by Conlon and his fellow Nationalist MP Eddie McAteer, the Anti-Partition League (APL) was born,[70] and Conlon became its organising secretary till his death in 1950. The APL's function was partly to supply some organisational structure to Nationalist politics in the wake of the decision taken after the 1945 election to abandon abstentionism and attend both the Stormont and Westminster parliaments. Beyond this, however, it was also designed to bring about the ideal held up by Conlon of Nationalist unity, to bond Nationalists from the old Home Rule tradition such as the 'Devlinites' of the North with those of the Republican camp. The APL, indeed, went on to achieve an impressive degree of such unity, and, notwithstanding its Northern Irish origins, quickly assumed a strong all-Ireland presence.[71] This entailed the support of many Catholic clergy, and of the South's major political parties. From 1945 through to the 1950s the APL operated as the main body coordinating anti-partitionist propaganda activities in Britain, North America and other parts of the Irish diaspora. It was a campaign of formidable energy, breadth and intensity which involved Ulster Unionism in a struggle for its political life.[72] An assessment of the Unionist Party in this era has to take full account of the 'pressure cooker' created politically by the global profile of the APL.

Conlon's views, as set out above, undermine in a moral sense the anti-partitionist case he and the APL pursued. Conlon's racist, sectarian and anti-Semitic address was made at a time when the full horrors of the Nazi concentration camps had been revealed. They seem to have made little impact on him, and the notion that he was exceptional in this respect is exploded by the many APL statements over the next few years which made preposterous equations between the Holocaust and the plight of Catholics in Northern Ireland.[73] It was all indicative of the kind of 'solipsism' discerned in Irish Republicanism in the 1930s by Richard English.[74] While Conlon's sentiments may not have been shared by others associated with the APL, there is no evidence of members publicly repudiating them. Criticism of the APL from within what might loosely be termed 'Nationalist Ireland' came only from the Republican Socialist MP for Falls in West Belfast, Harry Diamond, who denounced it as right-wing and sectarian.[75] Overall, in the years after the war Nationalist Ireland again mobilised, with at least the appearance of unity between its political and physical force tendencies, as *Catholic* Ireland. The vagaries of Southern politics, particularly the emergence of a coalition government to replace Fianna Fail in 1947,[76] provided incentives for the parties to rival each other in anti-partitionist zeal and Catholic piety.[77] Southern politicians, such as Frank Aiken, crossed the border to address rallies. In the North the tone was set by the local businessmen, farmers, teachers and journalists who formed the bulk of the APL,[78] and whose anti-communism recalled the emotions whipped up in Ireland, North and South, during the 1930s, particularly around the issue of the Spanish Civil War. Conlon's manifesto, indeed, was very 'Francoist' in its conspiratorial and crusading language.

Irish Nationalists believed that the return of the Labour government in Britain augured well for the cause of Irish unity, and the formation of a 'Friends of Ireland' group within the Labour Party, led by the Ulster-born and Protestant Geoffrey Bing MP, reinforced their optimism.[79] The 'Friends' group attempted primarily to highlight the position of the minority in Northern Ireland, and it reproduced the allegations against the ruling Unionists which had long been a stock of Nationalist argument and which had been put vividly as recently as 1943 in the pamphlet *Orange Terror*, by an anonymous Catholic author styling himself 'Ultach'.[80] This pamphlet, along with a critical reference made by the Roman Catholic Archbishop of Westminster in 1944, provoked several Unionists into retaliatory broadsides which tended to side-step the charges and take refuge in the suggestion that increasing numbers of Catholics, and immigrant Catholics from the South, in Northern Ireland did not support the picture of persecution painted by Nationalists.[81] For a time the united propaganda offensive of the APL and the 'Friends' put the Unionists decidedly on the defensive, capitalising as it did on the local government franchise issue and presenting it as a flagrant denial of rights to the minority.[82]

However, cracks began to show in the APL–'Friends' alliance over the former's right-wing flavour and its concentration on the partition issue above all else. Eddie McAteer's advocacy of a civil disobedience campaign in the North to end partition played straight into Unionist hands.[83] Moreover, it became clear that for all the back-bench activity of the 'Friends' group, senior figures in the Labour Party such as Home Secretary Herbert Morrison and Prime Minister Attlee himself were not favourably disposed to anti-partitionist demands in the light of the South's wartime neutrality and the North's crucial contribution to the war. Given the new common bond forged in wartime between Northern Ireland and the rest of the UK and the Allies, the times were hardly propitious for appeals to the British and indeed American governments; the South, internationally, bore something of a stigma on account of its decision to remain neutral, and memories of de Valera's gratuitous offer of condolences over Hitler's death to the German Legation in Dublin remained fresh. The Labour government, as will be discussed below, conducted generally positive working relations with the Unionists at Stormont.

Finally, in 1948, the decision of the Southern coalition government to declare Ireland a Republic and to break off all connection with the Commonwealth represented an over-playing of the Nationalist hand. An accompanying remark by the Taoiseach, the Fine Gael party leader John Costello, that he considered himself Prime Minister of all Ireland, 'no matter what the Irish in the North say',[84] was provocative in the extreme, as indeed were some of the contemporary outbursts of de Valera on his anti-partition speaking tour. In October 1948 in Glasgow de Valera warned those who supported partition in the North (the Unionist majority) that they would have to choose to be Irish or British, and that if their choice was not the former then, he exclaimed, 'In God's name will you go to the country that your affections lie in'.[85]

Obliged to respond to the Costello government's stroke, and advised in a 'backstairs' memorandum, to Brooke's gratification, that for strategic reasons Northern Ireland should not under any circumstances cease to be part of the UK,[86] the British Labour government passed the Ireland Act of 1949. This stipulated that Northern Ireland could only cease to be part of the UK with the consent of the Stormont parliament. By this time Northern Ireland was again in a sectarian ferment, due in no small measure to the behaviour of Southern politicians. First there was the coalition government's declaration of a Republic which prioritised the breaking of relations with Britain,[87] and then there was the sponsoring by all parties of collections (usually taken at the gates of Catholic chapels) of funds for Nationalist unity candidates at the election called by the Unionist government in Belfast for February 1949.[88]

The main losers when the tumult died down were again the minority in Northern Ireland. The campaign against the issue of partition as such, as opposed to the treatment of the minority, was conducted with reckless disregard for Unionist rights and beliefs, at a junction unfavourable for what appeared to be Irish Nationalist special pleading. It complicated the case for redress of injustices against the minority, and ultimately, in view of the ideological baggage it had carried since Conlon's election, weakened it.

The Unionist election campaign in 1945 had to concern itself much more than previously with issues other than the constitution.[89] The party committed itself to replicating the social welfare legislation which would be passed in London, and over the course of the following three years did so. Thus measures on Family Allowances, housing, health, National Insurance, and education put in place a stronger 'safety net' for the less well off in society, and expanded opportunities for social and economic improvement. Much was also done to attract new industries, if only in the majority of cases to the east of the Province. Re-insurance agreements with the Treasury under the new Labour government underwrote the progressive programme.[90] Northern Ireland marched in step with 'welfare state' Britain.

However, the Unionists had also made clear in 1945 that they rejected the 'socialist claim' that 'the State machine is all-wise'.[91] Indeed, the election of the Labour government caused consternation among those Unionists for whom the spectre of nationalisation was anathema.[92] Neither of course was it forgotten that the Labour Party had always been favourable to Irish unity. Just as Nationalists were encouraged to hope that Labour would deliver what they wanted, so Unionists regarded the prospect of a Labour government with such a large majority with some foreboding.[93]

As early as November 1945 Brooke talked to his cabinet colleagues about a 'difficult situation arising', namely the possibility of 'more extreme socialistic measures' which would have to be followed and which would be resented by many in the Unionist Party. Brooke went on to predict 'chaotic' conditions and asked his colleagues to consider the alternatives: Dominion status for Northern Ireland, or a return to Westminster.[94]

A protracted debate within the party followed, focusing on the feasibility of the Dominion status option.[95] Those in favour of it – such as Sir Roland Nugent, the Minister of Commerce from 1945 – saw in Northern Ireland's association with Labour's new welfareist Britain mainly a significant tightening of financial controls and the further constriction of Northern Ireland's autonomy. Those who took Nugent's view argued in effect that Northern Ireland should chart a different course by building on her devolved powers perhaps to the end of becoming a self-governing Dominion. 'The Dominion status lobby', as it has come to be labelled, made much of the argument that a conservative Northern Ireland electorate was having socialism foisted upon it. However, they were reluctant to pursue the implications of their case regarding the viability of the welfare state measures in the context of a fiscally autonomous Northern Ireland more responsive to Conservative policies of lower taxation. This was a weak link in their argument which was never properly addressed. More convincingly, they contended that the Province's Imperial Contribution was a drain on resources and that the situation called for a reconstruction of Northern Ireland's social and economic foundations appropriate to local conditions.

On the other side of this issue were those, such as cabinet ministers William Grant[96] and Robert Moore, who counselled against any weakening of the British link, and played what had for some time been the trump card of the party's dependence on the support of the Protestant working class. The latter argument was all the more powerful for the evidence of the leakage in that support at the 1945 election to parties of the left. In 1947 Brooke declared that 'the backbone of Unionism' was the UULA and asked rhetorically if it would be satisfied if the government rejected the social benefits gained through the British link.[97] In fact, the UULA was in a relatively weak condition and was not pulling its weight in the Unionist Party; Brooke's intervention was really intended to send a message to Protestant working-class voters who were suspicious of the party's intentions.

Brooke, therefore, despite initiating discussion on Dominion status and revealing himself worried about the prospect of the Labour government, had come to a firm position against any change to the relationship and to the minimalist use of devolution. Northern Ireland was effectively 'roped in' to Labour's centralising schemata which overrode regional and national distinctiveness throughout the UK.[98] A memorandum from Nugent in the same month as Brooke's UULA remarks reiterated the dangers of socialist legislation and cited the internal party and back-bench trouble which had already arisen over the issue. Brooke's answer was a refusal to deviate from 'the policy of maintaining quality of social services between Northern Ireland and the rest of the United Kingdom', the need to work in cooperation with the Labour government, and a suggestion that cosmetic changes be made to Northern Ireland's legislative measures to secure an easier passage through Stormont.[99] In the same cabinet Brooke lent his weight to those, like Brian Maginess, Minister of Labour, who advised against the Ulster Unionist MPs at Westminster being unreservedly associated with the Conservative Party: 'The Government of Northern Ireland was not a Tory Government; it was a Unionist Government'.[100] The situation regarding the Westminster MPs did lead to some embarrassment for the Unionist Party as certain members voted against Labour legislation which the Unionists would later introduce at Stormont. However, in the bulk of cases abstention was the path followed.[101] The issue, if nothing else, resulted in closer liaison between the 'Ulster Party' at Westminster and the party and government in Northern Ireland,[102] and post-war Unionist Westminster MPs were generally to make a greater impact on Unionist Party deliberations than their predecessors, particularly in the realm of propaganda and publicity.[103] In 1951, with the return of the Tories to power at Westminster with a slim majority, the votes of Ulster Unionist members became a valued commodity. Nevertheless, the political opportunities created by these events were largely spurned by the Ulster MPs, who, equally, appear not to have been directed from Belfast to extract concessions from Churchill's government. It was only in the second half of the 1950s, when the Conservatives were in a more secure position, that Ulster MPs began to make a nuisance of themselves regarding the issues of unemployment and economic regeneration of the Province.[104]

The Unionist government, with the creation of the Housing Trust before the end of the war, had in a sense moved significantly to the

left in practice if not in theory, and later measures such as the creation of a Northern Ireland Transport Authority confirmed the trend
towards centralisation. The establishment of a Northern Ireland
Tuberculosis Authority in 1947 represented further evidence of the
government's preoccupation with social welfare problems, and the
achievements of this body were to be considerable.[105] However, discontent within the party did not abate, and Brooke did not have his
difficulties to seek with the UUC, in which disgruntled supporters of
Andrews still held influence. In February 1948 a resolution carried
at that body's conference stated: 'That the introduction of
indigested [*sic*] socialist legislation by the Northern Ireland government, tending to curtail further the liberty of the people and the
expansion of business, is not in the best interests of Ulster'.[106] This,
of course, was the voice of middle-class Ulster, and it represented
the business interests which were also vital to the party. Elements of
the business community were supportive of moves towards Dominion status, although at the aforementioned UUC conference resolutions rejecting this option and any change to the principle of parity
in social services were carried unanimously.[107] It thus appears that
the UUC functioned in this period as a safety valve for the largely
middle-class membership of the party, a sizeable proportion of
which was female, to let off steam about socialism while reconciling
itself to the status quo of Northern Ireland's subordination to Westminster.

The UUC conducted a further re-organisation of the Unionist
Party after the war,[108] utilising the energies and idealism of younger
members such as Brian Faulkner, although no constitution for the
party as opposed to the Council was introduced and anachronisms
from the early twentieth-century battle against Home Rule
abounded. The UUC Annual Report of 1946 claimed that the
organisation had been put on a 'much more democratic basis', and
referred to 'an unbroken line of communication direct from the
members of the Association to the Leader'.[109] There was a renewed
emphasis on propaganda capabilities, which, in the context of the
APL onslaught, were quickly tested.

If Brooke had to risk displeasing many in his party by reproduc-
ing Labour legislation, he was equally prepared to confront the
British government. He did so over two issues which he could use to
appease his critics: the local government franchise and the curtail-
ment of immigrant workers from Eire. The pre-war decision to
retain the existing system of electing local councils was given

A history of the Ulster Unionist Party

legislative shape in 1946 against the wishes of the government in London; the latter chose in this case and others to justify non-intervention with reference to the parliamentary convention that Northern Ireland business could not be discussed at Westminster. In one intervention at Westminster the Labour minister Chuter Ede erroneously put Northern Ireland's position on a par with that of the Dominions.[110] Ede may simply have been confused, but the suspicion remains that this was a way of obfuscating the issues involved and releasing the government from the obligation to interfere in the messy affairs of Northern Ireland. However, if it had been true to its centralist credo in this respect it would have done so, and it could have insisted that Ulster come into line on matters such as the local government franchise and put a stop to the gerrymandering of local government boundaries for partisan – and in this case sectarian – ends.[111] It was, in retrospect, a vital missed opportunity to ensure fairer government in the Province.

Relations between the governments were also strained by the Eire workers question. The Unionist government came under pressure from its supporters, particularly in border areas, who feared that migrants from the South would upset the delicate population balance in such areas, and consequently voting strengths. The Northern Ireland government's proposal in 1945 to withdraw work permits caused a diplomatic row between London and Dublin, and a temporary setback to Unionist plans. However, in 1947 the Safeguarding of Employment Bill was passed at Stormont, permitting the control of Eire labour and the withdrawal of permits, and this time the Labour government complied. In such ways did the Unionists cash in the credit they had built up in the war, and Eire feel the backlash of British antagonism over her wartime neutrality.

This latter issue was unsurprisingly the mainstay of the Unionists' propaganda response to the anti-partitionist pressure in the post-war years.[112] A series of pamphlets were published by the UUC which highlighted Ulster's contribution to the war and the gratitude expressed by such statesmen as Churchill and Eisenhower. In *Twenty Questions for Mr de Valera*,[113] fourteen pertained to Eire's neutrality and its alleged consequences. In this respect the Unionists had a strong hand and they played it unsparingly. It was also an issue which, along with Northern Ireland's share in the social changes of the post-war United Kingdom, lent credibility to a portrayal of the Province as a participant in a new progressive world order while Eire remained insular and backward. As Jennifer Todd

108

has argued, Unionism utilised a modernising rhetoric in this period,[114] and gave a new twist to the old theme of Northern progress and Southern stagnation. Unionist propaganda drew a veil over the party's right-wing 'angst' as it compared Ulster's social services and benefits with those of Eire. In January 1949, prior to the general election in Northern Ireland, the UUC issued 'A Warning to the Ulster People' that 'It's Your Money Eire is After'. Urging voters to think in terms of 'pay packet politics', it concluded: 'the advantage of being a working member of the British team has its own rewards, and the present and future economic well-being of Northern Ireland is dependent on the preservation of the Union'.[115] The slogan 'Break with Britain and go broke with Eire'[116] might have been a conventional Unionist appeal, but it also seemed to contain a message for those who had toyed with the idea of Northern Ireland going it alone.

The materialist benefits of Britishness and the shared experience of war were the main Unionist propaganda selections from their repertoire of appeals, yet complexities of ethnic and national identity were not entirely overshadowed. In November 1948 in the pages of the party's new monthly, *The Voice of Ulster*, Edmund Warnock recalled the events of 1920 and stated: 'You tried us to breaking point but we did not break. Nowhere in the world will you find a more resolute people than the Ulster Scots.'[117] Ulster Unionist attitudes in this period, particularly towards the broadcast media, could be critical of perceived English metropolitan condescension,[118] and suspiciousness about English tendencies to entertain anti-partitionist arguments was vented in the Unionist press.[119] All the while, of course, Catholic Ireland functioned as the ethnic 'other' which carried the ever-present threat of cultural absorption. The Olympian posture adopted by Reverend MacManaway in his dismissal of 'the racial factor' as an argument 'dear to the heart of the Nationalist'[120] rather ignored the proto-nationalism of many of his fellow Unionists whether in the form of British, Ulster or Ulster-Scots sentiment. The secular Unionist form of argument, while deeply rooted in the history of Ulster Unionism and intellectually substantial, was less than convincing when it appeared to portray nationalism as something in which only Catholic Ireland indulged. Hugh Shearman's work, an important part of Ulster Unionist historiography, is germane in this respect: in 1949 he wrote of symbols, heroes and traditions of Irish Nationalism which appealed to the 'emotional and rhetorical temperament' of the people of Eire and bored and repelled 'the practical and executive temperament of the people of Northern Ireland'.[121] Shearman, at the time of writing this, needed only to observe the tribalist outpouring of often violent emotion on the part of those of a 'practical and executive temperament' who felt – once more – that they could rely only on themselves to fight to maintain a distinctive identity: distinctive both in Ireland and in the context of the UK. In many ways the swingeing polemics of another slice of Unionist historiography produced at this historical moment – the dramatist St John Ervine's biography of Craigavon[122] – were more insightful regarding the ambiguous mentality and cultural edginess of Protestant Ulster in its quest to remain in control of its own destiny. Moreover, the strand of Unionist thought represented by Shearman and MacManaway was prone to take for granted an undifferentiated Britishness as a fixed cultural norm: in the mid-twentieth century, no less than the late nineteenth, British identity and allegiance throughout the UK were fluid phenomena marked by greater diversity than these authors appreciated.[123]

Against the background of Eire's withdrawal from the Commonwealth, the election in Northern Ireland in February 1949 was the most intensely fought since 1921. Sectarian emotions dominated the campaign, notwithstanding instructions from the Unionist Party Chief Whip, Colonel Topping, that members should not attack anyone's religion. However, in the same appeal Topping had also felt obliged to advise his party workers not to discuss the 1947 Education Act, which had aroused much ultra-Protestant fury over its provision of increased capital grants to voluntary (mainly Catholic) schools. In addition, he warned them to steer clear of 'British socialism' while emphasising the social benefits enjoyed by Northern Ireland.[124] Clearly, there were fears of intra-Unionist divisions damaging the party's vote even in the charged circumstances brought about by Nationalist propaganda and manoeuvring.[125]

In the event, as Brooke acknowledged in his diary,[126] anti-partition attacks rebounded to Unionist advantage in a campaign which saw the Unionist business community come up with funds in response to the 'Chapel gates' collections,[127] and working-class Protestants rally to the flag notwithstanding socialist leanings.[128] A remarkably solid degree of Unionist unity was achieved, and the result told the story: 37 seats and over 234,000 votes. The APL won 9 seats out of 17 contested and polled over 101,000. The NILP lost its 2 seats and suffered a severe drop in its vote,[129] the decision taken at the end of January to endorse the constitutional position of Northern Ireland coming too late to make any impact. From a situation in 1945 when the 'national question' appeared to be losing some ground to a left–right model of political competition such as obtained in Britain,[130] it was an emphatic reinstatement of ethnic political priorities and imperatives. Yet it was always going to be difficult for the NILP, as was the case in the inter-war years, when the Unionist Party gave no social welfare hostages to fortune.

After the election the spotlight shifted to negotiations in London over the coming legislation to redefine Britain's relationship with both parts of Ireland. Brooke confided to his diary on 28 April that 'we have got what we want', with the exception of the name 'Republic of Ireland' remaining with the South.[131] Indeed, Unionists had every reason to feel pleased. The most significant passage of the bill, from their point of view, read:

> Northern Ireland remains part of His Majesty's dominions and of the United Kingdom and it is hereby affirmed that in no event will Northern Ireland or any part thereof cease to be a part of His Majesty's dominions and of the United Kingdom without the consent of the parliament of Northern Ireland.[132]

Referring to this affirmation of Northern Ireland's position, Herbert Morrison observed: 'That is not banging doors, but it is not unlocking doors either. It is leaving the situation fluid if the Parliament of Northern Ireland should wish to make a change …'.[133] Morrison well knew there was little likelihood of this, but he was aware of how the external circumstances of the war had altered the context of the question, and of how that context might be altered again in the future. He was stating what he saw as commonsense realities, yet he had little appreciation of how much his approach – like that of previous British statesmen – was at odds with an Irish Nationalist conception of unity as a 'divine right' to be delivered as of right, whatever the political difficulties; and to a degree also it was at odds with the Ulster Unionist quest for a permanent settlement. Craigavon had wished to believe that 1921 brought such a settlement, and he considered 1925 in the same light. Brooke, in 1949, thought indulgently also of matters being finally laid to rest. Both sides shared an endgame mentality and dealt in absolutes.

Accordingly, the bill, although stating that Ireland was not to be regarded as a foreign country and that Irish citizens in Britain would continue to enjoy British citizenship rights (including the vote), drew a furious response from Dublin and Irish Nationalist opinion in general. However, their outrage found little echo internationally,[134] and the general response of the regional and metropolitan British press was gratifying for Unionists, who were used to seeing their position misrepresented or their opponents' argument taken more seriously.[135] Unionists felt vindicated in their longstanding belief about the separatist character of all varieties of Irish Nationalism; the South's declaration of a Republic, said Brooke, was 'the last stage of that deplorable journey' stretching back to the settlement of 1920–22.[136]

In addition, the Unionists got what they thought they wanted without a *quid pro quo* from the Labour government, which arguably wasted another chance to curb electoral malpractices and discrimination on the part of local authorities in Northern Ireland. Again, excessive Nationalist stress on the implications for the partition issue above all else clouded a situation in which carefully applied pressure might have forced adjustments to the benefit of the minority in the Province. Although their vulnerabilities had only been disguised, the greater part of 1949 was the best of times for Ulster Unionists.

Towards the end of the year, however, the party's sense of well-being was again upset. Brooke recorded in his diary on 22 November that he had told the editor of the *Belfast Newsletter* that he saw signs of the Unionist Party breaking up on economic questions 'once the peril of the Border abated'.[137] What lay behind these thoughts was the continuing divisions within the party over the shadowing of the Westminster Labour government. Brooke, a fortnight later, was to write irritably in his diary about a resolution passed at the Women's Unionist Conference criticising the government for being 'slavish' in this respect: '[They] do not realise that our finances and other matters are integrated with Great Britain. They cannot have it both ways.'[138]

In this Brooke was justifiably impatient. As noted above, those in the party who criticised the government for following Labour usually also supported the welfare measures which had proved such a potent electoral weapon. The latest champion of increased autonomy, the South Tyrone MP W. F. McCoy, was in this sense loud in his advocacy of Northern Ireland acting with more fiscal independence while inaudible regarding the economic and welfareist implications of such a change. The intellectual and liberal barrister figure of Brian Maginess, Minister of Home Affairs from 1949 to 1953, pursued the case for more independence with greater sophistication and well-intentioned references to the interests of the minority, yet was hardly less evasive in this crucial regard.[139] Brooke evidently felt that, if Labour continued for some time in power, the issue would rupture the party, particularly in view of the apparently greater measure of security on the constitutional question granted by the Ireland Act. Thus, in a way, the succour delivered to Unionists by the Act carried with it seeds of danger: what price the party's continuing health without the unifying issue of the border? From this perspective it was fortunate for the Unionists that the partition issue was certainly not about to be dropped by Irish Nationalists and Republicans, however rebuffed they felt by the Labour government; indeed, in the new post-war world taking shape, there emerged international forums such as the United Nations at which the issue could be pressed.[140]

The Unionist Party was also struck at the close of 1949 by serious in-fighting over education. This was the culmination of tensions dating back to the Education Act of 1947, and beyond that to the dismissal of the Reverend Corkey in 1944. Corkey had conveyed the views of the Orange Order and the people whom his successor Hall-Thompson was to label the 'strong' Protestants,[141] in asserting that proper 'Protestant' education was not provided in schools transferred to the state in the way that the Catholic Church was able to ensure Catholic education in its schools.[142] The 1947 Act, drawn up mainly by the senior official in the Education department, Sir Reginald Brownell, and deputy minister Dehra Parker,[143] repealed the guarantees – inserted in the amending legislation of 1930 – for the provision of religious instruction to children in all transferred and grammar schools, and increased the capital grants to voluntary (mainly Catholic) schools from 50 to 65 per cent. Corkey had had Brownell in mind when he complained about officials with no sympathy for Protestant religious demands;[144] a picture was painted of treacherous influences covertly at work at the heart of the Northern Ireland governmental system undermining Protestantism, especially Presbyterianism.[145] The protests which had been heard back in the 1920s against the equally suspect Lord Londonderry were echoed in the 1940s: Protestants had transferred their schools in good faith and were being treated with contempt, while Catholic schools, fully controlled by their Church, were improving their position. Hall-Thompson, who bore the brunt of Protestant anger when he introduced the bill in 1947, was not an Orangeman, in itself unusual for a cabinet minister and therefore confirmation in the eyes of his opponents of his untrustworthiness. The Orange and 'strong' Protestant furore, in whipping up sectarian emotions, clouded serious points about the 1947 Act's maintenance of a selective secondary school system and grammar school privileges, and its raising of capital grants to those voluntary schools, overwhelmingly the Catholic ones, which refused to accept the principle of state representation on their management committees.[146]

Matters came to a head when Hall-Thompson attempted to introduce a bill to enable the Ministry to pay the employers' proportion of teachers' National Insurance contributions in voluntary schools. Unionist back-benchers gave vent to the extra-parliamentary Protestant rumblings, and opposition to the minister also emerged from within the cabinet itself.[147] On 8 November Brooke recorded:

> The Ministry of Education are having trouble and I think have not watched the political side as well as they ought. I have mentioned this to Hall-Thompson, the Minister. It is dynamite in this country and may crack the whole political set-up and, in turn, would affect the whole of the educational system, no matter how it goes. I suggested that it would be wrong politically to set up Roman Catholic grammar schools in Protestant areas.[148]

Brooke's diary contains evidence of his colleagues' deference to the Orange Order on this issue,[149] although Brooke himself was anxious not to do anything that could be interpreted as anti-Catholic and be used as 'propaganda' against the party.[150] Hall-Thompson, in whom too few in the cabinet and in the party had confidence, was duly made the sacrifice. He resigned on 14 December and Brooke tried further to calm the situation by promising the House a general re-examination of educational matters,[151] without, however, a commitment to changing the law.[152] Cabinet, in fact, re-endorsed the 1947 Act[153] and the protestors were given nothing tangible other than the head of Hall-Thompson, unless, that is, the appointment of Harry Midgley as his replacement is counted as such a concession. Midgley had been one of Hall-Thompson's fiercest critics, something that helped him to be accepted after his entry into the Unionist Party in 1947.[154] However, the constraints of office and the peculiar problems presented by educational administration permitted Midgley little latitude for his own personal goals, and he announced, in March 1951, that no fundamental changes in the educational system were possible.[155] By this time Brooke was feeling confident enough to consider disciplining the few back-benchers who still made trouble on the issue, and he noted later in his diary that the Orange Order had decided to do nothing.[156]

The education question in the 1940s and 1950s provides both ammunition for Unionist critics and arguments for the Unionists' defence. The government appeared to pay too much heed to dissent-ers from its own ranks whose views were motivated by anti-Catholicism rather than the fine points of the controversy. Such was the trepidation on the part of ministers about the danger the issue held for their own positions that the case for the building of new Catholic grammar schools in certain parts of the Province was dis-countenanced.[157] Minority perceptions of unfairness were not modified by the outspokenness of Midgley even if words were not significantly translated into deeds.[158]

On the other hand, Protestant protests over Bible instruction and the 65 per cent capital grants for voluntary schools were faced down, and a political price was later paid.[159] It is easy to forget, amidst the plight of Hall-Thompson, that his 1947 Act did provide the framework for the dramatic expansion of education in post-war Northern Ireland which had far-reaching social and economic ef-fects for both Protestants and Catholics. The Catholic Church was able to resist any secular input into the management of its schools without any revision of the increased capital grants provision of the 1947 Act; moreover, the full running costs of Catholic schools, in-cluding teachers' salaries, continued to be paid out of public funds. The arrangements, indeed, were more favourable to Catholics than in England, the USA and many other countries.[160] The separation of children at school age, insisted upon most emphatically by the Catholic Church, played its part in perpetuating divisions in North-ern Ireland;[161] in the eyes of most Protestants, whether of an 'Or-ange' cast of mind or not, Catholic schooling ensured the passing on of anti-British and anti-Protestant antagonism as well as pride in Irish Catholic identity. To be sure, separate schools militated against any mutual discovery exercise and respective myth-debunking necessary for the rebuilding of communal relations and the develop-ment of tolerance and respect.[162]

In this late 1940s to early 1950s period, the cabinet, however grudgingly, came down in favour of boarding scholarships for

Catholic pupils, overriding the decision of a Unionist local author-ity,[163] and also decided to consider a loan for the financing of St Mary's Catholic Teacher Training College due to the 'valuable part' played by the latter in 'the essential task of training teachers'.[164] Irish language and literature was a curriculum option for secondary school pupils, taught by teachers paid from public funds.[165] In 1954, G. C. Duggan, a former Comptroller and Auditor-General for Northern Ireland who had made scathing criticisms of the gov-erning Unionists since departing his post,[166] nevertheless felt obliged to point out that spending on education (affecting all parts of the community) in Northern Ireland compared favourably to that in the South. He wrote:

> there is a far greater margin of the educational budget left over in Northern Ireland, and the whole of this goes to the benefit of the children themselves. Though education authorities there grumble at the growing cost to the rates, everyone puts up with it, and one can only ascribe this acquiescence to the Ulsterman's being much more education-conscious than the general run of parents in the twenty-six counties.[167]

Bigotry may well have played a prominent role in the education controversies which disturbed post-war Northern Ireland, but so too did a passion for learning and better educational standards, however narrowly defined.

Education was just one of several issues that the Unionist leadership had to handle delicately in the post-war years. Housing was an-other. The NIHT was perceived to be biased against Protestants by certain Unionist elements, and such was the volume of complaints within the party that the UUC Executive Committee sent a deputa-tion to see the Trust's Chairman, Sir Lucius O'Brien. The report that came back quoted allocation figures for that year (1950) in Strabane and Keedy and Sir Lucius's comments about the lack of Protestant applications. It was then decided to impress upon local Unionist associations 'the need to help applicants obtain houses by early and correct applications and by acquiring knowledge of future schemes and developments'. There was then minuted a vote of con-fidence in the Housing Trust and its Chairman.[168]

Such manoeuvres were motivated by Unionist fears that the allo-cation of new housing was going to upset the electoral balance in those localities where the Unionist advantage was marginal.[169] It was therefore an issue of particular concern to Unionists in the west of the Province and in border areas. The Housing Trust, from its inception, was one of the most progressive innovations on the Unionist record, and its impartiality and effectiveness have been attested to in scholarly commentaries on the wider question of how much discrimination was practised by the Unionist regime.[170] It should be noted, moreover, that Brooke displayed a determination to stand up for it against those in his party who were critical. In February 1951 he wrote in his diary regarding a UUC meeting on the Trust:

> I insisted we must be fair to the minority, that I was not going to be responsible for discrimination etc. I finished up by saying that if they wanted another administration who could perhaps solve their domestic problems from a new viewpoint, or if they thought we were not handling the Socialist government right and wanted a Government which would discriminate against Roman Catholics they could do so. I would not take on the job.

He went on to note that he was then given a unanimous vote of confidence.[171]

Brooke thus again faced down extremist opinion, and the Northern Ireland government's house-building record, particularly in the early 1950s, compared favourably to the UK average.[172] Nevertheless, allocation was not conducted fairly by local authorities in respect of their housing stock, whether Unionist or Nationalist controlled.[173] Given the Unionist preponderance of local councils, it was the Catholic minority who were especially disadvantaged. The damaging potential of this issue for Unionism would become clearer with the passage of the post-war years. Again, in retrospect, it may be argued that Brooke should have seized the moment of deliverance supplied by the Ireland Act of 1949 to bring his local councils to order and ensure fairness regarding housing allocation, thus limiting further the propaganda weapons of his opponents of which he at the time showed such awareness.[174] This, however, overlooks the extent to which Brooke had a fight on his hands over the Housing Trust, never mind the local authorities, and the treacherousness involved in maintaining the balance of interests and influences within the Unionist Party. In this case, the claims of 'outpost' Unionists could not be ignored, lest the movement be seen to shrink to an eastern Ulster core. It was very politically difficult, in view of party anxieties over the Housing Trust, to move against Unionist local authorities on housing matters. Brooke's prioritising of party balance at this juncture nonetheless left discrimination issues largely untackled, with ramifications for the future. This was a period in which local Unionist councils in areas with large Nationalist populations exacerbated societal divisions by responding in a partisan fashion to what was regarded as the official bureaucratic bias towards Nationalists practised by the Housing Trust.

The Unionist government suffered a similar outbreak of disaffection among sections of its party and supporters over a decision taken by the Minister of Home Affairs, Brian Maginess, to ban an Orange Order march near Annalong in County Down in June 1952. Ironically, the legislation used by the minister – the Public Order Act of 1951 – had been drawn up to appease extremist Unionists, who had also been gratified by a government ban on an Ancient Order of Hibernians parade back in 1948.[175] This was now forgotten as the Orange Order led a campaign against Maginess. In 1953 incidents allegedly involving the IRA in Dungiven and Pomeroy at the time of Queen Elizabeth's coronation brought further Protestant pressure on the government.[176] It was, indeed, just as notable an era for populist appeals by maverick Unionists, both inside the party and out. In 1952 the Executive Committee of the UUC felt compelled to deliver a strong rebuke to Nat Minford, a Stormont party member, on account of a speech during the British general election campaign of the previous year. The UUC statement expressed regret over Minford's insults to the religion of 'their Roman Catholic fellow citizens', going on to record 'detestation of such statements, which are entirely opposed to the principles of the Unionist Party'.[177] Clearly, the party was trying to send a strong message that sectarian outbursts were not in Unionism's best interests, and that the movement had to take care to show a better public face and keep the friends that its wartime role had won. Nevertheless, any hint of a less than emphatic response to Nationalist displays of defiance strained the party's capacity to keep its members and supporters in line.

The 1953 Northern Ireland election was to provide ample such food for thought. With Maginess up against an Independent Unionist challenge in his constituency of Iveagh, County Armagh, Brooke felt it necessary to campaign for him and to defend the government on questions of public order, parades and the flying of emblems. 'Commonsense must be exercised', he told the voters, 'we all know … that some well-recognised routes and areas are definitely Unionist or Nationalist and the commonsense thing is to allow each side to have its meetings and processions in its own areas and use its own routes so as to avoid stirring up the other side'. Brooke, anxious not to lend colour to charges of minority rights being denied, went on: 'It may be irritating to loyalists that Southern Ministers are allowed to address meetings in Northern Ireland, but we gain more than we lose by giving positive proof that liberty of free speech exists'.[178]

It was too subtle an argument for many, and Brooke suffered the indignity of being heckled.[179] Maginess won the contest, but only after a strong Independent vote.[180] In the wake of the election Clarence Graham, an ally of Maginess and later to become Chairman of the UUC, wrote solemnly to Brooke:

Undoubtedly there is a substantial volume of opinion which feels that we are too much inclined to placate our opponents at the expense of our friends and if we fail to pay attention to this body of opinion they will either become supporters of the NI Labour Party or set up a separate Independent Unionist organisation.[181]

Elsewhere the albatross of his Education Act was too much for Hall-Thompson, who was defeated in Belfast Clifton by the Independent Unionist – 'For God and Ulster' – Norman Porter.[182] Porter had campaigned hard on education and tapped the deep well of Unionist discontent on the matter. Hall-Thompson admitted as much in an acidly worded communication with Brooke afterwards in which he conveyed his sense of being let down by his colleagues.[183]

Overall, the Unionist Party again won a comfortable majority of seats at the election. However, its vote dropped by almost half in an admittedly low poll. The NILP vote increased, and some 33,000 voted for Independent Unionists. In the Unionist Party inquest which followed, besides the issues already discussed, there were references to Unionist voters' apathy on account of the number of unopposed returns; there was concern about the lack of Unionist working men as candidates; there were again complaints about 'socialistic' legislation and welfare benefits going to 'disloyalists'; and there was the suggestion that many voters felt that supporting an Independent Unionist was the best way of ensuring opposition at Stormont.[184]

All of this was indicative of the constant dilemmas and hard choices facing the Unionist leaders, even in a contest where their grip on office was unassailable. Again, class questions emerged:

right-wing middle-class elements continued to be unhappy about certain legislation and called for closer identification with the Conservatives in Britain, while working-class electors were dissatisfied with the lack of working-class representation among party candidates and ruling circles. The UULA had not regained its pre-war strength or vitality, and the NILP's clear pro-British stance was beginning to alarm many in the Unionist hierarchy. Campaigning for Midgley in Willowfield, Brooke felt it important to repudiate the NILP charge that the Unionists were Tories.[185] For some years, indeed, Brooke had tried to damp down this question within the party and to avoid having it cause divisions and possible defections.[186] It was certainly the case that Unionist MPs at Westminster voted in the great majority of cases with the Tory government after 1951, and there was a mutual exchange of delegates at Tory and Ulster Unionist Party conferences. Nevertheless, the Unionists tried to be discreet about this in Northern Ireland itself, since developments such as lay-offs of workers, which occurred in the heavy industries in the early 1950s, especially textiles, had the potential to result in moves to the left and were certainly exploited by the NILP, which was becoming harder to stigmatise on the constitutional question.

The 1953 election provided proof of the continuing menace of Independent Unionists – as eager, willing and usually able to capitalise on perceived government 'softness' regarding questions such as public order and education – yet there was the equal danger of apathy resulting from walkovers. The question of opposition – the need for one yet the elusiveness of the 'right' kind – remained a difficult political conundrum. In the wake of the contest, the government moved to appease those veering towards opposition from within its own tribe. In early 1954 the Flags and Emblems Act – dubbed 'the Orange Order Appeasement Bill' by Nationalists[187] – was piloted through parliament with the object of providing protection for 'loyal subjects' to fly the Union Jack, whilst in effect giving the police power to remove the Eire tricolour where its display was thought likely to lead to a disturbance.[188] In the course of a stormy debate Unionists were accused of being in thrall to the Orange Order, and the charge was made that Unionist back-benchers only helped their careers by taking up the Order's agenda.[189]

These were penetrating criticisms and they have become hardy annuals of anti-Unionist commentary. While containing substance, they do not tell the whole story. For example, they do not help to explain why, in the immediate wake of the Flags and Emblems Bill which he introduced, full cabinet approval was given to the decision of the Minister of Home Affairs, George Hanna, to ban an Orange Order march in the disputed territory of the Longstone Road (Annalong) which had been proposed for Easter Monday 1954.[190] They also do not explain the Orange Order's failure to get its way on key issues like education in the post-war era. It might be objected that such examples of frustrated extremist goals do not remove the grounds for characterising Unionist rule in this period as 'hegemonic',[191] but too zealously theoretical an approach to the subject can obscure the changing political significance of day-to-day developments, and over-simplify the motivations and interests involved. In this regard it can be said that the failure to achieve its objectives over education was, from the point of view of the Orange Order's professed defence of 'true' Protestantism, a watershed in the Order's relationship to Unionism. Subsequent concessions on other matters aside, the Order never recovered the pressure-group clout it had demonstrated most notably over education in the 1920s and 1930s. Unionists of course still exercised firm control, but there had at least been an alteration in the nature of their rule. The quite determined pursuit at certain times of class interests by a section of the Protestant working class which held to a pro-Union position on the constitution, partly for reasons of those class interests, is likewise a phenomenon which cannot be reduced to a common, ideological denominator surrounding 'a settler colonial outlook'.[192]

The Brooke government, in the light of the Unionist Party's complexion and delicate balance of interests, played a 'give and take' game, conceding some matters to keep the lid on discontent, and rebuffing extremists on others.[193] Brooke, in private at least, seems to have been sympathetic to the liberal line pursued by such figures in the party as Brian Maginess[194] and Morris May who in 1950 urged the party to distance itself from the Orange Order.[195] However, Brooke was concerned also to listen to the views of people like the veteran Joseph Cunningham and the young Brian Faulkner who stressed the Order's importance.[196] Brooke was too cautious to risk the storm which would inevitably have rocked the party and the government if he had attempted to weaken links with the Order or appear to discount its role. The Order comprised an ethnic core in a party which ultimately depended on an ethnic vote, however important more liberal strains of ideology might be to its overall character.

Early in 1953 an article appeared in the *Belfast Telegraph* by its political correspondent in which the Stormont political world was shrewdly assessed.[197] The thrust of the piece was that insufficient numbers of talented people were attracted to a local political career, and that Stormont had come to be held in low regard on the part of the public. University graduates were conspicuous by their absence, and those who served on statutory authorities were disdainful about local politicians. It was further suggested that it fell especially to the Unionist Party to bring in new blood and improve the general calibre of political representatives. For this to happen the constituency associations of the party had to look 'beyond their own immediate interests' and give more serious consideration to 'outsider' candidates.[198] The correspondent also observed the 'eclipse of the Unionist Labour wing', and warned that it would cost the party dearly if not repaired.

This was timely commentary. Years of unbroken Unionist rule had left the public apathetic and detached from local politics. The capacities and limits of devolved government were still not widely appreciated. Apart from lawyers who were either able to combine careers or take career 'breaks' in politics, professional people were indifferent. Local industry was still well represented,[199] and also still able to influence economic policy from a narrow, self-interested perspective. The lack of proper opposition detracted hugely from the value of the parliamentary proceedings. The Unionist Party, at least in theory, possessed a democratic internal structure, but it was clear that local constituency associations were often vehicles for sectarian, class or other grievances to be pressed, and that selection of candidates was about more than ability. A few years later, indeed, the small-mindedness of the party's grassroots in North Belfast thwarted the re-selection of their Westminster MP, Montgomery-Hyde, in what became a highly publicised row.[200] The majority of local party members in this case were quite happy to spurn a figure whose cosmopolitanism and liberal views on specific issues more than offset for them his wealth of learning and high standing at Westminster.

The Unionist Party needed to take account of critical evaluations of the Stormont scene and consider how the future health both of itself and of local politics might be served. Brooke (created Viscount Brookeborough in 1952) and other party officers were aware of the dearth of quality among many of their MPs, councillors and party candidates, but their energies were to a great extent absorbed by the task of persuading the talented people there were, such as government ministers Brian Maginess and Dehra Parker, to remain in politics.[201] It was also an issue relegated down the list of Unionist priorities: keeping the party prepared for the defence of its record and for the repelling of propaganda attacks necessitated a combative reflex inimical to the long-term recasting job required to change the political culture of the Province. The party also considered such a change to be largely dependent on the cessation of hostility to the state on the part of Nationalists.

On this matter the portents remained gloomy from a Unionist point of view even as living standards through welfare improved the lot of Unionist and Nationalist, Protestant and Catholic.[202] Anti-partition propaganda persisted, and Brookeborough undertook de Valera-style speaking tours of the USA and Australia to counter it in his own unruffled, uncompromising and withering style.[203] Brookeborough attempted in the USA to exploit the cold war climate by claiming that Ulster was vital not only to the British Commonwealth, but to America itself in the fight against communism.[204] The Republic of Ireland was portrayed endlessly by Unionists as inward-looking, bound to the past and cut off from the main trend of world events.[205] This was a propaganda tactic which fed eagerly off the South's post-war economic woes and the consequent waves of emigration, and the 'Mother and Child' controversy of 1951 which seemed proof positive of a society in which the Roman Catholic Church pulled the levers of power behind the scenes and thwarted attempts to enter the age of enlightened social welfare provision.[206] The 1950s, like the late 1940s, provided Unionists with good propaganda tunes, and the UUC machine was still geared effectively to playing them.[207]

When it became clear that the anti-partitionist propaganda and publicity strategy was getting nowhere – the APL splintered into smaller groups in 1953 – Republicans began to prepare for a return to physical force methods. The relatively high poll for Sinn Fein candidates in the 1955 British general election seemed to convince them that there was sufficient popular support for such a campaign. It was duly launched in 1956 and continued sporadically until 1962 when it ended in failure.[208] The violence claimed several lives (two of policemen) and much damage to property, and kept the Northern Ireland government on a permanent state of alert. The level of support anticipated from the Catholic community did not materialise, and Brookeborough himself acknowledged gratefully the condemnations of the IRA made by Catholic clergymen and Nationalist politicians.[209] Unionists, on the other hand, were unconvinced that the Republic was doing everything possible to curb the IRA activities or to prevent the South being used as a 'sanctuary'.[210] Brookeborough made what Unionists felt were impressive television broadcasts denouncing the campaign and explaining the plight of Ulster to the British people.[211] However, his comments to the UUC after a trip to London for this purpose late in 1956 revealed Brookeborough as less than enamoured of the Tory government's level of support. He characterised its attitude as 'we are your friends but don't tell anybody about it', going on to say that he had had great difficulty in getting permission to say in his broadcast that the defence of Northern Ireland was as dear to the hearts of the government as the defence of any other part of the UK.[212]

The painful realisation on the part of many Unionists that they were not considered 'quite as British' as the other parts of the UK may have helped to feed a greater emphasis in the post-war era on an Ulster regional identity, something related also to literary and popular cultural developments of the period.[213] In a sense the extravagant displays of Britishness on royal occasions and the like might have contributed to perceptions on the part of people in Britain itself of a corner of the UK caught in an imperial time-warp,[214] yet 1950s Britain was by no means post-imperial in its assumptions and outlook, and fervent 'Union Jackery' street partying to celebrate the coronation was a feature of Scottish and Northern English working-class areas as well as Belfast. The tendency to disregard Northern Ireland in the context of UK calculations stemmed mainly from its distinctive governmental arrangements, and was arguably more marked in British ruling circles than in public opinion.[215]

The IRA's campaign, like that of the APL in the late 1940s, had the effect of helping Brookeborough to keep the Unionist Party united in the face of the threat of internal divisions. In 1956, along with the customary sniping from 'strong' Protestants about the government's propensity to favour its enemies,[216] there emerged tensions around specific social and economic matters.

The most troublesome was probably that of the Housing Miscellaneous Provisions Bill, commonly known as 'the Rent Bill', which enabled landlords to increase rents. The minister responsible for the bill, Dehra Parker, who made the issue something of a personal crusade, had an unfortunate history of arousing antagonism: indeed, she epitomised the 'fur coat' image of the Unionist Party promoted especially by Independent Unionists to portray the government as out of touch with the realities of ordinary people's lives. The honour of being the first, and only, female Unionist cabinet minister also seemed a mixed blessing in terms of how she was received at the grassroots.

Disquiet within the party was voiced in February 1956, Brookeborough's defence being that in the long term the government would only face criticism for allowing houses to fall into disrepair if it did not proceed with the measure.[217] In spite of this, opposition to it grew and involved most notably the Minister of Labour, Ivan Neill,[218] and the Attorney-General, Edmund Warnock.[219] The former abstained on the vote in parliament and was then forced by the Prime Minister into making a statement saying that he had been prevented from voting by 'force of circumstances', a good illustration of Brookeborough's ability to be ruthless when he wished. The price of a refusal would have been departure from the government.[220]

Warnock by contrast did resign, and it seems Brookeborough in this case gave him no choice.[221] Clearly, the Prime Minister's patience with this lucid and suave yet self-destructive political figure was at an end. Warnock had a taste for sounding alarmist,[222] and had been predicting a dire fate for the government long before the Rent Bill issue gave him a cause to gain more public attention. It was not, of course, the first time that Warnock had resigned from a Unionist government, and he was to enjoy more years of spicing up the local political scene. However, his talent for so doing was out of proportion to his personal base of support. In effect he was an isolated siren voice, and if he was attempting to use the rents controversy as a way of bidding for the Unionist leadership then it was a doomed enterprise from the beginning. 'It is curious', confided Brookeborough to his diary when the dust had settled on the affair, 'that an intelligent man such as he [Warnock] should lack completely in judgement.'[223] As ever, this was shrewd: Warnock played the game ineptly, his exploratory cast of mind being trained too much on risk-taking and on directing what invariably turned out to be short-lived dramas. He should have taken care, as Brookeborough had done in the war, to avoid giving the impression of plotting disloyally. Meanwhile, the man the Prime Minister might have wished eventually to succeed him, Brian Maginess, found the

'Lundy' tag too much of a burden.[224] In taking the vacant post of Attorney-General in 1956 Maginess effectively shifted the orientation of his career from politics back to the law, although he was still to make political waves.

Warnock, on the back benches, spoke out even louder against the Rent Bill, and the Unionist Party was soon to discover just how far it had upset the working-class electorate. The measure, when taken in conjunction with a concession to right-wing pressure such as Maginess's reduction of death duties in the wake of the previous election, tilted the balance too far away from working-class interests, especially against a background of the continuing unemployment problem.

The Unionist governments of the 1950s were plagued by an unemployment rate significantly higher than the UK average.[225] Their hopes that the Conservative government in London, in office from 1951, would intervene to help came to nothing; in fact, the Tory counter-inflationary measures of the time resulted in a credit squeeze and further blows to Northern Ireland's staple industrial base.[226] Brookeborough continued to set his face against any increase in Northern Ireland's financial powers, arguing that this would not help the export industries – linen was especially troubled – or inward investment. Northern Ireland's economic ills, as defined in government files in London in the 1950s,[227] derived from inbuilt disadvantages such as distance from the British mainland necessitating higher transport costs, and the lack of indigenous raw materials, resulting in the import at a high cost of coal in particular. In addition, there was the factor of the school leaving age, which was not increased to 15 until 1957, and the absence of national service. All of these factors combined to inhibit economic competitiveness and to create a higher rate of unemployment.

The Unionist government commissioned an economic survey the conclusions of which were so unpalatable that its publication was delayed from the time of submission in 1955 until 1957. The survey was highly critical of local industry's lack of dynamism, and of the government's failure to stimulate modernisation and diversification.[228] The government did what it could in providing investment grants and inducements, but perhaps not enough care was taken to ensure that the grants were wisely used in terms for instance of research and development.[229] The government seemed to focus less on industries with growth potential than on the ailing established ones which of course employed many of their supporters. It should, how-

126

ever, be noted that an economic survey carried out in Scotland at this time revealed a similar tale of over-dependence on an old heavy industrial base, as well as indifference to the need for new equipment and knowledge.[230] There was thus failure too on the part of Scottish elites to adapt. Devolved government, whether legislative or administrative, faced economic challenges in both places, arising from similar industrial histories and their respective dependent relationships to the broader British economy. The authors of the Northern Ireland survey did not advocate greater fiscal powers for Stormont, and they concluded quite firmly that the Province's economic performance was – and was likely to be for the foreseeable future – largely governed by economic conditions and policy in Britain.[231]

An Advisory Development Council was set up in 1955 which brought together officials for both the London and Belfast governments, but it proved to be a cosmetic gesture. The Tory government was certainly not prepared to risk the ire of heavy industrial interests in other parts of the UK by giving special privileges or concessions to Northern Ireland.

The economic survey's criticisms were given wider currency by Warnock and by the NILP, and the demand in particular for a Development Corporation to raise the capital to expand Northern Ireland's industrial base was used as an effective stick with which to beat the government in the run-up to the election. An unusually nervous Brookeborough recorded in January 1958 that he had a 'horror of being the cause of a split in the party',[232] and in the following month he had reason again to rebuke Ivan Neill for a speech on the economic situation which 'implied criticism of the government'.[233]

The government brought greater pressure to bear on its London counterpart to take the unemployment issue seriously,[234] but its efforts could not prevent significant losses to the NILP in the election which was held in March. The seats lost, four in number, were all in Belfast and contained large numbers of Protestant working-class voters.[235] The unemployment question, general economic sluggishness, and the Rent Bill all took their toll in an election campaign in which, IRA activities notwithstanding, there was a greater stress than usual on social and economic questions.[236] Indeed, it might be hazarded that without the IRA's campaign serving to preserve essential party unity and the bulk of the support base, there could have been a much more damaging outcome. As it was, the Unionist vote slumped to just over 100,000, and the total anti-government vote (of all parties and candidates) in Belfast was only marginally less than that for the government.

After the election Brookeborough addressed the UUC and remarked candidly that 'today the battle was being fought on economics and it was more difficult'.[237] This reflected a real concern about the potential of the NILP and Independents to make further inroads into Unionist Party working-class support against a background of relative security on the constitutional question. That combination would soon be upset again, but the difficulties for the Unionist Party would multiply.

Notes

1 Ulster Unionist Council (UUC) Papers, Public Record Office of Northern Ireland (PRONI), UUC Report 1940, D1327/18/224.

2 PRONI, D3015/1A/7/5/1–19, Spender to Douglas Savory, 21 February 1941; Spender to Savory, 1 March 1941. Savory was an Ulster Unionist MP at Westminster from 1940 to 1955.

3 The official history of Northern Ireland and the Second World War is John W. Blake, *Northern Ireland in the Second World War* (Belfast, HMSO, 1956). See also R. Fisk, *In time of war: Ireland, Ulster and the price of neutrality, 1939–1945* (London, Andre Deutsch, 1983); B. Barton, *Northern Ireland in the Second World War* (Belfast, Ulster Historical Foundation, 1995).

4 See Fisk, *In time of war*, pp. 88–91.

5 Something admitted by the Minister of Public Security, J. C. MacDermott. See Barton, *Northern Ireland*, p. 24.

6 Barton, *Northern Ireland*, pp. 37–40.

7 Ibid., p. 28; also B. Barton, *Brookeborough: the making of a Prime Minister* (Belfast, Institute of Irish Studies, 1988), p. 149. Warnock had exempted Brooke from criticism in June 1940 following his resignation in protest at the government's performance.

8 See criticisms by the young Harold Wilson, a junior minister at the Board of Trade in the London wartime coalition government under Churchill. Wilson reported damningly in January 1941 on the Northern Ireland war effort. Fisk, *In time of war*, pp. 452–3.

9 See PRONI, CAB 4/473 for 'Post-Blitz problems'.

10 The government seemed more concerned with the protection of Carson's statue in the Stormont grounds. See PRONI, CAB 4/476.

11 The Moderator was J. B. Woodburn, author of *The Ulster Scot* (1914). See Chapter 2.

12 PRONI, CAB 4/473; Barton, *Brookeborough*, pp. 198–9; J. Colville,

The fringes of power (London, Hodder and Stoughton, 1985), p. 463.

13 PRONI, D3015/1A/7/5/19, Spender to Savory, 8 May 1942. See also J. Bowman, *De Valera and the Ulster question 1917–73* (Oxford, Oxford University Press, 1982), pp. 244–6.

14 See Barton, *Northern Ireland*, p. 199 regarding Andrews's apparent late change of mind. It should also be noted that assistance was given by the South in the form of fire-fighters dispatched from Dundalk.

15 See PRONI, CAB 4/495; Barton, *Northern Ireland*, pp. 56–7.

16 PRONI, CAB 7/CD/208, Morrison to Andrews, 13 May 1941.

17 See G. S. Walker, *The politics of frustration: Harry Midgley and the failure of Labour in Northern Ireland* (Manchester, Manchester University Press, 1985), pp. 125–9 for an account of the Willowfield by-election.

18 For Douglas, see J. F. Harbinson, *The Ulster Unionist Party 1882–1973* (Belfast, Blackstaff Press, 1973), pp. 52–3.

19 UUC Papers, D1327/18/233, letter dated 12 December 1941.

20 UUC Papers, D1327/12/1.

21 PRONI, PM4/20/6, Andrews to Hugh Montgomery, 11 February 1941.

22 PRONI, PM5/9/1, Andrews to Brooke, 27 September 1944; also documents in UUC Papers, D1327/12/1.

23 For Bailie, see Harbinson, *The Ulster Unionist Party*, pp. 53–4.

24 UUC Papers, D1327/12/1.

25 Ibid., document entitled 'How to run a Unionist association'.

26 UUC Report 1943, D1327/20/2/26.

27 Ulster Women's Council Report 1942, D1327/20/2/26.

28 See PRONI, D3292/A1.

29 UUC Papers, D1327/12/1, document entitled 'A few suggestions to meet grievances'.

30 Walker, *Politics of frustration*, p. 127.

31 See PRONI, CAB 4/518 for the opposition of some Unionist MPs to the Belfast Corporation Bill.

32 UUC Papers, D1327/12/1.

33 Barton, *Brookeborough*, p. 201.

34 UUC Papers, D1327/12/1, letter from R. M. Connell to William Douglas, 31 December 1941.

35 See PRONI, PM4/20/6, letter from Hugh Montgomery to Andrews, 26 December 1941.

36 Ibid., Lavery to Andrews, 13 December 1941.

37 See Fisk, *In time of war*, pp. 453–4.

38 See PRONI, CAB 4/496, 502, 504; Barton, *Brookeborough*, p. 201; Fisk, *In time of war*, p. 463.

39 PRONI, PM4/20/6, letter from Andrews to Montgomery, 18 December 1941.

40 See discussion in P. Bew et al., *Northern Ireland 1921–94* (London, Serif, 1995), pp. 83–7.
41 PRONI, CAB 9/CD/231/2.
42 Bew et al., *Northern Ireland*, p. 86.
43 See G. Walker, *Thomas Johnston* (Manchester, Manchester University Press, 1988), ch. 6.
44 *Belfast Newsletter* (editorial), 10 December 1942.
45 *Belfast Newsletter*, 5 December 1942.
46 See UUC Papers, D1327/20/2/26.
47 See UUC Papers, D1327/22/1.
48 Ibid.
49 Barton, *Brookeborough*, p. 223.
50 The most detailed account is Barton, *Brookeborough*, ch. 10.
51 See famous tribute from Churchill quoted in Barton, *Northern Ireland*, p. 89.
52 Barton, *Brookeborough*, ch. 10.
53 The Northern Ireland parliament had its life extended beyond 1943 in the light of the wartime circumstances.
54 See Barton, *Brookeborough*; Fisk, *In time of war*, pp. 455 and 473. Brooke was a cousin of the wartime general Viscount Alanbrooke.
55 See PRONI, PM4/6/21.
56 Ibid., MacManaway to Brooke, 21 July 1943.
57 Walker, *Politics of frustration*, ch. 7.
58 *Northern Ireland House of Commons Debates*, XXVI, c. 468.
59 Barton, *Brookeborough*, p. 229.
60 PRONI, PM4/6/21, Brooke to Major J. S. Henderson, 21 June 1943.
61 PRONI, PM5/9/1, A. Robinson to Gransden, 22 August 1944. The system as it stood also allowed companies the right to up to six votes depending on the rateable value of their property.
62 PRONI, CAB 4/597.
63 PRONI, CAB 4/541; Walker, *Politics of frustration*, pp. 151–3.
64 PRONI, CAB 4/597 (Midgley memo); also CAB 4/614 and CAB 4/623.
65 Corkey's allegations of anti-Presbyterian bias in the Ministry of Education echoed similar complaints in the 1920s and 1930s (see Chapter 3).
66 PRONI, CAB 4/623.
67 Bew et al., *Northern Ireland*, p. 96.
68 The Communist Party in Northern Ireland, in accordance with Soviet Russia's change of position, became a supporter of the Allied war effort from 1941. The party's apparent pro-Britishness resulted in a good electoral showing in Protestant working-class areas in 1945.
69 PRONI, PM4/20/8, Election Address dated 5 June 1945.
70 For which see B. Lynn, *Holding the ground: the Nationalist Party in*

Northern Ireland (Aldershot, Avebury, 1997), chs 1 and 2; Bob Purdie, 'The Irish Anti-Partition League, South Armagh and abstentionism', *Irish Political Studies*, 1 (1986), pp. 67–78; Bowman, *De Valera*, ch. 7.

71 The APL was organised along different lines in the South.

72 See D. Kennedy, *The widening gulf* (Belfast, Blackstaff Press, 1988), ch. 15.

73 See, for example, statement by Henry Harrison, President of Paddington branch in London: 'Catholics were treated with as abominable and as barbarous cruelty as were the Jews in Hitler's Germany', in PRONI, D2784/12/3/3. See also B. Purdie, 'Lessons from Ireland', in T. Gallagher (ed.), *Nationalism in the nineties* (Edinburgh, Polygon, 1991), fn. 17; A. C. Hepburn, *The conflict of nationality in modern Ireland* (London, Edward Arnold, 1980), pp. 167–8.

74 R. English, '"Paying no heed to public clamor": Irish republican solipsism in the 1930s', *Irish Historical Studies*, 28:112 (1993), pp. 426–39.

75 T. Cradden, *Trade unionism, socialism and partition* (Belfast, December Publications, 1993), pp. 148–9. Diamond was to make sectarian interventions of his own a few years later. See G. Walker, *Intimate strangers: political and cultural interaction between Scotland and Ulster in modern times* (Edinburgh, John Donald, 1995), p. 141.

76 This government was led by Fine Gael's John Costello, but also included a new, fiercely Republican party, Clann na Phoblachta, led by ex-IRA man Sean MacBride.

77 See Cradden, *Trade unionism*, p. 149 for the letter by former Labour Party leader Tom Johnson to Ernest Blythe in 1949.

78 See Purdie, 'The Irish Anti-Partition League'.

79 B. Purdie, 'The Friends of Ireland, British Labour and Irish Nationalism, 1945–49', in T. Gallagher and J. O'Connell (eds), *Contemporary Irish studies* (Manchester, Manchester University Press, 1983).

80 This pamphlet was banned by the Northern Ireland government in the context of wartime security considerations. However, this was exceptional and in terms of the freedom of the press and censorship legislation Northern Ireland was generally more liberal than Eire.

81 See UUC Papers, D1327/20/3/9, the Very Rev. W. S. Kerr's 'Slanders on Ulster'; also D3015/1A/8/13/1 and /3.

82 UUC Papers, D1327/20/4/27, APL pamphlet *Discrimination, a study in injustice to a minority*. Strictly speaking, however, more Protestants were disenfranchised by the local government Election and Franchise Act of 1946, a price the Unionist Party was prepared to pay, and the risk it was prepared to run, to preserve its hold on several councils.

83 See E. McAteer, *Irish action* (Belfast, Athol Books, 1979).

84 Reported in *The Scotsman*, 8 September 1948.

85 *Glasgow Herald*, 18 October 1948.

86 PRONI, D3004/D/40, Brooke diary, 4 January 1949.

87 See D. Harkness, *Ireland in the twentieth century* (Basingstoke, Macmillan, 1996), p. 82 (Attlee statement).

88 See next section.

89 See UUC Papers, D1327/16/3/15.

90 These were based on the guiding principle of parity in social services and taxation. The insurance funds of the two administrations in London and Belfast were effectively amalgamated, and there was now no longer any requirement that part of the excess Northern Ireland cost should be met from the Northern Ireland Exchequer.

91 UUC Papers, D1327/16/3/15, leaflet entitled 'What Ulster Unionists stand for'.

92 Complaints about 'socialistic' measures had been made by these Unionists before the end of the war. See Walker, *Politics of frustration*, pp. 161–4.

93 For detailed assessments of relations between the Unionist government and the Labour governments 1945–51, see B. Barton, 'Relations between Westminster and Stormont during the Attlee premiership', *Irish Political Studies*, 7 (1992) pp. 1–20; B. Barton, 'The impact of World War II on Northern Ireland and on Belfast–London relations', in P. Catterall and S. McDougall (eds), *The Northern Ireland question in British politics* (Basingstoke, Macmillan, 1996).

94 PRONI, CAB 4/642.

95 For which see D. Harkness, *Northern Ireland since 1920* (Dublin, Helicon, 1983), ch. 5; Bew et al., *Northern Ireland*, pp. 99–107. These are the sources for what follows on this subject.

96 For Grant see comments of Terence O'Neill in *The autobiography of Terence O'Neill* (London, Hart-Davis, 1972), p. 32. Grant, of course, had been a leading figure in the UULA since its inception. He died in 1949.

97 Bew et al., *Northern Ireland*, pp. 103–4.

98 In Scotland this led to something of a nationalistic backlash which revived the campaign for a Scottish parliament.

99 PRONI, CAB 4/735.

100 Ibid.

101 See J. Ditch, *Social policy in Northern Ireland between 1939 and 1950* (Aldershot, Avebury, 1988).

102 See, for example, PRONI, CAB 4/732 and CAB 4/812.

103 For example, the contribution of Sir Douglas Savory such as his booklet *The war effort of Northern Ireland* (UUC, 1947).

104 See next chapter.

105 Harkness, *Northern Ireland*, p. 110.

106 UUC Papers, D1327/6/9. In addition, a Statistics of Trade Bill created a furious row in 1946 and had to be diluted in its Stormont form. See H. Patterson, *Ireland since 1939* (Oxford, Oxford University Press, 2002), p. 120.

107 UUC Papers, D1327/6/9.

108 UUC Papers, D1327/12/4.

109 UUC Papers, D1327/20/2/29.

110 See Hepburn (ed.), *Conflict of nationality*, pp. 169–70.

111 Unionists challenged Nationalist claims on this point with the argument that Nationalist figures were based on the census and equated being Catholic with being Nationalist. See PRONI, D3015/1A/7/5/ 1–19, Savory to Sir Wilfrid Spender, 21 July 1943.

112 For which in general see UUC Papers, D1327/6/1, Executive Committee minutes for 20 May 1949 and 1 July 1949.

113 Published by the UUC in 1948.

114 J. Todd, 'Unionist political thought, 1920–72', in D. G. Boyce et al. (eds), *Political thought in Ireland since the seventeenth century* (London, Routledge, 1993).

115 *A warning to the Ulster people* (UUC, 1949).

116 Ibid.

117 UUC Papers, D1327/20/3/12.

118 See G. McIntosh, *The force of culture* (Cork, Cork University Press, 1999), p. 70.

119 UUC Papers, D1327/20/3/12, *Voice of Ulster*, March 1949. The wartime offers of unity to Eire were not forgotten, if seldom mentioned.

120 Rev. J. G. MacManaway, *Partition. Why not?* (UUC, 1948).

121 Quoted in McIntosh, *The force of culture*, p. 187.

122 St John Ervine, *Craigavon: Ulsterman* (London, Allen and Unwin, 1949).

123 Something of the same criticism might be levelled at the nonetheless valuable work of James Loughlin in his *Ulster Unionism and British national identity since 1885* (London, Pinter, 1995).

124 UUC Papers, D1327/16/3/24.

125 PRONI, PM4/20/12, Terence O'Neill to Brooke, 1 November 1948.

126 PRONI, D3004/D/40, 26 January 1949.

127 Ibid.; also PRONI, PM4/20/12, Brooke speech, 8 February 1949.

128 PRONI, D3004/D/40, 31 January 1949.

129 A drop of 40,000. The Independent Unionist vote was virtually wiped out also.

130 See the hopes of Herbert Morrison on this point. Walker, *Intimate strangers*, pp. 83–4.

131 PRONI, D3004/D/40.

132 Quoted in Harkness, *Ireland*, p. 81.

133 See Hepburn (ed.), *Conflict of nationality*, pp. 170–2.

134 See Harkness, *Ireland*, pp. 81–2.

135 See PRONI, PM4/20/12 and PM5/9/2.
136 See Kennedy, *Widening gulf*, p. 239.
137 PRONI, D3004/D/40.
138 Ibid.
139 See H. Patterson, 'Brian Maginess and the limits of Liberal Unionism', *Irish Review*, 25 (1999/2000), pp. 95–112.
140 Ibid.
141 See Hall-Thompson memo in PRONI, CAB 4/798.
142 See resolution in half-yearly report of Grand Lodge, 8 June 1949, in PRONI, D2222, Box 8. Both Brooke and Andrews were in attendance.
143 Parker had long been a figure of suspicion among more fundamentalist Unionists. For example, she was at the centre of a bizarre controversy in the 1930s over a painting which was alleged to depict Prince William of Orange being given a papal blessing. See G. Walker, '"Protestantism before party!": the Ulster Protestant League in the 1930s', *Historical Journal*, 28:4 (1985), pp. 961–7.
144 See W. Corkey, *Episode in the history of Protestant Ulster* (Belfast, Dorman & Sons, 1947); M. Dewar et al., *Orangeism: a new historical appreciation* (Belfast, Grand Orange Lodge of Ireland, 1967), pp. 182–3.
145 PRONI, D3004/D/35, January–March 1944. See especially entries for 8 March and 10 March. Brooke in the latter entry cited Edmund Warnock as comparing the Presbyterian agitation to the shop stewards movement then behaving in militant fashion.
146 In the form of 4x2 committees in which the secular component would be in the minority. See D. H. Akenson, *Education and enmity: the control of schooling in Northern Ireland, 1920–50* (Newton Abbot, David and Charles, 1973), pp. 177–80; S. Farren, *The politics of Irish education 1920–65* (Belfast, Institute of Irish Studies, 1995); M. McGrath, *The Catholic Church and Catholic schools in Northern Ireland* (Dublin, Irish Academic Press, 1999).
147 PRONI, CAB 4/799.
148 PRONI, D3004/D/40.
149 Ibid., 13 December 1949.
150 Ibid.
151 *Northern Ireland House of Commons Debates*, XXXIII, c. 2276.
152 See PRONI, CAB 4/803.
153 Ibid.
154 See Walker, *Politics of frustration*, ch. 10, for discussion.
155 *Northern Ireland House of Commons Debates*, XXXV, c. 345. Midgley could not get his wish that 65 per cent grants be dropped to 50 per cent if the 4x2 committee option was not accepted. Midgley, *pace* Corkey, also had his troubles with Brownell at the Ministry. See P. Shea, *Voices and the sound of drums* (Belfast, Blackstaff, 1981).

156 PRONI, D3004/D/40, 8 March 1951.

157 See PRONI, CAB 4/798 and CAB 4/865.

158 See M. McGrath, 'The narrow road: Harry Midgley and Catholic schools in Northern Ireland', *Irish Historical Studies*, 30:119 (1997), pp. 429–51. McGrath argues that Midgley created difficulties for Catholic schools. See Walker, *Politics of frustration*, ch. 11 for a defence.

159 The Unionist Party lost seats to Independent Unionists in the 1953 election – see next section.

160 See T. Wilson, *Ulster: conflict and consent* (Oxford, Blackwell Press, 1989), pp. 140–1; also comments of Desmond Fennell in his *The Northern Catholic* (Dublin, Irish Times, 1958).

161 In this connection see statement of Bishop Farren quoted in T. Hennessey, *A history of Northern Ireland* (Dublin, Gill and Macmillan, 1997), pp. 118–19.

162 See discussion in Walker, *Intimate strangers*, ch. 4.

163 PRONI, CAB 4/798 and CAB 4/865.

164 PRONI, CAB 4/912; also D3004/D/44, 20 May and 24 July 1953.

165 See T. Wilson, 'Conclusion', in T. Wilson (ed.), *Ulster under home rule* (Oxford, Oxford University Press, 1955). Irish was compulsory in schools in the Republic, and for entry to the Civil Service.

166 See G. C. Duggan, *Northern Ireland: success or failure?* (Dublin, Irish Times, 1950).

167 UUC Papers, D1327/20/4/34, pamphlet by Duggan entitled *A united Ireland*.

168 UUC Papers, D1327/6/1, Executive Committee minutes, 28 April 1950 and 9 June 1950.

169 UUC Papers, D1327/20/2/34, UUC Report 1951. 'We realise the importance of the allocation of houses and are always open to investigate any allegations of unfair treatment which reach us.'

170 See J. H. Whyte, 'How much discrimination was there under the Unionist regime, 1921–1968?', in Gallagher and O'Connell (eds), *Contemporary Irish studies*; also Patterson, *Ireland since 1939*, pp. 123–4.

171 PRONI, D3004/D/42, 16 February 1951.

172 UUC Papers, D1327/20/3/10, 'Progress Report 1949–52'.

173 See Wilson, *Ulster*, ch. 13; White, 'How much discrimination'.

174 See PRONI, CAB 4/936 for film 'Fintona' on housing discrimination.

175 See PRONI, CAB 4/745.

176 See H. Patterson, 'Party versus Order: Ulster Unionism and the Flags and Emblems Act', *Contemporary British History*, 13:4 (1999), pp. 105–29 for fuller discussion.

177 UUC Papers, D1327/20/3/4, UUC Report 1951.

178 Details of speech in PRONI, PM4/20/15.

179 Ibid., Maginess to Brooke, 28 October 1953.

180 And possibly only with the help of Catholic votes. See Patterson, 'Party versus Order'. On the subject of cross-community support, it might be noted that Nationalist Eddie McAteer, in his campaign for seat of Foyle, declared himself proud of not appealing to any Unionist voters in the constituency. See *Derry Journal*, 6 March 2001.

181 PRONI, PM4/20/15, Graham to Brooke, 27 October 1953.

182 Porter led the pressure group the National Union of Protestants in Ulster, and was one of those behind the *Ulster Protestant*, a newspaper which frequently attacked the Unionist government in the 1950s.

183 PRONI, PM4/20/15, Hall-Thompson to Brooke, 23 October 1953.

184 See material in PRONI, PM4/20/15 and UUC Papers, D1327/16/3/45. In addition to the party's electoral problems it had lost Maynard Sinclair in January 1953 in the *Princess Victoria* disaster, and some Unionists refused to have anything to do with former Attorney-General and Carrick MP Sir Lancelot Curran after his daughter was murdered in mysterious circumstances in November 1952. See letter from Sydney Frazer to Brooke, 9 December 1953, PM4/20/15.

185 *Belfast Newsletter*, 13 October 1953.

186 PRONI, D3004/D/40, 11 and 16 November 1949. See J. Sayers, 'The political parties', in Wilson (ed.), *Ulster under home rule*. 'The spirit of the [Unionist] party ... is foreign to the oligarchic conceptions of the extreme right wing of Toryism.'

187 Speech by Cahir Healy, *Northern Ireland House of Commons Debates*, XXXVIII, c. 518. See Patterson, 'Party versus Order' for fuller discussion.

188 *Northern Ireland House of Commons Debates*, XXXVIII, c. 589–91.

189 Ibid., c. 593–6 and 604.

190 PRONI, CAB 4/936.

191 See J. McGarry and B. O'Leary, *The politics of antagonism* (London, Athlone Press, 1993), ch. 3.

192 Ibid., p. 140.

193 The observation was made from within the party after the 1953 election that different parts of the party had become 'isolated units' pulling in different directions. See UUC Papers, D1327/16/3/45.

194 See Patterson, 'Brian Maginess'; also PRONI, D3004/D/44, 1 December 1953 and 6 January 1954.

195 UUC Papers, D1327/6/1, Executive Committee minutes, 13 January 1950.

196 Ibid.

197 *Belfast Telegraph*, 23 February 1953.

198 See also in this respect Sayers, 'The political parties'.

199 See Bew et al., *Northern Ireland*, p. 126.

200 See material on the episode in Montgomery-Hyde Papers, PRONI,

D3084/I/A/2/4.

201 See *Belfast Telegraph* article of 23 February 1953.

202 There was disaffection among some Unionists over the matter of Family Allowances, which were perceived to benefit the Catholic community disproportionately. There was pressure applied on the government to restrict the benefits to the minority, but this was not yielded to. See *Belfast Newsletter*, 15 April 1955.

203 PRONI, D3004/D/41, 5 April 1950: on arrival in New York Brooke 'gave a press conference on the plane and a good deal of shouting from the Micks outside'.

204 Ibid., 8 May 1951.

205 See, for example, Brian Maginess's contribution to *Why the border must be* (Belfast, HMSO, 1956).

206 UUC Papers, D11327/20/4/28, Unionist publication *Church and state*; also D1327/20/2/34, UUC Report for 1951.

207 UUC Papers, D1327/6/1, Publicity Committee Reports; D1327/20/2/34, UUC Report 1951 on use of film.

208 For a recent evaluation see Hennessey, *A history*, pp. 104–7.

209 See, for example, PRONI, D3004/D/45, 19 January 1956.

210 UUC Papers, D1327/20/2/39, UUC Report 1956.

211 Ibid. The IRA attacked Brookeborough's home village, and he and his wife Cynthia were obliged to sit at home with shotguns at the ready. See PRONI, D3004/D/45, January 1957.

212 PRONI, D3004/D/45, 8 March 1957.

213 See Patterson, 'Brian Maginess'; McIntosh, *Force of culture*, ch. 6.

214 For which case see Loughlin, *Ulster Unionism*, passim.

215 The suggestion here is not that Northern Ireland was not in many ways (not least public order) different – differences abounded throughout the UK and characterised it as a state organised on principles of territorial management – but that Northern Ireland, in many official channels, was not *included* in the manner of other parts of the UK for whatever purpose.

216 In 1955 a former Attorney-General, Anthony Babington, wrote to the then Minister of Education, Harry Midgley, complaining that 'Militant Roman Catholicism has been allowed too much rope' and that 'it gives me a pain in the stomach when I hear our people saying that the Nationalists are coming over and voting Unionist or even abstaining'. Letter dated 14 August 1955 in Midgley Papers, privately held.

217 PRONI, D3004/D/45, 21 February 1956.

218 See I. Neill, *Church and state* (Dunmurry, 1995), pp. 52–3; also O'Neill, *Autobiography*, pp. 33–4.

219 See speech in *Northern Ireland House of Commons Debates*, XXXX, c. 837–40.

220 PRONI, D3004/D/45, 2 May 1956.

221 Ibid., 6 April 1956.

222 Ibid., 23 March 1956. 'Warnock wrote to say the Unionist Party was disintegrating before our eyes.' See also *Northern Ireland House of Commons Debates*, XXXX, c. 837 – 'the blackest day in the history of our Party for the past 35 years'.

223 PRONI, D3004/D/45, 31 December 1957.

224 Ibid., 17 March 1958. The term derives from the Siege of Derry of 1688 and means 'traitor'.

225 The Northern Ireland rate stood at 10 per cent in 1958.

226 See Bew et al., *Northern Ireland*, pp. 121–2.

227 See, for example, PRO, PREM 11/3447.

228 K. S. Isles and N. Cuthbert, *An economic survey of Northern Ireland* (Belfast, 1957); Bew et al., *Northern Ireland*, p. 124; also PRONI, CAB 4/1004, memo by Minister of Commerce.

229 See discussion in Wilson, *Ulster*, ch. 10.

230 See C. Harvie, *Scotland and Nationalism* (London, Routledge, 1998), pp. 121–2, 127.

231 See PRONI, CAB 4/1004. The Report's conclusions are attached to the memo by the Minister of Commerce.

232 PRONI, D3004/D/45, 27 January 1958.

233 Ibid., 20 February 1958.

234 See documents in PRO, PREM 11/3447.

235 The seats were Woodvale, Oldpark, Pottinger and Victoria. With the exception of the last, the Unionist Party had always found them difficult.

236 See material in PRONI, PM5/9/4.

237 Ibid., speech to UUC Standing Committee, 25 April 1958.

CHAPTER FIVE

CHALLENGES: LOSING CONTROL, 1958–1972

A thought came to him with the force of revelation. The Civil Rights were wrecking things because they said they were left out, but they didn't want to be part of them in the first instance. Like Francy, Mal had got it all wrong before; Francy was hated because he wouldn't join in, not the other way round. (Glen Patterson, *Burning your own*, London, Abacus, 1989, p. 113)

Brookeborough reacted to the electoral setbacks with a complacency reminiscent of his predecessor Andrews: 'not too bad on a bad unemployment wicket and strike'.[1] He announced neither cabinet changes nor policy initiatives. Behind the scenes, however, there was much concerned comment about the NILP's appeal to working-class voters in Belfast and the continuing economic difficulties. An analysis by Faulkner (Chief Whip) and William Douglas also highlighted internal squabbles among the party's 'City Hall' contingent and the decline of the UULA.[2] While Faulkner and other senior party leaders railed against the 'menace' of socialism,[3] other observers such as Warnock and Neville Martin (the defeated candidate in Woodvale) viewed the Unionist Party's identification with the Conservatives in Britain as a liability, and blamed the Unionist MPs at Westminster for not doing enough to lobby the Tory government on Northern Ireland's behalf.[4] The young activist John Taylor called for a better relationship between the government and trade unionists, and further stated: 'Our Party must never appear to be solely a right wing party but it must continue to be the party representative of Ulster loyalists of all classes'.[5]

As the correspondent of the *Belfast Telegraph* had foreseen five years previously, the Unionist Party's failure to maintain a thriving Labour wing had seriously weakened its position. In this respect the paternalistic Brookeborough, like Andrews before him, needed a 'broker' figure. After the death of William Grant in 1949 there was no such personal link between the cabinet and the world of the urban Protestant working class. Grant had been an invaluable conduit who was never replaced. Midgley, who survived Grant by eight years, had working-class and Labour movement credentials, and was Chairman of Linfield Football Club to boot, yet he was never completely trusted on account of his non-Unionist past. Senators Joseph Cunningham and Robert Armstrong, other crucial working-class influences from before the establishment of the state, were fading from public life by the late 1950s.[6] By this time, against a background of economic gloom in the Province's traditional heavy industries, the Unionist Party appeared too distant from working-class concerns, and, even more damagingly, insufficiently equipped to deal with the problems.

The roots of these problems were clearly summarised in a British government memorandum just before the 1958 election. Northern Ireland, it was noted, had no indigenous resources like coal and iron, it had to pay extra transport costs, and its main industries such as textiles were contracting. In a passage which encapsulated the Conservative government's attitude to Northern Ireland over the next five years of political wrangling and browbeating between London and Belfast, it was stated that the government's capacity to help was limited, and that the worst policy would be to make Northern Ireland 'unable and unwilling to stand on its own feet'.[7] During this time, in the face of London's inability or unwillingness to treat Northern Ireland like other regions of the UK, discontent grew at home on the part of the electorate and within the Unionist Party itself.

As lay-offs mounted at firms such as Shorts aircraft manufacturers and Harland and Wolff shipbuilders in Belfast, the British government set its face against measures such as freight subsidy to offset the increased transport costs.[8] The Northern Ireland Minister of Commerce, Lord Glentoran, also tried in vain to obtain relief for Northern Ireland firms hit badly by credit restrictions imposed at the centre, as well as a meaningful reduction in coal prices.[9] The latter issue was particularly difficult for the Unionists in light of the fact that Eire, as part of a trade agreement, was sold British coal at a cheaper rate. The irrepressible Warnock exploited the government's embarrassment at Stormont.[10] In November 1960 an exasperated Brookeborough – who seems to have come close to quitting over the economic situation[11] – visited Prime Minister Harold Macmillan in London to outline the political ramifications in person: the Unionists were facing the loss of the remaining seats held in Belfast and were under pressure from a 'highly active' NILP opposition and a trade union movement that had become very politically conscious; Unionist Party back-benchers were restive; 10,000 jobs were needed; the Ulster MPs at Westminster might be forced to take a much stronger line.[12] The response was minimal: all that was on offer was the renewal of capital grants to Northern Ireland industry for five years from 1962, and a suggestion that the British government might agree to conduct joint studies of the situation with Northern Ireland officials.[13]

The Unionist government attempted to put a gloss on this rebuff by suggesting that Macmillan had made firm pledges and that Admiralty and RAF orders would go to help the ailing firms. It also made much of the idea of a joint working party, so much so that a reluctant British government eventually agreed to it.[14] However, the less sycophantic branches of the Unionist press preferred to be realistic: the *Northern Whig* editorial was sceptical that the British government would offer any substantial help and observed that Macmillan would face pressure from the Clyde, the Tyne and the Mersey regarding the building of a new 'Queen' liner.[15] This fear turned out to be well-founded as the order later went to the Clyde, and it illustrated the difficulty of the Northern Ireland government in trying to persuade London that it merited some special treatment. The London government was always anxious, for its own political reasons, not to give other UK industrial regions cause to complain of being disadvantaged in respect of highly prized orders and new investment. In October 1960 Sir Arthur Kelly (Cabinet Secretary at Stormont) had conveyed Brookeborough's dismay over the support of the government for a new car manufacturing plant in Scotland.[16] The publicity given to such developments only increased the Northern Ireland government's political problems in trying to persuade working-class voters that their interests were being served. Plainly, the Unionist government was making no headway with its plea to London that the area in the UK with the greatest need, given Northern Ireland's significantly higher unemployment rate, ought to be given priority. Further disappointment awaited Unionist representations to London in March 1961, following which the Brookeborough government in effect placed all its hopes on the joint working party steered, after the death of its initial Chairman Sir Herbert Brittain, by Sir Robert Hall.[17]

The British government's attitude did not give grounds for such hopes. Its rejection of the latest Northern Ireland proposals, such as the reimbursement of employers' National Insurance contributions and an employment subsidy for shipyard workers, was compounded by its refusal to accept that unemployment in Northern Ireland was a 'joint responsibility'.[18] Essentially, London was using Northern Ireland's devolved government status to deny economic responsibility when its central policies were still affecting fundamentally the Province's economic outlook. As a memorandum by a Home Office official admitted while commenting on the additional problems with new industries:

> Recent experience has shown that some of the firms attracted to Northern Ireland since the war, particularly in the consumer goods industries, have not put down deep roots, and are vulnerable to restrictive economic measures taken by the United Kingdom Government in the interests of the country as a whole.[19]

This was an example of how devolution could put Northern Ireland at a disadvantage when the central government was unwilling to cater for the anomalies of the Province's position, and it is the kind of factor which was ignored by critics, Nationalist and otherwise, of what was seen as Northern Ireland's dependence on subsidies.[20] It reflected successive British governments' perceptions of devolution as a device to keep Ireland marginal to British politics rather than as a part of the complex challenges involved in the territorial management of the United Kingdom. Changing perceptions of devolution and territorial management for the UK on a broad scale, on the part of the centre, were to come too late for Northern Ireland and in particular the governing Unionist Party.

By March 1962 the Hall Report was ready and the Northern Ireland government was alerted to its downbeat findings. There was nothing in it to lift the Ulster Unionist Party out of its difficulties, and it reiterated the British government's opposition to the specific proposals Brookeborough had previously brought forward. Sir Arthur Kelly prevailed on Whitehall to tone down the more critical remarks before the Report's eventual publication in October 1962.[21] This perhaps saved the Unionists from a worse fate at the Northern Ireland elections of May 1962 when the NILP retained its four Belfast seats with increased majorities, and polled nearly

77,000 votes. The NILP also chose to give a clear run to 'left-wing' Unionist dissident Desmond Boal, who stood in the Protestant working-class seat of Shankill which had been badly affected by unemployment. Boal had indeed flirted with expulsion from the Unionist Party by tabling a motion seconded by David Bleakley of the NILP on the redundancies in the shipyards in March 1961. The party whip was later removed from him.[22] In this election Boal and the similarly motivated Warnock (representing St Anne's) were 'Independent Unionists' in all but name, and the party was also having difficulty in restraining other outspoken back-benchers such as Nat Minford and Robert Nixon, although their rebelliousness was less concentrated on economic questions.[23]

Brookeborough warned Macmillan just prior to the publication of the Hall Report that his government would be left in a vulnerable position and that Stormont MPs were likely to blame the Westminster government. He asked for an assurance about the immediate future of Shorts which Macmillan conceded, but had also to swallow the British Prime Minister's austere counsel that 'the industrial economy of Northern Ireland could never be secure while it rested on aircraft and shipbuilding. It was important to do in Northern Ireland what had been achieved in South Wales, namely to diversify industry ...'.[24] The trouble with this for Brookeborough was that it presented in the short term no way out of his perceived political problem, that of repairing the damage done to the Unionist Party's relationship with a significant section of the Protestant working class.

By this time there was a real sense of the Northern Ireland Labour challenge becoming 'normal' as in the rest of the UK, at least in urban Ulster. In Maurice Leitch's novel *The Liberty Lad*, published in 1965, a Unionist MP observes the closure of another textile mill: 'Yes ... Kildargan Mill be another headache for the Minister of Commerce. More bloody unemployment figures for those Labour gets to crow about.'[25] Moreover, it was no accident that Protestant shipyard worker and NILP activist Sam Thompson's explosive play *Over the Bridge* should have made Ulster theatrical history at this juncture, replete as it was with such a strong condemnation of the Unionist Party's role in the perpetuation of bigotry among workers.[26]

At Westminster the Unionist MP for North Belfast, Stratton Mills, railed against the Hall Report's 'implicit acceptance of the continuation of unemployment at a level of about 7 percent'.[27]

Stung by criticism at home that they were not defending Ulster's interests, the 'Imperial' Unionist MPs indeed began to stir themselves. In January 1963 they obtained an audience with Macmillan and Butler, the Home Secretary, about the unemployment situation. At the meeting the point was emphasised that 'The Ulster Unionist Members were under heavy local pressure to show that Northern Ireland's interests were not being overlooked or given lower priority than those of Scotland or the North East'. Hence more evidence of cooperation between the two governments was required to create greater public confidence in Northern Ireland – evidence that ministers for different regions were working together to produce solutions which would not adversely affect other areas. Butler said that anxiety might be relieved if more could be done to show that he had a special interest in coordinating the central government's measures for Northern Ireland in a similar way to the Secretary of State for Scotland, to the Minister of Housing for Wales and to the Lord President for the North-East.[28] This appeared to be a step towards 'integrating' Northern Ireland administratively and governmentally and ironing out the kinks to which Northern Ireland's distinctive status gave rise. Moreover, Butler observed that the case for establishing a joint committee of UK and Northern Ireland ministers had in the past been opposed by the Northern Ireland government on the grounds that it would produce unnecessary speculation and raise false hopes.[29]

If Butler was right about this then it might be said that successive administrations in Belfast connived in sustaining an unsatisfactory set of inter-governmental relations, the baleful results of which for Northern Ireland were plainly in evidence over the economic problems of the late 1950s and early 1960s. A Home Office memorandum prepared in response to the January 1963 meeting re-stated the position of Northern Ireland's economy in relation to the UK, and by implication the requirement for more coordinated political action:

> As the Working Party's report [the Hall Report] shows, the Northern Ireland economy is very closely linked with that of the United Kingdom; Northern Ireland enjoys parity in social services, in agricultural subsidies and in wage rates. Fiscal policy in Northern Ireland is determined by the United Kingdom Government. For these reasons the general prosperity and level of unemployment there are mainly determined by United Kingdom factors.[30]

Northern Ireland had chosen, repeatedly, not to go further down the devolutionary road towards greater autonomy, particularly in fiscal matters. The wisdom of this can be debated, but in the light of that choice it made little sense for British governments, with the apparent blinkered compliance of their Northern Ireland counterparts, to act as if the Province was more like a Dominion than a subordinate unit within a United Kingdom state distinguished by distinctive governmental and administrative territorial arrangements.[31] Brookeborough, it might be suggested with hindsight, would have been well advised to have built an institutionalised inter-governmental body into the post-war settlement he reached with the Labour government, against the background of Northern Ireland's full participation in the welfare state and its rejection of the 'Dominion status' option. However, the short-term and narrow party political perspective, doubtless wary of British government scrutiny of an unwanted variety, precluded such a course to the longer-term detriment of Northern Ireland.

Ulster Unionist anxieties and difficulties of this 'late Brookeborough' period have also to be viewed in the context of changes in the Republic of Ireland. From the advent of Sean Lemass as Taoiseach in 1959 and his repudiation of 'Sinn Fein economics' it was clear that both North–South and British–Irish relations were entering a new phase.[32] Lemass's pragmatic approach, which appeared relatively free of the grievance-bound anti-partitionism of de Valera, commended itself to the British government. Negotiations on trade issues opened up almost immediately and were to culminate in the benchmark Anglo-Irish accord in 1965. During this period the Northern Ireland government came under pressure from London to adopt a more cooperative stance towards the South.[33]

Politically, this was extremely tricky, especially against the background of an IRA campaign in the North which stuttered on till 1962. In 1958–59 in particular Unionists were absorbed with the task of persuading London to apply pressure on Dublin to cooperate more effectively on security matters.[34] In November 1959 the Ulster Unionist MPs at Westminster urged Home Secretary Butler to take away some of the 'privileges of the Commonwealth' which they believed the Republic enjoyed, and warned him that 'they might not be able to restrain their people if these incidents [border raids and attacks on security forces] continued'.[35] However, even this kind of language failed to move the British government into

altering its approach to economic talks with the Republic in accordance with political considerations relating to the North. The coun-
ter-argument from Butler was that any such pressure being seen to
be brought on the Republic would necessarily limit its ability to act
effectively.[36] This rebuff exacerbated the frustration of the Unionists
over the question of goods from the South making their way tariff-
free to the North and affecting the competitiveness of Northern Ireland products; calls from Unionist cabinet ministers for London to
impose retaliatory tariffs on goods entering the UK from the South
got nowhere. In short, British government policy was moving towards free trade with the Republic and Northern Unionist
sensitivities were ignored.

Moreover, there followed a confrontation between the London
and Belfast governments over an Electoral Law Bill which curtailed
the voting rights in Northern Ireland of immigrants from the South.
In the event London decided, after much hand-wringing, not to
force Belfast into dropping the measure.[37] Nevertheless, Ulster Unionists could not mistake the general trend towards closer British–
Irish relations to which the Northern Ireland government's
priorities were subordinated.

Lemass's government in Dublin saw an opportunity to
strengthen the all-Ireland economic context and floated the notion
of a reduction in tariffs on some Northern goods coming into the
Republic. The North's Minister of Commerce, Lord Glentoran,
supported this, as did many leading Northern manufacturers and
industrialists, but the Unionist cabinet would not allow economic
pressures to override the political sensitivities around partition. In
February 1960 the Northern government refused the offer.[38] Nevertheless, it was clear that Brookeborough would place no obstacle in
the way of Northern businessmen taking action on their own.[39] For
some time leading Ulster business figures such as Sir Graham
Larmour of the textile industry had signalled their frustration with
the inertia of the Unionist government. In September 1962, arising
out of consultations with these business figures, the Dublin government reduced some duties on goods in the linen and furniture
trades, to a fanfare of cheering by the Nationalist press.[40] Taken in
conjunction with the gloom induced by the Hall Report, the North's
economic prospects now appeared less optimistic than the rejuvenated South, and Unionists were placed further on the political
defensive with no sympathetic London government to give succour.
Although Macmillan, perhaps influenced by his Parliamentary

Secretary, the Ulster Unionist Samuel Knox-Cunningham, gave no personal impetus to North–South dialogue,[41] there was little credence given in London to Brookeborough's view of the Lemass dispensation as essentially anti-partitionism by other, more diplomatic means.[42]

Lord Brookeborough's tenure as Prime Minister came to an end in March 1963, twenty years after it had begun. A combination of political setbacks and failing health forced him to stand down.[43] In a profile written a year before Brookeborough's departure, the distinguished journalist W. D. Flackes had observed that the Prime Minister 'never fights unnecessary battles'.[44] This was certainly an insight into Brookeborough's longevity, yet it was also an indication of how far he would go to avoid confronting the kind of issues which require true statesmanship to resolve.

It was to Northern Ireland's enduring detriment that Brookeborough did not consider the battle over Catholics being encouraged to join the Unionist Party a necessary one. He was clearly in sympathy with the Liberal Unionism of Brian Maginess and Morris May in the 1950s and distressed by the grassroots hostility towards the former in particular.[45] Nevertheless, he did not give Maginess strong enough public backing, and made too many – arguably unnecessary – appeasement gestures to the Orange Order. Brookeborough could not have been unaware of the campaign led by the *Belfast Telegraph* editor Jack Sayers to modernise Unionism,[46] but chose to carp about that paper's occasional praise for the NILP rather than engage with its 'constructive Unionist' prospectus for the future. After the 1958 election the paper had called on the Unionist Party to develop a proper political philosophy and appeal to a moderate centre of both Protestants and Catholics, and to risk courageously the loss of the 'true blue incorruptibles'.[47] Sayers, like Maginess, was convinced that Catholics could be persuaded to get more involved in public affairs.

The matter erupted into open controversy in November 1959 when Maginess and Sir Clarence Graham, Chairman of the Standing Committee of the UUC, made speeches widely interpreted as an encouragement to Catholics to join the party. Brookeborough wrote in his diary of the 'rage' among his cabinet colleagues and commented: 'The point is, there is no indication from either the Nationalists or the Church that they agree with us in the general policy of maintenance of constitution'.[48] Graham was given a rough time at a meeting of the UUC executive before Sir George Clark, Grand Master of the Orange Order and party 'patriarch', pronounced firmly against Catholic membership.[49] Sir David Campbell, leader of the Unionist MPs at Westminster, wrote to Brookeborough to say that while he and his colleagues 'generally agreed' with Graham they felt the timing was 'most inopportune'. Campbell went on to repudiate Clark's speech. Brookeborough replied that timing and occasion were important and that public discussion should be avoided. 'There are variations', he wrote, 'of the interpretation of "tolerance" as between Belfast and the country areas.'[50] A week later Brookeborough spoke on the matter to a Young Unionist dinner and remarked insouciantly that the discussion was 'academic' and that (party) unity was the only thing that mattered.[51]

For Sayers it was clear that the ruling Unionist Party clique at their Glengall Street headquarters in Belfast, headed by UUC Secretary William Douglas, had acted to 'extinguish' Maginess. The perception was of a Glengall Street 'Tammany Hall' machine working closely with leading Orange Order figures such as Harry Burdge, who was rumoured to have written Clark's speech.[52] Brookeborough's ability to exercise control over this clique was called into question. Certainly, he appears at the very least not to have relished any such confrontation or the consequences for Unionist Party organisation of upsetting the experienced and electorally battle-hardened Douglas and his team.[53] Even the liberal-minded Unionist MP Connolly Gage, a friend, correspondent and co-campaigner of Sayers in this period, paid warm tribute to Burdge's political skills on the latter's death in March 1963.[54] Throughout Brookeborough's premiership the political dilemmas produced by the respective claims of party and government marked a significant evolution of a motif which had been fastened to the movement since the creation of Northern Ireland, and which, by virtue of the party's unbroken grip on power, was unparalleled in the rest of the British Isles. It would prove also to be the central preoccupation of Brookeborough's successor.

Carrying out fundamental change to the party's organisation as a means to the end of preparing it to meet challenges such as an appeal to the Catholic minority, a new relationship with the South, and indeed a new outlook for Northern Ireland more widely in respect of Britain and the European Economic Community (EEC), was simply not attractive to the ageing and unwell Brookeborough by the late 1950s and early 1960s.[55] It was a task for a younger, more energetic and purposeful figure. Brookeborough did not lack tolerance or indeed a certain liberalism in outlook, but he never allowed such qualities their true political expression. He employed his personal charm and his array of political and diplomatic arts in the continuing quest to maintain Unionist Party unity and keep extremist elements in check and in house. Within the narrow confines of his own criteria for success Brookeborough's achievements over twenty years were substantial: the Unionist Party maintained essential unity, the anti-partitionist project was thwarted, and a potentially difficult post-war relationship with Britain under Labour was managed to the long-term benefit of Northern Ireland's full participation in the welfare state and new educational opportunities, if not always, as noted, its broad economic interests.

Indeed, any assessment of Brookeborough has to take account of his failure to respond positively – or force the British government to respond – to the economic woes of his latter years. Brookeborough then presided over the most serious breakdown in the confidence of the Protestant community, especially the urban working class, in the Unionist Party, something which would have far-reaching effects. Brookeborough's awareness of the importance of this relationship is reflected in the way he concentrated his efforts – in vain – on the question of support for the traditional industries. What one historian has referred to scathingly as the 'pampering of the Protestant working class',[56] Brookeborough recognised as an affirmation of Northern Ireland's economic life-blood and the symbolic cultural and psychological importance of industries like shipbuilding to the community's self-image. The playwright and Unionist critic Sam Thompson contemporaneously claimed that the pattern of all Belfast life was to be found in the shipyards, and similar popular cultural sentiments were to be found in Glasgow, Newcastle, Barrow and Birkenhead.

The place of Catholics in the 'community' of this Belfast context was at the very least ambiguous. Brookeborough simply took refuge in the argument that attitudes to the minority would only change when the minority changed its attitude to the state. This was a recipe for stagnation in community relations and the permanent postponement of reforms which may have been more within the capacity of a Unionist leader to carry through and remain in office than at any time previously. However, the trials of Maginess in the 1950s provide a cautionary qualification to this, and it bears repeating that the Unionist Party was in reality a highly diverse movement in which local power bases, particularly in border areas heavily populated by Nationalists, made it politically treacherous not to extend solidarity, far less attempt to override their wishes. Brookeborough's facing down of the opposition to increases in financial provision for Catholic schools, the setting up of the Housing Trust, and his occasional rebuff to Orange pressure over marches deserve more acknowledgement, in the light of this volatile context of Unionist politics, than has been generally granted. Through it all Brookeborough, a patrician figure, retained a genuine popular touch;[57] he was perhaps the last Unionist leader to command respect, loyalty and affection across the social and political spectrum of the movement.

Brookeborough's languid style could be deceptive; so too, frequently, was the publicity-conscious zest of Captain Terence O'Neill who succeeded him. His premiership was to promise much and to collapse in chaos amidst Unionist Party divisions of unprecedented political impact. In hindsight O'Neill has tended to be viewed either as a reforming figure too far in advance of his party or as an inept strategist whose failure to reform in time plunged Northern Ireland into conflagration.[58]

O'Neill was appointed by the Governor of Northern Ireland following consultations with Brookeborough. It is not known for certain if O'Neill was his predecessor's choice, although as Minister of Finance, O'Neill was by convention next in line. More to the point he was not elected by the Unionist Party – the last Prime Minister of whom this was the case – and it has been observed that he had no strong personal base of support.[59] Of his rivals, Brian Faulkner was particularly willing and able, and many, including Faulkner himself, were to nurse a sense of injustice over the favouring of the Eton-educated O'Neill with his service record in the Irish Guards during the war. This was something of a reprise of the contrasts played out between Andrews and Brooke: the business and largely Presbyterian versus the landed and military Anglican 'establishment' sides of Unionism.[60] After twenty years of aristocratic leadership there was perhaps a widespread feeling in the party ranks that the new leader should emerge from the alternative social and cultural wing of the movement. What is not in doubt is that O'Neill's position was insecure from the outset, and that niggling resentments took root before he got down to work.

O'Neill seems to have been conscious that his image as a toff was no longer an advantage by the early 1960s.[61] He thus strove to be viewed as a technocrat and made it his mission to modernise Ulster. His style was presidential, favouring the advice of civil servants such as Ken Bloomfield[62] and Jim Malley over that of his cabinet colleagues, and he arrived determined to instil a new professional service ethic into the often informal and irregular world of Stormont. He attempted to catch the spirit of the times which, politically, was expressed most colourfully by President Kennedy in the USA. O'Neill delighted in the media soubriquet of himself as 'Ulster's JFK',[63] and indeed spent much energy in the early part of his premiership in an obsessive and ultimately fruitless pursuit of the diplomatic coup of a Kennedy visit to the Giant's Causeway.[64] In retrospect this highly involved and at times farcical quest assumes significance as being emblematic of O'Neill's 'gesture politics', many more examples of which were rapidly to follow in the considerably more risky form of visits to Catholic schools and words of condolence over the death of the Pope. The problem was that it was unclear both to the Catholic minority and to Ulster Unionism what such gestures signified. O'Neill plunged into the politics of public relations with little thought about the actual Ulster public.

O'Neill set a new upbeat tone which dispelled the gloom of Brookeborough's last days, dogged with disappointment as they were. He raised expectations of economic improvement and rising prosperity through challenging rhetoric and a promise to tap the potential of devolved government as never before. 'This is Government with a Forward Look', ran the title of a UUC pamphlet produced in January 1964 which reproduced the purple passages of the Prime Minister's early speeches:

> We intend to write upon this Province with the hand of progress. We intend to participate fully in a social and economic revolution as far-reaching and overall more benevolent than the industrial revolution. We can and will make Ulster a place where every man's head is held high.[65]

O'Neill pledged that the Unionist Party was going to give a lead on planning, the vogue concept of the time and anathema, it was later claimed by O'Neill, to Brookeborough.[66] Indeed, implicit criticism of his predecessors was characteristic of O'Neill's prospectus: 'The day for a defensive attitude is over ... we are succeeding – for the first time since 1930 – in spreading some understanding of what

Northern Ireland stands for'.[67] 'For the last twenty years Northern Ireland has been administered', O'Neill wrote to Jack Sayers on becoming Premier, 'I expect it will kick and scream before it will agree to be governed.'[68]

O'Neill thus launched an Economic Plan for Northern Ireland six months into his premiership, to be conducted by Professor Tom Wilson, an academic economist.[69] In addition, he took up the proposals of Sir Robert Matthew's Belfast Regional Survey and Plan and embarked on the promotion of economic growth centres in different parts of the Province which would include the establishment of a new city in County Armagh.[70] Diminution of the railway network was to be offset by the construction of motorways, and commitments were made to new housing and employment targets. A report, under the guidance of Sir John Lockwood, was commissioned on the situation of a new university. By 1965 the Ulster Unionist Party was presenting itself as the champion of a youthful ethos – 'the party of the young at heart'. Ulster was becoming 'an opportunity State', and in the Unionist Party any 'old-fashioned approach to Administration of our affairs' was as 'outdated as the horse tram'.[71] For one historian of the O'Neill years all this was in essence a change from Brookeborough's concentration on acquiring support for traditional industries to a new programme of 'self-help' designed to realise the Province's potential for growth.[72] However, O'Neill's approach was no less about winning subsidies from the British government. As Mulholland has pointed out, O'Neill's achievement was 'to shift Treasury expenditure on to a higher level within the framework of a revivified home rule'.[73]

O'Neill simply grasped the changing emphasis and priorities of the day, attuned as he was to the mandarin thinking in both Whitehall and Stormont, and re-fashioned Northern Ireland government policy according to the new gospel of planning, regional development and modernisation. In so doing, as Bew, Gibbon and Patterson have stressed,[74] he repositioned his party to appropriate much of the ideological armoury of the NILP, which then found its room for making a distinctive political appeal on social and economic questions further constricted. The O'Neill government's recognition in 1964 of the Northern Ireland Committee of the Irish Congress of Trade Unions (ICTU), notwithstanding the friction this gave rise to in the party and the cabinet,[75] was another sign of the government attempting to deal with its 'Labour problem' and cast off old shibboleths which were perceived as an impediment to progress.

O'Neill appeared to be more in step with the times and told Westminster and Whitehall what they wanted to hear. In February 1964, despite earlier misgivings, the Chief Secretary to the Treasury wrote to the Home Secretary to say that the Treasury would agree a programme of £32 million, on top of Northern Ireland's existing subvention, to fund a roads programme over the next five years.[76] Late in 1964 O'Neill set up a new 'super' Ministry of Development,[77] to which he switched his Minister of Home Affairs, William Craig, whose enthusiasm for a new direction in devolved government matched that of the Prime Minister. Craig, in his mid-thirties, took on this challenge with relish and soon began to threaten the powers of local authorities.[78] He also began to rival Faulkner at the Ministry of Commerce as the main influence in the government. The Minister of Finance, the less than youthful Ivan Neill, felt sufficiently overshadowed and ignored to resign from the government in the spring of 1965.[79]

Amidst the fanfare over a rejuvenated Ulster, however, the Province's communal and ethnic divisions remained fundamentally unaltered. O'Neill's approach trusted to economic prosperity to act over time as a solvent; there seemed to be an implicit assumption that rising living standards and better conditions would of themselves take the pain out of Northern Ireland politics. O'Neill's vision was about a shared pride in Ulster: indeed, no Unionist government had taken so positive a line in the strengthening of regional identity and in being prepared to diverge from Britain in a legislative sense more often, notwithstanding the continuance of a financial relationship which could fairly be described as dependent.[80] Nevertheless, a shared Ulster identity was a remote hope while the minority laboured under the weight of structural disadvantage, and the Unionist Party remained preoccupied by a culture of sectarian head-counting. A year into O'Neill's premiership this was vividly illustrated at a parliamentary party discussion of the proposed new city. On this occasion O'Neill himself made his pitch by saying that Unionist majorities in Armagh had fallen by 5,000 over the past ten to twelve years and that something had to be done. However, some of his colleagues feared that the new city would mean houses 'occupied by people other than Unionists', and that from 'a Protestant and Unionist view' it was felt that the situation could not be 'kept in hand'.[81] Although the scheme for the new city went ahead, the insensitive decision to name it 'Craigavon' assured the further alienation of the minority.[82] This was followed by another part of the modernising flagship, the new university, taking the character of a Unionist snub to Catholics on account of the Lockwood Committee's recommendation that it be sited in Protestant Coleraine rather than predominantly Catholic Derry City.[83] O'Neill, moreover, chose not to complement his attempts to acknowledge the minority by inviting Catholic representatives in proportion to their community's numbers on to statutory boards or any of the committees which had been set up with the purpose of shaping the new Ulster with which he wished everyone to identify.[84] Clearly, modernising the Unionist Party[85] and beyond that the political culture of Northern Ireland was a prerequisite for the success of O'Neill's vision, but there is little evidence that he began to face up to this in the early part of his premiership. Ominously, there also occurred serious sectarian rioting in Belfast during the British general election of October 1964 which brought Harold Wilson's Labour government to power in London with a slim majority.

Unionists, including O'Neill, still generally considered the Conservatives their natural allies, and a similar wave of anxiety to that caused by Labour's ascent to power in 1945 swept the movement. O'Neill once styled himself a 'Progressive Conservative' in the Canadian sense[86] – indeed he had espoused federal-sounding ideas[87] – yet there was a side to him which enjoyed cosying up to the Tory grandees and drawing upon his similarly privileged background. In April 1964 he wrote in very familiar terms to the then Tory Prime Minister Sir Alec Douglas-Home proffering advice on when the latter should call the election.[88]

There was little chumminess with Wilson, who had made promises to the recently formed Campaign for Social Justice (CSJ) in Northern Ireland that he would deal with 'infringements of justice' in the Province.[89] At their first meeting in November 1964 O'Neill, in all probability steering a diplomatic course, said he would be happy if the new government gave special responsibility for Northern Ireland affairs to a junior minister at the Home Office. However, Wilson, probably to O'Neill's relief, replied that he was not proposing such a special appointment.[90] The significance of this was that O'Neill was spared a mechanism entailing closer scrutiny by the central government, and what his own government and party would have considered interference.[91] Wilson's promise to deal with injustices came to nothing, and a pattern was quickly established at Westminster where the government sheltered behind the 'convention' that Northern Ireland business could not be discussed.[92] This, moreover, was in the face of sustained pressure by Labour back-benchers such as Paul Rose, who was Chairman of the party's Campaign for Democracy in Ulster (CDU) lobby.[93] This body functioned in a similar way to Geoffrey Bing's 'Friends of Ireland' in the late 1940s, concentrating on issues like discrimination rather than partition itself. The Wilson government took the option of leaving matters to O'Neill to resolve in his own way; a chance was therefore lost to regulate inter-governmental relations to the end of bringing Northern Ireland into line with current democratic standards in Britain and removing anomalies which bedevilled the Province's economic position within the UK. The Ulster Unionists, at this stage, were not geared to force a constitutional confrontation over the issue whatever their views on it. The most recent historian of the Wilson government and Northern Ireland has indicted Labour for not intervening at various junctures during its tenure of office, particularly in the period immediately following its re-election with a comfortable majority in March 1966.[94]

This election was prompted by the wafer-thin Labour majority for 1964 – 3 seats falling to 2 – and this factor guided Wilson towards another aspect of the Britain–Northern Ireland relationship, namely the voting rights of the Ulster MPs at Westminster. These MPs, all Unionists in the 1964–66 parliament, invariably voted with the Tories and on occasion their votes threatened the government with defeat, notably on the issue of steel nationalisation in 1965. Wilson took advice on whether he could address 'the apparent constitutional anomaly' whereby these Ulster MPs could vote on matters pertaining to other parts of the UK, while Northern Ireland business was not discussed or voted on at Westminster.[95] This constitutional question had been around since the time of Gladstone's first Home Rule Bill, and was to resurface during debates on Scottish and Welsh devolution in the 1970s.[96] Wilson also raised the issue with O'Neill, who explained that voting rights offset the fact that there were fewer MPs from Northern Ireland than population numbers warranted.[97] Wilson suggested that O'Neill might advise the Unionist members not to vote on certain controversial subjects.[98] Rose observes that the MPs did not 'keep their heads down' but that Wilson had other priorities than confronting them;[99] additionally, the Ulster Unionist voters made little difference after the 1966 election. The leader of the Westminster Unionist MPs, Captain L. P. S. (Willy) Orr, made much of Wilson's threat to alter the constitutional convention,[100] but his and his colleagues' outrage contrasted with attitudes at Stormont, where it was felt that Orr and company were drawing unwelcome attention to the party.[101] The leadership of Orr and the similarly blimpish Samuel Knox-Cunningham served Ulster Unionism ill; their anti-Labour spleen took little account of the broader questions for their party. The shrewdness and tact of Sir David Campbell and the Liberal Unionist advocacy of Montgomery-Hyde and Douglas Savory – characteristics of Westminster Ulster Unionism in the 1950s – were sorely missed.

If Wilson was not prepared to get involved in Northern Ireland affairs to the extent of clashing with the Unionist government, he nonetheless steered O'Neill into taking a warmer approach to relations with Dublin. O'Neill may not have required much persuasion: he was aware of the trend towards greater British–Irish cooperation over matters like trade, and his close advisers such as Bloomfield had for some time been on friendly terms with their Dublin counterparts.[102] Lemass, moreover, held a modernising perspective analogous to O'Neill's, although it has been well said that he had prepared his party, Fianna Fail, for the political changes this entailed, in contrast to O'Neill and the Unionist Party.[103] Aside from this, Lemass's pragmatic willingness to leave the resolution of partition to the long-term mercy of economics – notwithstanding the assumption that it would thus be ended – was compatible with O'Neill's priorities. After nearly two years of overtures and diplomatic hiccups, and motivated partly by a desire not to concede the initiative to the energetic and ambitious Faulkner,[104] O'Neill invited Lemass to Belfast in January 1965.

This historic visit was hailed by the press in both North and South as a great breakthrough, and applauded by Wilson in London. With the exception of a few disgruntled back-benchers led by Boal who complained of lack of notice, the reception in the Unionist parliamentary party was positive.[105] Even Brookeborough and Sir George Clark, still Grand Master of the Orange Order, gave it their blessing. Certain cabinet ministers were unhappy about not being informed sufficiently,[106] but this was a well-established trait of O'Neill's by this time. In the immediate aftermath of this meeting and a reciprocal one in Dublin a month later, there were two notable consequences: first, further trading concessions granted to the North at the behest of Faulkner and in defiance of the 'cold war' outlook of the Ulster Unionists at Westminster and a minority at

Stormont;[107] and second, the assumption by the Nationalists at Stormont, prompted by Dublin, of the role of official opposition. As London and Dublin drew closer, O'Neill made sure that Northern Ireland was swimming with the prevailing diplomatic current.

In 1965 the Secretary of the NILP, Sam Napier, received a report on the activities of a group called Ulster Protestant Action (UPA).[108] This organisation was strong in Protestant working-class areas of east and west Belfast, particularly Shankill/Woodvale, and its membership consisted of 'the very extreme type of Protestant'. Some older members were alleged to have been active in sectarian riots in the 1920s and 1930s. Certain Belfast city councillors, including Unionist Party representatives, were said to be connected with it, a sitting member at Stormont was its 'virtual nominee', and an MP at Westminster received its full backing. The organisation's central officers were labourers, it put forward people for election as shop stewards, and, in a struggle with Catholic Action, campaigned against the Northern Ireland government 'pandering' to the Roman Catholic Church. The UPA's leader was said to be the Reverend Ian Paisley.[109]

Paisley, the son of a Baptist preacher and leader by this time of his own 'Free Presbyterian' Church, had dabbled in politics since the late 1940s when his mentor was the extremist Independent Unionist John W. Nixon, MP for twenty years for Woodvale and leading light of the UPL in the 1930s.[110] Paisley's mission, like that of Nixon, was to promote an ultra-Protestant Loyalist political agenda by campaigning against perceived treachery on the part of the governing Unionist Party. At times this could also mean supporting members of factions of the Unionist Party whose credentials in relation to 'Protestant interests' were felt to be trustworthy and whose position *vis-à-vis* the weak-kneed leadership might be strengthened. Paisley, in a new age of media technology, took this kind of 'Independent Unionism' to new limits. He imbibed the populist rumbustiousness of a tradition which stretched back from Norman Porter, Nixon, Tommy Henderson and William Wilton to Tom Sloan.[111] He realised the potency of a cocktail which comprised fidelity to 'Protestant and Loyalist' principles and an appeal to working men and women on 'bread and butter' issues. In 1964 Paisley capitalised upon a Unionist alderman's comment about the flying of the Union Jack being a 'narrow issue' to describe the Unionist Party policy at Belfast City Hall as 'Down with the Flag ...

Up with the Rates, Rents and Bus Fares'.[112] The cocktail was further shaken by a depiction of Ulster as the cockpit of the life and death struggle between 'Bible Protestantism' and 'Romanism'. For Paisley the religious ecumenism of the age, arising out of the Second Vatican Council (1962–65), was a Popish con trick, and Terence O'Neill's brand of Unionism was in this respect the political equivalent of the perceived treachery of those Protestant churches who were being 'ensnared' into ecumenical activity.

Paisleyite infiltration of the Unionist Party occurred in various places, feeding off grassroots disaffection with the direction O'Neill seemed to be taking.[113] If the parliamentary party did not baulk at the Lemass visit, the local associations certainly did. Paisley appealed in particular to rural small farmers and labourers, and to urban workers who had either experienced unemployment or faced the threat of it. What the Unionist Party could no longer use the UULA to do – supply a political role to Loyalist working men – Paisley managed with increasing success in a context of economic uncertainty and political flux. It turned out to be Paisley, rather than the NILP, who would benefit most from the Unionist Party's Labour problems. The NILP report on the UPA predicted as much.[114] The urban Protestant working class's confidence in the Unionist Party – never solid at the best of times – was at its lowest ebb from the late 1950s through into the 1960s. Votes went in different directions: to the NILP, to Unionist dissenters like Boal, and eventually to Paisley's own political organisation. The instability of this vote was a major aspect of the crumbling of the Unionist Party monolith and the constitutional crisis to come.

In 1964 the Court Ward Unionist Party (Woodvale) ran candidates all with experience of unemployment for the local elections on a classic Paisleyite platform: they pledged to maintain 'our Protestant Sunday' as well as to re-house people and provide better facilities. They also slammed the 'sentimental promise' of the NILP, and reserved the right to criticise and 'if principle demands it' oppose the Unionist Party.[115] One of these candidates, the dock worker Johnny McQuade, duly won back the seat of Woodvale from the NILP in the 1965 Northern Ireland election and became a dogged opponent of O'Neill within the party. In the 1964 British general election in which he played a prominent role in the disturbances, Paisley was credited by Unionist Party candidate Jim Kilfedder as having won him the seat of West Belfast. Kilfedder at Westminster and Boal at Stormont seem to have been the MPs referred to in the

NILP report on the UPA.

The 1965 election was a setback to the NILP, which was severely weakened by infighting and campaign problems, some of which arose from the desire on the part of two of its MPs to try to combat the Paisley challenge by appearing equally staunch sabbatarians.[116] However, the party enjoyed a swing back in the British general election of 1966, and it should not be forgotten that it polled 103,000 votes in the previous British election in 1964. There was a significant Labourist culture in the Protestant working class; the difficulty for the NILP was that it often coexisted with sectarianism and with an unshakeable suspiciousness about the intentions of the Nationalist minority, and was thus vulnerable to Paisleyite populism.[117] Attempts by the NILP to raise the issue of discrimination and to acquire more Catholic support were jumped on by the likes of McQuade, and the NILP's Paddy Devlin had his IRA internee history dragged out.[118]

In 1966 Paisley was transformed from an irritant in the wings to a centre-stage scene-stealer, largely through the rise in inter-communal tensions surrounding the Republican commemorations of the 50th anniversary of the Easter Rising. As O'Neill was to reflect later, this event helped to focus opposition to him and to dash his hopes for community harmony.[119] Paisley then became a martyr to his followers by being jailed for his part in an unruly protest at the General Assembly of the Presbyterian Church in June. In the same month, a murder gang in the Shankill Road, laying claim to the name of the UVF, gunned down two Catholics, provoking O'Neill into proscribing the organisation.

Paisley's influence, later indicted by members of the UVF, was all the more dangerous for his colourful and compelling 'theatre'. His was a form of evangelical vaudeville – intolerance laced intoxicatingly with humour and knockabout vilification of enemies. Paisley's pre-modern message found an ironic ally in the modern media, which he and his followers, including those in the Orange Order, alleged was Catholic-dominated. He was supremely 'telegenic', and television coverage, in spreading his notoriety, turned him into a phenomenon. His withering lampooning of O'Neill met with no effective response, whatever the opportunities for a satirical counterattack might have been.

For many members of the Unionist parliamentary party and UUC there was no doubt that the atmosphere created by Paisleyism had contributed to the tragedies in the Shankill and to the dangerous conditions now obtaining. Sir George Clark said that the time had come to ascertain who were their friends and who were their enemies;[120] while John Dobson MP advised that Sir George and others in similar positions 'should examine the background of "Paisleyism" and try to put this across when speeches were delivered'. Dobson added that the time had come when the front bench as well as the back bench should try to point out that the policies of Paisleyism would destroy the constitution rather than protect it.[121]

Yet further Paisleyite demonstrations and rioting prompted not a closing of ranks but a serious challenge to O'Neill's leadership.[122] Boal, a Paisley ally whom O'Neill had sacked in June as Junior Counsel for the Attorney-General, referred at a meeting of the parliamentary party[123] to 'the lack of understanding by the Prime Minister'; he accused O'Neill of acting in a 'provocative and infantile manner'. Boal added that he had no confidence in O'Neill on account of the Lemass talks, which he saw as evidence of the Prime Minister's lack of wisdom in the field of 'liaison'. McQuade objected to the word 'extremism' and said that he did not like what had happened at the commemoration of the Easter Rising and 'felt that West Belfast had been sold'. Brookeborough hardly helped by suggesting that O'Neill be put, in effect, on probation to heal the rift in the party, while Senator Barnhill thought that the Prime Minister had 'moved too far and too fast', going on to articulate the concerns of Unionists west of the Bann about neglect and unwelcome changes. Basil Kelly MP blamed back-benchers for much of the trouble, while Lord Robert Grosvenor commented that they had come close to 'committing suicide' and putting themselves in a position where Westminster would take over. He supported the Prime Minister. John Taylor said that the party had created Paisleyism and argued that there was not sufficient liaison and that there was 'a lack of confidence'. Sir George Clark, calling for unity, also observed that many people felt alarmed by the Lemass meeting and that there should 'not be any more rapid changes', but rather 'a period of consolidation'. Clark's comments about the Lemass meeting were typical of the way many were looking back at it in 1966 in a very different vein.

The parliamentary party was thus a melting pot of grumbles, denunciations, indignant rebukes, and exasperated pleas for unity. It was in fact a very ill-organised *putsch*, with O'Neill's most credible rival for the premiership, Faulkner, absent (perhaps purposefully) in the USA. O'Neill, at the same parliamentary party meeting, got the vote of confidence he needed.[124] As Mulholland contends, there was no declared candidate to challenge O'Neill and the rebels lacked a central aim.[125] Some malcontents such as Warnock, by now advancing a more liberal line, simply felt that O'Neill had to make way for someone who could deal effectively with Paisleyism.[126] The Paisley agitation had shaken a party already troubled over what precisely O'Neill's grand visions would mean in reality. It was also a party some of whose local interests looked askance at the changes which the greater degree of central planning would entail and the threat to their own powers,[127] or were resentful of measures taken such as the cutting back of the railway services or the neglect of their areas in the setting up of new businesses, the new city and the new university.[128]

Paisley had also found the Orange Order in a similarly troubled and uncertain condition, and had successfully influenced sections of it.[129] In a way he was pushing at an open door since the Order's relationship with the Unionist Party had deteriorated during the 1950s, and many rank-and-file members were easily seduced by comforting messages and slogans. Protests at 12 July demonstrations in 1965 and 1966 gave great momentum to the anti-O'Neill cause. Sir George Clark's decision to stand down as Grand Master in 1967 appeared to be a victory for Paisleyism in the Order and anti-ecumenism certainly ran deep, although the power struggle between left and right was not clearly resolved.[130] The Order's link to the Unionist Party continued in the form of its 122 delegates (out of a total of 718) to the Ulster Unionist Council, and its 12 seats on the UUC Executive Committee.[131] However, more than ever it smacked of political amateurism.

The opposition to O'Neill, unfocused as it was, seriously weakened his capacity to respond to the promptings of Wilson in London to introduce reforms in the area of the local government electoral system and the allocation of housing. In Britain the media spotlight was now turned on such abuses, to the embarrassment of Unionists. Wilson himself later claimed, and Unionists like Craig believed, that financial subsidies to Northern Ireland were under threat of being withheld.[132] O'Neill pointed to the appeal of Paisleyism to the poorer sections of the community and the danger of a 'backlash' of ultra-Protestant feeling.[133] He warned that intervention by London would 'invite a revival of the spirit and policies of 1912'.[134] At the end of 1966 O'Neill announced modest reforms, far less than Wilson demanded, so constrained did he now feel by pressures at home. The new temper of political controversy also prevented any further development of cooperation with Dublin, where Jack Lynch had replaced Sean Lemass as Taoiseach. On the occasion of his retirement from politics in 1965 the arch-moderniser Lemass has been quoted as saying: 'The Irish people should never forget that it was more humane to be murdered in the Gas Chambers than to be dragged to death by a Black and Tan tender'.[135] The spirit of the Anti-Partition League was not dead, and the bitterness in Irish Nationalism, as in Ulster Unionism, would not easily be dissolved.

In January 1967 the Northern Ireland Civil Rights Association (NICRA) was formed to take agitation over issues such as the local government franchise, gerrymandering, and discrimination in housing and employment to a higher level.[136] Along with other developments around the same time, this signalled a radicalisation in Catholic politics and terminal discontent with the approach of the old Nationalist Party led by Eddie McAteer.[137] Despite its status of official opposition from 1965, the latter was treated dismissively by O'Neill and the Unionist Party: historians differ as to whether O'Neill might have been able to do a deal on reforms through a more cooperative approach towards the Nationalists, and indeed towards the NILP.[138]

O'Neill preferred instead to invest his energies and hopes in projects such as 'civic weeks' in which all sections of the community were urged to participate.[139] However, it was soon plain that making another type of cosmetic gesture to the minority rather than fashioning for them a proper political role was not going to be enough. Catholics, without ceasing to be Nationalists, began increasingly to demand the full rights of British citizenship to embarrass the Unionists; through the civil rights movement they came to exploit the differences between Stormont and Westminster.[140] The issues had a long history, and the civil rights arguments about Ulster falling short of British democratic benchmarks had for some years been used by the NILP. Indeed, if it had been purely a 'British rights for British citizens' affair and had had the rights of disenfranchised Protestants as well as Catholics been highlighted,[141] the NILP would appear to have been the natural channel for protest. Perhaps if the NILP had succeeded in its attempts in the early and mid-1960s to get proper backing from the British Labour Party and to become affiliated to it, then the advances which the NILP had made by the early 1960s would not have so rapidly eroded.[142] Certainly, the

NILP was the only credible cross-community, non-sectarian political force with a firm commitment to reform.[143]

But the new politics of protest were also, inescapably, about the profound sense of 'resentful belonging' on the part of the Catholic minority.[144] As Jennifer Todd has observed, civil rights also involved the rights of the Catholic community to the expression of their Irish Nationalist identity; righteous indignation was as much fuelled by the denigration of that identity by Unionists over the years as by specific issues such as the 'one man, one vote' demand for local government elections.[145] Protests over the various issues tended to be expressed in the language of, and the musical tribute to, Irish Nationalist and Republican struggle. This, and NICRA's failure to campaign about cases of discrimination on the part of Nationalist-controlled councils, contributed to a hardening of Protestant community antagonism to the movement.[146] While NICRA broke with Nationalist political tradition in formally restricting itself to demanding legal and constitutional rights within the UK,[147] testimonies of activists made clear that many Nationalists and Republicans got involved precisely because they believed the campaign would end partition.[148] As one scholar has put it: 'The intellectual linkage between nationalism and civil rights was the belief that Northern Ireland was an artificial entity which required systematic discrimination to survive'.[149] There was thus a belief that if reforms were forced on the Unionists the state would be unable to survive, and this, ironically, was how extremist Protestants also read the situation. So, either the endurance of militant anti-partitionism made inevitable an extremist Loyalist backlash, or extremist Loyalism in putting a brake on O'Neill put paid to the new mood of pragmatism within the minority community which might have been accommodated by speedy reforms and a redress of grievances regarding discrimination.[150]

The extent of the discrimination suffered by the minority has been debated, and clear exaggerations have been identified, but the findings of an impressively nuanced scholarly inquiry are critical enough of a Unionist Party all too indulgent of its 'border tendency's' obsession with keeping growing Catholic populations out of power.[151] The parliamentary party evidence already cited in addition to cabinet documents and the testimonies of outsiders provide a clear picture of a ruling party determined to hang on to power in defiance of contemporary democratic norms.[152] A repentant Edmund Warnock even came clean in 1968 about Craigavon's gerrymandering of Derry City in 1936 as a way of strengthening the constitutional position.[153]

But, as Mulholland comments, 'Discrimination was less winner takes all than a means to preserve a perceived balance'.[154] Contrary to the influential school of thought which depicts them as motivated by an ideology of supremacism,[155] Unionists acted in a defensive manner. Among less-well-off Protestants there was a strong perception of not being given what they believed to be their due or their reward for loyalty. This was a perennial difficulty for the Unionist Party leadership and, as has been illustrated, fed various forms of Independent Unionism and protest politics. A sense of 'Protestant superiority' was a myth for the bulk of Protestants.[156] However, there still was a collective ethnic commitment to the survival of 'Protestant Ulster' in the face of daunting Irish Nationalist odds and recurrent IRA offensives such as the 1956–62 campaign.[157] The 1920 Act, buttressed indeed by that of 1949, was still regarded as a guarantee, as a permanent settlement within which the Unionists had the right to preserve their position of power, even by dubious means. A 'covenant' had been made with Britain to this end.[158] A perception of Irish Nationalism as prepared to use any means necessary to pursue *its* goals always served as an excuse for this Unionist perspective.

It was a mentality never properly understood by O'Neill, far less by the British political classes. Paul Rose and the other CDU Labour MPs acclaimed the return of Gerry Fitt, the Republican Labour candidate, for the seat of West Belfast in the 1966 election and were subsequently so dazzled by Fitt's garrulous polemics that they could not see his Catholic tribalism.[159] Indeed, Rose and his colleagues seemed not to know what they were meddling with; they possessed no insight into the overlap between questions of reform and rival Unionist and Nationalist perspectives on the 'national question' in Ireland. There was no appreciation of Unionist ideas of preserving 'balance' in the interests of the constitutional position, as opposed to sectarian hegemony, or of what Nationalists really meant when they demanded political reform and change.

As an inward-looking movement geared to preserving structures and arrangements which it considered crucial for survival, Ulster Unionism was ill-equipped to deal with outside scrutiny of Northern Ireland affairs, media attention and British government pressure. It was not versed in the same political language. Catholic Nationalism, on the other hand, proved adept at political bilingualism: ethnic tribalism where appropriate at home and impeccably reasoned and evidentially based advocacy of human rights for the outside world.[160] Catholic society also gave the impression of being on the move to the achievement of a better tomorrow while Protestant Ulster reeled from the attacks on its state or 'statelet', bewildered, angry and utterly divided within itself about how to respond.

O'Neill attempted to move his party and government towards meaningful reform, and he showed himself prepared to tackle formidable opponents like Harry West, whom he sacked over a case of improper ministerial conduct in April 1967. However, this was at the cost of upsetting West's Fermanagh Unionist fiefdom and was symptomatic of O'Neill's problems in dealing with his party's deeply rooted clientelism especially in rural areas.[161] The West sacking caused ripples of discontent throughout the party, and Faulkner came out in criticism from the comparative safety of his high-achieving Ministry of Commerce base – Faulkner knew he was in effect indispensable. Moreover, the administration's other ministerial 'star', William Craig, became increasingly erratic, and caused O'Neill embarrassment over his advocacy of greater autonomy for Northern Ireland and the breaking of the parity arrangements in social services.[162] After the leadership crisis of 1966 O'Neill had moved Craig back to the Ministry of Home Affairs so that he would have someone firm to deal with Paisleyite trouble. Craig felt this was a demotion, became a fractious colleague, and was to demonstrate his firmness with disastrous consequences against the civil rights demonstrations as their agitation built during 1967–68.

The eruption of Catholic anger in Londonderry, following clashes between civil rights protesters and the police on the afternoon of 5 October 1968, provoked a Pavlovian defensiveness among most Unionists.[163] It was symptomatic of the crisis, although entirely consistent with the nature of his five-year tenure, that O'Neill, as leader and Prime Minister, could not orchestrate the response he favoured. The record shows him to have grasped the implications of the 'wholly adverse' media coverage of the RUC's batoning of unarmed civilians, and the certainty of the Wilson government's insistence on reform. O'Neill and his Minister of Finance, Kirk, justifiably raised the spectre of possible financial penalties being imposed on the Province from the centre, and O'Neill slammed 'idle talk' of a unilateral declaration of independence. The target of this sideswipe was of course Craig, who seemed intoxicated by battle and utterly unapologetic about the police.[164] Before the showdown with Wilson in Downing Street, O'Neill issued further warnings, but the two colleagues who were to accompany him, Faulkner and Craig, both considered it unlikely that Wilson 'would proceed to any extreme course which would be wholly unacceptable to majority opinion in Northern Ireland'. Craig declared himself opposed to change in the local government franchise ahead of the proposed review of the system, saying that it could have 'disastrous political consequences'. O'Neill, in reference to deputations of party members from Fermanagh, Tyrone and Londonderry who awaited him to press for guarantees of no such franchise change, appeared gloomily to concur. Faulkner suggested that Wilson be told that they had 'no dogmatic views' regarding the franchise; he himself did not share the reservations felt by others in the party. Wrangles ensued over whether to set a time limit for local government reform, while the Chief Whip (Bradford) and Kirk said they should have something concrete to offer to Wilson. Craig demurred at this, arguing that it was tantamount to allowing Wilson to tell them how to act. He repeated his view that Wilson would not do anything to provoke 'a constitutional crisis' or 'a massive uprising of the Loyalist community', and Faulkner readily agreed: devolutionary government could not be conducted under 'duress'.[165]

It was against such a background that O'Neill led his two ministers into Downing Street on 4 November to be harangued by Wilson and Home Secretary James Callaghan. O'Neill later acknowledged the error in going without clear proposals of their own or a properly agreed view;[166] it was an embarrassing display of weakness at a crucial juncture. O'Neill stressed the recent increase in capital grants (to 80 per cent) for Catholic schools and the progress of the bill to abolish the business vote at local government and Stormont elections and the university seats; Faulkner highlighted the new jobs which were going to the minority, particularly in the expanding service sector;[167] and Craig claimed that local government reorganisation was being energetically pursued. Nevertheless, Wilson and Callaghan were of the view that reforms should include without delay 'one man, one vote' at local elections.[168] Moreover, it was made clear that any overthrow of O'Neill by extremists would not be tolerated, and Wilson issued stern warnings of punitive action if reforms were not instituted. Craig thought he was bluffing but a recent study of the Wilson government has revealed the seriousness of British government plans for a possible intervention.[169]

There followed a series of acutely fractious cabinet meetings in Belfast, conducted against a backdrop of turmoil in the Unionist Party and increasing tensions in the wider community. O'Neill advertised his dilemma by impressing upon his ministers the need to convince back-benchers of the seriousness of the situation. They had to be told that 'the maintenance of the overall constitutional position depended upon control at Stormont and not upon the control of certain local authorities in ways which were often difficult to justify'. Bradford weighed in on O'Neill's side with the injunction that the Unionist Party 'existed to defend the Union, not to defy the British government'.[170] Yet Craig and Faulkner continued to play on resentments over 'dictation' by the Wilson government, a theme which resonated damagingly in party ranks outside the cabinet room. On 20 November Craig declared in cabinet, contrary to the interpretation offered by Attorney-General Basil Kelly, that the powers reserved to the British government in the 1920 Act would be 'quite unconstitutional' to exercise.[171] Later he pointed to the Attlee 'guarantee' of 1948 (embodied in the Ireland Act of 1949) that there would be no change in Northern Ireland's constitutional status without Northern Ireland's 'free agreement', to support his case.[172]

Over the course of these critical weeks the significance of 'one man, one vote' as the civil rights movement's headline demand and the theme of British government 'dictation' and threatened intervention became interlocked in the calculations of the Unionist government. Among a majority in cabinet, it became an issue of principle that the government avoid complete capitulation to London's instructions, and that to this end it should refuse to proceed with the franchise issue until the local government reorganisation had been accomplished. Bradford warned that if 'one man, one vote' was not included in the proposed package of reform the agitation would continue, and he counselled that Catholic votes had to be secured if the constitutional position was to be maintained in the long run. This undoubtedly reflected O'Neill's own outlook. However, James Chichester-Clark (Minister of Agriculture) and Ivan Neill (Minister of Development) argued that the timing was not right for the franchise change, and they urged a demonstration 'to the party' of independent action.[173] O'Neill was painfully aware of the party factor, and thus proceeded to settle on a policy of reviewing the franchise issue when the local government reorganisation was complete.[174] 'One man, one vote' was missing from the package of five measures unveiled by O'Neill on 22 November: a points system for the allocation of public authority housing; the appointment of an ombudsman; the abolition of the company vote; a Development Commission to replace the Londonderry Corporation; the eventual withdrawal of some of the Special Powers.

O'Neill wrote to Wilson saying that universal suffrage at local election was 'not possible in political terms' at that time, and that the real issues were, in any case, 'predominantly social'.[175] The reforms, coupled with a statesmanlike broadcast to the Northern Ireland public on 9 December (the 'Ulster at the Crossroads' address), bought O'Neill some breathing space.[176] Helped by a campaign in the *Belfast Telegraph*, O'Neill appeared, briefly, to have raised a hitherto dormant 'middle Ulster' strand of opinion to bolster the cause of a reformist Unionism. He also appealed to the civil rights movement to take the heat out of the situation, and it responded by suspending demonstrations. Above all, however, O'Neill was concerned to clear his own leadership path: his address on 9 December contained thinly disguised condemnation of the position taken by Craig, who was increasingly cutting an Ian Smith figure both in relation to suggestions of a unilateral declaration of independence and in loathing of Harold Wilson.[177] Two days later, following a defiant reply from his minister, O'Neill duly sacked Craig, prompting criticism from Faulkner and further rancour within the parliamentary party. At the party grassroots the jettisoning of Craig raised concerns about the signals being sent out over the particularly vital issue of law and order. It might be said to have exposed the party and the government to the Paisleyite charge of lacking the resolve to deal with 'Ulster's enemies', notwithstanding the continuance of trouble instigated by Paisley's followers in their quest to counter civil rights and Nationalist demonstrations.

It was, indeed, the attack by Loyalist counter-demonstrators on a march organised by the Marxist student group People's Democracy – in breach of 'the truce' – at Burntollet, County Londonderry, on 4 January 1969, which plunged the Province back into the political maelstrom. Catholic outrage met a rather dismissive response by O'Neill, whose next move was to set up a Commission of Inquiry into the disturbances of the previous October, to be headed by the Scottish judge Lord Cameron. This was too much for Faulkner, whose resignation shredded the credibility of the government at a stroke.[178] To sack one high-flier might have shown the requisite guts; to lose another smacked of political carelessness. The further resignations of William Morgan (Minister of Health) and Joe Burns (Assistant Whip) hardly registered on the same scale of political earthquake, but did nothing to help the Prime Minister.

And it is certainly arguable that on the issue of the Cameron Commission Faulkner judged more shrewdly. O'Neill's reasoning was that an inquiry would 'demobilise' the moderate support of the civil rights movement, and that its findings 'could hardly fail to bring out in an objective way the real difficulties of the situation and the real aims of some of those involved'.[179] O'Neill was certain that the inquiry would recommend 'one man, one vote' but that this would make it easier for the government to sell the reform to the party. It is clear that the franchise reform was accepted by virtually everyone in the government as inevitable; the issue was rather one of bringing the Unionist Party along in the light of the loss of control in certain local areas which was implied. O'Neill felt that the government's task in selling his five-point package to the party was proving hard enough without the symbolic issue of the franchise, which he was nonetheless well aware would have to be addressed before long if the British government and the civil rights movement were to be appeased. Later, in March 1969, the moderate Robert Porter, just installed by O'Neill as Minister of Home Affairs, stated in cabinet that the change in the franchise was 'inevitable', but that the government 'should retain some degree of initiative as to how and when it was introduced'.[180]

Faulkner, at the original cabinet meeting in January, took the position that an inquiry would be 'abdication of the government of responsibilities which were properly its own', and would have an adverse effect on police morale.[181] He worried about the 'potentially embarrassing inquest' which would result, and preferred to tackle the 'one man, one vote' question instead, leaving the party in no doubt that if it did not give its backing then the government would resign. However, only Morgan supported his stance in cabinet.

With hindsight Faulkner was proved correct in his prophecy about the inquiry's findings. The report when published in September 1969 was severely critical of the Unionist government and party and gave much ammunition to their critics.[182] Its damning indictment of Unionism completely overshadowed the critical reflections on certain aspects of the civil rights movement, and O'Neill's prognosis of January 1969 was proved far too sanguine. Moreover, setting up the inquiry was always unlikely to appease those demanding immediate reform: it was, as Faulkner judged, a defining moment which demanded the courage to confront the party in the interests of long-term stability. O'Neill and the bulk of his ministers believed the franchise had to be reformed yet they prioritised what they knew could only be a very temporary face-saving gesture. There is no evidence that the Unionist Party as a whole appreciated it, or felt more confidence in the government on account of it. Faulkner had been something of a slippery operator, and had no previous 'form' in respect of support for 'one man, one vote'.[183] Yet his advice, if taken in January, might have enabled the government to proceed on a morally more secure basis and would have sent an emphatic message after Burntollet to the Loyalist wreckers.[184]

On 3 February 1969 O'Neill dramatically dissolved parliament and called a general election for the 24th of that month. He was reacting to the escalation of voluble dissent from within the Unionist Party – twelve back-benchers signed a petition calling for his removal as leader[185] – which had followed the ministerial resignations. It was an impulsive move, notwithstanding the strength of the factors which might have justified it; and it seems not to have weighed as heavily on O'Neill as on his predecessor (who had reason to know[186]) that the implications of fighting an election with a fractured party were profound. O'Neill revealed himself as incongruously cavalier at the vital moment, and he placed on the line his party's future as well as his own with apparent insouciance. Debilitating as the divisions in the party had been for some time, O'Neill might have made an attempt at least to address the stated concerns of his critics, if only to signal that he still prioritised the unity and health of Ulster Unionism. However late in the day, he should have considered his much-arraigned style of leadership; for some time his detractors had concentrated their fire on his aloofness and his often dismissive approach to those outside of his charmed circle.[187] During the election campaign, indeed, the anti-O'Neill Unionists did not come out against O'Neill's package of reforms of the previous November.

The election witnessed the bizarre spectacle of pro-O'Neill Unionist candidates being chosen by most local associations, anti-O'Neill Unionists by some others, and pro-O'Neill unofficial Unionists being backed discreetly by the official party machine in Glengall Street and not at all discreetly by the Prime Minister against anti-O'Neill Unionists. The outcome was just as complex.[188]

Of the 36 Unionist Party seats won, 24 were pro-O'Neill and 12 anti-O'Neill. There were 3 pro-O'Neill Independents returned. O'Neill himself narrowly held on to his seat of Bannside in County Antrim in the face of a strong challenge from Paisley, whose 'Protestant Unionist' organisation (fielding 6 candidates) won over 25,000 votes in total. On the Nationalist side of the communal divide, figures brought to prominence by the civil rights movement such as John Hume and Ivan Cooper defeated the old Nationalist Party runners.

O'Neill had appealed to the electorate for an emphatic show of support. His plea was certainly answered by an unprecedented turnout on the part of the well-off, traditionally apathetic ranks of the professional and gentry classes. The election saw the highest participation rate since 1921, and the highest Unionist Party vote, notwithstanding the distinguishing pro- and anti-O'Neill labels, in the history of the Northern Ireland state. Moreover, it is important to note that the pro-O'Neill Unionist vote was over twice that of the anti-O'Neill, and that there was much vocal support in particular from the Women's Unionist Association.[189]

Yet the party was dealt a major dilemma by having to fight in a split condition. Ulster Unionism's capacity to contain the dangers of internal dissension, within electorally acceptable limits, had been broken. Supporting non-official candidates against official ones made a mockery of the values of party loyalty and solidarity to which core activists subscribed. The extent of the offence caused was reflected in a series of party votes following the election: a vote of support for O'Neill in the parliamentary party of 23 out of 35; a vote for O'Neill passed by 183 to 116 at the Standing Committee of the UUC; and a similar vote at the UUC when the margin in O'Neill's favour was only 338 to 263.[190] The emergence during the election campaign of the New Ulster Movement (NUM) as a 'solidly middle class' pro-O'Neill ginger group only created a further sense of fragmentation.[191] The NUM was to step up the crusade for liberal Unionism before breaking with the Unionist Party and forming the nucleus of a new party – Alliance – in 1970. The return of the anti-O'Neill Unionists, however much several (including Craig in Larne) had suffered slashed majorities, of itself cancelled out the plusses for O'Neill; this guaranteed the persistence of splits and more criticism of his leadership. The strength of anti-O'Neill feeling in the west and south of the Province, and in urban Protestant working-class areas especially West Belfast, testified to the persistence of a zero-sum mentality which equated the maintenance of local power with the wider survival of the Unionist cause. In these areas the surrounding Catholic and Nationalist presence bred an inflexible tribalism. O'Neill's apparent trust in the impact of the Wilson government's warnings about the consequences of ousting him, and his stress on the threat to financial subsidies, only succeeded in stiffening the thrawn resolve of those in sectarian cockpits who were hostile to him.[192] To all this has to be added the personal near-humiliation of Bannside, and the failure to attract significant support, against his personal expectations, from the Catholic community. The latter indeed chose to vote in great numbers for those who had most strongly indicted the Northern Ireland Unionist regime. The unedifying episode concerning the party nomination for South Down, which resulted in a rebuff for the Catholic party member Louis Boyle, only underscored for many Catholics the futility of voting Unionist whoever was supposed to be in charge.[193] It would not be long before O'Neill would refer to Catholics in tones of crass condescension while advocating fair treatment.[194]

The election, far from clearing the air, increased the mood of foreboding in Northern Ireland society. A series of explosions, disrupting electricity and water supplies, served to deepen the crisis during April. In October 1969 they were revealed to be the work of Loyalists, some alleged to have links to Paisley,[195] and O'Neill was to claim in his memoirs that this indeed had been his own hunch at the time.[196] However, the logic of anti-O'Neill Loyalists resorting to violence to bring down the Prime Minister, and perhaps secure the release of the then incarcerated Paisley, was lost on the police. The main suspects were the 'old enemy', the IRA, and Protestant Ulster once more perceived the fact of siege for which mythically they were ever ready. The victory of People's Democracy activist Bernadette Devlin, standing as a 'unity' candidate in the mid-Ulster by-election of 17 April, put the rebel icing on the cake. 'There can be no justice while there is a Unionist Party', she declared in an incendiary maiden speech at Westminster five days later.[197]

With the Unionist Party and the wider Protestant community in torment, O'Neill reversed his position of January and plumped for universal suffrage at local elections. The cabinet deliberated on it on 22 April, O'Neill and Porter informing the meeting that they would resign if the parliamentary party did not comply with it. The Minister of Agriculture, Chichester-Clark, and the Minister of Development, Captain Long, pronounced themselves doubtful about the timing and feared 'massive resistance from militant Protestants'.[198] The following day, prior to the crucial parliamentary party meeting, Chichester-Clark resigned on these grounds while accepting the measure in principle. A stunned O'Neill proceeded to get the backing of the party, after another ill-tempered meeting, by 28 votes to 22. The main civil rights demand had been conceded, but in circumstances arguably less acceptable to traditionalist Unionist opinion than six or even three months previously. Perhaps reading the Orange runes, Chichester-Clark, a landowner of essentially moderate views, made a populist gesture which was to do him no harm a week later when the Unionist Party decided on a new leader.

For O'Neill finally walked away on 28 April. The prospect of leading a bitterly divided party stretched before him, if, indeed, it were not to be cut off by further resignations. He may have viewed the pushing through of 'one man, one vote' as a guarantee of an honourable place in the history books regardless of whether earlier political miscalculations and failures of nerve had ensured that its eventual passage would be accompanied by his own political extinction. O'Neill had never been truly convincing as the leader to reclaim civic Unionism and restore the balance between it and the ethnic character of the party and movement over which he presided frigidly. The 'narrow ground' of Northern Ireland as a political unit would have made this an acutely difficult project even for a Carsonian figure who commanded affection and trust and brought a clearly justified and argued programme. O'Neill was not that figure, and failed politically to pursue a civic Unionist project with clarity and purpose.

Mulholland highlights the ways in which O'Neill alienated the traditional power blocs of the Unionist alliance in local government, the west of the Province, and different interest groups.[199] Yet there was nothing new in this: Brookeborough too had annoyed Unionists in local authorities over the Housing Trust; the Belfast Corporation had been suspended during the Second World War; the west always felt neglected; and groups like farmers and urban workers made troublesome noises as a matter of course. The difference between O'Neill and his predecessors essentially lay in the nature of the threat to the Unionist Party's grip on power in the 1960s: the civil rights movement ruptured Unionism because it was the first opposition movement to emerge in Northern Ireland which was sufficiently strong and politically astute simultaneously. Conditions in Northern Ireland determined that this opposition would in effect be drawn from the other side of the ethnic divide, but civil rights proved an opponent much more problematic to Unionism than the physical force tactics of the IRA during 1956–62 or the bellicose sterility of straightforward anti-partitionism before that. From within the pro-Union community, moreover, the turmoil created by Paisley was on a markedly greater scale – commensurate with the effectiveness of the civil rights protest – than anything hitherto contrived by disaffected Independent and maverick Unionists.

Major James Chichester-Clark was elected O'Neill's successor at a Unionist parliamentary party meeting on 1 May. He was the first leader in the party's history to be elected in such a fashion. The margin of victory over his opponent, Brian Faulkner, was 'one man, one vote': 17 to 16. Faulkner later suggested that Chichester-Clark had hatched a plot with O'Neill, in which his resignation of 23 April had been a crucial manoeuvre to deprive Faulkner of the succession.[200] It is more likely, as Chichester-Clark's biographer has suggested, that the resignation had been a ploy on the part of the Major to position himself for the consequences of an increasingly probable departure from office of O'Neill.[201] O'Neill appears to have favoured Jack Andrews as his successor, and only turned to his kinsman when that old trouper declined.[202] Had Andrews assented there would have been something of an ironic reversal of his father's fortunes in 1943. The increasingly beleaguered position of O'Neill in 1969 bears resemblances to that of the wartime Premier, and Chichester-Clark's resignation could be said to have killed off O'Neill much as Brookeborough's finished Andrews.

As in 1943 there were mutterings about a gentry and Anglican Unionist 'establishment' suppressing the business-minded and largely Presbyterian wing of the party.[203] Faulkner did arouse opposition in the more privileged bastions of Unionism, but this was probably more on account of appearing too politically smart by half. His dynamism was flatly distrusted. However, Chichester-Clark's margin of victory does not suggest a party jumping to squirearchical commands. The young solicitor and O'Neillite Basil McIvor, for example, was probably typical of several in voting against Faulkner on the basis of the latter's history of friction with O'Neill and ambiguous position in relation to reform, rather than any class or caste factor; McIvor was much closer to Faulkner in social background than to Chichester-Clark.[204] Faulkner's appeal to the party meeting featured economic progress, housing, jobs, respect for the rule of law, party unity and, perhaps significantly in this context, ministerial posts on merit. Yet he brazenly took the position on the local government franchise which he had castigated O'Neill for adopting in January, namely that the timing was not right although it was inevitable. Chichester-Clark by contrast performed the reverse volte-face and proclaimed that under him there would be no going back on 'one man, one vote'.[205] O'Neill himself voted for Chichester-Clark on the grounds, he was later to claim, that Faulkner had been stabbing him in the back for a lot longer.[206] It should also be remembered that if Chichester-Clark came to the contest with a relatively low public profile, Faulkner was considered by some in the Unionist Party not to be particularly well known at grassroots level.[207] Overall, Faulkner may have paid the price for appearing to a nervous party to be the more risky choice in a fraught situation. Speculation that he would have provided the kind of leadership necessary to deal with the crisis and to reunify the party is not very soundly based. At the juncture in question Faulkner appeared no more solid a prospect than the ponderous yet evidently wily figure of Chichester-Clark.

Chichester-Clark also displayed tact and good political sense in immediately including Faulkner in his cabinet with the vital brief of Minister of Development, charged with steering through local government and housing reforms. Two of Faulkner's backers in the contest, and long-standing opponents of O'Neill, John Taylor and John Brooke, were promoted to junior ministerial posts. Then the Prime Minister declared a political amnesty ensuring that no criminal proceedings should continue or be initiated in relation to political protests since 5 October 1968.[208] As well as civil rights leaders, Paisley benefited from this and was released from jail. Chichester-Clark met with him in an attempt to defuse his agitation,[209] leading to speculation about Paisley being brought within the Unionist fold. This was always unlikely, and it was put beyond any doubt by the rise in communal conflict as the summer wore on. Outbreaks of trouble in July and early August necessitated the use of CS gas, and anxieties over the Apprentice Boys of Derry march on 12 August in that city were expressed at cabinet on 4 August.[210] The following day Porter, Minister of Home Affairs, informed his colleagues of his intention to use the 'Specials' to guard threatened Catholic homes in Protestant areas to show that the USC existed to help preserve law and order in the interests of all.[211]

The harsh reality was that the government's good intentions, or at least those of its genuine moderates like Porter, had been over-taken by the acrid atmosphere which had been developing for months. The long history of antagonism on the part of the Catholic community towards the security forces, and the 'B' Specials particularly, could not be dissolved by gestures. The foreboding about the Apprentice Boys march proved well-founded: riots followed it and the police entered into a protracted battle with the residents of the Catholic Bogside area. Subsequent days saw Belfast engulfed in sectarian strife with Catholics bearing the brunt in lost lives and homes. Again, allegations were levelled at the RUC and hastily mobilised Special Constabulary of collusion with Protestant mobs.

At Stormont Chichester-Clark's government, which had hardly enjoyed a political honeymoon, made noises about pressing on with reforms and set up a welfare committee to try to deal with home-lessness and other issues.[212] However, the security situation was obviously out of control: on 14 August Wilson and Callaghan acceded to the request of the Stormont government, and the pleas of Catholic political voices such as Gerry Fitt and Bernadette Devlin, to send in the army. Chichester-Clark's cabinet was well aware of the significance of this step: that it would call into question the extent to which the government in Belfast controlled the security issue, and the position of the RUC and the Specials.[213] Nevertheless, it was agreed that Downing Street should be told that any question of dis-banding the Specials was 'quite unrealistic'.[214] The government was also inclined towards a defiant stand by the intervention of Irish Taoiseach Jack Lynch and his broadcast of 13 August, in which a threat to invade the North seemed to be implied, along with a re-statement of the Nationalist orthodoxy that partition was the root of the current problem.[215] Indeed, in the weeks and months that followed, members of the Irish government were party to an organ-ised effort to aid the minority in the North which allegedly involved procuring and running guns.[216]

On 19 August Chichester-Clark met Wilson and Callaghan, the result of which was the 'Downing Street Declaration'. The Specials were to be withdrawn from riot duty, and control of security mat-ters was transferred to the General Officer Commanding of the army.[217] In cabinet discussion the following day Roy Bradford, Minister of Commerce, accurately perceived this as 'a fundamental shift of power to Westminster'.[218] That was not all: a committee under the chairmanship of Lord Hunt was set up to inquire into policing in the Province, a development which cast further doubt on the future of the Specials. The Chichester-Clark dispensation, barely on its feet, was thus lumbered with the image of being a 'puppet' regime; it also became widely perceived by the majority community as losing the battle to preserve a symbol of Ulster's capacity to maintain its British connection against the mobilisation of Irish Nationalism in its contemporary preference for multiple disguises, North and South.[219] Such perceptions only deepened in the coming weeks as barricades were erected in Catholic districts barring entry to the security forces, and the Northern Ireland government was reduced to a spectating role as the army, and on occasion Callaghan himself, negotiated with leaders of Catholic and Nationalist opinion like Fitt.[220]

The Hunt Report, coming shortly after the publication of the Cameron Report which criticised the long years of Unionist rule, brought about the disbandment of the USC and its replacement by a new force, the Ulster Defence Regiment, to be incorporated into the army.[221] Riots ensued on the Shankill Road, resulting in the deaths of a police constable and two civilians. The significance of the Specials lay in their symbolism: they were seen by the Protestant masses as a people's militia, the only trustworthy force to combat the IRA. They were also, more arguably, part of a pact between the Unionist government and the Protestant people, a source of employment for some and thus essential to the 'pork barrel' politics of Unionism in Northern Ireland from the inception of the state. Their passing weakened still further the capacity of the Unionist Party to convince the Protestant workers that it could look after their interests. In a desperate attempt to save some face, the Stormont cabinet pressured Callaghan, who tentatively consented, to give assurances that the new force would not be disbanded without the consent of the Northern Ireland government.[222]

The Unionist government was certainly placed in an invidious position, and any appreciation on the part of London ministers for Chichester-Clark's difficulties with the Protestant community was purely rhetorical. It was in many ways the worst of all worlds to continue the operation of devolved government in circumstances in which the centre had taken effective control and was dictating the terms of the management of the crisis.[223] However, the Wilson government, notwithstanding the drawing up of plans for such an eventuality in the winter of 1968–69,[224] baulked at imposing Direct Rule simultaneously with troop involvement. Callaghan, it has been argued, thought it important to leave Stormont in place to implement reform; and he felt that it was politically impossible, in relation to the readiness of public opinion for such a step, to suspend Stormont at this juncture.[225] Much speculation has been offered since about the possible avoidance of the subsequent troubles which could have resulted from a decisive and total assumption of responsibility by London.[226] It is certainly the case that the next three years, the final ones of this particular devolution experience, established a culture of political violence, spanning the community divide, which was decisive in shaping the Province's future for a generation.

The events of 1969 brought the Unionist Party to a state of chaos. Beyond the conflicting viewpoints among members about how to respond to the political crisis, there was the related problem, for some time evident, of a cumbersome and ambiguous party structure and mode of operation. There was still no Unionist Party constitution, only that of the UUC to which the constituency associations and other bodies were affiliated. In its December 1969 issue, *The Unionist* newspaper commented succinctly: 'As a political party the Ulster Unionist Council and its various member organisations and extensions are a very loosely constituted body with little provision for discipline'.[227]

This state of affairs gave rise to conflict over questions such as who had a right to call him or herself a Unionist, and whether members should be able to join other political movements. The continuing activities of Paisley's 'Protestant Unionists' and of the New Ulster Movement highlighted the latter issue in particular.[228] There was, as *The Unionist* pointed out, no clear indication of how far any formulation of policy by the cabinet, by the Standing Committee of the UUC or by any other authority, was to be binding upon the Council as a whole or upon the members of the various bodies represented upon it.

Within the party it became widely felt that modernisation was long overdue, a matter which dominated the party conference of April 1970. At this gathering, Chichester-Clark made his pitch around the theme of loyalty and discipline, and promised to set up a committee to review the rules, membership and structure of the party. 'I sometimes think', he pronounced plaintively, 'we do not have a single Unionist Party at all, but a multiplicity of separate Unionist parties throughout the country.'[229] He was simply the latest in a line of Unionist leaders to have to grapple with such an unwieldy political vehicle; however, in Chichester-Clark's case above all the others, the party's sense of being ill-equipped organisa-tionally to adapt to rapid changes was especially debilitating in view of the extraordinary gravity of the crisis from the summer of 1969.

A strong reminder of how difficult it would prove to reform the party in the way the Prime Minister desired was provided at the April conference by Harry West, one of five MPs recently sacked from the parliamentary party for continual criticism of the govern-ment. West deplored what he regarded as more centralisation and less of a voice for 'the people'.[230] West, indeed, was to be instrumen-tal in forming the West Ulster Unionist Council later in 1970 to add to Chichester-Clark's travails. He spoke for those in the party who prided themselves on an independent approach, but for whom criti-cism of the government essentially reflected fear of the volume of change which had taken place in the space of a year. This lobby was directly addressed by Robert Porter when he attempted to answer the charge against the government of 'steamrollering' policies through the party. Porter pointed out that since May 1969 there had been fifteen meetings of the parliamentary party, five meetings of the Standing Committee, a special meeting of the UUC itself, two meetings of county representatives and several meetings of the Back-benchers' 66 Committee, at which he and his colleagues had explained government policies.[231]

Meanwhile, with reference to the situation at Westminster, Cap-tain Orr lamented that such 'tragic divisions' as were only too ap-parent within the Unionist Party as well as the 'Unionist people' were preventing the Unionist MPs from making the most of the Labour government's difficulties in Britain.[232] This was special pleading on the part of Orr, whose own band of MPs at Westmin-ster was not itself a shining example of unity, and whose defence of Unionism had been subjected to effective ridicule first by Fitt and then by Devlin.[233] Nothing done by the Westminster Unionist MPs as much as tempered the poor representation of the Unionist case in the British media; nor were the frequent inaccuracies regarding the civil rights issues successfully highlighted and countered.[234] The Unionists at home and abroad were painfully aware of how badly they were losing the propaganda war. As Gailey has observed, it was the Catholic demands which were much more in tune with metropolitan British opinion by the late 1960s,[235] while the ten-dency on the part of the British media to represent the opposing sides by means of attention to the personalities of Paisley and

Devlin distorted the complexities of the situation and posited an antediluvian Bible-basher against a revolutionary firebrand. Within this picture the Unionist Party was not only misrepresented, but all but invisible.

Chichester-Clark, for example, received little credit for the appointment of a Minister for Community Relations in October 1969. Nor did his emphatic message that Catholics were welcome in the Unionist Party, delivered in November 1969, substantially alter outside perceptions of the party he led as exclusivist and bigoted.[236] In large part this was understandable given the party's continuing link with the Orange Order. The new Minister of Community Relations, Robert Simpson, resigned from the Order on taking up his post,[237] and Chichester-Clark declared that membership of the Order should be regarded as a 'private affair'.[238] In early 1970 Roy Bradford, Minister of Commerce, questioned the Orange link publicly and urged the Order to think about its future relationship to the party and the question of its representation on the UUC.[239] Bradford also alluded to the issue of other affiliated organisations, the implication being that there was a long overdue need for review of arrangements which, for example, privileged the moribund UULA and, for reasons lost in the mists of time, the Willowfield Unionist Club. However, the case of the Orange Order was the most salient: the Order, as a high-profile institution, provided a convenient channel through which much Protestant 'angst' of the time could be discharged. Inevitably, much of this came across as critical of the government and helped to reinforce the impression of a Unionist Party devouring itself in its hour of greatest peril.

The party was not, therefore, well placed to face the challenge of Paisley and his ally William Beattie at by-elections in Bannside and South Antrim respectively in April 1970. These contests have been viewed as 'probably the most vital in the history of the Stormont House of Commons'.[240] They arose from the retirement of O'Neill and, in relation to South Antrim, of Richard Ferguson, a liberal Unionist and supporter of the former Premier. They were a test of the government's ability to turn the Paisleyite tide and reassert the position of the Unionist Party. They were seen as crucial to the prospects of a Unionist government pursuing a reformist course and stabilising Northern Ireland as both a society and a political entity.

Against this background of high stakes, it should be recognised that the Unionist Party, and particularly its Bannside candidate Bolton Minford, a local doctor, fought a campaign distinguished by a resolutely non-sectarian and inclusivist message. It was, indeed, perhaps the most convincing expression of the civic and pluralist strand to Unionist ideology in the history of Northern Ireland. At Bannside, the Unionist Party chose to define the terms of the struggle with Paisley as between 'Greater Britishness' and 'Little Ulsterism', the former being depicted as progressive and accommodating, the latter reactionary, narrow and sectarian. However disingenuous this may have seemed to those with reason to recall much in the party's history which resembled the latter, it was a courageous demonstration of the party's will to meet Paisley head-on and clear the way for its progress along an unequivocally liberal Unionist route.

The campaign featured some of the most significant, if forgotten, speeches ever made by leading Unionists. Senator Jack Andrews referred to Carson, Craigavon and his father having 'no hatred for any man because of his religion' and said there should be 'a fair place for everyone who was prepared to be loyal'. Andrews paid tribute to his father's dedication to the 'step by step' policy which had brought British standards in social services to everyone in Northern Ireland. 'This has been the course and policy of Official Unionism', he stated, going on to ask what 'Protestant Unionism' was to be taken to mean: 'Does it mean that you should put a sign over the door of the Unionist Party reading "Protestants only"? For if it does do not be in any doubt that Carson and Craigavon would never have approved of it.' Andrews went on to comment on Paisley's use of ridicule, particularly in relation to Sir Arthur Young, who was parachuted into Northern Ireland from England by Callaghan to head the RUC late in 1969: 'He is of course an Englishman but we would not have got very far if we had acted on the basis of "only Ulstermen can help Ulster". That would have ruled out Lord Carson, the Dubliner, F. E. Smith, and Bonar Law.' The choice, declared Andrews, was between 'full partnership with Britain in the UK' or 'going off on a solitary course', reflecting that some of official Unionism's opponents appeared to want 'Home Rule', 'to turn our backs on Great Britain and the rest of the world and follow a sectarian interest to its disastrous conclusion'.[241]

Brian Faulkner then took up Andrews's theme, referring to an 'element in our midst' (by which he meant on this occasion members of both communities) which was 'frankly anti-British'. Many who were eager to demand 'the privileges of British citizenship' were also 'keen to create trouble'. He thus equated Paisleyite rhetoric about 'the Protestants of Ulster' with Nationalist tub-thumping about 'the Irish people'.[242] Bolton Minford himself observed that Paisley never mentioned the word 'British' in his election address and asked: 'Is he not proud of his British nationality? Has he forgotten that the British link is the foundation of our Constitution? Is he ashamed of that or does he think that Britain is ashamed of him?' Paisley, Minford asserted, 'has divided families, churches, Orange lodges and bands but he must not be allowed to divide this country in the eyes of Great Britain and the rest of the world'.[243]

Clearly, the Unionist Party was trying to convince the electorate that the bad press the Unionist case was receiving in Britain was due to the image created by Paisley, and that it was obviously in the voters' interests to prevent him doing more damage. The Unionists were risking all on an appeal to British loyalty and to the British connection as the defining feature of Unionism, at a time when many ordinary Ulster men and women felt betrayed by the media portrayal in Britain of the crisis, and by the London government. They were also airbrushing out of their own history the conspicuous defiance against the British governments of the day displayed by Ulster Unionism in the battles over Home Rule when, it has been noted,[244] a powerful sense of Ulster 'independence' was forged. This was later exploited by the Unionist Party in power in the Northern Ireland polity which succeeded those struggles. Paisley, indeed, can be viewed as reviving and laying claim to this part of Unionist and Loyalist history. In the circumstances of 1969–70, what is significant is that the Unionist/Loyalist solidarity of the Home Rule dramas – the ethnic bonds fastened by the civic-minded Carson – was a broken reed, and that the Unionists at this juncture were prepared to cede a part of themselves to Paisley which they felt they could not politically sustain. To fight off Paisley, the party – to the great disquiet of many within it – gambled on identification with a secular 'mainstream' Britishness: it swapped the party tunes for the symphonies of state. It abandoned, temporarily but crucially, the balancing act it had always sought to perform, and appeared to drop outright, rather than merely relegate, the grim and determined persona of the 'Ulsterman'. Such a refurbishment exercise on Unionism seems wittingly to have been attempted by Minford when he stated that he did not identify with 'a Protestant Parliament for a Protestant people' – the well-remembered declaration of Craigavon elided from the story told by Jack Andrews – but rather with 'a progressive parliament for a prosperous people'.[245]

While electoral calculations and strategising might have led Unionists to appear less than honest about the party's own role in bringing about the troubles, there were honourable interventions made by party spokesmen which merit the attention of historians. Minford, for example, challenged Paisley to condemn violence: 'Let him condemn the man who turns out his neighbour or burns his neighbour's house, be he Protestant or Catholic, Atheist or Jew. If he does this, this Election, whatever its result, will achieve something.'[246] Chichester-Clark, referring to the disruptive tactics of Paisley's supporters, made the telling point: 'it's really no good criticising the Irish Republic for a censorship of books and films, if we hand our own Province over to those who have consistently shown little regard for the right of free speech'. He went on to add that there could be no place at all for the words or the tactics or the policies of 'sectarian bigotry'.[247] The Bannside Unionist campaign, taken along with many other speeches and interventions by Unionists like Simpson, Porter, Ferguson, McIvor, Chichester-Clark and Faulkner, bear witness to the distance travelled by some in the party – and at this time its leadership – towards a genuine attempt to rebuild community relations. It should also be noted that in May 1970 the party newspaper carried a remarkable article in which it was frankly admitted that members of the Catholic community 'have suffered far more cases of innocent people having their homes destroyed, intimidation of the defenceless, attacks on schools and places of worship and general anxiety. These are the people who have most needed special consideration.' This, the article went on, remained true in spite of the fact that there had been 'subversive elements' seeking to exploit this situation.[248] As previously noted, there was also a disposition on the part of the leadership of Unionism in late 1969 and early 1970 to distinguish itself from the Orange Order in the eyes of outsiders, although this did not extend, on 12 July 1970, to ministers refraining from the public spectacle of marching with their lodges.[249]

The Unionist strategy at Bannside and South Antrim came to grief. Both Paisley and Beattie were returned, albeit that there was undoubtedly substance to the Unionist claims that some Nationalists and Republicans would have voted 'Protestant Unionist' to deal another blow to the government. There was also the vital factor of an NILP candidate in Bannside who polled significantly, and both an Independent and an NILP candidate in South Antrim.[250] In the election post-mortem there were Unionists who identified the party's major failure as the inability to convince those who voted Independent and NILP that the Unionist Party was the best vehicle to achieve a programme of tolerance, peace, social justice, welfare and prosperity; they pointed to the fact that the major swing took place not in favour of Protestant Unionists but Independents and the NILP.[251]

Nevertheless, it was a hugely symbolic triumph for Paisley and the brand of Unionism or Loyalism which he promoted. He articulated with more conviction in the circumstances the defensive mentality which had long been a pillar of Unionism; a holler of 'No Surrender' comforted a substantial number of habitual Unionist Party voters whose confidence in their own government had been shattered. The Unionists were left to rue the fragmentation of a once united party, and, in the case of Faulkner among others, to argue that a preoccupation with the law and order issue had weakened the impact of the government's programme among its own supporters.[252] Appeals to voters to behave in ways calculated to win sympathy across the water had not worked well enough: as in the 1969 election a stubborn and prickly Ulster sense of resentment over perceived mistreatment or lack of understanding in Britain damaged the party leadership.

The Unionist Party was the chief victim of the collective sense of humiliation and consequent resentment borne by 'Protestant Ulster' from 1969.[253] Attempts to engender a more positive outlook around a non-sectarian celebration of being British were overwhelmed by this sense of offended honour. The tendency to view the situation as a 'zero-sum' struggle against the Catholic minority was too strongly rooted after generations of Unionist political propaganda to this very effect. The notion that everyone could emerge winners out of the crisis of 1969–70 did not convince, a foreshadowing of future difficulties for similar liberal Unionist projects.

A memorandum submitted by the Presbyterian Church (still the largest single Protestant denomination) to Callaghan on 29 August 1969 had pointed out that 'while greatly valuing the British connection, emotionally as well as economically, culturally and politically', their people 'vigorously wish to maintain their own identity'. The memorandum went on to state that while extremism was deplored by a majority, we are deeply disturbed by evidence of a serious hardening of attitude among our solid membership of farmers, trades and businessmen. In general our people are rather slow to speak or move but hard to stop once they are determined; we dread the prospect of a Protestant explosion or dour resistance on a scale not yet encountered. Their loss of morale could only bring disaster on the whole community.[254]

This was a warning of 1912 vintage, emanating from the Presbyterian tradition which had so coloured the original campaign of resistance. Presbyterians, as in the past, took it upon themselves to speak for the entire Protestant community.[255] The warning was to prove prophetic enough, and it was to rebound to the detriment of the Unionist Party's relationship with the wider Protestant community.

The initiative after Bannside swung significantly towards Paisley, who capped his triumph by seizing the Westminster seat of North Antrim at the general election of June 1970.[256] Overall, the Unionists were reduced to 8 of the 12 seats at this election, the loss of Fermanagh and South Tyrone to the (Nationalist) Unity candidate compounding the misery of the return of Fitt and Devlin. The tired excuse of 'apathy' could not disguise the demoralisation in the Unionist Party over these setbacks, coming so soon after the shattering blows of Bannside and South Antrim.[257] The party dissidents, concentrated in groups such as the Young Unionist Council, turned up the heat on the leadership.[258] The only consolation for the Unionist government, it was widely believed at the time, came in the return of the Conservatives to government in London.

When the Tories took power Chichester-Clark moved to dispel the assumption held by many that Unionist policies would change, that the Northern Ireland government had simply been doing Wilson's bidding. The new security arrangements would be maintained, declared the Ulster Premier, adding that the centralised system of house-building (which issued in the creation of the Housing Executive) would go ahead, and that local government reorganisation (involving the implementation of the new franchise, the redrawing of electoral boundaries and the centralisation of certain services) would be carried through.[259] Refuting rumours that Paisley would be brought into the cabinet and would soon run the Unionist Party, Chichester-Clark again stressed that 'loyal Roman Catholics' were as welcome as 'loyal Protestants' in the party.[260] For the credibility of the Prime Minister and his administration it was imperative that the impression of having been simply the tool of the Wilson government with no reforming impetus of its own be challenged. How sensitive Chichester-Clark remained on this point was illustrated by a letter he wrote to the new Home Secretary, Reginald Maudling, on 12 July, in which he sniped at the Labour government for encouraging the view that the latter had to compel its Ulster counterpart to take action after August 1969.[261]

Chichester-Clark was buoyed by the initial talks with Maudling, telling the Unionist parliamentary party that there was 'now relationship and trust' in place of 'suspicion', the term he chose to describe relations with the previous government.[262] However, Maudling did not intend to depart significantly from the course pursued by Callaghan: the army's role in coping with the security crisis would continue in the short term to be primary, while the reform programme was expected to do its healing work and the reorganisation of the police would make the RUC acceptable.[263] To many in the Unionist Party, not to mention the wider majority community, this 'softly softly' approach raised hackles. It was felt that reforms had not brought a generous response, that there was confusion over the roles of the army and the police respectively, and the relationship between them, and that the continuing problem of 'no go' areas undermined the Northern Ireland government. At the parliamentary party meeting discontent was vented over the army negotiating with 'citizen defence associations' in Catholic areas and with political figures such as John Hume and Eamonn McCann in Derry. Joe Burns, a long-established hard-line dissident, suggested that the army either go into the Bogside area of that city and 'clear it up', or prevent supplies getting into it. Burns spoke for many others in calling for the resignation of Sir Arthur Young, Inspector General of the RUC.[264]

The day after the parliamentary party meeting the dissidents got some satisfaction. A curfew – lasting thirty-four hours with a two-hour break – was imposed on the Catholic Lower Falls area of Belfast. This was an operation mounted against the emerging threat of the IRA, particularly the breakaway wing styling itself 'the Provisionals' which took its ideological cue from Patrick Pearse.[265] Provisional IRA (PIRA) snipers shot dead five Protestants in Belfast in June, a good example of how a rhetorical struggle against 'imperialist oppression' could be reduced to a grubby sectarian war on the ground. The curfew resulted in gun battles, at the conclusion of which five Catholics lay dead, and this episode is widely thought to have radically transformed relations between the army and the Catholic population, relations which had at first been cordial. It may also have helped the Provisionals' claim to be their community's 'defenders', an image they were to trade off far into the future. However, as O'Doherty has argued, the PIRA's true intentions may have been to provoke the security forces so that a reaction might indeed serve to destroy relations with the Catholic community, and the PIRA's aim was the greater radicalisation of the Catholic people behind republican objectives rather than the simple matter of that community's protection. Certainly, it can be pointed out that the emergence of the PIRA and the escalation of conflict after 1970 resulted in far greater Catholic suffering: 'The fact is that the Provisionals articulated not defence but defiance, and the cost of that defiance was increased casualties among the Catholic working classes'.[266] By the middle of 1970 the PIRA's campaign had changed the terms of the Northern Ireland problem. 'Discrimination', Bob Purdie has written, 'shrank back in importance when compared with the problem of political violence.'[267] It may be added that in the response of the security forces the Catholic minority acquired fresh grievances which nullified the improvement they had seen through the Northern Ireland government's reforms.[268]

The Unionist government justified the curfew with reference to the discovery of arms and ammunition, and ministers were gratified to note that the army, in the light of this, promptly severed connections with the citizens' defence groups.[269] However, there was fury over the clandestine visit paid to the Falls Road following the curfew by the Irish Minister for External Affairs, Dr Patrick Hillery; this action was also deplored by British Premier Edward Heath. Much anxiety surrounded the annual Orange marches to celebrate the Battle of the Boyne, with the Minister of Agriculture, Phelim O'Neill, suggesting the 'diversionary effects' of scheduling 'really good TV programmes'![270] It was later decided not to rearm the police for the occasion of the marches.[271] In the event there was relatively little trouble, the deployment of extra troops perhaps the decisive factor.[272] Prior to the Boyne celebrations, Chichester-Clark had written to Maudling to seek his help in bolstering the image of his government, in particular removing the impression that the army was above the local political establishment: 'To put it bluntly, if we cannot be seen to govern, we cannot in conscience remain in being as a government'.[273]

This was the nub of the issue, and Chichester-Clark was to be progressively disappointed by inter-governmental developments. He felt unfairly pressured towards further reforms when his position was so precarious. Heath and Maudling were certainly anxious that he should not be toppled and replaced by a hardliner;[274] they were fully aware of the hardening of grassroots Unionist opinion.[275] Yet documentary evidence suggests that the Heath government was seriously considering the option of suspending Stormont virtually from the start of its tenure in office.[276] In August, against a resurgence of disorder, Heath received a briefing paper which came down in favour of suspension, whether on a temporary or permanent basis, either with or without the agreement of Stormont. The paper noted that Chichester-Clark's government did not enjoy popular support, that the relationship between Westminster and Stormont had been changed by the use of troops, and that a Tory government could suspend Stormont with less trouble than, by implication, a Labour one.[277]

Security issues plagued the remainder of Chichester-Clark's premiership. They were the basis of the chorus of internal party criticism which never let up;[278] William Craig, moreover, re-emerged to join Harry West as a chief tormentor, and demanded the rearming of the police. West's West Ulster Unionist Council produced a manifesto to which the cabinet felt obliged to respond. In the process of cabinet deliberations, the allegation of Northern Ireland not receiving 'fair shares' *vis-à-vis* the financial relationship with London was raised and repudiated by a Ministry of Finance official, who nonetheless identified unwittingly part of the problem: 'We would prefer not to be put into a position where we had to argue the case for the present attribution system publicly, because to a large extent it has been evolved in confidential discussions between this Ministry and the Treasury'.[279] The great extent to which Belfast–London relations were conducted in such a mysterious bureaucratic fashion did nothing to alleviate the Unionist government's difficulties with its own supporters at this juncture; as in the case of the latter years of Lord Brookeborough, the perception of a Northern Ireland government being putty in the hands of Whitehall contributed significantly to the unrest. Being British was not widely believed to mean simple compliance with the London government of the day. The flaws in this aspect of the operation of devolution, arguably long felt, proved a contributory factor to the destabilising of Northern Ireland from 1969. So too did the continuing ambiguities of the Province's status: the West Ulster Unionist Council stressed what it believed were the inviolable rights accorded to the Northern Ireland parliament by the Ireland Act of 1949, an issue William Craig was to highlight persistently before long. Chichester-Clark tried in vain to impress upon the party as a whole that to seek assistance from London on the scale required by the crisis meant that it was illogical to expect London not to become more involved.[280]

The Prime Minister, on the resignation of his minister Robert Porter in August 1970, took on the Home Affairs brief along with his other duties. This, coupled with the appointment of the combative John Taylor to the junior post of Minister of State in the same department, has been widely viewed as mistaken.[281] Almost immediately Chichester-Clark fell ill. Dealings with opposition politicians – most by now having grouped into the Social Democratic and Labour Party (SDLP)[282] – were not improved by their distrust of Taylor. The Prime Minister failed repeatedly to get the backing of the Conservative government for the additional security measures he sought.[283] Breaking point came in March 1971 when the murder of three Scottish soldiers by the IRA triggered crisis talks and a demand by Chichester-Clark for 3,000 additional troops and, according to Heath, political control over them.[284] What was granted fell significantly short, and he resigned on 20 March. Heath informed his cabinet that Chichester-Clark had been persuaded to tone down his resignation statement so as not to jeopardise the formation of a new administration. Chichester-Clark, ever the gentleman, 'avoided any recrimination against the United Kingdom government'.[285]

The outgoing Premier's monument was a series of courageous declarations of a civic-minded Unionism to his party and to society at large, and a raft of reforms the commendable and forward-looking character of which was in effect neutered by the mayhem in the streets. For many Unionists he would always be identified with the demise of the Special Constabulary, but a respectful political obituary in the Unionist Party newspaper condemned those who had attacked Catholics and their homes in 1969:

> For these stupid barbarities Major Chichester-Clark had to a substantial extent to carry the can in Downing Street. He had also to carry the entangling burden of every event in the Ulster past which could cast doubt and discredit upon the viability of the Northern Ireland Constitution.[286]

This was a fair measure of Chichester-Clark's task, and an appropriately weary commentary on his failure.

Faulkner defeated Craig by 26 votes to 4 at a parliamentary party meeting to decide Chichester-Clark's successor. The new leader subsequently got a vote of confidence satisfactory by recent standards at the Standing Committee of the UUC (199 to 71) and 'overwhelming support' at the UUC AGM.[287] The emphatic nature of Faulkner's victory evidently reassured the Heath government, whose dilemma over whether to intervene decisively would have been made much more acute by the return of Craig.[288] As it was, Faulkner was widely viewed as Northern Ireland's last chance to keep itself in devolved government business; this was both an incentive to the IRA to push on and a tremendous burden of pressure for the new Prime Minister to carry.

Faulkner constructed his new cabinet on a broader base. He took advantage of an obscure provision in the Government of Ireland Act of 1920 to appoint David Bleakley, a former NILP Stormont MP, as Minister of Community Relations, and he brought in the liberal Robin Baillie – to be scornfully tagged an *arriviste* by right-wing critics – as Minister of Commerce.[289] In the interests of balance, he persuaded West to take the Agriculture portfolio, a coup which wrong-footed the malcontents in the party, if only in the short term. This was remarkable in as much as Faulkner declared that he would persist with the government's reform programme, attempt to make the existing security policy more effective, and resist calls to rearm the police. In his speech to the UUC on 29 March he further asserted that his administration would be 'scrupulously fair' and that there would be no 'get tough with Catholics' policies. He stressed 'positive government' geared to practical problems and not to 'doctrinaire points of view', appealing to party members to 'throw away your labels' and help him.[290]

The constructive tone was matched with action shortly into Faulkner's premiership when he produced proposals to enable the opposition, the SDLP, to play a more meaningful parliamentary role and contribute to the governance of Northern Ireland.[291] This would be through a system of committees half of which would have salaried chairmanships held by non-Unionists. These committees were envisaged by Faulkner as contributing to policy formation and providing a check on the executive. The SDLP appeared interested if cautious. The proposals were later incorporated into a Green Paper.

Faulkner could also point to the more representative character of the new Housing Executive and the proposed area boards for education and libraries, and health and social services, as well as the expected transfer of control of new district councils to Nationalists.[292]

The prospect of reaching a parliamentary *rapprochement* was, however, soon scuppered. Rioting in Derry in July resulted in two civilians being shot dead by the army. The SDLP's demand for an inquiry was rejected, leading to its withdrawal from Stormont and establishment of an alternative Assembly. Curiously, the SDLP did not withdraw from Westminster, which would have been more logical given that the inquiry was a matter for the British government. It seems, indeed, that the SDLP merely used this as a pretext to retreat to the unequivocal politics of anti-partitionism.[293] It was a serious setback to Faulkner's plans and left him exposed to a renewed campaign from the Unionist right. The Prime Minister immersed himself in the security problems in an embattled frame of mind and emerged convinced that the gamble should be taken to employ the weapon of internment without trial.

For Faulkner the extent to which the IRA had become 'dug in' behind the barricades necessitated a drastic tactic to root its activists out. There was also the precedent of the IRA's 1956–62 campaign and the use of internment then to render it ineffective. Heath's retrospective view is of British government reluctance, although internment had been considered in March and opposed by Chichester-Clark.[294] On 22 July in cabinet it was felt that the introduction of Direct Rule might be required to prevent Faulkner being succeeded by an extremist, but this was to be a last resort; before it was adopted 'it might well be right to agree that the Northern Ireland government should invoke their powers of internment'.[295] Heath was aware that the military arguments against internment were still strong,[296] but he was led to the conclusion that Faulkner needed something to stave off the extremist challenge which, in British governing circles, was considered to be partly the result of the demoralisation of the 'squirearchy' in Ulster and their unwillingness to give effective leadership to the community.[297] Chichester-Clark's resignation was clearly viewed as signalling the political collapse of this brand of Ulster Unionism. On 5 August Heath, supported by his usual team of Maudling, Carrington and Douglas-Home, attempted to get Faulkner to agree to an indefinite ban on marches to accompany internment, but the latter said this was 'impracticable' and stood his ground. 'Since the government would need full Protestant support for any new initiatives on political reconciliation which they might be able to undertake', argued Faulkner, 'it would be foolish to alienate Protestant support by an indiscriminate ban on marches.'[298] After further discussion it was decided to limit the ban to six months, which implied the cancellation of the proposed Apprentice Boys march in Derry later in the month. At the end of the meeting Heath informed Faulkner that if internment failed then the next step, 'and the only remaining step', would be Direct Rule.[299]

Announcing the introduction of internment to his cabinet, Faulkner acknowledged that the measure would involve the UK government in derogation of the European Convention on Human Rights: 'the matter was obviously one of concern ... but they [the British government] had nevertheless accepted the deed for the course proposed as a means of achieving the restoration of law and order'.[300] The cabinet, with the exception of Bleakley who later resigned, expressed full support.

Internment in retrospect assumes the character of Stormont's gravedigger. In terms of security alone it was an abject failure, notwithstanding Faulkner's periodic claims of success from its introduction through to early 1972. Out-of-date intelligence resulted in many innocent Catholics being lifted while IRA leaders largely evaded capture. The sense of Catholic community outrage over the manner of its implementation was compounded by the fact that it was one-sided. Heath had raised the issue of impartiality at the meeting of 5 August,[301] and Bleakley did likewise in cabinet in the course of resigning, only to be informed by the Attorney-General Basil Kelly that 'the police had been genuinely unable to furnish him with any information suggesting that a subversive organisation existed in the Protestant community'.[302] This might have been a subtle way of saying that Protestant violence, being 'pro-state', was to be tolerated, or it more likely reflected the need to justify an operation which was politically and militarily treacherous enough without having to cope with the alienation of both sides, or Faulkner simply could not afford the political risk of offending his own side. Whatever the interpretation, the result was a reaffirmation on the part of the minority of the time-worn perception of being 'second-class' citizens who would never receive fair dealing in the political entity of Northern Ireland. Certainly, Nationalist and Republican propaganda to this effect, along with lurid tales of brutality meted out to internees, engaged outside sympathies, and Jack Lynch's Fianna Fail government was to the fore in its condemnation. Lynch claimed to Heath that the Stormont regime was being influenced by the Orange Order.[303] Against such a background, the fond imaginings of the Heath government about the prospects of Faulkner's initiatives and reforms in the expectation of the gunmen's demise are remarkable. Sir Alec Douglas-Home, the Commonwealth Minister, for example, advised against the option of Direct Rule (which would have been seen as a triumph for the IRA) with the observation that 'the embryonic proposals outlined by Faulkner were sound politics'.[304]

Whatever the intrinsic merits of these proposals, they stood no chance after August 1971, especially since Faulkner was adamant that there was no question of any participation by the minority's representatives in the executive.[305] Faulkner made it plain to the British government that he could not sell the idea of a coalition to his party, and even doubted he could deliver proportional representation for parliamentary elections.[306] In October Faulkner did appoint a Catholic, G. B. Newe, as Minister of State in the Prime Minister's department, but this historic event dimmed against the backdrop of intensified community polarisation,[307] and in the circumstances smacked of tokenism.

The impact of internment on the issue of political violence was substantially to worsen it, rendering political dialogue between the Unionists and the SDLP unattainable.[308] Faulkner was soon accusing the SDLP of having chosen to 'ride on the back of the IRA tiger' and having escalated its demands to the point of the destruction of Stormont.[309] Internment simply made a mockery of initiatives in community relations. Outright civil war was probably closer in the summer and autumn of 1971 than at any other time before or since. In September the Unionist Party headquarters suffered the first of several bomb attacks. Later the same month the Ulster Defence Association (UDA) was formed out of the existing Protestant vigilante and paramilitary groups. Following this, Ian Paisley and ex-Unionist Party MP Desmond Boal brought the Democratic Unionist Party (DUP) into being and propped up proceedings at Stormont by becoming the opposition. The new party was largely based on Paisley's old 'Protestant Unionist' support base owing to the failure of talks between him and Craig to produce a new party comprising the supporters of both.[310] Craig, in the company of UDA members and a group called the Loyalist Association of Workers (LAW), was to launch his own vehicle – Ulster Vanguard – in February 1972, while still remaining in the Unionist Party. At Stormont in December 1971 he spoke of the terrorists' threat to the Northern Ireland parliament and referred to the 'colossal blunder' of 1969 when *de facto* responsibility for security was handed to Westminster. 'It is a certainty', he declared,

> that when the present terrorist campaign ceases there will remain a belief in military action. Because of its successes the gun is again a credible political instrument in Ireland. We are going to have to live with these consequences. They can add up to only one thing. We must have a Parliament in Northern Ireland with real authority and power extending over the whole range of our internal affairs.[311]

At the end of 1971 Senator Jack Barnhill became the first Unionist politician to be murdered by the IRA in the new round of troubles.

The guns belonging to the British army, specifically the Parachute Regiment, then wrote another bloody page into the history books on 30 January 1972 when thirteen civilians were shot dead in Londonderry following a banned civil rights demonstration. 'Bloody Sunday' brought international opprobrium down on the British government, as well as taking Catholic Nationalist fury to new peaks. IRA (Official not Provisional) retaliation took the form of the bombing of an army barracks at Aldershot in which nine died, as well as the attempted murder of John Taylor. The repercussions of 'Bloody Sunday' were indeed far-reaching, and are still being felt today. The tribunal of inquiry set up by Heath held that the army had been fired at, outraging Nationalist opinion. It has been respectively claimed by John Taylor and Ken Bloomfield (Deputy Secretary of the Northern Ireland cabinet at the time) that Faulkner had no knowledge of security meetings prior to the day concerning army tactics and the decision to send in the Parachute Regiment, and that he would have been horrified by the prospect of any action being taken outside of the law.[312] If the calamitous result of internment set the British government on course towards the suspension of Stormont,[313] then the disaster of 'Bloody Sunday' significantly hastened the pace.

Heath met with Faulkner on 4 February and sounded him out regarding several options which, according to a later account in the Unionist Party newspaper, included the involvement of the minority in government; the transfer of law and order power to Westminster; the transfer of areas close to the border to the Republic; periodic referenda on the border question; and an easement of internment.

Faulkner was said to have opposed the first as unworkable and rejected totally the next two; he acquiesced in the fourth and agreed to the fifth if circumstances permitted.[314] Faulkner indicates in his memoirs that the option of transferring law and order powers was not raised, and that Direct Rule was still not favoured. The talk had essentially been about 'initiatives'.[315] The Ulster Premier carried on promoting his Green Paper ideas about a more participatory system of parliamentary government, and lambasting the Republic for confining its sympathy to one set of victims in the Province and being obstructive about the return of murder suspects to the North.[316]

If Faulkner was thus inclined not to ponder the unpalatable, his opponents within Unionism had started to agitate against what they took to be a looming threat. Appearing to imitate Paisley imitating Carson at a Vanguard rally in Ormeau Park in Belfast, and flanked by Unionist Party notables such as the Reverend Martin Smyth, Ernest Baird and Sir Samuel Knox-Cunningham, William Craig hammered home the point he had been at pains to make since the mid-1960s: that it had become a long-standing British constitutional practice and convention that once powers were given from the centre they could not be diminished or taken back. For Craig, the 1949 'guarantee' overrode the 1920 Government of Ireland Act in respect of Westminster's capacity to retrieve the powers devolved to Northern Ireland. This was not, indeed, an idle point at a time when there was a government commission deliberating on the wisdom and practicalities of devolution for other parts of the UK.[317] Craig could also have cited the 'federal' interpretation offered of Northern Ireland's status by both Northern Irish and British government ministers over the years, and he was to be given polemical ammunition by the venerable Unionist historian Hugh Shearman, who argued that some of the powers of the parliament and government of Northern Ireland actually derived from the 1925 Agreement reached by the British, Free State and Ulster governments, and were thus part of international law on account of that agreement being registered at the League of Nations.[318]

Faulkner dismissed Craig's Vanguard movement as a 'comic opera',[319] but he was the tragic figure in the unfolding drama. On 22 March Heath informed Faulkner that it was the view of his government that law and order powers should be transferred to Westminster, that a constitutional referendum should be held, that moves should be made to end internment, that there should be a Secretary of State appointed for Northern Ireland, and that talks should be held with the SDLP with a view to reaching a 'community government'. The Northern Ireland cabinet in theory could have decided to carry on, and at least one scholarly analyst later contended that they should have.[320] Harry West counselled against resignation and was sceptical that Heath would close down a democratically elected parliament and government.[321] But in the belief that the lack of law and order powers would deny them essential credibility, the Northern Ireland cabinet duly offered their resignation, which was accepted on 24 March.[322] Stormont was to be 'prorogued' and Heath made it clear that Direct Rule was intended as a temporary expedient while efforts were made to produce an arrangement more widely acceptable to both communities in the Province. The road to power-sharing was thus prospected, and outside outraged Unionist circles the urgent quest to find a formula for a better future effectively stilled the debate over constitutional niceties and possible breaches of constitutional practice.

It has been well noted that the Unionist MPs at Westminster failed to have any impact on these events, notwithstanding the fears of Maudling back in July that they might persuade more Tories to criticise the government.[323] The Unionist MPs' story had been one of hesitant and incoherent parliamentary tactics, internal divisions and lack of influence in the right places at the right time. Soon after the imposition of Direct Rule these MPs revealed differences over future options, mirroring the situation among Unionists back in Northern Ireland. Many felt that Direct Rule was certainly not a blow to the Union as such, however much it was depicted as a blow to the Unionist Party. They took the view that full political integration ought to be the next step, a perspective subsequently endorsed by the scholarly commentator and former consultant to the O'Neill government Tom Wilson. Wilson argues that integration would have provided stability, whereas the British government's actual course sent out the wrong signals about its commitment to Northern Ireland's place in the Union and thus perpetuated constitutional uncertainty.[324]

However, certain factors weighed strongly against the integrationist option. It has been pointed out that, in contrast to other parts of the UK, Northern Ireland's right to secede from the UK had been acknowledged by different British governments,[325] and there was a pronounced tendency at the centre of British government and in the London-based media to regard Northern Ireland as a questionable member of the British 'family' with fewer entitlements than the rest. Later in 1972 Sir Alec Douglas-Home put it revealingly:

> I really dislike Direct Rule for Northern Ireland because I do not believe that they are like the Scots or the Welsh and doubt if they ever will be. The real British interest would best be served by pushing them towards a United Ireland rather than tying them closer to the United Kingdom. Our own parliamentary history is one long story of trouble with the Irish.[326]

This effusion, from the heart of the establishment, underlined the extent of the misconceptions at the heart of the Republican 'Brits Out' case over the following twenty years.

Moreover, it had been *de facto* policy on the part of successive governments since the early 1920s to keep Northern Ireland apart, politically, in terms of the discussion of business in parliament and the organisation of the major parties of the state. This was a convention, unlike the one concerning the transfer of powers, which the British political establishment was determined to maintain. Integration may have been a sensible and logical choice to make, but it came up against the arguably specious 'they're not like us' line of thinking which was deeply rooted and all but unshakeable.[327] The vaguely imagined, although deceptive, sense of British coherence, comprising England, Scotland and Wales and posited against Northern Ireland, proved at this point credible enough to carry hardened assumptions about how Northern Ireland should face the future. The deconstruction of this particular view of Britishness, long a reality culturally, took place politically too late to influence the debate on Northern Ireland at this caesura in its history.

Notes

1 Public Record Office of Northern Ireland (PRONI), D3004/D/45, 21 March 1958.
2 PRONI, PM 5/9/4.
3 PRONI, D3816/15, Queen's University Yearbook 1958–59.
4 PRONI, PM 5/9/4, 'Analysis of Unionist defeats in city seats'.
5 PRONI, D3816/15, Queen's University Yearbook 1958–59.
6 See Armstrong Papers, PRONI, D4242.
7 Public Record Office (PRO), PREM 11/3447, memo dated 10 March 1958.
8 PRO, PREM 11/3447; see documents on the issue dated October and November 1960.

9   Ibid.
10 See PRONI, D1327/22/2, 1 July 1958; CAB 4/1103.
11 PRO, HO 284/62, memo from Dennis Vosper to R. A. Butler, 29 September 1960: 'Lord Brookeborough is quite clearly most upset at this prospect towards the end of his career and did at one time seem to suggest that he might want to throw in his hand'.
12 PRO, PREM 11/3447, notes on meeting of 18 November 1960.
13 Ibid.
14 See PRO, HO 284/63.
15 *Northern Whig*, 19 November 1960.
16 PRO, HO 284/62, 12 October 1960.
17 PRO, HO 284/63.
18 Ibid.
19 Ibid.
20 For example, discussion of Hall Report by Garret Fitzgerald, *Irish Times*, 31 October 1962.
21 PRO, HO 284/63; PRONI, CAB 4/1206.
22 See PRONI, D1327/22/3, 7 March, 4 July and 7 November 1961.
23 See J. H. Whyte, 'Intra-Unionist disputes in the Northern Ireland House of Commons, 1921–72', *Economic and Social Review*, 5:1 (1973), pp. 99–104.
24 PRO, PREM 11/3897, 'Note for the record', 15 October 1962.
25 Maurice Leitch, *The liberty lad* (London, Panther, 1968), p. 54.
26 See review of the play by Louis MacNeice in S. H. King and S. McMahon (eds), *Hope and history* (Belfast, Friars Bush Press, 1996).
27 PRO, HO 284/63.
28 PRO, PREM 11/4387.
29 Ibid.
30 Ibid., memo dated 28 January 1963.
31 For scholarly discussion of the issues involved in UK territorial management see, for example: J. Bulpitt, *Territory and power in the United Kingdom* (Manchester, Manchester University Press, 1983); P. Madgewick and R. Rose (eds), *The territorial dimension in UK politics* (London, Macmillan, 1982); B. Crick, *Political thoughts and polemics* (Edinburgh, Polygon, 1990).
32 For Lemass see P. Bew and H. Patterson, *Seán Lemass and the making of modern Ireland* (Dublin, Gill and Macmillan, 1982).
33 See M. Kennedy, *Division and consensus: the politics of cross-border relations in Ireland 1925–1969* (Dublin, Institute of Public Administration, 2000), ch. 8.
34 See Eamon Phoenix's discussion in *Irish News*, 3 January 1989.
35 PRO, HO 284/45.
36 Ibid.
37 PRO, HO 284/50.

38 PRONI, CAB 4/1115.
39 Kennedy, *Division and consensus*, pp. 182–4.
40 Ibid, p. 189.
41 See R. Aldous, 'Perfect peace? Macmillan and Ireland', in R. Aldous and S. Lee (eds), *Harold Macmillan: aspects of a political life* (Basingstoke, Macmillan, 1999).
42 See PRONI, D3004/D/45, 15 September 1960.
43 See account in Terence O'Neill, *The autobiography of Terence O'Neill* (London, Hart-Davis, 1972), pp. 40–3. Brookeborough died in 1973.
44 PRONI, D1327/20/4/42.
45 See H. Patterson, 'Brian Maginess and the limits of Liberal Unionism', *Irish Review*, 25 (1999/2000), pp. 95–112.
46 For which see A. Gailey, *Crying in the wilderness. Jack Sayers: a liberal editor in Ulster 1939–69* (Belfast, Institute of Irish Studies, 1995).
47 Ibid., pp. 48–9.
48 PRONI, D3004/D/45, 4 November 1959.
49 There were, however, Catholic members, apparently discreetly enrolled. See M. Mulholland, *Northern Ireland at the crossroads: Ulster Unionism in the O'Neill years, 1960–9* (Basingstoke, Macmillan, 2000), p. 8.
50 See *Irish News*, 2 January 1991, Eamon Phoenix article.
51 PRONI, D3004/D/45, 20 November 1959.
52 See Gailey, *Crying in the wilderness*, pp. 52–61; also Harry Burdge Papers, PRONI, D1609.
53 For an indication of Glengall Street's power see the comments of Ivan Neill in his autobiography, *Church and state* (Dunmurry, 1995), p. 34, about being made to feel an 'interloper' in the party headquarters.
54 PRONI, D1609/1.
55 See criticisms of Sayers in Gailey, *Crying in the wilderness*, p. 71; also Mulholland, *Northern Ireland*, p. 27.
56 Mulholland, *Northern Ireland*, p. 58.
57 See reflections of Maurice Hayes in his *Minority verdict* (Belfast, Blackstaff Press, 1995), p. 65.
58 For notable assessments of O'Neill see Mulholland, *Northern Ireland*; F. Cochrane, 'Meddling at the crossroads', in R. English and G. Walker (eds), *Unionism in modern Ireland* (Basingstoke, Macmillan, 1996); D. Gordon, *The O'Neill years* (Belfast, Athol Books, 1989); Gailey, *Crying in the wilderness*. See also O'Neill's *Autobiography*, and his *Ulster at the crossroads* (London, Faber and Faber, 1969).
59 Neill, *Church and state*, pp. 59–60; Mulholland, *Northern Ireland*, pp. 24–5.

60 Mulholland, *Northern Ireland*, pp. 24–5.
61 O'Neill attempted to cultivate an earthier image by celebrating 'Ulster-Scots' or 'Scotch-Irish' history: see Mulholland, *Northern Ireland*, pp. 70–1; Gailey, *Crying in the wilderness*, pp. 96–7.
62 K. Bloomfield, *Stormont in crisis* (Belfast, Blackstaff Press, 1996). This memoir is a valuable source for the O'Neill era and beyond.
63 Gailey, *Crying in the wilderness*, p. 77.
64 For relevant documents see PRO, PREM 11/4385; also O'Neill, *The autobiography*, pp. 48–9.
65 PRONI, D1327/20/3/21.
66 O'Neill, *The autobiography*, p. 47.
67 PRONI, D1327/20/3/21, 'The pattern of the new Ulster' (UUC, 1964).
68 Quoted in Gailey, *Crying in the wilderness*, p. 79.
69 PRONI, CAB 4/1239.
70 Mulholland, *Northern Ireland*, pp. 22–3.
71 'Are you an under 30 voter?', Linenhall Library Political Collection.
72 Mulholland, *Northern Ireland*, pp. 21–3, 34.
73 Ibid., p. 50; also P. Bew et al., *Northern Ireland 1921–94* (London, Serif, 1995), p. 136.
74 Bew et al., *Northern Ireland*, pp. 134–40.
75 See Mulholland, *Northern Ireland*, pp. 34–7; also PRONI, CAB 4/1238 and CAB 4/1259. Arguably the Brooke government had been moving towards this in October 1962: see CAB 4/1207. For the parliamentary party see D1327/22/3, 23 April 1964.
76 PRO, PREM 11/4964.
77 Incorporating Transport and Local Government.
78 See PRONI, D1327/22/3, 15 June 1965.
79 See Neill, *Church and state*, p. 61.
80 For a discussion of legislative divergence in the 1960s see W. D. Birrell, 'The mechanics of devolution: Northern Ireland experience and the Scotland and Wales Bill', *Political Quarterly*, 49 (1978), pp. 304–21.
81 PRONI, D1327/22/3, 13 May 1964.
82 Mulholland, *Northern Ireland*, pp. 50–2.
83 Ibid., pp. 53–4; for *Unionist* anger about this decision see D1327/22/3, 8 April 1965 and 18 May 1965.
84 Bew et al., *Northern Ireland*, pp. 137–9; also Brian McGuigan, *The day of O'Neill*, pamphlet in Linenhall Library Political Collection.
85 It should be noted that the personification of the party 'old guard', Secretary William Douglas, was persuaded to resign shortly after O'Neill took over.
86 Mulholland, *Northern Ireland*, p. 170.
87 Ibid., pp. 30–1.
88 PRO, PREM 11/4965, letter dated 7 April 1964.

89 See P. Rose, *How the troubles came to Northern Ireland* (Basingstoke, Macmillan, 2000), p. 13.

90 PRO, PREM 13/457, record of meeting, 6 November 1964.

91 See Gordon, *The O'Neill years*, pp. 27–9 on the Unionist response to a NILP proposal for a Special Minister to coordinate economic affairs, and for Northern Ireland economic development to be controlled centrally.

92 This convention did not – as was argued by some Unionists – have the force of law. See Rose, *How the troubles came*, ch. 1 for discussion.

93 Rose, *How the troubles came*, ch. 1; B. Purdie, *Politics in the streets* (Belfast, Blackstaff Press, 1990).

94 Rose, *How the troubles came*, pp. 56–7.

95 PRO, PREM 13/1663, various documents.

96 When it was dubbed 'the West Lothian Question' following the constituency of Tom Dalyell, the Labour MP who was mainly responsible for highlighting it.

97 PRO, PREM 13/1663, meeting between Wilson and O'Neill, 19 May 1965.

98 Ibid. Subjects suggested included race relations.

99 See Rose, *How the troubles came*, pp. 62–3.

100 Ibid., p. 61. See also PRONI, D1327/20/1/31, UUC Year Book 1967.

101 Kennedy, *Division and consensus*, p. 273.

102 See Bloomfield, *Stormont in crisis*.

103 Mulholland, *Northern Ireland*, p. 27.

104 Kennedy, *Division and consensus*, p. 233; Faulkner had established cross-border business networks. See B. Faulkner, *Memoirs of a statesman* (London, Weidenfeld and Nicolson, 1978).

105 See PRONI, D1327/22/3, 3 February 1965.

106 Ibid., 8 April 1965. The ministers included Faulkner.

107 See Kennedy, *Division and consensus*, pp. 254–6, 263. See also PRONI, CAB 4/1303.

108 PRONI, D3702/C/1/12, Sam Napier papers. This is the source for what follows on UPA.

109 The most authoritative works on Paisley are S. Bruce, *God save Ulster!* (Oxford, Oxford University Press, 1986); C. Smyth, *Ian Paisley: the voice of Protestant Ulster* (Edinburgh, Scottish Academic Press, 1987); E. Moloney and A. Pollak, *Paisley* (Dublin, Poolbeg Press, 1986).

110 See Chapter 3.

111 A. Jackson, *Ireland 1798–1998* (Oxford, Blackwell, 1999), p. 371, has likened Paisley's achievements to those of Sloan. It should be noted that Paisley patronised the revived Independent Orange Order, Sloan having been one of the founder members of the original.

112 Election leaflet, May 1964, Linenhall Library Political Collection.

113 See Mulholland, *Northern Ireland*, p. 117; Gailey, *Crying in the wilderness*, p. 111.

114 PRONI, D3702/C/1/12.

115 Election leaflet dated 20 May 1964, Linenhall Library Political Collection.

116 See PRONI, D3702/C/8.

117 See Mulholland, *Northern Ireland*, ch. 5 fn. 97 on the views of Belfast shipyard workers; also F. Wright, 'Protestant ideology and politics in Ulster', *European Journal of Sociology*, 14 (1973), pp. 213–80.

118 See election leaflet for Spence, McQuade and Co. published by UPA, Linenhall Library Political Collection.

119 Mulholland, *Northern Ireland*, p. 113.

120 PRONI, D1327/22/3, 28 June 1966.

121 Ibid.

122 See Mulholland, *Northern Ireland*, pp. 105–14 for discussion of this conspiracy and its failure.

123 PRONI, D1327/22/3, 27 September 1966. This is the source for what follows on this meeting.

124 Boal left the meeting and remaining malcontents Warnock and Taylor agreed to make it unanimous.

125 Mulholland, *Northern Ireland*, p. 113.

126 Ibid., p. 111.

127 For commentary on the tensions between Stormont and local authorities in this period see Hayes, *Minority verdict*, pp. 60, 69–70.

128 See PRONI, D1327/22/3, 8 April 1965.

129 See PRONI, D4234/A/2, Clark papers. Paisley was offered various Orange Order platforms in this period.

130 Mulholland, *Northern Ireland*, pp. 126–8.

131 PRONI, D1327/20/1/30, UUC Yearbook 1966.

132 See Rose, *How the troubles came*, pp. 50–7.

133 Kennedy, *Division and consensus*, p. 272; PRO, PREM 13/2266.

134 See *Irish News*, 1 January 1997, Eamon Phoenix article.

135 *Irish Times*, 21 October 1983, letter to the editor.

136 The best account of the background to, and emergence of, NICRA is Purdie, *Politics in the streets*. See also E. McCann, *War and an Irish town* (London, Pluto Press, 1974) and M. Farrell, *Northern Ireland: the Orange state* (London, Pluto Press, 1976) for perspectives of those who saw the civil rights challenge in terms of its potential to achieve an Irish socialist republic.

137 See Bew et al., *Northern Ireland*, pp. 146–58; M. Elliott, *The Catholics of Ulster* (London, Penguin, 2000), p. 401.

138 See Henry Patterson's review of Mulholland's *Northern Ireland* in *Bullan*, 5:2 (2001).

139 See Mulholland, *Northern Ireland*, pp. 128–33.

140   See Gordon, *The O'Neill years*, p. 51.
141   On the topic of disenfranchised Protestants see evidence presented by trade union leader Andy Barr, *Belfast Newsletter*, 14 July 1969.
142   See PRONI, D3702/C/10, various documents.
143   See PRONI, CAB 4/1344 for an NILP memo on citizen rights. For a critical appraisal of the NILP in this period see P. Devlin, *Straight left: an autobiography* (Belfast, Blackstaff, 1993), chs 5–7.
144   The term is used by Elliott, *Catholics*, ch. 12.
145   J. Todd, 'Northern Irish Nationalist political culture', *Irish Political Studies*, 5 (1990), pp. 31–44.
146   Mulholland, *Northern Ireland*, p. 158; T. Wilson, *Ulster: conflict and consent* (Oxford, Blackwell Press, 1989), p. 154.
147   Purdie, *Politics in the streets*, p. 2.
148   See, for example, McCann, *War and an Irish town*.
149   C. Hewitt, 'The roots of violence: Catholic grievances and Irish Nationalism during the civil rights period', in P. J. Roche and B. Barton (eds), *The Northern Ireland question: myth and reality* (Aldershot, Averbury, 1991).
150   One of the best treatments of the complexities of the situation remains R. Rose, *Governing without consensus* (London, Faber and Faber, 1971). See especially his 'loyalty' survey (Appendix).
151   Hewitt, 'The roots of violence', points out, for example, that Nationalists often argued on the basis of total Catholic numbers rather than Catholics of voting age. See also Wilson, *Ulster*, chs 11–14; Elliott, *Catholics*, pp. 384–94.
152   See PRONI, CAB 4/1254 and /1277; also Rose, *How the troubles came*, pp. 72–3. See A. J. Walmsley, *Northern Ireland: its policies and record* (UUC, 1959) for a defence of the ratepayers' franchise. Walmsley was a Unionist Party senator.
153   PRONI, CAB 4/1414. See also *Irish News*, 21 January 1999.
154   Mulholland, *Northern Ireland*, p. 138.
155   For example, see J. J. Lee, *Ireland 1912–85* (Cambridge, Cambridge University Press, 1989), ch. 1.
156   See G. Walker, 'Protestant Ulster in Lee's *Ireland*', *Irish Review*, 12 (1992), pp. 65–71.
157   See J. Oliver, *Working at Stormont* (Dublin, Institute of Public Administration, 1978), ch. 8 for discussion of this campaign's significance in the persistence of defensive attitudes.
158   See comments of Unionist MP Teddy Jones in Mulholland, *Northern Ireland*, p. 140.
159   See speech reported in *Irish News*, 30 May 1967; also discussion in P. Walsh, *From civil rights to national war* (Belfast, Athol Books, 1989), pp. 24–35.
160   See discussion in C. C. O'Brien, *States of Ireland* (London, Panther, 1974), ch. 8.

161   See Mulholland, *Northern Ireland*, p. 120; Kennedy, *Division and consensus*, p. 293.

162   See Bloomfield, *Stormont*, pp. 85–6 on Craig.

163   The civil rights march which led to the clashes had been banned by Craig, Minister of Home Affairs.

164   PRONI, CAB 4/1405.

165   PRONI, CAB 4/1409.

166   O'Neill, *The autobiography*, p. 105.

167   See Elliott, *Catholics*, p. 408. Progress was also made regarding the issue of the Mater Hospital – see CAB 4/1413.

168   See report of meeting in CAB 4/1413. James Callaghan in his *A house divided* (London, Collins, 1973), pp. 10–11 refers to the meeting and to Craig's belief that the IRA was behind NICRA.

169   See Rose, *How the troubles came*, pp. 121–5; ch. 7.

170   PRONI, CAB 4/1413.

171   PRONI, CAB 4/1418.

172   PRONI, CAB 4/1423.

173   PRONI, CAB 4/1418.

174   PRONI, CAB 4/1419.

175   PRONI, CAB 4/1423. 'The franchise is primarily an issue appealing to political activists; but it is jobs and houses which most concern the mass of the people.'

176   Included in O'Neill, *Ulster at the crossroads*; see also Mulholland, *Northern Ireland*, pp. 170–3.

177   Ian Smith was then the Rhodesian Prime Minister in conflict with London and prone to threaten unilateral declaration of independence.

178   The resignation was followed by a bitter exchange of letters between Faulkner and O'Neill. Letters reproduced in O'Neill, *The autobiography*, Appendix. See Faulkner, *Memoirs*, pp. 51–2.

179   See memo in PRONI, CAB 4/1427/12.

180   PRONI, CAB 4/1432.

181   PRONI, CAB 4/1427.

182   *Disturbances in Northern Ireland* (Belfast, HMSO, 1969), Cmd 532. The report highlighted, for example, the gerrymandering of local government boundaries and the question of local authorities' allocation of council houses. However, see the Unionist stress on Richard Rose's findings in his *Governing without consensus* (London, Faber and Faber, 1971); *Ulster Times*, October 1971.

183   See PRONI, CAB 4/1413.

184   Paisley and his then right-hand man Major Bunting were sentenced to three months imprisonment for unlawful assembly in Armagh on 30 November. Paisley went to jail in March 1969.

185   This revolt was dubbed 'the Portadown Parliament' on account of the conspirators meeting in a hotel in the town. The signatories in-

cluded West, Taylor, Craig and Boal.

186 For Brookeborough's despair, see Gordon, *The O'Neill years*, p. 146.
187 See quote in Moloney and Pollak, *Paisley*, p. 178.
188 For discussion of the election see Mulholland, *Northern Ireland*, pp. 181–92; F. W. Boal and R. H. Buchanan, 'The 1969 Northern Ireland election', *Irish Geography*, 6:1 (1969), pp. 78–84; *The Unionist*, March 1969.
189 Mulholland, *Northern Ireland*, p. 193.
190 See O'Neill's comments on the effects of the explosions at vital installations on the latter vote, *The autobiography*, p. 122.
191 Mulholland, *Northern Ireland*, p. 183.
192 See remarks of Sir David Lyndsey Keir in Rose, *How the troubles came*, p. 139.
193 Mulholland, *Northern Ireland*, p. 185.
194 This, the 'frightfully hard' speech, was made after his resignation. See comment of O'Brien in his *States of Ireland*, p. 163.
195 Moloney and Pollak, *Paisley*, ch. 6.
196 O'Neill, *The autobiography*, pp. 122–3.
197 P. Bew and G. Gillespie, *Northern Ireland: a chronology of the troubles 1968–93* (Dublin, Gill and Macmillan, 1993), pp. 14–15.
198 PRONI, CAB 4/1437.
199 Mulholland, *Northern Ireland*, p. 199.
200 Faulkner, *Memoirs*, p. 55.
201 C. Scouler, *James Chichester-Clark* (Killyleagh, 2000), p. 69.
202 Mulholland, *Northern Ireland*, p. 196.
203 See Hayes, *Minority verdict*, p. 124. Chichester-Clark was the nephew of Dame Dehra Parker.
204 See B. McIvor, *Hope deferred* (Belfast, Blackstaff Press, 1998), p. 55.
205 PRONI, D1327/22/4, 'Notes of meeting'.
206 See critical comment on this by David Bleakley in his *Faulkner* (London, Mowbrays, 1974), p. 77.
207 PRONI, D1327/22/4. See comment by Taylor, who nonetheless backed Faulkner.
208 See PRONI, CAB 4/1441.
209 PRONI, CAB 4/1453.
210 PRONI, CAB 4/1456.
211 PRONI, CAB 4/1457.
212 PRONI, CAB 4/1461.
213 See J. O'Brien, *The arms trial* (Dublin, Gill and Macmillan, 2000), pp. 35–6, 43.
214 PRONI, CAB 4/1463.
215 O'Brien, *Arms trial*, pp. 42–3.
216 The fullest treatment of this episode is O'Brien, *Arms trial*.
217 See Scouler, *Chichester-Clark*, p. 88 on the difficulty caused to Chichester-Clark by Wilson's television broadcast subsequent to

their meeting in which it was implied that the Specials were to be phased out.

218 PRONI, CAB 4/1465.

219 For insider comment on the impact of the Hunt Committee on Chichester-Clark's government, see Neill, *Church and state*, p. 65.

220 See PRONI, CAB 4/1474.

221 Other recommendations included the disarming of the RUC.

222 PRONI, CAB 4/1484.

223 Callaghan gave a strong impression of running the show. See K. O. Morgan, *Callaghan: a life* (Oxford, Oxford University Press, 1997), p. 349. Morgan's book is all too typical of a tendency in much writing about the Northern Ireland troubles to dismiss the Unionist case without a proper understanding of it, or indeed a proper grasp of the facts of the political situation – see, for example, pp. 345–6.

224 See Rose, *How the troubles came*, ch. 7; O'Brien, *Arms trial*, pp. 35–9.

225 Rose, *How the troubles came*, p. 161.

226 For example, see Bew et al., *Northern Ireland*, pp. 19–20.

227 *The Unionist*, December 1969.

228 On 21 March 1969 the UUC issued a statement to the effect that while membership of another organisation was permissible, members may not play a part in an organisation which has in the past, or may in the future, sponsor or support candidates for election other than official Unionist candidates.

229 *Ulster Times*, May 1970. This paper succeeded *The Unionist*. This committee delivered a report in July 1971 which proposed a tightening up of membership rights and responsibilities, and a reduction in Young Unionist representation on the UUC. See J. F. Harbinson, *The Ulster Unionist Party 1882–1973* (Belfast, Blackstaff Press, 1973), p. 170. It should be noted that Chichester-Clark was himself 'deselected' in 1970.

230 *Ulster Times*, May 1970.

231 Ibid.

232 Ibid.

233 Westminster MP Samuel Knox-Cunningham was a major critic of both O'Neill and Chichester-Clark.

234 See critical note in *Ulster Times*, June 1970, on the 'drum beating' of the Westminster Unionist MPs; also UUC pamphlet on Public Relations Fund, Linenhall Library Political Collection.

235 A. Gailey, 'The destructiveness of constructive Unionism', in D. G. Boyce and A. O'Day (eds), *Defenders of the Union* (London, Routledge, 2001). See also Alan Parkinson's article in the same volume regarding the Unionists' media problems.

236 See speech to Larkfield Unionist Association, 20 November 1969, included in the collection of Unionist Party press releases, Linenhall

Library. It should also be noted that a public committee on community relations had been set up, headed by Maurice Hayes, a Catholic
civil servant.

237 For comment see Hayes, *Minority verdict*, pp. 76–7.
238 *The Unionist*, December 1969.
239 *Ulster Times*, March 1970.
240 W. D. Flackes, *Northern Ireland: a political directory* (London, BBC,
1983), p. 264.
241 Andrews speech, 8 April 1970, Linenhall Library Unionist Party
press releases.
242 Faulkner speech, 10 April 1970, Linenhall Library Unionist Party
press releases.
243 Minford speech, 13 April 1970, Linenhall Library Unionist Party
press releases.
244 See Chapters 1 and 2.
245 Minford speech, 9 April 1970, Linenhall Library Unionist Party
press releases. This bears comparison with the notable speech by
David Trimble in 1998 – see Chapter 6.
246 Minford speech, 14 April 1970, Linenhall Library Unionist Party
press releases.
247 Chichester-Clark speech, 14 April 1970, Linenhall Library Unionist
Party press releases.
248 *Ulster Times*, May 1970. The identity of the author of the article was
not disclosed.
249 See discussion of this in cabinet, PRONI, CAB 4/1533: Bradford's
attempt to dissuade ministers from so doing failed.
250 See Flackes, *Northern Ireland*, p. 264 for details of the election
outcome.
251 *Ulster Times*, May 1970.
252 Faulkner speech, 21 April 1970, Linenhall Library Unionist Party
press releases.
253 See O'Brien, *States of Ireland*, pp. 214–16.
254 *Northern Ireland. Hearings before the Subcommittee on Europe of
the Committee on Foreign Affairs, House of Representatives Ninety-
Second Congress, Second Session* (US Government, Washington,
1972), p. 357.
255 See discussion in Chapters 1 and 2 of the Presbyterian contribution
to the shaping of Ulster identity and to the campaign against Irish
Home Rule. Contrast the Presbyterian statement with those of the
other churches contained in the Congress hearings: ibid., pp. 355–
60.
256 The constituency, which included Bannside, was heavily Presbyterian with a large number of small farmers. There was a history of
tensions with the Unionist Party – see discussion of Sir Robert Lynn's
candidature in 1929 in Chapter 3. There is an illuminating discus-

sion of Paisley and Bannside in Owen Dudley Edwards, *The sins of our fathers* (Dublin, Gill and Macmillan, 1970), ch. 3.

257 See *Ulster Times*, July 1970.

258 See Report on Council meeting, 2 June 1970, Linenhall Library Unionist Party press releases. Among officers elected were Craig, Knox-Cunningham, Boal and West, and lesser known figures who were to make an important political impact in later years, namely Clifford Smyth, Roy Garland, Reg Empey, John Laird and Dennis Rogan. The contrasting display of loyalty to the leadership by the women's associations should be noted.

259 Chichester-Clark speech, 23 June 1970, Linenhall Library Unionist Party press releases.

260 Ibid.

261 PRO, PREM 15/101, Chichester-Clark to Maudling, 12 July 1970.

262 PRONI, D1327/22/4, 2 July 1970. Maudling's outlook was less up-beat. See Bew and Gillespie, *Northern Ireland*, p. 28.

263 Maudling wanted responsibility transferred as soon as possible back to the police, whom he felt should share the 'odium' of enforcing law and order – see PRO, PREM 15/100, cabinet minutes, 22 June 1970.

264 PRONI, D1327/22/4, 2 July 1970.

265 For the 'official' / 'provisional' IRA split at the end of 1969 see O'Brien, *Arms trial*, preface and ch. 1.

266 M. O'Doherty, *The trouble with guns* (Belfast, Blackstaff Press, 1998), p. 73.

267 Purdie, *Politics in the streets*, p. 250.

268 See Wilson, *Ulster*, ch. 16.

269 PRONI, CAB 4/1532.

270 Ibid. O'Neill, the Prime Minister's cousin, regularly despaired about the character of the Unionist Party, and later joined and became leader of the Alliance Party.

271 PRONI, CAB 4/1533.

272 See PRO, PREM 15/101, Chichester-Clark to Heath, 14 July 1970.

273 PRO, PREM 15/101, Chichester-Clark to Maudling, 12 July 1970.

274 PRO, PREM 15/101, memo to Heath, 20 July 1970.

275 The Stormont government had been ridiculed for lack of firmness at a meeting of the Standing Committee of the UUC on 8 July.

276 PRO, PREM 15/101, memo to Heath, 9 July 1970.

277 PRO, PREM 15/101, paper by Michael Lathan of the Conservative research department.

278 As the Chief Whip, John Dobson, remarked, even on the issue of Lough Neagh eel fishing, 'the Unionist Party is in a state of supersensitivity' – see PRONI, CAB 4/1548/23.

279 PRONI, CAB 4/1548. An investment package drawn up by the Wilson Labour government was endorsed by the Tories. For a contemporary defence of Northern Ireland's position see H. Shearman,

'Conflict in Northern Ireland', *The year book of world affairs*, 24 (1970), pp. 40–53: 'In terms of financial flows of all kinds, of which taxation revenue is only ɔne, it is clear that Northern Ireland more than pays its way'.

280 For example, Heath in his memoirs, *The course of my life* (London, Coronet, 1999), p. 425, says he insisted that Chichester-Clark ban 'sectarian parades' from the end of July 1970 for six months.

281 See Scouler, *Chichester-Clark*, pp. 110–11; Bloomfield, *Stormont*, pp. 131–2.

282 Gerry Fitt became the party's first leader, with John Hume deputy.

283 See Maudling's infamous remark about 'an acceptable level of violence' in D. McKittrick and D. McVea, *Making sense of the troubles* (London, Penguin, 2001), pp. 62–3.

284 Heath, *The course of my life*, p. 426; also PRO, CAB 128/48, 18 March 1971.

285 PRO, CAB 128/48, 22 March 1971.

286 Editorial, *Ulster Times*, April 1971.

287 *Ulster Times*, April 1971.

288 See Heath, *The course of my life*, pp. 426–7.

289 *Ulster Times*, October 1971. Bleakley could only hold office for a maximum of six months. See commentary in Bleakley, *Faulkner*, pp. 80–2.

290 *Ulster Times*, April 1971.

291 See Faulkner, *Memoirs*, pp. 102–7; Bleakley, *Faulkner*, pp. 87–91; Bloomfield, *Stormont*, pp. 142–5, 152–5.

292 However, for a critical Nationalist assessment of Faulkner and his schemes see H. Kelly, *How Stormont fell* (Dublin, Gill and Macmillan, 1972), chs 2 and 3.

293 See Walsh, *From civil rights*, pp. 62–6.

294 Heath, *The course of my life*, p. 428.

295 PRO, CAB 128/48, 22 July 1971.

296 PRO, PREM 15/478, letter from Tony Stephen (Ministry of Defence) to Peter Gregson (Private Secretary to Heath), 21 July 1971.

297 PRO, PREM 15/478, Gregson memo, 22 July 1971.

298 PRO, PREM 15/478, notes of meeting, 5 August 1971.

299 PRO, PREM 15/478, letter from Burke Trend (Cabinet Office) to Robert Armstrong, 6 August 1971.

300 PRONI, CAB 4/1607; see Faulkner, *Memoirs*, ch. 11.

301 PRO, PREM 15/478, notes of meeting, 5 August 1971.

302 PRONI, CAB 4/1609.

303 PRO, PREM 15/478, text of telephone conversation, 10 August 1971. The report of the committee set up by Chichester-Clark to reform party structures which appeared in 1971 did not include a recommendation to change the Orange Order link (see Kelly, *How Stormont fell*, p. 40).

304 PRONI, CAB 4/1607/19, note of meeting held at Chequers, 19 August 1971.

305 Ibid.

306 PRO, PREM 15/478, memo dated 15 August 1971.

307 So too did the agreement reached between the Northern Ireland government and the Mater Hospital for the transfer of the hospital to the state system from the beginning of 1972.

308 See B. O'Duffy, 'The price of containment: deaths and debate on Northern Ireland in the House of Commons, 1968–94', in P. Catterall and S. McDougall (eds), *The Northern Ireland question in British politics* (Basingstoke, Macmillan, 1996).

309 Speech at Newtownards, *Ulster Times*, December 1971.

310 See S. Bruce, *Conservative Protestant politics* (Oxford, Oxford University Press, 1998), pp. 60–1.

311 Quoted in *Ulster Times*, December 1971.

312 *Observer*, 3 February 2002, on Taylor (Minister of State for Home Affairs at the time); *Belfast Newsletter*, 30 May 2002, on Bloomfield. Faulkner was killed in a horse riding accident in 1977.

313 See *Irish News*, 2 January 2002, Eamon Phoenix articles on cabinet memo.

314 See *Ulster Times*, April 1972.

315 Faulkner, *Memoirs*, pp. 142–4.

316 Speech quoted in *Unionist Review*, 2:2 (March 1972), Linenhall Library Political Collection.

317 The Royal Commission on the Constitution 1969–73, Cmd 5460 (HMSO, 1973), usually known as the 'Kilbrandon Report'. This recommended devolved assemblies for both Scotland and Wales and drew significantly on the Northern Ireland experience in reaching its conclusions about the form the devolved arrangements should take.

318 *Ulster Times*, April 1972.

319 It probably deserved a more serious appraisal given the menacing nature of Craig's quasi-fascist leadership cult and the extremism of his rhetoric. For Vanguard see S. Nelson, *Ulster's uncertain defenders* (Belfast, Appletree, 1984), ch. 9; Kelly, *How Stormont fell*, pp. 121–9.

320 Wilson, *Ulster*, p. 172. See also A. Aughey, *Under siege: Ulster Unionism and the Anglo-Irish Agreement* (London, Hurst & Co., 1989), p. 38.

321 McIvor, *Hope deferred*, pp. 82–3.

322 See Bloomfield, *Stormont*, pp. 164–5 for an inside account.

323 PRO, CAB 128/48, 22 July 1971, on Maudling. For Unionist MPs at Westminster see P. Norton, 'Conservative politics and the abolition of Stormont', in Catterall and McDougall (eds), *The Northern Ireland question*. The profile of these MPs remained one of elderly males – see discussion in Harbinson, *Ulster Unionist Party*, ch. 9.

324 Wilson, *Ulster*, p. 164.

325 See A. Guelke, *Northern Ireland: the international perspective* (Dublin, Gill and Macmillan, 1988), p. 4. However, the notion of conditional membership also arguably applied, and applies, to Scotland – at least in practical terms. See discussion in G. Walker, *Intimate strangers: political and cultural interaction between Scotland and Ulster in modern times* (Edinburgh, John Donald, 1995), ch. 6. See also points made in the article on Northern Ireland's constitutional status in *Ulster Times*, June 1972.

326 Quoted in R. Weight, *Patriots* (Basingstoke, Macmillan, 2002), p. 535.

327 It seems to have been a belief that 'they're just like us' which prompted a contributor to the *Ulster Times* (March 1972) to comment that Bernadette Devlin's new home in London was 'in a Protestant area just off Battersea's Lavender Hill'!

CHAPTER SIX

ALTERED STATES: THE UNIONIST PARTY AND THE NORTHERN IRELAND CONFLICT, 1972–2002

> Unionists are reactive and serial thinkers when they need to be proactive and dialectical thinkers. By dialectical I mean that Unionists always want a line to be drawn in concrete and the constitutional question settled for ever. But nothing in life is settled for ever, including a United Ireland, and all lines are drawn in sand. (Eoghan Harris, *Selling Unionism*, Belfast, Ulster Young Unionist Council, 1995, p. 30)

The introduction of Direct Rule reduced overnight the Unionist Party from a party of government with patronage at its disposal, to a body of incoherent and ineffectual protest. In a sense Ulster Unionism was being invited to return to its state of political nature: it had been shaped as a movement out of the campaign against Irish Home Rule and it had preserved unity behind skilled leadership. In between, however, it had been forced to mutate into a governing machine while continuing to embody a communal will; hence when deprived of the reins of government it stood as a symbol of tarnished ethnic honour. It could not easily re-emerge out of the confused resentments of its constituents to perform another spectacular political enactment of the 'Ulster will fight' script. 'Ulster' was not saying no to a fight, but in 1972 in contrast to 1912 it was by no means clear how and to what end the Unionist Party should attempt to direct that fight. In its April 1972 issue, the Unionist paper, the *Ulster Times,* called on the party to undergo the 'radical changes' necessary to give voice to the 'many diverse shades of Loyalist opinion'. However, the successful catch-all Unionism of the Home Rule era was to prove unattainable.

It was natural for Unionists to regard the suspension of Stormont as a victory for Nationalism, and especially for the violence of the

IRA. Northern Ireland had become a global by-word for atrocities; another Unionist publication observed mordantly that gruesome murders in the city of Chicago were being labelled 'Belfast-style' outrages.[1] Moreover, it appeared that violence worked. Unionist antipathy towards the new governing arrangements presided over by British Secretary of State William Whitelaw fed off the persistence of the security crisis and Whitelaw's vain attempts to parley with the Provisional IRA leadership. The mounting anger and frustration found release initially in protest rallies, and later in UUC propaganda publications[2] which were designed to jolt the watching world out of the misconceptions Unionists believed had been maliciously fostered; yet this was no substitute for clear political thinking.

Faulkner railed against the 'semi-colonial' form of government which Direct Rule entailed, and the 'coconut commission' of advisers on whom Whitelaw depended to run the show,[3] and he attempted to marshal the Unionist Party behind a constitutional campaign for the restoration of Stormont. He saw the party's role as essentially that of the major opposition force with a brief to bring the Whitelaw administration to its 'political senses' and to deal with the IRA.[4] Faulkner set up a policy committee in May 1972 to redefine the way forward for the party and he managed to persuade Craig to join it. This was significant in the light of Craig's leadership of Vanguard and his militant profile. After the prorogation of Stormont Faulkner had shared the limelight with Craig at demonstrations, and endured the latter's involvement with the UDA in a two-day industrial stoppage. In the immediate aftermath of the introduction of Direct Rule, Vanguard thrived as the main outlet for Unionist and Loyalist protest and Craig appeared poised to become the tribal chief for which his activities since the beginning of the year had been careful preparation. Vanguard was designed to reconstruct the 'umbrella' nature of Unionism and Loyalism and to pilot Craig to the leadership of the Unionist Party, and for a brief period this seemed quite plausible.

Craig certainly eclipsed Paisley as a potential messiah figure at this juncture. Paisley, having predicted the suspension of Stormont from late 1971, pronounced himself unperturbed when it occurred, and proceeded to line up his party, the DUP, behind a demand for the political integration of Northern Ireland within the UK. The fact that Paisley's integrationist enthusiasm proved temporary did not detract from its significance in the context of Unionist community dynamics after the fall of Stormont. For Paisley clearly misread the mood: anger at what seemed to be a reward for Republican violence and an unjust punishment for the majority fastened on to Vanguard's excoriating attacks on the British government and arguments about infringements of Ulster's rights.[5] There was, of course, a respectable case to be made for integration, but this was not the moment for it to be sympathetically heard; additionally, Paisley's espousal of it was incongruous in the absence of any liberal or secular change in his brand of populist politics. It was ironic that two years on from the battle for the soul of Unionism at Bannside the position of Paisley and the Unionist Party should have been reversed, but this was more apparent than real in his case.

In the case of the Unionist Party there was a very real sense in which the party's populist credentials around the theme of Ulster identity were recovered by the fact of Craig's prominence and Vanguard's appeal to party members and voters. Faulkner still held the centre, but his position was weakened by defections of moderates to the Alliance Party, a development which would have profound consequences before long.[6] Attempts were made late in 1972 to have Vanguard membership declared incompatible with membership of the Unionist Party, but failed.[7] Faulkner knew that in the circumstances the party could not afford to lose the campaigning strength of Vanguard,[8] however distasteful he may have found the menacing nature of Craig's declarations of intent. Vanguard itself attracted disparate elements of Ulster Protestant society, its largely middle-class and right-wing activists standing in awkward alliance with the trade unionists of the Loyalist Association of Workers (LAW) and the working-class paramilitaries of the UDA whom Craig cultivated.[9] Had Craig become Unionist Party leader it is likely that his inclinations towards a more independent Ulster would have brought him up against the difficulties faced by earlier advocates of the same line such as W. F. McCoy, of breaking the outlook of many in the working class which valued the relative economic security of existing arrangements, particularly those relating to welfare and subsidised industry.[10] His attempts to revive the Unionist Party practice of incorporating 'Loyalist Labour', while notable in the short term, posed dilemmas in relation to the direction in which he wished to take Unionism. The increasingly pro-Dominion status and indeed Ulster independence noises emanating from Vanguard were to prove highly significant in dissuading many important Vanguard activists within the Unionist Party from following Craig out of it when the moment came.[11]

Morally, it would have been noble for the Unionist Party to dissociate itself from the threat, and the fact, of violence – Loyalist paramilitaries contributed amply to the overall pattern of terror and the first of their number were interred late in 1972 – but this would have been at the cost of the loss of Vanguard and the reduction of the party to a middle-class moderate rump. It is an inconvenient yet compelling conclusion that the accommodation of Vanguard in 1972 and early 1973, coupled with Paisley's identification with integration, ensured the Unionist Party's continuation as the main political voice of Protestant Ulster. The extremism of Craig inhibited Paisley's progress,[12] and the looseness of Unionist Party discipline permitted Craig's rebellious-sounding variety of Loyalism to prosper.[13]

Yet ultimately there was to be no Vanguard takeover. With hindsight Faulkner might have wrong-footed Craig by getting him on to the policy committee out of which a party document, *Towards the Future*, emerged in September 1972.[14] This policy statement bore the Faulkner stamp in its advocacy of a new Stormont legislature with a USA-style committee system to ensure maximum minority participation: it was essentially what Faulkner had offered the SDLP in 1971. But the document also contained a proposal for a joint Irish governmental council, and to this along with the rest Craig signed up. The document was unanimously approved by the Standing Committee of the UUC[15] and formed the substance of the party's contribution to talks about new constitutional arrangements for Northern Ireland convened by Whitelaw in September. However, Craig declined to attend these talks and distanced himself from Faulkner.[16]

The Unionist Party, in the absence also of the SDLP and the DUP, was seen to be pulling its weight. This impression was accentuated by the granting by Whitelaw of a 'Border Poll' on the constitutional status of Northern Ireland as part of the government's Green Paper of October, although the suggestion in the paper that any new Northern Ireland devolved arrangement would have to receive cross-community support was seized upon by Craig and repudiated. The plebiscite was duly held in March 1973 and, against a background of mass Nationalist abstentions, delivered a resounding verdict in favour of the Province remaining within the Union.[17] This provided the measure of communal reassurance required for the UUC's vote, by 381 to 231, accepting the British government's

White Paper of the same month on arrangements for a future Stormont assembly as a basis for negotiation. The outcome of this vote prompted Craig to leave the Unionist Party and set up what he termed the Vanguard Unionist Progressive Party (VUPP). For Craig and those who followed him, and for many others who did not, the White Paper's clear indication that the minority would have a share in executive power and that there would be an institutionalised Irish dimension was too much. The VUPP joined with the DUP (Paisley having now abandoned integration), the UDA, LAW, and sizeable elements within both the Unionist Party and the Orange Order to oppose the White Paper and demand the defeat of the IRA, the rejection of the Council of Ireland idea, full parliamentary representation at Westminster, and control of the RUC by Northern Ireland elected representatives.[18]

Unionism and Loyalism thus presented a jumble of disaffected groups and competing visions. Out of it all the Unionist Party emerged, still under Faulkner, weakened but not prostrate. Discontent and debate over the future spread itself across the party as it remained, with prominent former Vanguard figures such as the Reverend Martin Smyth, James Molyneaux, John Taylor and Willie Ross opting to stay inside the Unionist Party to carry on the struggle for what they viewed as traditional values and goals. All were to become important forces within the party.[19] Craig's increasingly belligerent pro-independence statements and his close association with Loyalist paramilitaries – he and Vanguard were discredited by the violent chaos of a strike in February 1973 over the internment of Loyalists – alarmed such former supporters who had always viewed Vanguard as a means to the greater good of the Unionist Party rather than an end in itself.[20] It was another crucial moment: had Smyth, Taylor, Molyneaux and others followed Craig the Unionist Party would have been fatally deprived of the claims it could still make to being a 'broad church'. Smyth,[21] a quiet 'party man', stolid and rather inarticulate yet firm and thoughtful in his convictions and judgements, was perhaps the key player: he was initially a delegate to the UUC of Belfast County Orange Lodge and his Orange connections helped to keep that organisational link intact at this time of crisis. There had been a split from the left, a split from the right, and there would be a split, in a manner of speaking, from the centre, but the Unionist Party with its unwieldy structures and antiquated organic links was proving more resilient than the tempestuous political environment suggested it should.

Nevertheless, the damage done to the party's organisation by the Vanguard breakaway was enormous.[22] It resulted in the closure of branches and even divisions within staunchly Unionist families. The party machinery took a long time to be re-established in areas like North Antrim, Mid-Ulster and parts of Belfast, although it proved stronger in areas such as South Down, Armagh and Fermanagh. The strength of Orangeism in rural and small town areas, particularly west of the River Bann, was a signal feature of the party's ability to survive, and factors such as these help explain the durability of the Orange link in spite of calls for its removal.

The party may also have been helped substantially through the lean periods of the early troubles by the work of its women members, both in constituency associations and the Women's Unionist Council. In May 1973 the *Unionist Review* discussed whether women should be given a guaranteed role in the new assembly which was being planned, and noted that the party's encouragement to women to play an active part had earned it the jibe from Paisleyite and other opponents that it was controlled by 'the fur coat brigade'. The jibe confused – deliberately no doubt – the evidence of women at the constituency work level with their profile in the ranks of party politicians and councillors and UUC office-holders, which in general was a very low one.

The impact of the troubles has been widely viewed as resulting in a lost generation of political talent generally in Northern Ireland, and David Hume certainly concurs with regard to the arena of local government, where of course the incentives in terms of the amount of power and patronage to be enjoyed were now severely limited.[23] The collapse of Stormont removed what had hitherto been the main local political focus, although the efforts to restore it from 1972 would have kept warm the ambitions of at least some aspiring legislators and rulers. The Unionist Party did undoubtedly suffer from a stuffy image, and young politically minded individuals were to be found in greater proportions in the DUP; moreover, those who joined Craig's VUPP possessed youthful talent which would much later find its way to the top of the Unionist Party.

Socially, the business and professional classes described by Harbinson[24] had dominated the Unionist parliamentary party in the old Stormont parliament, and this continued in slightly diluted form into the Direct Rule era. A study of 28 Unionist Party candidate profiles for the elections to the proposed new assembly in 1973 reveals 7 professionals, 5 farmers, 4 businessmen, 3 company directors, 3 managers, an architectural technician, a secretary, a voluntary welfare worker (female), a production supervisor, a parliamentary consultant, and a housewife.[25] Thus working-class and female candidates tended to be as conspicuous by their absence as before. On the other hand, Hume has noted that the profile of Westminster Unionist MPs after 1972 was markedly less elitist and more middle-class and lower-middle-class; Unionist representatives at Westminster in the Direct Rule era were much more than in the past the product of grassroots Unionism.[26] More interest, not surprisingly, was taken in the members who were sent to London and how they performed there.

The assembly elections, conducted under proportional representation for the first time since the 1920s, were reminiscent of the 'Crossroads' election called by O'Neill in February 1969 in as much as the electorate was presented with two classes of Unionist Party candidate. This arose out of the refusal of anti-White Paper candidates to sign up to a statement of party policy issued by Faulkner. The party leader had earlier taken refuge in an ambiguous form of words to circumvent the awkward issue of power-sharing: the party was not, he said, prepared to participate in government with those whose 'primary objective' was to break the Union with Great Britain. The object was to allow for the possibility of sharing power with the SDLP and it seems to have worked up to a point for Faulkner. Of the 39 'pledged' (as in signing up to the statement) or 'Official Unionist' candidates, 22 were returned. Ten 'unpledged' candidates were elected and in alliance with the DUP, VUPP and other Loyalists they formed a block of 28. The risks of pressing on to the kind of arrangements obviously favoured in the White Paper were thus already plain to Whitelaw, although the balance of opinion within the Unionist electorate was still quite fine. The British government was buoyed by the prospect of a deal being cobbled together between the Ulster Unionist Party (now increasingly referred to as the 'UUP'), the SDLP, Alliance and the NILP which would command cross-community support and also involve Dublin.

The 'pledged' and 'unpledged' divide in the UUP festered after the election when the 'unpledged' members, led by Harry West, complained of being the victims of 'a most deliberate and vicious campaign initiated from Party Headquarters and financed from party funds'.[27] Faulkner later admitted 'a tactical error' in not inviting the 'unpledged' to a meeting of the party in the assembly,[28] to which the 'unpledged' Jim Kilfedder, Chief Whip of the Unionist group of MPs at Westminster, retorted: 'I am not a second class Unionist representative. And I – and my colleagues – who are similarly placed, require no special invitation to join the Party, of which we are already members, in the Assembly.'[29] This round of infighting, however, was a mere prelude to more serious stuff surrounding the materialisation of a power-sharing deal.

This deal was carved out of a conference at Sunningdale in England in December 1973 in the wake of a narrow vote by the UUC against a motion rejecting power-sharing (379 votes to 369). The fine detail of the composition of the power-sharing executive raised fewer difficulties than the proposal for a Council of Ireland with executive powers.[30] The SDLP and the Irish government strove together to attain the latter on top of the 'double-barrelled' proportional representation of both assembly and executive, while the British government, in the person of Heath and new Secretary of State Francis Pym, prodded Faulkner into acquiescence. It was neither the first, nor would it be the last time that the negotiating odds were thus stacked against the Unionists. Even so there was surprise in government circles that Faulkner bowed to the pressure; veteran Stormont civil servant Ken Bloomfield, deeply involved in the process, says he doubted at the time that Faulkner could sell the package to the Unionist community.[31] As it was, the competing Nationalist and Unionist interpretations of what the deal meant pointed to obvious problems ahead: as Gillespie has commented, Nationalists wanted the Irish dimension to be strong and to develop into an all-Ireland administration, Unionists the exact opposite; Nationalists wanted reform of the RUC and the ending of internment, while Unionists wanted the scrapping of articles 2 and 3 of the South's constitution (which lay claim to the territory of Northern Ireland) and the South's cooperation on security, particularly on the matter of extradition.[32] The Irish government issued a declaration recognising the fact of Northern Ireland's existence although not its right to do so, and a court case in the Republic in January 1974 produced the verdict that Sunningdale did not contravene the Irish constitution and that the sovereignty claim remained.

Anti-Sunningdale Unionists, organised into a 'United Ulster Unionist Council' (UUUC), pounced on this; concentrating their fire on the Council of Ireland part of the deal ('Dublin is just a Sunningdale away'), they significantly shifted Unionist opinion further against it. Prior to the outcome of the case, Faulkner had lost a

UUC vote on the Council of Ireland by 457 to 374 and had resigned as leader of the party, to be replaced by one of his arch-critics, Harry West. UUP constituency associations began 'de-selecting' pro-Sunningdale candidates in favour of hardliners. The isolation of Faulkner, who later set up his own Unionist Party of Northern Ireland (UPNI), was probably the death knell for the agreement, although it is possible to speculate that the new executive which took office at the beginning of January might have worked to change minds had it not received another mighty blow at the British general election of February. The UUUC received just over half the vote in this contest, winning 11 out of 12 Westminster seats with only Gerry Fitt (now Faulkner's deputy in the executive) being re-turned for the SDLP. As they were returned on an anti-Sunningdale basis, Heath did not seek the support of the Ulster Unionist MPs, who included future party leader Molyneaux, the mercurial Kilfedder, and newcomers Willie Ross and Harold McCusker. Faulkner and his supporters got only 13 per cent of the vote. Worse for the executive in a sense was the fact of a new Labour govern-ment in London with no sense of proprietorial concern for the Sunningdale agreement beyond the general hope that it might bring peace to Northern Ireland. This was soon dashed by the Ulster Workers' Council (UWC) strike of May 1974.

The demand of the strike was either that the Council of Ireland should not be ratified by the assembly, or that an assembly election should be called. Frantic attempts to get the SDLP to agree to a dilution of the Council of Ireland proposals succeeded too late to prevent the stoppage, which, aided by paramilitary intimidation, soon became widespread and involved workers in the key power industry. The new Secretary of State, Merlyn Rees, chose not to use the police or army against the strikers, to the fury of the SDLP and the Irish government.[33] During the strike more than thirty people were killed by Loyalist bombs in Dublin and Monaghan. Harold Wilson, Prime Minister once again, made a broadcast in which he accused the strikers and those who backed them of 'sponging' on the British state. It was an ill-advised remark, although James Molyneaux has put on record his belief that Wilson had the ulterior motive of hastening the end of the executive by deliberately harden-ing the strikers' attitude.[34] Wilson, though, had a long history of antipathy towards Ulster Unionists dating from his baleful regard for the efficacy of the Ulster Unionist government's contribution to the war effort when he was a junior minister in the 1940s, and his 'spongers' accusation stands comparison – on a personal level – with 'the enemy within' indictment issued by Premier Margaret Thatcher of the striking miners in Britain ten years later. Both Wilson and Rees employed the facile 'they're only loyal when it suits them' argument, ignoring the complex bargaining at the heart of the workings of the UK as a whole, and judging Ulster Protestants by a criteria which would not be applied to other groups in the state.[35] Rees's anglocentric myopia (ironic given his Welshness) about the nature of the UK was crassly revealed in his memoirs when he justified the assertion that 'the Province was different' by the fact that Northern Ireland had a separate statute book, either neglecting to mention or being in ignorance of Scotland's separate legal system, to take but one further example of the institutional diversity within the polity.[36]

Rees, on the other hand, was well aware of what Nationalists refused to acknowledge, namely the breadth of support across the majority community which the strike commanded.[37] This included the UUP now led by West, Faulkner's supporters having largely followed him to a new political home. West formed a united front with Paisley and Craig as the politicians attempted, to the workers' annoyance, to claim credit for the success of the stoppage which was ensured by the resignation of Faulkner and the rest of the executive on 28 May.[38] If Republicans could boast of bringing down the old Stormont regime, Loyalists signalled that they could scupper any replacement for it of which they did not approve. It was a portent of the long political stalemate which was to ensue.

The hopes entertained by the British government that the pro-Sunningdale Faulknerite Unionists might regain lost ground were emphatically curtailed by the results of the British general election of October 1974. The UUUC increased its share of the vote and Faulkner's UPNI performed dismally. Faulkner had suddenly become a marginal figure, an undeserved fate yet an eloquent commentary on the risks involved in trying to alter the paradigm of ethnic politics so deep-rooted in Northern Ireland, and sufficient perhaps to warn off others who might have wished to do the same. The problem facing anyone from the Unionist side who sought to de-tribalise Ulster politics was the strength of the perception in that community of this being a weakening of the collective will to preserve the Union which would inevitably be exploited by Nationalists. There was a pessimistic belief that significant change would

automatically be to the Nationalists' advantage since the latter perceived no gain in the status quo. Against this background, it was not
at all surprising that the Unionist community considered the
changes prospected at Sunningdale to be weighted overwhelmingly
against them, and to herald a new political context in which the
initiative would pass to Nationalists to pursue their traditional
goals with their hopes enhanced.

The election was also notable for the defeat of Harry West in
Fermanagh and South Tyrone, which left him with the task of leading a party whose parliamentary activities were for the moment
confined to Westminster. Here, James Molyneaux was nominated
to lead the UUUC group, whose parliamentary strength could not
be ignored by a Labour government with so slim a majority in the
House of Commons. The acquisition for the UUP of the services of
Enoch Powell, returned for the seat of South Down after the sitting
member Captain Orr had been pressured into retirement,[39] decidedly strengthened the UUUC as a parliamentary force, and was an
indication that Westminster was to be regarded more seriously by
the UUP than at any time since 1921.

These developments created the conditions for the uneasy interaction and at times outright struggle between different political
approaches and brands of Unionism within the party. Powell's promotion of integration and his unequivocal faith in British parliamentary institutions was to clash with what he regarded as the
parochial emphasis on 'Ulster's' concerns and rights and demands
borne unflaggingly by West and other prominent party figures of
the period such as Austin Ardill and Martin Smyth. These Unionists
still put a premium on the return of devolved government, a cause
for which Powell had no time. Powell's influence over Molyneaux
resulted in the latter paying lip-service to the devolution goal while
in practice pursuing more integrationist ends. Of these, the efforts
of Powell and Molyneaux were successful in achieving an increase
in the representation of Northern Ireland in the House of Commons
from 12 to 17 seats, and they claimed credit for various other measures on issues such as security.[40] In the integrationist view Unionists
had to prioritise the redress of the democratic defects of the Direct
Rule system, such as the Orders in Council procedure for Northern
Ireland legislation by which there could be no amendments, just
debate. Thus Powell and Molyneaux argued doggedly that Northern Ireland had to be brought into line with other parts of the UK
such as Scotland in terms of the conduct of parliamentary business,

and that the Province should have local government powers and institutions on a par with the rest of the UK. Over the period of the Labour government of Wilson and James Callaghan from 1974 to 1979, the Unionist Party MPs, excepting the maverick Kilfedder,[41] played a careful tactical parliamentary game, attempting to extract as much as they could from the government.

This approach troubled Harry West back in Northern Ireland in what it omitted to prioritise and address. For the bulk of the party in Ulster there lingered a palpable sense of bitterness over events in 1972 and the subsequent trend in British policy away from local majority rule. In 1976 a party publication was still claiming that Northern Ireland had 'squatter's rights' which should not have been infringed by the suspension of Stormont:

> It can be seen ... that Northern Ireland as a constitutional entity within the United Kingdom, has been destroyed by processes which involved a reckless disregard for legality, constitutional precedent, the sanctity of agreements or the veracity of government spokesmen.[42]

This was the classic Vanguard line of argument from 1972 and an indication of the durable influence of that group's outlook on the party, represented of course by figures such as Smyth, Ardill, Taylor and indeed West.

Along with such arguments went a distinct current of anti-Englishness. There was the complaint that the Direct Rule regime was a way of giving top jobs to Englishmen,[43] and that the Secretary of State and his junior ministers were primarily concerned with their constituencies in England.[44] For party leader Harry West, the London 'establishment' was the enemy of Ulster's interests,[45] and in 1976 he contemptuously dismissed the suggestion, cultivated chiefly by Powell, that the Ulster MPs were truly influential at Westminster.[46]

In part this variety of Ulster Unionist politics constituted a chorus of renewed resentments and protests due to the failure of the Constitutional Convention of 1975–76. The Convention was the British government's attempt to let the local parties devise a solution for themselves, but, in the light of the election result of May 1975 in which the UUC won 47 out of the 78 seats, there was little likelihood of success. After much deliberation a majority report was produced rejecting both the idea of power-sharing as of right and an institutionalised Irish dimension.[47] The SDLP was not interested and the Convention was finally dissolved by Rees in March 1976. In late 1975 to the surprise of many, including some of his own followers who promptly repudiated him, Craig came out in favour of a 'voluntary' power-sharing scheme with the SDLP which did not involve an Irish dimension. It was a brave attempt to salvage a deal from the wreck of the Convention, but the SDLP's agreement was far from likely, and it proved a step too far for Craig, whose prospects of leading Unionism receded rapidly. Some of Craig's acolytes, such as the young David Trimble who supported his stance, would find their way back to the Unionist Party.[48] Meanwhile, disillusioned Vanguard party members formed the United Ulster Unionist Movement (UUUM) and elected Ernest Baird as their leader.

Feelings of being 'slapped down' again by the British government thus gripped the UUUC politicians, and within the Unionist Party such views contributed to tensions with the 'integrationists'.[49] While West, Ardill and others were flaying the British government for dismissing the Convention's recommendations and accusing it of encouraging the SDLP to be inflexible on the issue of guaranteed places in government, Powell was making friendly noises about the government and assuring Unionists that 'the Union is now less in danger and more secure than it has been at any time since 1968, and probably further back still'. He went on:

> With every passing month, as Parliament and Government accept Northern Ireland substantially as they accept the other parts of the United Kingdom, the bonds of Union grow gradually stronger with the strength of habit and common sense, which in time hardens into the strength of inevitability.

The House of Commons, according to Powell, was still 'the beating heart of political Britain' and the representatives of Northern Ireland now 'an integral part' of it, 'the living evidence of the reality and permanence of the Union'.[50] Powell, indeed, positively exulted in the collapse of the Convention.[51]

Powell stood for an ideal of fidelity to British political institutions which was much less subscribed to in the different parts of Britain, far less Northern Ireland, than he chose to believe. Just as he had clashed with Craig over the theme of unconditional loyalty in 1975,[52] so he could be found in May 1976 chiding his Unionist constituents and by implication his party leader about retreating into themselves and threatening to take the law into their own hands.[53] Powell could not fathom the ethno-nationalism inherent in

Ulster Unionism which found such expression as West's reference to 12 July as 'Ulster's national day' and his declaration that 'the Ulster people feel they are under attack in many subtle ways, all with the object of demoralising us, of breaking us up, of forcing us to accept institutions of government that we do not want and of taking from us our identity as a people'.[54] Unionists like West preferred to depict themselves as 'the dour Ulster-Scot in the last bastion' of 'true' British values.[55] Theirs was an essentialist abstraction as much as Powell's, and both were incapable of addressing the Northern minority's national, as opposed to social and economic, demands.

Powell, however, possessed a conception of the Union which in effect repudiated the interpretation of it as a partnership, or a series of partnerships. This was arguably how most Ulster Unionists, like most Scots, wished to view it, as Margaret Thatcher's later experience of Scottish perception of her rule indicated. Like Thatcher with the Scots, Powell could not forge a proper rapport with grassroots Ulster Unionists. 'Creeping integration' may have been an apt way to describe the political scene in relation to Northern Ireland from the mid to late 1970s, but it has also to be remembered that devolution was very much on the agenda for Scotland and Wales, and a consequent restructuring of the UK state seemed more than possible. All of this found expression within the Unionist Party in the 1970s, which still very much encompassed the 'two traditions' of 'Ulster Britishness' and 'Ulster Loyalism' analysed in seminal fashion by Todd.[56] Although West's utterances place him in the 'ethnic' or 'Ulster Loyalist' rather than the 'civic' or 'Ulster British' category – and it might be observed again that the categorisation is oversimplistic – he also made significant pronouncements as leader about the overriding priority of holding on to their broad and 'inclusive' character in order 'to hold the centre'.[57] This distinguished the UUP from other political parties and groups which appealed to the electorate, and thus bore down on the overall politics of the conflict. By 'holding the centre' it might be argued that the UUP kept the terms of the debate about Northern Ireland's constitutional future within certain bounds, although, as will be seen, attempts would be made to extend them.

For the remaining period of the Labour government, however, it was Nationalists rather than Unionists who complained more intensively. James Callaghan took over as Prime Minister from Wilson in May 1976 and installed Roy Mason as Northern Ireland

Secretary in September. Mason put the emphasis on security matters and the strengthening of the economy rather than constitutional initiatives. While devolutionists in the UUP were somewhat appeased by a tougher line on terrorism and public sector investment, the integrationists could point to SDLP discontent over issues such as the increase in the Province's representation at Westminster as proof of the effectiveness of their strategy. The tensions between the two were still rife throughout the party, but overall the period 1976–79 was a far less traumatic experience for Ulster Unionists than the years from the start of the troubles.

A greater sense of stability was reflected in the party's electoral performances. In the 1977 local government contests it made many gains, winning some 34 per cent of the council seats. This represented a marked recovery from the low point of the party's fortunes at the Assembly election of 1975 when it won only a quarter of the total vote. A party publication observed that the local election results had not yet fully restored it to 1973 'pre-crisis' strength, but that they were a reward for 'three years of steady and decisive leadership in an exceptionally difficult situation'.[58]

Shortly after these elections, moreover, the party withdrew from the UUUC, which promptly collapsed. This was ostensibly on account of attacks made on the party during the elections by other members of the UUUC, in effect Paisley and the DUP.[59] However, the ignominious failure of the attempt by Paisley, Baird and the UDA in May 1977 to conduct another Loyalist workers' strike, the aims of which were to restore majority rule Stormont and bring about more draconian security action against the IRA, made it imperative that the UUP should be seen to distance itself. The party had indeed come out against the strike when plans were announced in April.

Paisley was discredited by this episode, and its effects were probably still felt in the 1979 British general election when the UUP showing of 36.6 per cent of the vote contrasted starkly with that of 10.2 per cent for the DUP, although the latter's low share was also the result of its decision not to contest certain seats and divide the pro-Union vote. The DUP, it should also be said, gained both North and East Belfast, the latter seeing the triumph of the DUP deputy leader, Peter Robinson, over Craig, who had returned to the 'Official' Unionist fold, by just 64 votes. Craig then departed from public life. The Unionist Party's self-estimation in the wake of the election was that the party clearly held 'the major area of the "middle ground" in Ulster politics', and that it was 'the main body that has to be considered in any party-political negotiations'.[60]

This was fair enough, but events rather overtook the party's exercise in reassuring stocktaking. One month after the Westminster election, the European Assembly poll was held. On this occasion Paisley won a massive personal vote and John Hume performed impressively for the SDLP, but the UUP leader Harry West was humiliatingly eliminated and fellow candidate John Taylor only elected to the last of the Northern Ireland seats with 11.9 per cent of the vote. The result was undoubtedly due punishment for the party's ambiguous stance on the EEC. Since Heath had taken the UK into the European Community in 1973, the party had had no clear line for or against. Powell's opposition was well-known, but West and other leadership figures were more ambivalent, particularly since future decisions in Brussels pertaining particularly to agricultural issues looked set to be crucial. Many anti-EEC party voters thus probably plumped for Paisley to register their views.

The upshot was the resignation of West as party leader in September 1979. In a letter to 'Fellow Unionists' West apologised for the embarrassment caused to the party in his European defeat and acknowledged that he had lost the support and confidence of 'a large section of our party'. He went on to admit that the UUP also suffered from poor organisation, particularly in areas which had traditionally been strongholds, pointing to 'a distinct lack of active party workers on the ground'. The situation, he added, was reflected in 'the deplorably small and quite inadequate financial contributions coming from such areas, hence our party's present ridiculously precarious financial position'. In a clear reference to his own difficult experience of the past five years West recommended that the party

> fully support the future leadership in its rigorous insistance [*sic*] that precise and clear cut decisions properly taken by the appropriate organs within the party are adequately communicated to all levels and that no suspicion of confusion, disunity or deviation from party policy is allowed to develop in Ulster or Westminster.

He asserted that controversies over the EEC and devolution had cost the party dearly, before proceeding to restate firmly his own convictions on the necessity of devolved government being returned and the risks inherent in leaving Northern Ireland's fate to British governments to determine.[61]

West's parting shots reflected his own inability as leader to prevent the 'broad church', which he was on record as desiring the party to be, from nonetheless appearing to be a 'family at war' over certain key issues. In the circumstances of the Labour governments of the 1970s, especially from 1976, the Unionist Party managed electorally to cope with the open split in its ranks over devolution and integration. This was due to Unionist and Loyalist rivals discrediting themselves, and a generally more stable political context than 1972–74. The Unionist Party still 'held the centre' sufficiently to get votes from all directions of the majority community, left, right and centre depending on the circumstances of the different polls. It was also much more likely to receive Catholic Unionist support than any Unionist rival, although the small 'u' Alliance Party was probably the main beneficiary of these votes. However, on the EEC the party was decisively eclipsed by Paisley, and this was an issue which many voters clearly felt was separate from the ones they were normally obliged to pronounce on. Nevertheless, it was a warning sign for the UUP, and coupled with West's observations about the parlous state of party finances and organisation, it added up to a complicated overall profile. This was a party which found its way through the political chaos of the early 1970s to preserve and then strengthen its position as the main Unionist political voice absorbing many former defectors; but this was also at the cost of structural damage incapable of quick repair, and a drastic reduction in grassroots activism.[62]

The leadership of the Ulster Unionist Party passed to James Molyneaux, whose army service and 'Loyal Order' connections commended themselves to many in the movement. He saw off the challenges of the Reverend Robert Bradford, MP for South Belfast, and Austin Ardill to win comfortably at a specially convened UUC meeting in September 1979. This brought to an end the unhelpful conundrum of the party appearing to have a dual leadership: West in Ulster and Molyneaux – or as some critics alleged, Powell – in London. By the time of his resignation West had become exasperated by the situation and felt that Molyneaux was undermining him.[63]

Molyneaux had become 'Powellite' in practice even if he was in theory still in favour of a full measure of devolution. His preferred objective for the time being, evident in parliamentary interventions such as a notable speech in December 1976,[64] was for an 'administrative devolution' compromise, and he felt vindicated when the Conservatives included a pledge in their 1979 election manifesto to the effect that they would legislate for a new Regional Council for Northern Ireland through which the people would be given back control over major local government services. For Molyneaux this was what his party needed: it promised to bring Northern Ireland more into line with wider British practice and thus gave cheer to integrationists, while it was also capable of being interpreted as a step towards the restoration of devolved government. However, the author of this part of the manifesto, Airey Neave, to whom Molyneaux was close, was murdered by the Republican terrorist group the Irish National Liberation Army (INLA) in March 1979. When the Tories came to power under Margaret Thatcher the commitment was dropped in favour of another round of party talks convened by the new Secretary of State, Humphrey Atkins, aimed at achieving cross-community agreement.[65]

The Atkins conference was boycotted by Molyneaux, who was bitter over the about-turn by the Tories on the Regional Council scheme. There was some disquiet in the party about this, and West was later to claim that the boycott was a cardinal error in as much as it destroyed a chance for progress more acceptable to Unionists than what was imposed upon them later.[66] Molyneaux, somewhat ironically given West's past arguments of a similar nature, later defended his position by saying that he had opposed the attempt to move towards compulsory power-sharing since it involved permanent coalitions rather than coalitions which could be dissolved and replaced.[67]

As the Atkins conference was being wound up in March 1980, Molyneaux was telling Unionists that the days when they could hope for the kind of devolved government they believed was rightfully theirs had 'passed away', and that arrangements which allowed issues to be dealt with 'in a sort of committee spirit and without acute party-political contention' constituted a more worthwhile and realistic goal.[68] Molyneaux in effect hankered after the political and constitutional stability which he perceived as having crystallised during Mason's period as Secretary of State. However, it was dry stuff and not the most obvious way of keeping the DUP challenge at bay. On a personal level Molyneaux's pedestrian style and lack of charisma ensured that Paisley much more often commanded the media attention.

The Thatcher government, to Unionist dismay, chose to cultivate

Dublin in the aftermath of the demise of the Atkins talks. This was the beginning of a process of Anglo-Irish summitry which, notwithstanding many stoppages and diversions on the way, would lead to a crisis for Unionism. Molyneaux's inclination was to downplay it, and Paisley was left to exploit the sense of fear among many in the majority community. The impact of the Republican hunger strikes of 1980–81, which included the political breakthrough of Sinn Fein, produced even more rigid polarisation. Republicans strove to imitate their predecessors in a cult of blood; Pearse's pious injunctions found their late twentieth-century echo:

> Whenever death may surprise us, let it be welcome provided our battle cry reach some receptive ears, that other hands may reach out to pick up our torch and march in tune with our funeral dirge to the staccato of machine gun fire and new cries of battle and victory.[69]

This was the apostolic succession of the militaristic guardians of Ireland's 'honour'. The obstacle in their way, though it was never admitted in the rhetoric of 'the struggle', was still Protestant Ulster.

In the local government elections of May 1981, following first the election for Fermanagh and South Tyrone, and then the death of hunger striker Bobby Sands, the DUP polled marginally better than the UUP although the latter remained the strongest party in terms of seats. After the assassination by the IRA of Robert Bradford in November 1981, the DUP and the UUP got into an acrimonious row over the former's wish to put up a unity candidate at the subsequent by-election for the South Belfast seat. In the event, the DUP put forward one of its best-known personalities, gospel singer the Reverend William McCrea, while the 'Official' Unionists nominated Martin Smyth, still a leading Orange Order figure. Smyth won this battle of the dog collars comfortably, by over 5,000 votes from the Alliance candidate with McCrea a poor third. It was an indication that the UUP had again weathered the storm in an emotional and politically volatile period. Paisley's attempt in the second half of 1981 to bring into being a 'third force' to meet the security crisis seemed to backfire on him; it was looked upon largely as an exercise in bluster and alienated those Unionists for whom paramilitarism in all forms was anathema.

In 1982 the latest Secretary of State, James Prior, proposed elections to an Assembly which he envisaged as having power devolved to it in stages: this was dubbed 'rolling devolution' and its success or failure would turn on a threshold figure of 70 per cent agreement among representatives, thus meeting the criteria for cross-community consensus. Prior's plans got a dusty response from the UUP and its weak provision for an Irish dimension ensured the non-participation of the SDLP and Sinn Fein, although both fought the election.

Molyneaux and Powell led the charge against the government at Westminster. In the light of the Falklands War, from which Unionists were inclined to draw the conclusion that the government cared more about aggression against 2,000 people in the South Atlantic than against a million closer to home, Molyneaux sarcastically asked in the House of Commons if the government proposed to establish an 'Anglo-Argentine Council'.[70] Prior's venture was viewed darkly as the latest attempt to weaken Unionist resolve, and decidedly in the tradition of Heath and Whitelaw, 'the architects of power-sharing and the Irish dimension'.[71] The Unionist Party, indeed, somewhat turned the tables of militant posturing on Paisley, who involved the DUP purposefully in the committee work of the Assembly after the election.[72] The results of this contest left the Unionist Party as the largest group, with 26 seats to the DUP's 21, but perhaps the most notable, and ominous, performance was that of Sinn Fein in securing more than 10 per cent of first preference votes.[73]

The Prior Assembly carried on a rather nominal existence until fully dissolved in 1986. By then it had been superseded by an intergovernmental agreement between London and Dublin which dispensed with the principle central to 'rolling devolution' that the structures of government had to be acceptable to both sides of the community.[74] In the meantime the UUP retained its electoral supremacy in the 1983 British general election, winning 11 out of the 17 seats now provided for Northern Ireland, and 34 per cent of the poll to the DUP's 20 per cent. A pact between the parties had operated in three marginal seats.[75] The Unionist Party manifesto, 'The Only Way', was strongly integrationist and Powellite in its attacks on the 'autocratic' nature of Direct Rule and allegations about the Foreign Office and the Northern Ireland Office being in league with Dublin and Washington to undermine Northern Ireland's constitutional position.[76] On the Nationalist side Sinn Fein edged closer to the SDLP, and its main spokesman, Gerry Adams, was returned for West Belfast. The SDLP clearly required a tangible political achievement to reinforce its position within the minority community. The trend towards Sinn Fein was confirmed in the 1985 local elections, giving rise to havoc in local councils where Unionists of all shades refused to work with Sinn Fein. The Unionist Party scored nearly 30 per cent of the vote in these elections to the DUP's 24.3 per cent. In respect of local government, the UUP was still receiving a critical press over alleged discrimination in the matter of nominees and candidates for public bodies, and was reluctant to follow the direction of the Fair Employment Agency of which it scarcely held a more benign view than the DUP.[77]

The early 1980s also saw the emergence of potential party leaders in Harold McCusker and Robert McCartney, along with the continuing prominence of seasoned campaigners such as Smyth and Taylor. McCusker made a strong impression with reasoned arguments during the hunger strikes when Paisley was indulging in his 'Carson Trail' rallies, and he was instrumental in delivering the party support in border areas. McCusker, a trained school teacher and former training officer, identified with the Labour Party's social and economic critique of Thatcher, and was aware of how vital it was that the Unionist Party dispelled the image of being hidebound by entrenched interests. In 1981 he frankly admitted that the DUP's organisational structure and aggression compared favourably with those of his own 'constipated' party.[78] McCusker in effect styled himself in opposition to the party establishment.

Robert McCartney QC similarly presented himself as an outsider, but in his case there were also strong hints of an attempt to appear as a saviour. Playing strongly on his personal rise from the Shankill Road to the Bar, McCartney held out the promise of a radical transformation of the Unionist Party from its political thinking through to its *modus operandi*, and his rise to prominence from the time of a public clash with Paisley in December 1981 was suitably rapid. The party had by this time lost much of its appeal to such professional figures, and his arrival was initially welcomed. McCartney also supplied a relatively sophisticated brand of liberal Unionist polemics, which he had earlier in a professional capacity presented to the Dublin government.[79] His arguments centred on the Catholic nature of the Southern state and echoed the concerns of those liberal Unionists like Thomas Sinclair in the days of Irish Home Rule. In his impatience with the party's sluggish intellectual and organisational dynamics, and indeed physically, McCartney would, however, most closely resemble the troublemaking lawyer of the party's past, Edmund Warnock. McCartney's relationship with the Molyneaux-led Unionist Party proved turbulent and, within a short time, unsustainable. Ironically, this was largely on account of

McCartney's pressing the integration case too strongly for Molyneaux's comfort.

Nonetheless, McCartney could be said to have pointed Unionists towards engagement with the South, a task the party had resolutely refused to acknowledge as such. McCartney recognised that the Unionists had to challenge the ease with which simplistic narratives about the Irish problem and its historical roots dominated Nationalist Ireland and commanded such a sympathetic reception outside Ireland. David Trimble, a law lecturer, was engaged in a similar attempt to gear Unionists to a more informed appreciation of their cultural heritage and a sharper defence of the Unionist view of history.[80] In this respect, it was grossly remiss of the party not to take the opportunity of addressing the New Ireland Forum.[81] This was an exercise on the part of the 'constitutionalist Nationalist' tradition, North and South, to review and restate their position in relation to Northern Ireland and partition. The Forum Report did reflect a more considered appreciation of the Unionists' distinctiveness and their attachment to the Union, but it was also replete with time-worn assumptions and stereotypes, and a partisan historical narrative.[82] As Wilson suggests, it was incumbent on the Unionists to use the Forum to raise awkward questions and put the Republic of Ireland on the spot before a wide audience over issues such as articles 2 and 3.[83] As it was, the only Unionist voices to be heard were those of the McGimpsey brothers, Christopher and Michael, acting in a personal capacity. Both were to make their mark on the party.

The recommendation of the Forum Report was the traditional Nationalist objective of a 32-county unitary state. However, two other ideas were floated: that of a federal Ireland, and that of joint authority. Thatcher at first dismissed all three as possible political solutions, but it was to become clear before long that the joint authority option, as an influence on the deliberations between the two governments, had been taken forward.

The accord signed by the British and Irish Prime Ministers at Hillsborough on 15 November 1985, colloquially known as the 'Anglo-Irish Agreement', traumatised Ulster Unionism.[84] There had been warnings, but little inclination to heed them. At the Unionist Party conference back in April 1985 Molyneaux dismissed what he chose to regard as 'disinformation' about Thatcher's plans for Northern Ireland, and called her a 'straightforward politician'. He denied that Ulster's friends in parliament were 'a shrinking band' and referred phlegmatically to speculation about new initiatives and novel structures by saying that 'we have been put through all these hoops before'.[85]

Such complacency and trust in highly placed Tory allies, such as Thatcher's Parliamentary Private Secretary Ian Gow, left the Unionist leader signally discredited when the Agreement appeared to call the basis of the Union itself into question.[86] The Agreement formalised the joint British–Irish governmental approach to the Northern Ireland problem which had been foreshadowed since at least 1980 and previously at Sunningdale. It stopped significantly short of joint authority: the Irish government was given only a consultative role in the affairs of Northern Ireland. Nevertheless, it was a role designed to be meaningful in respect of Dublin's brief to look after the interests of the minority, and the 'determined efforts' (in the words of the Agreement) which were to be made to accommodate the South's views. Moreover, Dublin's supposed acceptance of the status of Northern Ireland within the UK was undermined by the different versions (British and Irish) of article 1 of the treaty, and by the direction in which the initiative pointed, namely a united Ireland.[87] The inter-governmental conference which was the fulcrum of the enterprise was to be concerned with sensitive issues such as security and justice. Indeed, improved security was the main objective of the British government in signing the agreement, while Taoiseach Garret Fitzgerald believed that a fairer deal for the minority would reduce their sense of 'alienation' and thus the likelihood of their supporting Sinn Fein.[88] The scope of the inter-governmental conference's deliberations could only be reduced in the event of devolved government being agreed and established in Northern Ireland.[89]

Unionists were furious at such an arrangement being foisted on them without consultation (the SDLP by contrast had been kept fully informed by Dublin). They believed it was the end of the Union as they knew it, and a flagrant attempt to demoralise them and reduce their capacity to resist being driven into a unitary Irish state.[90] They pointed to the ambiguities over Northern Ireland's status while articles 2 and 3 of the South's constitution remained intact. Indignation swept through the pro-Union community and almost of itself compelled the rival parties and leaders together in a show of defiant unity.

There ensued a protracted campaign of opposition which was steered by Molyneaux and Paisley, although the party leaders' evident desire to rebuild a negotiating platform with Thatcher was constrained by their followers. They were forced to stick to the position that the Agreement had to be scrapped before Unionists would consent to talks about an alternative. Unionist protests involved initially the mass rally in Belfast of 23 November at which Molyneaux counselled the need for staying power on the part of his fevered listeners, and the injured eloquence of Harold McCusker in the House of Commons.[91] Impassioned denunciations were then followed by a variety of strategies: the Unionist Party and the DUP turned the Prior Assembly into a vehicle of anti-Agreement commentary; they withdrew (with the exception of Powell) from participation in the Westminster parliament; a legal challenge was mounted; the Queen was petitioned; civil disobedience was resorted to; the work of local councils was boycotted leading to suspension in some cases; all Unionist Westminster MPs resigned their seats and fought by-elections in a 'referendum' on the Agreement in January 1986; and a general strike and 'Day of Action' took place in March 1986.

Assessments of such strategies – individually and collectively – have been critical:[92] they failed to remove the Agreement, the local councils boycott divided the body of Unionist Party councillors, the 'referendum' resulted in the loss of the Newry and Armagh seat to the SDLP, and the 'Day of Action' degenerated into violence against the police. Molyneaux declared in respect of the latter that he would have no truck with any such future event, and strains began to show in the party alliance. Furthermore, the 'Ulster Says No' slogan which fronted the whole campaign portrayed Unionists of all kinds as senselessly obdurate in the eyes of much of the British public and other outside opinion. As Aughey has observed, there was an unbridgeable gulf in understanding between Ulster Unionists and the British political classes over the Agreement.[93] What was widely viewed as a compromise essential to political progress and peace and stability, Ulster Unionists saw as a deadly threat to their survival, not only as UK citizens, but ultimately as a distinctive people. The Agreement for Unionists was an untrammelled victory for the SDLP, whose leader John Hume had indeed spoken of the need for the British government to 'lance the boil' of what he perceived as the Unionist veto on political progress. To Unionists, the British government had capitulated to the SDLP/Dublin agenda and accepted that moves had to be made towards the inevitable end of a united Ireland. In so doing, the government had played fast and loose with the Union in violation of the delicate balance of conditions and obligations which underlay it. The UK was regarded by Ulster Unionists, as the Scots regarded it, as a 'union state' in which the notion of parliamentary sovereignty could be trumped by that of popular sovereignty.[94] The maintenance of the Union required a particular form of statesmanship which entailed due recognition of the distinctive needs and histories of the territorial units. The Anglo-Irish Agreement did indeed raise many questions about the British constitution and the nature of the Union; 'People on the mainland', McCusker was later to say, 'who are never asked to define their Britishness, are now asking Ulstermen to abandon theirs.'[95] However, to the dismay of Ulster Unionists, there was no readiness on the part of the British politicians and parties to enter into such a debate. Weariness with the troubles of Northern Ireland resulted in a virtual consensus around the Agreement and a consequently baleful regard for Unionist objections. This situation was more than mirrored in the media, where the Unionist predicament was depicted, with a few exceptions, unsympathetically, and old clichés about stern-faced Ulster Protestants caught in a time-warp were given free expression. The Agreement was widely viewed in the British and Southern Irish media as spelling the terminal decline of Ulster Unionism.[96] Martin Cawley in the *Irish Times* struck such a note while barely able to suppress a sense of Nationalist triumphalism, yet also made an astute point about Unionism's relative lack of political skill:

> The swirling political process has left Unionist politicians battered and tense. Down the years under Stormont they have never felt the need to acquire the skills to play a deft role in a normal give-and-take political atmosphere. Now the learning process is more difficult than ever. They are in a corner unable to find a middle course between the knowledge that nationalism as an aspiration and philosophy is infinite and the suspicion that the Union may be finite.[97]

The Unionists' response to the Anglo-Irish Agreement indeed betrayed political naivety. They left themselves with no negotiating space and seemed to think that displays of defiance would bring Thatcher to her senses. As Wilson points out, they threw away another chance to highlight the issue of articles 2 and 3 and to create difficulties for Dublin.[98] Unionists generally failed to appreciate the damage to themselves in the adoption of certain tactics and stances in respect of outside opinion. Yet the other side of this coin was the unmistakeable, if negative, assertion of a collective will to let the world know that there would still be no united Ireland without an almighty struggle. Unionists had again demonstrated, if at a significant political cost to themselves, that they constituted a formidable problem for both governments. It might be added that the governments were forced to acknowledge the ferocity of Unionist objections, and that implementation of the Agreement was somewhat soft-pedalled.[99] Indeed, when the two governments began to bicker about security and legal matters the Unionists could afford to reflect that there was a post-Agreement future for them after all.

In this light it is perhaps more appropriate to indict Molyneaux's leadership in terms of a failure to grasp the changed priorities of the British government after such seismic episodes as the Republican hunger strikes and the clear swing towards Sinn Fein, as well as the joint British and Irish governmental agenda around this development. Moreover, it had been Molyneaux's decision to cold-shoulder Atkins and Prior, and he should have realised that this would entail a political price. It is less straightforward to conclude that Molyneaux's handling of the situation in the aftermath of the Agreement was disastrous for the Ulster Unionist Party. As will be shown, the party increased its electoral strength *vis-à-vis* the DUP, and Molyneaux generally kept Paisley in check, notwithstanding the latter's continuing propensity to be seen as the face and the voice of Ulster Unionism in its widest sense. The stress by both Molyneaux and Paisley on the paramount need for Unionist unity essentially benefited the Ulster Unionist Party.

Unity, however, also came at a price: the blunting of an ideological edge to the campaign against the Agreement. As Cochrane has shown in rich detail, the lack of ideological coherence within Unionism was particularly evident in the response to Hillsborough.[100] The framers of the Agreement had perhaps wished to trigger debate among Unionists about devolution and to encourage an acceptance of power-sharing. However, the debate which occurred was that between devolutionists and integrationists with the former very much on the defensive.[101] While devolutionists argued that the return of Stormont would prevent something like the Agreement being imposed again, they were handicapped by the widespread Unionist perception that devolution would be a 'trap' within the context of the Hillsborough Agreement; even the influential and liberal pro-devolution figure of Peter Smith, a lawyer who increased his profile in the Unionist Party in 1985, rejected devolution within the terms of the Agreement.[102] The task of promoting the devolution case within the UUP largely fell to those styling themselves 'the Charter Group', of whom former leader Harry West and David McNarry were the best-known representatives. The Charter Group made much of the appeal of regional autonomy, but its weak attempts to address the central question of power-sharing guaranteed a lack of response from the SDLP, whose priority in any case appeared, post-Hillsborough, to be the consolidation of the prize of an Irish dimension. Indeed, the UDA's power-sharing devolutionary proposals published in 1987 under the title 'Common Sense' elicited a more favourable political reaction across the spectrum.

In the wake of the Agreement integrationism came to be redefined as the right of the Northern Ireland people to participate fully in the politics of the UK, specifically through the British party system. From Molyneaux and Powell's 'minimalist' integration ideas concerning the regulation of Northern Ireland business in the Westminster parliament, the argument progressed to 'electoral' integration: the reason why Westminster had acted so 'despotically', it was claimed, was the absence of proper Northern Irish representation in the parties of the state, or the parties likely to form the government. Integrationists within the Unionist Party, fuelled by the lucid polemics of a small bunch of left-wing commentators outside of it,[103] raised the banner of 'equal citizenship' and demanded the right to join and vote for the British political parties. They were championed by Bob McCartney, who delighted in the irony of the language and slogans of the civil rights era being pressed into service for Unionism, and they included many younger activists in the party.[104]

The 'equal citizenship' campaign caught the imagination for a brief period, but it collided with the innate conservatism of the UUP and the party's refusal to sacrifice its uneasy internal unity. Molyneaux's approach was geared towards fostering an impression of the future from which both integrationists and devolutionists could draw comfort; the electoral integrationists, by contrast, demanded that a clear choice be made. Molyneaux, and the important 'fixer' figure of Frank Millar who was General Secretary of the party from 1983 to 1987,[105] saw the danger of a split and moved to head it off. The implications of the equal citizenship campaign involved Unionist Party members and voters being urged to ditch their own party in favour of one of the British parties. Moreover, McCartney was happy to condemn the past shortcomings of Stormont in the espousal of his argument that devolution had been discredited. It was thus no surprise that the familiar charges of disloyalty and betrayal emerged from the Unionist Party in its concern for what was seen as its honour as the voice of Protestant Ulster. McCartney lost a key vote at the party conference of November 1986 and was expelled in May 1987 as the party prepared for the British general election around the theme of Unionist unity and the alliance with the DUP and other Unionists against the Agreement.

In the joint manifesto for this election entitled 'To Put Right a Great Wrong', there appeared the uncompromising statements:

> The inter-governmental conference is joint authority with the Irish Republic. Politicians who spawned the Provisional IRA can now fly into Stormont to issue instructions and cross-examine Ulster's security chiefs.
>
> There cannot and will not be any return to normal parliamentary practice until the process of negotiating an alternative is under way.[106]

The election outcome saw the Unionist Party lose Powell's seat of South Down, although the pact between the party and the DUP rendered the latter much weaker than before. This led to much discontent within the camp of the Unionist Party's rivals, and in some constituencies a low turnout of DUP voters.[107]

Those who had supplied the arguments for the equal citizenship integrationists accused the Unionist Party of opting for 'Protestant communalism' and thereby maintaining the main obstacle to proper Catholic participation in the politics of the UK state.[108] A significant number of party activists, motivated it appears by such a non-sectarian and secular perspective, followed McCartney out of the fold. A moment which could have produced a genuinely new Unionism – although one which had no ultimate place for the Unionist Party and would assuredly have run into great difficulties of another sort[109] – thus passed.

The focus switched to the report of the Task Force which had been set up in 1986 by both Unionist parties, comprising Millar and McCusker and Peter Robinson of the DUP, to refortify the opposition to Hillsborough and to provide a political way forward. The report was delivered after the 1987 election, and proved too radical for the party leaders in its willingness to consider power-sharing and, it has been suggested, devolved government 'outside' the UK.[110] The latter appears to have been floated by McCusker, whose disillusionment with British politics led him to muse on independence.[111] The independence idea indeed received something of a fillip in the outraged post-Hillsborough mood among Unionists, and ventures such as the establishment of the 'Ulster Clubs' in 1986 could be said to have marked a certain degree of organisational preparation for such an eventuality.[112] Yet the most striking feature of the range of Unionist and Loyalist reaction was its incoherence: bitter arguments about tactics and the future of Unionism raged behind a screen of unity held together incongruously by Molyneaux and Paisley. As the Unionist war of attrition against the Agreement continued, able activists of both parties resigned and left political life, perhaps the most notable example being that of Frank Millar in protest at the Task Force's (abridged) report 'An End to Drift' being in effect shelved. In a frank interview in 1989 McCusker averred that Unionists were 'punch drunk' and all they could do was 'counterpunch'. They had no policies except obstruction, he said, and were 'leaderless'.[113] Ken Maginnis, a liberal Unionist figure (and a non-Orangeman) who perhaps salvaged something for the party in relation to the media during this period, disparaged what he saw as his party's tendency to procrastinate and simply wait and hope for some favourable turn of events.[114] This was a clear criticism of Molyneaux's approach.

Nevertheless, Molyneaux faced down his critics and weathered the storm of pessimism, if unable or unwilling to do anything to clarify his party's ideological confusion. He was fond of referring to the party's policy statement of 1984, 'The Way Forward', to deflect pressure. This document envisaged a purposeful devolved assembly with substantial administrative functions and a committee system composed on a proportionate basis to assume control of regional services.[115] It was clearly no basis on which to address post-Hillsborough realities, but in the absence of an alternative which commanded widespread support in the party, it was made to suffice. Additionally, and perhaps more crucially, Molyneaux could point by the end of the 1980s to the limits of the operation of the Agreement, and the sense that Unionists' worst fears had not been realised.[116] At the party conference in November 1988 Molyneaux observed that the realities surrounding the Anglo-Irish 'diktat' were becoming clear to people in London and Dublin: 'I am not ashamed of our strategy of battening down the hatches until those who have chosen the road of confrontation in the Anglo-Irish Agreement come to their senses'.[117] In the 1989 local government elections the

UUP polled over 31 per cent of the first preference votes in comparison with the DUP's 17.8 per cent and the SDLP's 21 per cent.[118] Molyneaux told the UUC in 1989 that 'firm constitutional guarantees will succeed where political solutions have failed, and where futile political initiatives result in yet more savagery'.[119] This was an expression of the Unionist leader's famous intolerance for political 'high wire acts'. By the end of the decade he believed his message was getting through.[120]

The British government was frustrated by the extent to which the Anglo-Irish Agreement became an impediment to reaching political agreement within Northern Ireland itself. A new Secretary of State, Peter Brooke, was installed in July 1989 and began a long and tortuous process of establishing a framework for talks between the Unionist parties and the SDLP. Brooke also put out feelers to Sinn Fein, raising the possibility of its inclusion if IRA violence ceased. In January 1990 he encouraged Unionists to believe that there could be a negotiated alternative to the Agreement. In November of the same year he somewhat dismayed them by stating that Britain had no selfish, strategic or economic interest in Northern Ireland, although many were inclined to conclude that this had been obvious for some time.

In March 1991 the UUC approved the Unionist Party's participation in a three-stranded talks process along with the DUP, the SDLP and Alliance.[121] Brooke agreed to suspend the operation of the Anglo-Irish secretariat for a fixed period of ten weeks. Wrangles soon followed about the venue for talks and the chairman. Some progress was apparently made in relation to strand one – the attempt to establish an agreed form of devolved government for Northern Ireland. However, the contentious nature of strand two – relations between Northern Ireland and the Republic (now with a Fianna Fail government led by Haughey) – hung ominously over deliberations. Unionists again demanded the removal of articles 2 and 3 of the Republic's constitution. The talks were wound up as the ten-week 'window' closed, and then resumed in September, but no breakthrough was achieved. This was hardly surprising since Unionists were trying to get rid of the Anglo-Irish Agreement to which Hume and the SDLP were so committed.

One interesting feature, however, was the presence on the UUP talks team of David Trimble, whose profile was steadily rising. Trimble had been elected to Westminster at a by-election in Upper

Bann in 1990 following the death of McCusker. In this contest the Unionist Party firmly rebuffed the challenge of a Conservative candidate, who lost her deposit and scuppered the momentum of her party which had begun to organise in certain constituencies in the Province a year earlier. Following the election, John Taylor referred derisively to the Tories flying 'Hooray Henries' into the constituency, and asserted that the UUP did not follow either Labour or Tory parties 'like sheep into their lobbies'. He added that while the party supported the general thrust of the Tory economic and foreign policies, it had also voted against the government on pensions, the freeze in family benefits, the imposition of student loans and hospital closures, as well as, of course, the Anglo-Irish Agreement.[122] In his maiden speech, Trimble raised the issue of electoral integration and claimed that the Unionist Party was 'the national British parties in Ulster' in that it was in effect a coalition of Tories, Liberals and Labour supporters.[123]

Trimble was assigned to strand three of the talks, that dealing with the relationship between Britain and the Republic. Unionists were unhappy that there was not a 'fourth strand' centring on the relationship between Northern Ireland and Britain,[124] but Trimble nonetheless was able to push the idea of a Council of the British Isles which dated back to his Vanguard days.[125] Molyneaux, indeed, signalled at the UUP conference in 1990 that such a framework would be appropriate for the resolution of the Ulster conflict.[126] The Unionist Party essentially insisted that the hated Hillsborough structures had to be transcended, and it was on firm ground in arguing that the Agreement did not provide an adequate context for east–west relations.

Brooke's attempts to restart the talks in early 1992 fell victim to his own blunder in singing on an RTE television show in the immediate aftermath of an IRA atrocity which killed seven Protestants. It was to be the way he was best remembered, since in April 1992 the UK went to the polls, and Prime Minister John Major received an unexpected, if marginal, endorsement.

The election saw the Unionist Party attempt to position Northern Ireland in the context of the debate on constitutional reform which was gaining momentum in Britain, and also in the context of an increasingly regional-conscious European Union. Molyneaux's message in the party manifesto was 'Alone no more'. He claimed that although Northern Ireland had been treated separately through various initiatives for many years, the goal of 'Union through parity' was in sight. Molyneaux referred to 'the great debate on decentralisation of powers to regions' and was particularly mindful of the Scottish question; he had indeed been involved in discussions with representatives of the Scottish Constitutional Convention which had been set up in 1989 to produce a blueprint for a devolved parliament.[127] The Unionist Party tried to take advantage of the sense in which thinking about devolution and constitutional re-structuring had caught up with Northern Ireland: the Province in the early 1990s now seemed less of a constitutional anomaly and more of a case study from which important lessons could be learned. As the Unionist Party manifesto put it:

> We have unrivalled experience of the mechanics of devolution. In the 'current discussions' we are designing blueprints and models which are attracting much interest in the other component parts of the United Kingdom. We have a head start on those who are just embarking on the great adventure.[128]

The party signalled its desire to join the process of the constitutional reshaping of the UK, but stressed that any system of government which could not equally be applied to any other regional entity within the UK would be unstable.[129] Chris McGimpsey, at the time of the election, suggested that Northern Ireland should receive a similar system of legislative devolution to that being floated for Scotland; he foresaw a 'coalition' government in Northern Ireland under such a set-up, while David Trimble envisaged Northern Ireland being part of 'a system of decentralisation' throughout the UK. Such interventions, along with Molyneaux's continuing efforts to have Northern Ireland business conducted along Scottish lines at Westminster, were directed towards the goal of removing the exceptionalism of Northern Ireland within the UK. It was an approach which combined traditional Unionist objectives with flexibility over reform and constitutional renewal and an apparent willingness to move with the times.[130] It blended with the re-emergence of 'federal' thinking in relation to the UK: politicians, academics and journalists all floated 'Home Rule All Round' or genuinely federal schemes for the UK which usually included Northern Ireland.[131] It was a context in which the profound diversity of the UK was properly acknowledged in public debate, and it was a crucial moment in the development of the political thinking which lay behind the constitutional reforms of the late 1990s.

The early 1990s was in fact a period in which the Unionist Party lifted its sights and avoided political navel-gazing. Its more thought-ful spokespersons attempted to assimilate the enormous impact of world events in the 1989–92 period, such as the development of the European Union, the collapse of Soviet communism, the ending of the Cold War and the recrudescence of ethno-national conflicts. The party woke up to the need to present its message more cogently outside Northern Ireland, and to expose the limitations of Nation-alist political thinking which still centred on the increasingly out-dated model of the nation-state. Michael McGimpsey was to write in the Unionist Party journal in 1994: 'Unionism as a philosophy remains strong and in its refusal to countenance the heresy of Nationalism, is remarkably in harmony with the spirit of the new Europe'.[132] The Unionists also began to play more effectively the 'identity politics' of the day and to exploit the trend towards plural-ist structures of government and the spread of self-determination opportunities. Martin Smyth asserted that self-determination was the 'core element' of the Unionist philosophy, and that the Province was distinctive both from the other parts of the UK and from the Republic of Ireland.[133]

John Major's return to power rather upset the calculations of the Unionists, who had been preparing themselves for the return of a Labour government with a reform agenda. Major's Conservative government was to stand firm against devolution for Scotland and any scheme of broad constitutional restructuring, and it was to em-ploy much rhetoric about the cohesion of 'the British family' to jus-tify its position. On Northern Ireland, the government took a very different line and continued to put it in an exceptional context. A new Secretary of State, Sir Patrick Mayhew, was given the task of re-igniting Brooke's initiative, and duly suspended the inter-govern-mental conference to allow for talks. The three-stranded approach was again adopted.

The process continued until November 1992 and was most nota-ble for the Unionist Party's decision to proceed to discussion on strand two before agreement could be reached on strand one. This involved the party in a historic trip to Dublin where it found the government led by Albert Reynolds unwilling to budge on the cru-cial issue of articles 2 and 3 of the Irish constitution. The Unionist Party was to bask in the novelty of a favourable press, as well as the widespread perception that its Nationalist opponents both North and South were also capable of intransigence.

In the course of the talks the UUP presented a range of proposals which included a power-sharing assembly based on proportionality; a change to articles 2 and 3; a Bill of Rights for Northern Ireland; a coordinating body in a Northern Ireland assembly to cover cultural expression and diversity; an Inter-Irish Relations Committee (IIRC) to deal with cross-border issues; and a Council of the British Isles to consider 'the totality of relationships'.[134] The party's flexibility and imaginative thinking contrasted with the DUP, which withdrew from the talks and condemned the UUP for going to Dublin. However, such criticism also came from within the Unionist Party ranks, and there were top-level disagreements over the nature of the IIRC in particular. Ken Maginnis's late submission to the process on strand two went beyond many prominent party members' bounds of acceptability, and Maginnis also clashed with Trimble in respect of the latter's desire to make the IIRC effectively subordinate to the Council of the British Isles.[135]

The failure of the talks was the result of many factors, but it became clear that John Hume's priorities were shifting in the direction of his dialogue with Sinn Fein and its leader, Gerry Adams. The British government too seems to have been edging towards the conclusion that a settlement would have to involve Republicans and indeed Loyalist paramilitaries. In December 1992 Mayhew, in a speech at Coleraine, echoed Brooke's 'no selfish interests' remarks but with a more ominous significance for Unionists, for whom the notion of the British government as a neutral 'referee' was an increasing liability.

Molyneaux, in the light of the potential leverage with which the post-election parliamentary arithmetic left the Unionists, refocused on that arena. Pressure was applied for concessions such as a Northern Ireland Select Committee and the UUP notably swung behind Major during the knife-edge vote on the Maastricht Treaty. Denials of deals being secretly agreed seemed disingenuous as the government indicated that the Select Committee would be provided and other parliamentary anomalies addressed.[136] The Unionist Party seemed to be playing a good tactical game, although it could not afford to overplay its hand: the Irish policy of the Labour opposition which would form any alternative government was being directed by the very 'green' Kevin MacNamara. Back in Northern Ireland the party won 29 per cent of the first preference votes at the local elections in May 1993, comfortably ahead of the DUP with 17 per cent.[137]

However, the extent to which the British government was

concerned to accommodate the agenda of 'pan-nationalism', comprising Hume, Adams and the Dublin government, was made evident in the 'Joint Declaration' at Downing Street by Major and Albert Reynolds on 15 December 1993. As one scholarly commentator has put it, this 'bought in' to the Republican analysis just as the Anglo-Irish Agreement had bought in to that of the SDLP.[138] It validated the idea of Irish self-determination although it stipulated that both parts of the island had to endorse any new settlement separately, if concurrently. Northern Ireland's destiny was still technically in its own hands, yet the signs on the constitutional map pointed, as at Hillsborough, to the one destination of a united Ireland.

The Unionist Party neither welcomed nor repudiated the declaration. It was to claim that Molyneaux had been successful in diluting the Nationalist and Republican content of it to the point where it no longer fundamentally threatened Unionists. Molyneaux, it was stated, ensured that anything implying joint authority or a place for Sinn Fein at the talks table or the idea of the British government 'persuading' for a united Ireland was not in the declaration. Although the Unionist Party still objected to 'overtly nationalist phraseology' and was dismayed, if not surprised, that articles 2 and 3 were left untouched, it was content to let the DUP monopolise the familiar Unionist rhetoric of betrayal.[139] This was a risky game and it worried a large number in the party. Molyneaux's role in the preparation of the declaration was applauded by some, but failed to convince many others such as the rising star David Trimble.[140] Molyneaux seemed to want to build on the party's improved image of being constructive peace-builders, forged through the Brooke–Mayhew talks, and he also felt that the procedural reforms he had wrested from the government at Westminster, such as the Select Committee, would soon come to be seen as more substantial developments. For Molyneaux the fact of the democratic deficit being addressed in a practical way outweighed a form of words designed to wean the IRA away from violence.

Signs of unrest in the Unionist Party were evident at the UUC AGM in February 1994 when certain figures deemed too moderate, including Chris McGimpsey, were ousted from their positions and replaced by hardliners. A group calling itself 'the Craigavon Society' appeared to be orchestrating an anti-Molyneaux chorus of criticism.[141] Paisley, after labelling Molyneaux a 'Judas', won his customary huge personal vote in the European election of June

1994, but the Unionist Party candidate Jim Nicholson improved his vote slightly on 1989. Then the occurrence of the IRA ceasefire in August and that of the Loyalists six weeks later appeared to herald a historic opportunity for a lasting peace after a quarter century of troubles. The Unionist Party in general did not disturb the mood of cautious optimism, although many in the party were sceptical.

The crunch for Molyneaux's leadership came with the publication of the two Framework Documents by the two governments on 22 February 1995.[142] These, generally referred to afterwards as the one 'Framework Document', built on the Downing Street declaration and reinforced that document's orientation towards an all-Ireland context. There were proposals for internal devolved structures in Northern Ireland, but more significantly there was a North–South freestanding executive dimension and a contrastingly weak provision for east–west relations. Indeed, there was a distinct absence of mechanisms for strengthening the links between Northern Ireland and the UK. Molyneaux's attempts, in the shadow of the Anglo-Irish Agreement, to slot Northern Ireland more firmly into the structures of UK governance appeared to have come to little. Notwithstanding the critical appraisals of the Major government's inconsistencies over constitutional reform issues, which came from Scottish and Welsh Nationalists and devolutionists and advocates of general UK reform as well as Ulster Unionists, the upshot appeared to be the belief on the part of another Conservative government that Northern Ireland was not part of the 'British family', or the Union, on the same terms at least as the other parts.[143]

The Framework Document was extensively trailed and the Unionist Party attempted to pre-empt it with a document of its own the day before the two governments announced their plan. The Unionist paper rejected the idea of all-Ireland institutions unrestrained by a Northern Ireland assembly. 'It would appear', the document stated, 'that the Government believes it can create a divide between the greater number of people in Northern Ireland and the Unionist leadership, and hopes to use a referendum to deliver Northern Ireland's affairs into the hands of All-Ireland political institutions.'[144] On 10 March a 'Response' by the party emphasised Major's inconsistencies on devolution for different parts of the UK and accused him of 'brain-washing our people that they must be made *different* so that they may be more easily detached!' It was claimed, moreover, that the Framework Document undermined the principle of consent and would lead inexorably to joint authority and a united Ireland.[145]

The Unionist Party now found it difficult retrospectively to justify its acquiescence in the Downing Street declaration and was roundly condemned by Paisley, who identified this as a key development in encouraging the governments to pursue a path inimical to Unionist interests. Molyneaux now appeared to have trusted in a British Tory government not once, but twice with deleterious results. An index of the loss of confidence in his leadership was to be found in the audacious challenge to his position at the UUC meeting in March when a 21-year-old student won 15 per cent of the vote. This was followed three months later by the North Down by-election victory of Bob McCartney, by this time a seasoned detractor of Molyneaux's minimalist style. The Unionist Party candidate vainly defended his leader: 'perseverance, consistency, and having the courage to get up and fight back after every set back'.[146] The trouble was that Unionists were getting fed up of setbacks thought to be caused in no small measure by a consistent failure to read the whole political game and play it incisively. McCartney pronounced the days of 'Wee Jim' to be over,[147] and two months later they indeed were.

Molyneaux resigned the day after his 75th birthday with a statement of characteristic economy and dryness. He had been leader sixteen years. There had been moments of statesmanship, and times when his calming influence had been beneficial. He was beyond question a respected parliamentarian. However, the regular tributes to his 'shrewd, tactical judgement'[148] seem over-generous against the failure to prevent, or even anticipate, the two momentous intergovernmental landmarks of 1985 and 1995. After all, Molyneaux himself set the terms by which he has to be judged: 'as a Privy Councillor I have an insight into what can and cannot be done by government'.[149] He made a virtue of low-key leadership and clearly saw it as appropriate to the party he led. 'The Unionist Party', he stated, 'as the only one with experience of government, possesses a degree of responsibility and a sobering realism which is unique here.'[150] But the party's experience of government counted for less with each passing year of Direct Rule, and political sobriety proved only partly successful overall in fending off the populism of Paisley and the DUP. There was a certain sense in playing the quiet man to Paisley's raucous political gunslinger during opposition to the Anglo-Irish Agreement; this produced a blend of styles which held the alliance together. Yet this was an ambiguous achievement. Unionist unity was bought at a price of serious estrangement from the British government and British political life more generally, and it probably hindered ideological development and the formulation of sharper policies. The Unionist Party was certainly a broad church with a conservative backbone and not a vessel to be moved rapidly or steered whimsically; nevertheless, minimalism bordered danger-ously on ossification. It was perhaps no accident that lively minds and able organisers often felt that they did not belong. The lack of a strategy to appeal to working-class voters was apparent until a half-baked attempt to reinvent the Unionist Labour Association in the final months of Molyneaux's leadership.

Despite being leader for so long Molyneaux failed to promote the party effectively outside Northern Ireland,[151] and made scarcely any impact on the vital issue of the modernisation of the party. Es-sentially there was still too much power resting in the constituency associations. The diversity between constituencies, including the criteria for membership, meant that the total membership of the party could not even be calculated. Internal discipline was still a chronic problem.[152] The party, moreover, remained resolutely male in Molyneaux's time: the participation of women did not receive the encouragement from the top it should have, and hidebound atti-tudes prevailed to the discomfort of some of those women who struggled to make their presence felt.[153] In the 1980s the percentage figure of women candidates for the party at local elections was four-teen.[154] There was a similar complacency on Molyneaux's part re-garding the party's relationship to the Orange Order. Asked about this by Roy Bradford, who had favoured breaking the link back in the 1960s, Molyneaux spoke of Orange audiences being a truer 'lit-mus test' of opinion than purely party audiences, and he thought it reasonable for the Unionist Party to appeal for Catholic votes without any change to the relationship.[155]

It would not be just in reaching a verdict on Molyneaux's leader-ship to lose sight of the parliamentary accomplishments of the early 1990s which seemed to reprise those of his period as Unionist leader at Westminster in the 1970s, or to ignore his alertness to the chang-ing nature of the constitutional debate in the UK as it developed over his time as leader. Nonetheless, as UUP leader he needed to be much better at appreciating changing political developments as they affected and were affected by Irish Nationalists and Republicans. His failure to realise the full political significance of the Republican hunger strikes, as well as that of John Hume's dialogue with Gerry Adams against a background of radical rethinking in the Republican movement, left Unionism at a distinct disadvantage at pivotal moments. Molyneaux proved to be an inadequate guide and teacher for his own party and beyond that the Unionist community. He left his party poorly prepared for the task of persuasion which faced all parties in 'the politics of solution seeking in Ireland' which was the crucial testing ground of leadership.[156]

Molyneaux was succeeded, to the surprise and consternation of many, by David Trimble. As a former law academic with a personal history of Vanguard activism, Trimble aroused suspicions in the Unionist Party on both counts. He was considered too intellectual as well as too personally ambitious. There was something of an echo of the wariness which had surrounded Faulkner – another 'clever wee man' – during his rise to the top, and the comparison with Faulkner would not stop there.

Several factors caused a doubtful UUC to elect him on a night of high drama at the Ulster Hall in Belfast. The leadership election contest of 8 September 1995 ranged the experienced figures of John Taylor, Ken Maginnis, Martin Smyth and Willie Ross against the relatively youthful Trimble (aged 50), who was, in fact, the last to declare that he would stand. He did so, it seems, after consulting close associates such as Gordon Lucy, John Hunter, Nelson McAusland and David Brewster, all of whom wished devoutly for a radical change of leadership style and were unenthused by the other runners. This pool of support came from those to the right of the party who imagined that Trimble would be more effective, particularly in relation to the media and the refashioning of Unionism's external image, in combating Nationalism. Trimble seemed to fit the bill of a proactive leader more convincingly than his rivals, and he had made a favourable impact as an able and energetic MP at Westminster. In addition, Trimble had also come to national prominence in the summer of 1995 over the bitter dispute at Drumcree in Portadown concerning the local Orange lodge's right to march its usual route from Drumcree Parish Church to the town centre along the Garvaghy Road, on either side of which there lived resentful Catholic residents. The conclusion of the 1995 struggle over the issue in the marchers' favour was crowned by a triumphalist gesture involving both Trimble, the local MP, and Paisley. Both were subsequently honoured by the Orange Order for their efforts on the

Portadown lodge's behalf. Trimble's prominence contrasted starkly with the absence of the Grand Master, Martin Smyth.[157] The support of the Orange Order delegates at the leadership contest appears to have switched in significant measure from Smyth to Trimble; the former polled a humiliating 60 votes on the first ballot and was eliminated.

Nevertheless, John Taylor was still the clear favourite before the election and it was his substandard speech on the night which has been identified as a key factor in the late transfer of support among delegates to Trimble.[158] Trimble and Taylor went into a final third ballot in which Trimble secured 466 votes against the latter's 333. Maginnis's liberalism limited his appeal, and he was thought to have been prepared to concede too much to Dublin back in 1992; Ross was primarily scuppered by his identification with Molyneaux.[159]

The fears of those inside, but mostly outside, the Unionist Party that Trimble's victory would herald merely a different style of uncompromising Unionism were confounded from the start. A symbolic meeting with the Southern Irish politician, Democratic Left leader and former IRA ideologue Proinsius de Rossa was followed by a meeting in Dublin with the Taoiseach, John Bruton. Gordon Lucy recalls being summoned to Unionist Party headquarters weeks after Trimble's election to talk about ways of involving the Republican movement in the political process. Lucy and others who had backed Trimble became quickly disillusioned with the direction they felt Trimble was preparing to take the party.[160] Trimble quite simply wasted no time in establishing that his approach would be more flexible than anticipated; if people had chosen him for his ability to articulate the Unionist case before the world then they would also have to accept that he would take the Unionist Party to the thick of the action where purist posturing yielded no results.[161]

With hindsight it can be divined that Trimble approached the task of party leadership in the spirit of an address he gave in October 1998 to an audience of disaffected Young Unionists. In this speech Trimble stressed that risks had to be taken and he called upon the august historical example of James Craig to support his contention. He also claimed that Craig took risks because he was confident in himself and his beliefs. Trimble saw his task, therefore, as building confidence within a party rather prone to defeatist perspectives since 1968, and educating it in the need to engage fully with the murky realities of politics in which there are 'no inevitabilities'.[162] This was a much taller order than most party leaders would face, since the UUP was not naturally geared to the politics of wheeling and dealing, and was characterised by a hankering after the mirage of a permanent settlement. As the Southern Irish political commentator and media expert Eoghan Harris informed the delegates at the Unionist Party conference in 1995, Unionists always wanted 'a line to be drawn in concrete and the constitutional question settled for ever', but 'nothing in life is settled for ever'.[163] Trimble, by his own efforts and through the exhorting of advisers like Harris (to whom Trimble encouraged his party to listen), attempted to pave the way for engagement with Sinn Fein.

Trimble's ascent to the leadership coincided with a growth in 'new Unionist' thinking and a marked increase in academic attention to Unionist politics.[164] Awareness of the need to 'sell' the Unionist message, both at home and abroad, was developing in the UUP before the change of leader occurred.[165] Along with this went a more pronounced tendency for that message to be of a secular Unionist variety: as Christopher Farrington has observed, secularism was a 'growth idea' within Unionism from the early 1990s, a process stimulated largely by the 'equal citizenship' integrationism which emerged in response to the Anglo-Irish Agreement.[166] By the time of Trimble's leadership victory, there was a new respectability surrounding Unionist political thought which prompted counter-blasts from Nationalists who believed that it was really the old sectarian Unionism in the fancy dress of fashionable language about citizenship and pluralism.[167] Less predictably, it led also to a philosophically oriented critique from a Unionist Party member whose alternative idea of Unionism, labelled 'civic', in effect urged Unionists to be less Unionist in their behaviour and less preoccupied with the Union, and to prioritise the goal of dialogue with Nationalists and Republicans in Northern Ireland.[168]

The UUP was the source of much of the new thinking, and was the party that many who promoted such ideas wished to influence. Trimble was by inclination a thinker and a doubter rather than a devout believer, although he was by no means indifferent to his Presbyterian roots and continued to worship regularly.[169] Trimble's leadership helped connect the UUP more purposefully to broader streams of thought and intellectual debate. However, the trend was wider than the UUP: it encompassed the party set up by McCartney, the United Kingdom Unionist Party (UKUP), and the Loyalist groupings the Progressive Unionist Party (PUP) and the Ulster Democratic Party (UDP), which had become more prominent since the ceasefires of the paramilitary groups to which they were respectively linked, the UVF and the UDA. The extent to which the PUP and the UDP became significant players in what had come to be called 'the peace process' helped shift the centre of gravity within Unionism away from the religious and ethnic pole towards the secular and civic one, and in so doing rather undermined the validity of the scholarly models of Unionism which had hitherto dominated the field.[170] There is some suggestion that Trimble, at the outset of his leadership, wished to forge a greater degree of Unionist unity, with the question of a return to the UUP fold of McCartney particularly uppermost in his mind.[171] In some ways both men's Unionist visions converged: they recognised the need for a modern pluralist prospectus consistent with the multi-cultural realities of the UK, and they were particularly conscious of Unionism's external relationships. There was much that McCartney might have signed up to in the statement of aims adopted by the UUC executive in November 1995 and authored by Trimble's close party associate and former academic colleague Dermot Nesbitt.[172] On the other hand, the history of the integration/devolution debate – artificial though that squabble in many ways was – and McCartney's repudiation of the context of the peace process as inherently and hopelessly biased against Unionists was to preclude any coming together.

Unionist unity, however, would have belied the name without the DUP, and this party still bore aloft the standard of what was in effect Protestant Unionism.[173] The balance of Unionist advocacy was still fine enough for factors such as the Drumcree dispute and other contentious parades to tip it back towards ethnic imperatives. Such factors were to hover troublesomely over the political deliberations of the coming years, always threatening to reduce Unionism to an arid tribal struggle.[174] Trimble's desire to redefine the party's link with the Orange Order, as part of a broader modernising process, came up against entrenched attitudes: Martin Smyth for example intervened at the party conference in October 1995 to denounce the idea of risking some 160,000 Orange votes in return for perhaps 50,000 Catholic pro-union ones as 'bad mathematics'.[175] The issue of the need to modernise the UUP in general, and reform the relationship with the Orange Order in particular, was to be problematic for Trimble in the manner of its relevance to his future course of direction as leader.

In the wake of the paramilitary ceasefires of 1994 the main obstacle to all-inclusive negotiations was the question of the decommissioning of weapons. Unionists of all shades were adamant that there had to be decommissioning before Sinn Fein could enter talks. The London government took the Unionists' side while Dublin vacillated on the issue. In the event it was agreed that an international commission to investigate decommissioning would be set up under the chairmanship of US Senator George Mitchell. In January 1996 this Commission proposed that decommissioning should occur in parallel with talks and it put forward six principles of democracy which all parties were recommended to accept. The British government added that there should be elections to provide a democratic basis for the process. This move pleased Trimble and fuelled Nationalist and Republican grievances about the perceived leverage the UUP was exerting on the weak government of John Major at Westminster. Shortly afterwards the IRA ended its ceasefire by bombing Canary Wharf in London with the loss of two lives. Such influence as the UUP may have exercised was insufficient to prevent the government adopting a form of electoral system for the elections to a new Northern Ireland Forum, held on 30 May 1996, which was the preference of DUP and the SDLP.[176] The UUP had traditionally always fared better in the 'first past the post' Westminster system, and party literature for the Forum contest condemned this hybrid system as 'designed to shred' the UUP vote.[177]

This looked like a case of getting the excuses in first, but the result turned out to be reasonable for the UUP. The party won 30 seats, six ahead of the DUP and nine ahead of the SDLP. Its percentage of the vote was a modest 24.2 per cent, the result of an even greater fragmentation of the vote among Unionist parties than usual. The smaller parties, the UKUP, PUP and UDP, all won seats to the Forum. On the other side of the communal divide the SDLP lost ground to Sinn Fein: the latter's showing of 15.5 per cent of the vote and 17 seats demonstrated that it could not be kept out of the process if there was to be any chance of a settlement which would stick. In the meantime it was excluded while the IRA continued to use violence both in Northern Ireland and in Britain; a massive bomb wrecked the centre of Manchester shortly after the Forum met for the first time. Trimble and the UUP, in accepting Mitchell as Chair of the all-party talks which opened after the election, defied the DUP and the UKUP. For the Unionists, the fear of what could be hatched against their interests if they excluded themselves from the process was clearly a determining factor in their approach. Unionists, as past experience suggested, only ended up with something worse if they were not part of what was going on.

For a long period the process seemed highly unlikely to produce a breakthrough. Drumcree again brought Northern Ireland to a heightened sectarian pitch, and Trimble's highly publicised dealings with the Loyalist terrorist Billy Wright damaged his image at home and abroad. His justification, that he was attempting to defuse tension, was not widely appreciated. The SDLP withdrew from the Forum, leaving it to become, in effect, a Unionist talking shop. At Westminster the Major government's willingness to set up a Northern Ireland Grand Committee with a remit similar to its Scottish counterpart in the scrutiny of legislation ensured that the Unionists would not bring the government's life to a halt before it naturally expired in May 1997. Trimble could claim that he had exploited the UUP's parliamentary position to good effect, although somewhat ironically this was very reminiscent of his predecessor. A change of government was to provide the conditions for the UUP to attempt to make political gains of a different kind.

Labour, led by Tony Blair, came to power after a landslide election victory and demonstrated quickly that peace in Northern Ireland was a top priority. The Unionist Party emerged stronger from the election, winning 10 seats (including the new seat of West Tyrone as a result of a split Nationalist vote) and polling 32.7 per cent. The DUP's share of the vote was 13.6 per cent. Overall, the Unionist vote slipped under 50 per cent and low turnouts in predominantly Protestant constituencies remained a cause for concern.[178]

Blair took office with a radical agenda of constitutional reform, at the centre of which were devolution proposals for Scotland and Wales. The UUP responded positively: 'the government's commitment to decentralisation and openness creates opportunities for us', Trimble declared in the House of Commons.[179] Trimble was keen to show that his party was amenable to 'New Labour's' plans for 'New Britain', and there was an important mutual respect between himself and Blair. Building on Unionist Party efforts from the early 1990s to 'muscle in' on the argument about UK constitutional change, Trimble pledged that his party would be in the thick of the debate, and that it would support devolution based on 'sensible cooperation' between the centre and the regions. Trimble was eager to see Northern Ireland incorporated into the broader restructuring process in the UK, and he was to find that Blair was more than willing to oblige. Blair's commitment to the Union, including Northern Ireland, was given clear expression in a speech in Belfast shortly after he became Prime Minister. Moreover, as events were to show, Trimble was able to orientate the British government more successfully than any previous Unionist leader to the strengthening of the east–west dimension to the Northern Ireland problem. He was able to seize the opportunity which Blair's expansive concept of the constitutional future afforded the Unionists to advance the idea of a Council of the British Isles. This idea had long been a favourite of Trimble's from his Vanguard days, and he and other former Vanguard members now prominent in the UUP, such as Reg Empey, had been able to make it a fixture of party policy.[180] Indeed, Trimble approached the negotiations with the other Northern Ireland parties with the view that any North–South arrangements should be within the context of a new isles-wide body.[181] This was at once traditional and modern: it echoed the pre-partition Unionist stress on the British Isles as the natural unit politically, economically and socially; and it seemed compatible with the post-nationalist ideas of the 1990s and the revival of 'federal' thinking in Britain. As Empey was to put it in 1998: 'We see ourselves playing a major role in the Europe of the Regions. We even aspire to play the same role in relation to the United Kingdom, as the German Länder do in the Federal Republic.'[182]

Trimble was relaxed about Blair's constitutional radicalism because he had long recognised that the UK had never in fact been a uniform, integrated state.[183] He also recognised that a loosened-up, decentralised UK was in many ways more congenial to Ulster Unionists than the anglocentric unitariness which characterised the vision of the Conservatives under Thatcher and Major. As Blair shifted the emphasis towards a 'union state' interpretation of how the UK should function and away from that of a 'unitary state', it was less easy to posit Northern Ireland (and Ulster Unionists) anomalously and arbitrarily against a spuriously monolithic concept of Britain.[184] Disaggregating Britain, the process of which truly began with Labour's victory in 1997, laid bare the extent of cultural diversity and the widespread nature of complex, multiple and layered identity issues. Blair's homage to Gladstone, ironically the original sinner of Unionist legend, offered Unionists the genuine hope that they could be made to feel that they belonged, notwithstanding the anxieties which were harboured by Unionists of all

kinds throughout the UK about the risks inherent in such a programme of constitutional recasting. As Edna Longley put it in a
lucid appraisal of the condition of Protestant Ulster in 1997:
'Belonging to the UK means engaging with what might be its crisis,
what might be its mutation'.[185]

Blair's project encouraged a more nuanced appreciation of the
varieties of Britishness, something eminently to the advantage of
Ulster Unionists. Trimble and his support base in the UUP saw this
and took heart from the trend of events both in the UK and further
afield. A more regionally conscious Europe held no fears for them,
and they could claim that Unionism was better equipped than Nationalism to address questions of the accommodation of different
identities and of multi-layered governance.[186] The future seemed to
hold out the promise of the kind of interaction between the different
parts of the British Isles which shaped the UK in the first place,[187] as
well as the consequent weakening of the politically damaging impression of freakish exceptionalism in regard to Northern Ireland.
Nevertheless, there remained great dangers: decommissioning deadlock and failure to reach agreement to allow Northern Ireland to
become part of the new devolved framework formed a formidable
riddle to resolve, and if it was resolved at a cost perceived by the
Unionist electorate to be too high then Trimble's future plans for the
UUP would be instant history. Former confidants of Trimble worried that he would follow Faulkner into the annals of tragic failures
on account of trusting too much in a British Prime Minister;[188]
while the Unionist 'nay sayers' bayed loudly about what they saw as
the treachery involved in any possible deal. Trimble thus took a
considerable gamble in agreeing to participate in multi-party talks
including Sinn Fein after the IRA called a second ceasefire in July
1997.[189] Sinn Fein was admitted without the guarantee of parallel
IRA decommissioning, and although Trimble insisted on the pro-
viso that there could be no bilateral meetings between his party and
Sinn Fein before decommissioning, he was condemned bitterly by
the DUP and the UKUP, and disowned by a clutch of his own Westminster MPs.[190] The Loyalist parties by contrast were decidedly
ready to join the process.

Both the absence of the DUP and the UKUP, and the presence of the
PUP and UDP, helped Trimble and his team of negotiators to rise to
the task before them. The former factor, as George Mitchell was to
point out, freed the party from daily attacks at the negotiating

table,[191] while the Loyalist parties added credibility to the notion that the days of the 'Ulster Says No' approach were at an end, and they were to provide the UUP with important backup. The UUP's decision seems to have confounded the expectations of the Republican movement that the party would buckle under pressure to stay out; it has even been suggested that an IRA bomb and the murder of two policemen in Trimble's constituency were expressly intended to force the UUP to withdraw.[192] The UUP certainly tried to have Sinn Fein expelled on account of Republican violence, but the party simply continued under protest when the governments refused to do so.

The negotiations, which were organised around the three-stranded structure of the early 1990s, were tortuous and fraught.[193] Minds were truly focused from January 1998 when the two governments produced a 'Heads of Agreement' document which provided comfort for Unionists and alarmed Sinn Fein. The latter found to its dismay that a Northern Ireland assembly would be the centrepiece of any settlement, and the symbolism of Republicans entering Stormont in the future seemed to sink in. Sinn Fein, however, had allowed the UUP and the SDLP to move too far on strand one to influence the eventual shape it took. This, essentially, was to the SDLP's liking: a power-sharing cabinet government and an assembly with legislative powers, rather than the UUP's administrative devolution proposals and a committee system which involved lower-level power-sharing. The power-sharing – 'consociationalist' – arrangements were organised around formal ethnic blocs with special weighted voting stipulations.[194]

The main UUP efforts were concentrated on strand two – the nature of the North–South dimension within Ireland. Here they had to try to combat the wishes of the SDLP, the Dublin government, and particularly Sinn Fein for a freestanding North–South body with executive powers, a step up indeed from what had been sketched out in the Framework Document. Early in April it seemed that something was emerging which the Unionists could not accept, and this resulted in a crisis of confidence in the British Secretary of State Mo Mowlam. However, Blair made a crucial intervention which led to a radical revision of the proposals, and the end product of a North–South ministerial council bound to the Northern Ireland assembly, as well as a limited number of North–South bodies concerned with relatively uncontentious issues, was a triumph for Trimble and the UUP. Moreover, it was accompanied by an undertaking on the part of the Dublin government to rewrite articles 2 and 3, as well as the acceptance by Nationalists and – in practice – by Republicans of the consent principle regarding the wishes of the majority in Northern Ireland to retain the Province's constitutional position within the UK.[195]

On strand three the Unionists also succeeded in their quest for a Council of the British Isles, to be called the British-Irish Council (BIC). This body would involve, in addition to the British and Irish governments, the governments of the new devolved administrations in Scotland, Wales and Northern Ireland, as well as those of the Isle of Man and the Channel Isles. This was the realisation of a personal goal for Trimble, and a genuinely innovative recognition of east–west relations; no longer could the Northern Ireland problem continue to be regarded in a purely one-island context. On the other hand, Trimble's desire to see the North–South dimension effectively controlled by the BIC was not fulfilled, and Unionists would be left having to ensure that the BIC did not degenerate into the talking shop which Nationalists and Republicans were inclined to hope, and rejectionist Unionists gloomily claimed, that it would become.

By far the most difficult issues for Unionists to agree were those of decommissioning, the release of paramilitary prisoners, and the prospect of policing reform. These almost prevented the UUP signing up to the final deal, and did result in one of the party's senior negotiators, Jeffrey Donaldson, walking out on the brink of it being concluded. Donaldson felt that the requirement for decommissioning was not toughly enough worded. Tony Blair again attempted to prop up Trimble and the UUP on this issue by giving personal guarantees; these proved enough for Trimble's deputy, John Taylor, to give his vital support.[196]

The Belfast – or 'Good Friday' – Agreement of 10 April 1998 took its place as another momentous landmark in Irish and British history.[197] The UUC Executive Committee and a full meeting of the Council subsequently gave Trimble the endorsement he needed, but there were many within the party, including MPs and senior figures, who were hostile and who lost no time in making common cause with the DUP and UKUP. Writing in the immediate aftermath of the Agreement, Henry Patterson stated that the success of Trimble's strategy would lie in persuading Unionists to distinguish 'the stabilising constitutional core' of the Agreement from 'the distasteful secondary aspects' which – as Trimble himself stressed – were matters of policy which the British government was likely to implement in any case.[198] Trimble had more to sell than Faulkner, and he had received the kind of support from the British Prime Minister which was a further contrast to 1974, yet this time there would be convicted terrorists being let out of jail, the RUC's future would be in doubt, and Sinn Fein, by virtue of the system agreed, would be likely to win seats in the executive while the decommissioning issue remained to be resolved. Detractors of Trimble who have since levelled the facile charge that he did not do enough to sell the Agreement simply fail to comprehend the difficulties which the above posed in the light of what Arthur Aughey has called the deeply rooted 'fatalism' of Ulster Unionist culture.[199]

Trimble tried to alter the mood of his community by positioning Ulster Unionism within Blair's optimistic prospectus for a 'new Union'. He tried to re-orientate Unionists, within and outside his party, from majoritarianism to pluralism, perhaps the defining characteristic of the 'new Unionism' which had provided the context for his rise and his leadership strategy. He talked up what he could: 'We have got the structures as good as they could be. They are safe. The Union is secure. Dublin cannot dictate to us. The British Isles dimension has been established.'[200] He further attempted to trace back what had been agreed to the overtures made jointly by Molyneaux (who lost little time in denouncing the deal) and Paisley to Thatcher early in 1987 as an alternative to the Anglo-Irish Agreement.[201] The latter, Trimble argued, was now part of the history books: Unionists had succeeded in replacing it with a better alternative.[202] Trimble claimed that he had turned back what appeared to be a tide towards joint authority. His mission was to make Unionists face up to hard choices in the present so that in the long term they would provide for their own healthy survival within a rejuvenated Union.[203]

In the event it was Unionist voters rather than Nationalist ones who showed themselves to be divided over the merits of the Agreement in the referendum in May.[204] Although the 'Yes' vote was 71.1 per cent overall, there was only a bare majority among Unionists. Moreover, it was clear that a significant portion of this, given the high turnout, came from the traditionally abstentionist ranks of 'middle Ulster' and was thus a 'soft' vote in favour.[205] The proof of this would come in the Assembly elections the following month when the Unionist Party vote – 21.3 per cent – represented the party's worst ever performance in a Northern Ireland election, and saw it fall for the first time into second place behind the SDLP in terms of vote share. The average turnout in 'Unionist' seats was 10 per cent lower than those of 'Nationalists'. The UUP still ended up the largest Assembly party, but this was due to transfers, many of them from 'No' Unionists.[206] With the support of the two PUP members in the new Assembly, Trimble mustered sufficient votes to be elected First Minister. Nonetheless, his position was highly precarious, with defections from his party likely, and the emotive issues of decommissioning and prisoner releases dominating debate on the Agreement to the detriment of the deal as a whole and the future of devolved government in Northern Ireland.

The tragedies surrounding the Drumcree controversy of July 1998, followed by the carnage of the Omagh bomb (the work of Republicans who repudiated the Agreement), appeared to dim the prospects of stable government being established, although there was also the hope that these were the grim darkness before the new dawn. Certainly, Trimble's careful choice of phrase in a speech of welcome to President Clinton in September – his desire to see 'a pluralist parliament for a pluralist people' – coupled with his ac-knowledgement in his speech of acceptance of the Nobel peace prize in December that Northern Ireland had been 'a cold house' for Catholics, signalled unequivocally a readiness for a new begin-ning.[207] Periodic Republican claims that the UUP in reality 'did not want a Catholic about the place' were disingenuous and mischie-vous. Neither did it help Trimble's task when there were interven-tions such as that of Barry McElduff of Sinn Fein in October: 'Our struggle is not about reforming the six counties ... it is about getting the British, especially the English, out of Ireland – it's as simple as that'.[208] Notwithstanding such aboriginal politics, Sinn Fein still managed generally to convey the impression that the Unionists were the main obstacle to a new era of peace. Far from this, it might be argued that Trimble's defence of the Agreement in relation to a vision of the forging of new relationships throughout the islands, including that between North and South in Ireland,[209] was as for-ward-looking and expansive as the Republican mantra concerning the one island and the alleged intentions of Unionism was dated and constrictive.

During late 1998 and early 1999 agreement was reached on the structure of the Northern Ireland executive and on the cross-border bodies, and the Dublin and London governments signed treaties ratifying the new North–South, British–Irish and inter-governmen-tal arrangements. Around the question of decommissioning, how-ever, there remained a stalemate. A joint plan by the Prime

Ministers, Blair and Bertie Ahern, in July 1999 to begin devolved
government with decommissioning to follow within days was
rejected by the UUP, which boycotted Stormont on the scheduled
occasion of the executive taking office. Trimble refused this time to
be persuaded by Blair; he knew he would imperil his own position
and the future of the Agreement by going along with the plan. Blair
and Ahern consequently recalled Mitchell to review the process,
and Mowlam was replaced by Peter Mandelson in a bid to rebuild
Unionist confidence. With the Patton report proposing radical
changes to policing, the UUP's scope to move away from the 'no
guns, no government' policy was apparently non-existent. Northern Ireland was about to enter a long period of strategic manoeuvring over the survival of the Agreement to which the Ulster
Unionist Party was central and on the development of which
Trimble's leadership depended.

Since November 1999 there have been several special meetings of
the UUC which have entailed votes on Trimble's strategy to make
the Belfast Agreement work commensurate with Unionist long-term
objectives. Besides their significance for the remarkable way in
which Trimble clung to the leadership through turbulent political
weather and for the survival of the Agreement, they served also to
focus attention on the nature of the UUP as a political party, and the
peculiarities of that 'large, unwieldy and unpredictable' body, the
UUC.[210] An adviser to Trimble, the young and percipient Steven
King, memorably described the party as 'run on the lines of Presbyterian anarchy with a whiff of Anglican arrogance'.[211]

That the meetings were held with such regularity reflected the
ease with which a faction within the party could obtain the necessary signatures for such a course, and then repeat the exercise if the
outcome was not to its satisfaction. The party's lack of an effective
centre aroused much comment, and the striking contrast with the
DUP, SDLP and Sinn Fein was stressed.[212] The UUC's antiquated
structure, by virtue of the special privileges granted to bodies such
as the Orange Order and the Young Unionists, allowed delegates
heavily influenced by other parties such as the DUP, and who in
some cases may not even have been members, to have a say in decid-
ing the party's destiny.[213] The Orange Order and the Young Unionists, both of which adopted strident anti-Agreement stances,
accounted for some 154 seats on the 860-strong UUC body in
2000.[214] Trimble was aware from the start of his leadership that

party reform was urgent and overdue, but the pressing commitments of the peace process diverted him from the task. He was given ample cause to regret this from 1999 to 2003.

The main issue remained the party's umbilical tie to the Orange Order. As long as this existed there were clear limits to the credibility of the party's commitment to a pluralist, civic-oriented future. The dilemma was a real one: the Orange Order was to the Ulster Unionist Party what the trade union movement was for so long to the Labour Party.[215] It represented a restraining and responsible influence on Protestant Ulster at least in equal measure to its capacity to promote ethnic exclusiveness and encourage intolerance and extremism.[216] Yet the political influence it tried to exert in the period of the peace process was unremittingly subversive of Trimble's brand of Unionism, Orange Order member though he remained. For the Order could see only a dire threat to itself, to its rituals and demonstrations, and to 'the Protestant way of life' as it was narrowly defined. To Orangemen the 'equality agenda' of the Agreement was code for attacks on Protestant culture. Their anguish over episodes like Drumcree led to the kind of confidence-sapping introspection out of which Trimble was trying to lead Unionism. The Order's importance as a unifying force within Unionism was by now greatly diminished, and it had been prey to Paisleyite disruptiveness for many years. Yet its role in maintaining the UUP as the main political player in Northern Ireland since 1972 was not inconsiderable. The Order, post-1972, still had the incentive to preserve as much Unionist unity as possible so that the Unionist Party might be strong enough to return to power. Arguably this incentive declined sharply after the Anglo-Irish Agreement, and the Belfast Agreement involved a return to government of a kind unpalatable to Orangeism in general.

An attempt in April 2000 to change the Order's relationship to the party came up against the obstruction of a two-thirds majority requirement in the UUC, according to rules agreed in 1989.[217] Warnings about a 'civil war' in the party over the issue forced Trimble to tread warily.[218] Shortly before this internal row, Trimble had had to fend off a leadership challenge from Martin Smyth, winning by an unconvincing margin of 57 per cent to 43 per cent. Smyth clearly won back much of the Orange support he had lost to Trimble in 1995 as well as gaining other malcontented delegates. The contest resulted from the neurotic response of many in the UUP to a Trimble speech in Washington on decommissioning designed to wrong-foot Sinn Fein.[219] This highlighted the leader's plight: making a clever move on the world stage to the discomfort of your opponents counted for nothing if it appeared to signal a softening of your stance. Trimble simply could not count on the latitude given to most other party leaders to play the political game. In their analysis of UUC members around this leadership contest, Tongue and Evans categorise the anti-Agreement, anti-Trimble Unionists as 'Orange sceptics', and draw attention to the significance of the variable of Orange Order membership in the voting behaviour of delegates.[220]

Trimble's lack of progress towards a modern 'one member, one vote' structure for the Unionist Party jarred beside his achievements in rendering the party more sophisticated in international terms. No previous Unionist leader enjoyed such serious external attention. Under Trimble's guidance the party made particular strides in the USA, even on the mundane level of running an office in Washington. The UUP presence in the American capital actually resulted from a party delegation led by the then leader Molyneaux in 1994 which met Vice-President Al Gore. During this trip a wealthy Ulster exile offered the party the office rent-free after hearing to his astonishment that the UUP's operating budget was then around £100,000 per year, a sum for which many Republican sympathisers in the USA wrote cheques without batting an eyelid.[221] This underlined the fact of the party's relative poverty, a situation which remained fundamentally unaltered under Trimble.

As the Orange influence on the party reinforced defensive political positions, so too did it help to preserve male dominance. Recent academic research has put the female membership of the party at nearly half of the total, yet women's issues remained marginal to party politics and policies.[222] Another survey has revealed that in 1999 only 2 of the UUP's 14 officers were women and of its 178 councillors 13.5 per cent were women.[223] There were 2 women out of 28 elected for the party to the Assembly in June 1998, as well as Lady Sylvia Hermon for the Westminster seat of North Down in 2001. Under Trimble's leadership there has been a greater recognition of the need to get more women adopted as candidates and into top positions in the party; a Women's Unionist Conference was held for the first time in 2000.[224] However, there is still opposition to quotas as a means of promoting women, and little has been done to challenge the traditionalist culture of the party in relation to gender issues. Up to the present, modernisers within the party such as

James Cooper and Alex Kane (also a journalist) have urged reform in order to tap a substantial portion of the secular Unionist electorate which is turned off by the Orange link and outdated attitudes. Kane has warned that the pro-Agreement faction of the party should not be taken for granted.[225] Indeed, for many pro-Agreement Unionists, Trimble has not imposed his leadership sufficiently, nor dealt firmly enough with his opponents.

The Mitchell review concluded on 18 November 1999 with what appeared to be a definite understanding between the parties on decommissioning. Trimble decided to seek the approval of the UUC to allow the establishment of the devolved executive finally to take place. In effect he was preparing to 'jump first' before any tangible handover of weapons, and it was thus the clearest example to date of his willingness to engage in the politics of brinkmanship. He succeeded on 27 November, if at the cost of having his level of support fall to 58 per cent, and with the help of an expedient: a post-dated letter of resignation which would be activated in the event of the Chairman of the commission on decommissioning, General John de Chastelain, having nothing to report in January 2000.[226] At a stroke Trimble overturned the stereotype of Ulster Unionism as reactive and obstructive. On the other hand, he might not have pulled it off without the resort to the post-dated letter (which angered Republicans) and the compliance of his deputy, John Taylor, whose criticisms stopped just short of outright opposition.

The executive was formed on 29 November in accordance with the d'Hondt method of allocating ministries.[227] Trimble became First Minister and the SDLP's Seamus Mallon Deputy First Minister. The three other UUP members were Reg Empey (Minister of Enterprise, Trade and Investment), Sam Foster (Minister of Environment) and Michael McGimpsey (Minister of Culture, Arts and Leisure). The Unionists' anxiety to prevent Sinn Fein taking McGimpsey's brief resulted in the former IRA army council figure of Martin McGuinness becoming Minister of Education. Sinn Fein also took the Ministry of Health and Social Services. Thus the Republicans controlled two of the big spending departments, and the anti-Agreement Unionists were handed the propaganda weapon of such a sensitive responsibility being held by someone whom Unionists perceived as especially culpable for almost thirty years of terrorism.[228]

Hopes and fears about the progress of devolution were put on hold soon after. No decommissioning moves were made by February 2000, whereupon Peter Mandelson suspended the institutions, provoking howls of outrage from Nationalists and Republicans who considered this reassertion of British sovereignty to be contrary to the spirit of the Belfast Agreement. It had the corresponding effect of reassuring Unionists.[229] However, perhaps feeling that Mandelson's action had given him political breathing space and anxious, as noted above, to show the world that Sinn Fein and not the UUP was stymieing the process, Trimble indicated in Washington in March that he might be prepared to return to government if firm guarantees on decommissioning were given. This provoked Smyth's leadership challenge, on the occasion of which Trimble also had his hands tied by a motion from David Burnside, a public-relations expert and former ally, linking the re-entry into government to retention of the name of the RUC.[230]

Early in May the IRA committed itself to putting arms 'beyond use' and re-engaged with the decommissioning commission. On the back of this Trimble again tested the willingness of the UUC to agree to the resumption of devolution, even though the signs clearly pointed to the mood being profoundly sceptical. Nevertheless, he scraped through once more, this time by a narrower still 53 to 47 per cent margin. Trimble's main critic by now was Jeffrey Donaldson, whose relative youth, forceful style of advocacy, and impeccable party credentials suggested leadership potential.[231] Perhaps crucially, however, Donaldson appeared to be in no hurry.

Trimble's support in the reconvened Assembly was down to 26 in his own party (including his own vote). The anti-Agreement Unionists of all kinds now had more than the 30 votes required to make 'parallel consent' for key decisions in respect of the Unionist and Nationalist blocs impossible. Trimble's predicament highlighted the UUP as part of the problem in the delivery of the Unionist bloc so crucial to the success of the consociationalist prescription of the Belfast Agreement. The requirement on the Unionist side for its 'elite' – the Trimble-led UUP – to maintain enough homogeneity to achieve a settlement appeared to be breaking down in the face of an increase in intra-ethnic conflict which scholarly critics of the consociationalist paradigm have argued is indeed a likely outcome of these very arrangements.[232]

More sectarian acrimony accompanied the 'marching season' in general and Drumcree in particular, and the death in a car crash of the UUC President, Josias Cunningham, added to Trimble's party troubles. Cunningham, descendent of the stockbroking family which had been identified with Ulster Unionism since the days of Irish Home Rule, had placed his skills as a political fixer and his personal authority at Trimble's service through the challenging times of the Agreement and its aftermath.[233] Within the ongoing context of pro- and anti-Agreement Unionist controversy, devolved government made a slow start, while the North–South institutions soon appeared much more active and politically driven than the BIC.[234] As rows about symbolism were added to those on decommissioning and policing, faith in the Agreement among the Unionist electorate plummeted.

At the end of October the UUC met to support, by another slim margin of 54 to 46 per cent, Trimble's wish to continue in office, but this was only after he announced that he would exclude Sinn Fein ministers from North–South meetings, an action later declared unlawful. It was a measure of Trimble's determination to fight for the Agreement that his somewhat pedantic academic approach yielded to a blunt and unambiguous one: 'There is no Unionist utopia out there. Politics is a rough business with limited choices. Will we sleep any sounder in our beds if we are seen to ditch this agreement? Will there be decommissioning? Will the Union be guaranteed? No, no and no again.'[235]

In January 2001 John Reid was chosen to succeed Mandelson in the apparent hope that being leant on to decommission by a tough Catholic Celtic-supporting Scot would move Republicans in that direction. Reid was also to address the sense of alienation among Protestants, particularly those in the working-class areas where paramilitaries had reverted to type. Trimble and the UUP were fast losing the unsteady ground they had in such constituencies, where the dominant perception was of a sectarian fight to the finish and the concepts of 'parity of esteem' and pluralism prompted puzzlement or cynicism.[236]

In May Trimble wrote another letter of resignation to take effect from 1 July, and this ploy may well have helped stave off a worse result in the British general election of the following month. As it was the UUP lost three seats and the DUP gained two: Trimble himself had to fight off a strong DUP challenge and, literally, an angry Loyalist mob at the count. The UUP share of the vote, 26.8 per cent, was nonetheless an improvement on the Forum and Assembly elections, and arrested a downward trend involving the Assembly and European elections of 1998 and 1999. Trimble's position was not so fatally weakened as many had anticipated, and there was no replay of the Faulkner election humbling of February 1974, although it was noticeable that the party tried to fight the election on the essentially deceptive basis of avoiding debate on the Belfast Agreement as such.[237] Trimble at least gained an ally in Lady Sylvia Hermon to offset the return of Burnside; Ken Maginnis and John Taylor both declined to stand. Within the other ethnic bloc, Sinn Fein eclipsed the SDLP.

Trimble's resignation duly took effect and crisis talks to save the Agreement resumed between the governments and parties. In August Reid suspended the institutions for a day to allow a six-week period for negotiations. Within that period the arrest of Irish Republicans in Columbia suspected of association with FARC guerrillas, followed by the terrorist attacks of 11 September in New York and Washington, altered the context radically, and brought forth a beginning to decommissioning. Trimble obtained the support of the UUC to return to government, although his re-election as First Minister in November came about in the most dubious of circumstances.[238] The future of the administration led now by Trimble and Mark Durkan of the SDLP looked decidedly healthier, and a Programme for Government and budget were agreed by the Assembly. Even on policing, the parties (minus Sinn Fein) came to an agreement. Against this, the end of year statistics showed that 2001 had been the most violent since the ceasefires of 1994.[239]

Trimble could claim at least some of the credit for the decommissioning breakthrough, but it was not long before the new mood of optimism faded. In 2002 an anti-Agreement drift within the UUP was evident in the selection and de-selection of candidates for the Assembly elections scheduled for May 2003. Persistent rumours about Trimble jumping ship to the Conservative Party and an easier life at Westminster were not laid to rest.[240] An attack on 'the pathetic, sectarian, mono-ethnic, mono-cultural state to our south'[241] was probably Trimble's way of reassuring his tribe, but the speech played badly across the rest of the political spectrum and hardly complemented the British Isles vision of interaction and cooperation with which he had taken pains to associate the UUP at the time of the Agreement. Such controversy also served to obscure the rational objections of pro-Agreement Unionist voters to the way matters had unfolded, as well as the extent to which many Nationalists flagrantly acted as if the consent principle was expendable.[242] Moreover, the piecemeal emergence of the new UK under Blair still carried with it a significant degree of constitutional uncertainty around the future of the Union itself, and that of British identity and citizenship. Like Irish Nationalism, and perhaps on account of the binary mindsets which the Irish question had long fostered, Ulster Unionism seemed too set in its ways, too prone to the reflex of asserting Britishness in order to oppose Irish Nationalism, sufficiently to embrace a post-nationalist recipe for exiting the 'end-game' with honour intact.[243] In this early twenty-first-century sense it still conformed most tellingly to an essentially nineteenth-century nationalist idea, notwithstanding its layered identities, its ambiguous relationship to nation-states actual or imagined, and the efforts of its more cerebral voices.

In September 2002 the UUC agreed that the party would withdraw its ministers from the North–South ministerial council, and that it would withdraw from the executive on 18 January 2003 unless Republicans offered 'real and genuine transition' to peaceful means. This was a formula which kept critics of the leadership happy and led some to conclude that Trimble was now a prisoner of his opponents, even if the best-known of them, Donaldson, could not make up his mind to seize the leadership.[244] The following month arrests and allegations of an IRA spy ring at Stormont led to another suspension of the devolved institutions. Speculation about the next Assembly elections increasingly centred on whether the DUP would become the largest Unionist party, and thus present the problem of how a deal could be struck with either the SDLP or, more likely, Sinn Fein, to reactivate devolution.

Anti-Agreement elements within the party manoeuvred industriously against the leadership as the gloomy mood settled over the Northern Ireland political scene in 2003. Trimble was embarrassed by a party executive vote going against any change to the Orange Order connection in February, while Donaldson, publicly backed by Martin Smyth, Molyneaux and Burnside, fed talk of Unionist realignment with an initiative designed in effect to tie the party leader's hands over negotiations about a return to devolved government. Trimble ally Esmond Birnie warned that there could be no 'ducking out' of the task of building a more up-to-date movement, and he seemed to identify a chronic organisational problem in his observations about newcomers being 'discouraged' for fear of established power bases being upset.[245] David McNarry, another Trimbleite, attempted to confound the critics by claiming that the leader's approach had brought the IRA close to disbandment, and that more of the same 'doggedness' would complete the job.[246]

However, so evident was the 'dysfunctional' nature of the UUP[247] that the decision by Blair to postpone the elections scheduled for May was generally assumed to have been taken to save the party from humiliating defeat and to preserve the leadership of Trimble. The subsequent publication of the 'Joint Declaration' on the part of the two governments concerning ways and means of restoring devolution only added to the crisis: the Donaldson faction came out against the declaration in its entirety and demanded that Trimble follow suit. The main objection, dismissed by pro-Agreement Unionists, was the role of the Dublin government in the context of a sanctioning procedure to be brought against parties not fulfilling their obligations under the Agreement. This was essentially a move meant to reassure Unionists and bring pressure to bear on Republicans, but the anti-Agreement Unionists saw only a back door for Dublin into the affairs of the Northern Ireland Assembly, and a further risk to the Province's security regarding the provisions for demilitarisation also included in the document.

Donaldson went through the tried and trusted channels to ensure yet another UUC showdown on 16 June, the result of which again favoured Trimble and again only by a slim (54–46) margin. Far from accepting the outcome stoically, Donaldson hinted heavily about quitting, before, on 23 June, joining with Smyth and Burnside in announcing that they were relinquishing the party whip at Westminster. This meant that the UUP President, Smyth, and Honorary Secretary, Donaldson, were in open repudiation of the party leadership and a vote of the party's ruling body; and it further meant that Trimble could count only on the support at Westminster of MPs Lady Sylvia Hermon and Roy Beggs. Comparisons with previous crises in the party's history such as that of 1973–74 were eagerly pondered.[248] Trimble's position was on the face of it stronger than Faulkner's, yet there were senior figures in the party such as Jim Nicholson who appeared to cast doubt on his ability to carry on.[249] The doubts increased as the party leader took steps to discipline the rebels, and Orange Order discontent rumbled. On 27 June the gang of three were controversially suspended pending a disciplinary hearing, fuelling speculation about a civil war in the party resulting ineluctably in a major split. The Reverend Martin Smyth, who had been such a key figure in limiting the damage done by the Vanguard rupture involving Trimble among others in 1973, seemed now prepared to play a decisive role in convulsing the party with his display of defiant traditionalism. In an astonishing intervention he appeared to concede Esmond Birnie's point about the reluctance on the part of entrenched interests to open up the party to newcomers.[250]

Trimble had concluded that he had been tolerant of his rivals' subversiveness for too long, and he thus gambled on a demonstration of bruising decisiveness. Whether such a gamble would come off turned on his hope that firm leadership would steady the party, convince the doubters and waverers, and rally the constituency of Unionism which such supportive commentators as Alex Kane had long identified as ripe for mobilisation if handled correctly.[251] In view of the inherited political reflexes of Ulster Unionism, the lingering factor of apocalyptic ethnic hallucinations induced by Orangeism, and the cautious inclinations of many in the party's ruling circles who favour compromise however messy, this was a tall order.

The crisis represents a long-running struggle pushed to the point at which Trimble has risked his leadership for the accomplishment of a party placed securely on a modernising footing. If at the end of it there is no such outcome it is highly likely that the party's historic claim to be the largest and broadest Unionist political organisation, along with its Britannic aspirations, will face the prospect of being terminated and mocked. Those within Unionism who agitated against Trimble will have consigned the party to a political context in which, ideologically, it will slowly suffocate.

Notes

1 *Ulster Review*, 2:5 (August 1972).
2 See Public Record Office of Northern Ireland (PRONI), D1327/20/3/28. The best example was *The terror and the tears* (Unionist Research Department, 1972).
3 See report of Faulkner speech to Bow Group in *Ulster Times*, May 1972; also B. Faulkner, *Memoirs of a statesman* (London, Weidenfeld and Nicolson, 1978), p. 157.
4 Faulkner, *Memoirs*, pp. 165–6.
5 See *Ulster Times*, June–December 1972, various articles; also Vanguard publications *Ulster: a nation* and *Government without right*. D. Miller, *Queen's rebels* (Dublin, Gill and Macmillan, 1978), Epilogue, provides a discussion of these arguments, viewing them as another variation on the theme of contractarianism or 'conditional loyalty' (see discussion in Chapter 1 above).

6 Faulkner, *Memoirs*, p. 146.

7 Ibid., p. 183; also D. Hume, *The Ulster Unionist Party 1972–1992* (Lurgan, Ulster Society, 1996), p. 47; S. Nelson, *Ulster's uncertain defenders* (Belfast, Appletree, 1984), p. 104.

8 See H. Kelly, *How Stormont fell* (Dublin, Gill and Macmillan, 1972), p. 127.

9 See Nelson, *Ulster's uncertain defenders* for discussion of class tensions within Vanguard.

10 See discussion in Chapter 4 above.

11 See Hume, *The Ulster Unionist Party*, p. 47; A. Purdy, *Molyneaux: the long view* (Antrim, Longstone Books, 1989), p. 65.

12 It is worth noting that Conor Cruise O'Brien believed at the time that integration would be the cause around which Ulster Protestants would rally: see C. C. O'Brien, *States of Ireland* (London, Panther, 1974), p. 272.

13 See Faulkner, *Memoirs*, p. 174 for comments on party organisation.

14 PRONI, D1327/20/3/38.

15 See report of Faulkner speech, *Ulster Times*, October 1972.

16 Faulkner, *Memoirs*, pp. 177–8.

17 591,820 said 'yes' to Northern Ireland remaining in the UK; 6,463 said 'no'.

18 See P. Dixon, *Northern Ireland: the politics of war and peace* (Basingstoke, Palgrave, 2001), p. 138.

19 The young activist David Trimble by contrast followed Craig.

20 See UUP press releases regarding Craig in PRONI, D1327/21/38.

21 See Hume, *The Ulster Unionist Party*, pp. 147–9; also PRONI, D4127/1/12/1, Smyth to James Kilfedder, 9 January 1976: 'Along with you and many others I had been concerned about the discipline in our Party and the individualism of members who were apparently prepared to take a Unionist patronage but not prepared to work together as a Unionist team …'. This passage might provide a clue to Smyth's attitude to events in 1973.

22 See Hume, *The Ulster Unionist Party*, pp. 13, 147–9.

23 Ibid., Introduction.

24 See J. F. Harbinson, *The Ulster Unionist Party 1882–1973* (Belfast, Blackstaff Press, 1973), ch. 10.

25 See candidate profiles in *Ulster Review*, June 1973.

26 Hume, *The Ulster Unionist Party*, pp. 18–19.

27 PRONI, D4127/1/9/1, West to J. O. Bailie (Secretary of UUC), 26 July 1973.

28 Faulkner, *Memoirs*, p. 198.

29 PRONI, D4127/1/9/1, statement by Kilfedder (n.d., c. July 1973).

30 For accounts of Sunningdale see Dixon, *Northern Ireland*, pp. 142–50; T. Wilson, *Ulster: conflict and consent* (Oxford, Blackwell Press, 1989), ch. 17; P. Bew and H. Patterson, *The British state and the*

Ulster crisis (London, Verso, 1985), ch. 2.

31 K. Bloomfield, *Stormont in crisis* (Belfast, Blackstaff Press, 1996), pp. 182–3.

32 See G. Gillespie, 'The Sunningdale Agreement: lost opportunity or an Agreement too far?', *Irish Political Studies*, 13 (1998), pp. 100–14.

33 See M. Rees, *Northern Ireland: a personal perspective* (London, Methuen, 1985), ch. 3.

34 See Purdy, *Molyneaux*, pp. 112–13.

35 Rees, *Northern Ireland*, pp. 79–80.

36 Ibid., p. 99.

37 Ibid., pp. 71, 76; also Purdy, *Molyneaux*, pp. 134–5.

38 The executive included fellow Unionist Roy Bradford, who went on to write a novel loosely based on these events, *The last ditch* (Belfast, Blackstaff, 1981). See Bloomfield's tribute to Faulkner, 'the man of principle of the seventies', in his *Stormont*, p. 221.

39 See S. Heffer, *Like the Roman: the life of Enoch Powell* (London, Phoenix, 1999), pp. 726–30 on wrangles over the South Down seat which also involved Glen Barr, who had come to prominence during the UWC strike.

40 Ibid., pp. 789–90; Purdy, *Molyneaux*, pp. 101–9. The bill became law in March 1979.

41 PRONI, D4127/3/5/1, press release by Kilfedder, 9 December 1975.

42 *Unionist Clarion*, 2 (May 1976).

43 Ibid.

44 PRONI, D1327/21/40, speeches by Harry West, 14 May 1976 and 28 May 1976. In the latter speech West highlighted the Irish Republican/Nationalist vote in certain British constituencies.

45 PRONI, D1327/21/40, speeches by West, 14 May 1976 and 28 June 1976.

46 PRONI, D1327/21/40, speech by West, 14 May 1976.

47 PRONI, D1327/20/3/29, 'A guide to the Convention Report' (UUC).

48 See H. McDonald, *Trimble* (London, Bloomsbury, 2000), p. 60.

49 PRONI, D1327/20/3/20, *Unionist Clarion*, March 1976.

50 PRONI, D1327/21/40, speech by Powell, 22 April 1976.

51 Rees, *Northern Ireland*, p. 277.

52 See Heffer, *Like the Roman*, pp. 758–9.

53 PRONI, D1327/21/40, speech by Powell, 28 May 1976.

54 PRONI, D1327/21/40, speech by West, 12 July 1976.

55 *Unionist Clarion*, 2 (May 1976). See West speech to UUC AGM, 19 March 1976.

56 J. Todd, 'Two traditions in Unionist political culture', *Irish Political Studies*, 2 (1987). Todd arguably does not explain adequately the complexities and blurred boundaries within, especially, the Ulster Unionist Party with its formal Orange link.

57 *Unionist Clarion*, 2 (May 1976), West speech to UUC AGM.
58 PRONI, D4127/5/13/3, *Ulster Unionist Bulletin*, 2 (n.d., c. 1977).
59 Ibid.
60 PRONI, D1327/20/3/31, 'Analysis of election'.
61 PRONI, D1327/20/3/33.
62 See also Kilfedder's damning verdict on 'old guard Unionists' and their effect on the party, delivered at the time of his resignation in February 1979, PRONI, D4127/1/15/1.
63 Purdy, *Molyneaux*, p. 70.
64 Ibid., p. 57.
65 Molyneaux and four other UUP MPs voted against the Labour government in the House of Commons, leading to the election. Two others, McCusker and Carson, voted with Labour.
66 Purdy, *Molyneaux*, pp. 78–9; also McDonald, *Trimble*, pp. 76, 83.
67 Purdy, *Molyneaux*, p. 80.
68 PRONI, D1327/20/3/33, Molyneaux speech to UUC AGM, 24 March 1980.
69 *Irish News*, 17 October 1980 (death notices).
70 PRONI, D1327/20/3/33, *Unionist '82*, 1 (May 1982). The editor of this journal, and party press officer, was Frank Millar.
71 *Unionist '82*, 3 (September 1982).
72 For which see C. O'Leary et al., *The Northern Ireland Assembly 1982–1986: a constitutional experiment* (London, Hurst, 1988).
73 For a contemporary scholarly discussion of 'rolling devolution', see P. O'Malley, *The uncivil wars* (Belfast, Blackstaff, 1983), ch. 11.
74 See Wilson, *Ulster*, p. 187.
75 The DUP opposed Powell in South Down but did not prevent him winning. There was considerable antagonism by now between Paisley and Powell.
76 *The only way* (UUC, 1983).
77 See the *Guardian*, 18 October 1982.
78 See profile in the *Guardian*, 6 June 1981.
79 See discussion in O'Malley, *Uncivil wars*, pp. 133–41.
80 See McDonald, *Trimble*, pp. 85–90. Trimble's law lecturer colleague and rising UUP star Edgar Graham was murdered by the IRA at Queen's University, Belfast, in December 1983.
81 See Wilson, *Ulster*, pp. 189–92; also P. Arthur, *Special relationships* (Belfast, Blackstaff, 2000), pp. 184–208 for an in-depth and sympathetic view of the Forum's work.
82 See critique in C. O'Halloran, *The limits of Irish Nationalism* (Dublin, Gill and Macmillan, 1987).
83 See Wilson, *Ulster*, p. 189.
84 There is a voluminous literature on the Anglo-Irish Agreement. A representative cross-section of views and interpretations might include: Wilson, *Ulster*, ch. 19; P. Bew et al., *Northern Ireland 1921–*

94 (London, Serif, 1995), ch. 6; J. McGarry and B. O'Leary, *The politics of antagonism* (London, Athlone Press, 1993), ch. 7; Arthur, *Special relationships*, pp. 208–20; A. Kenny, *The road to Hillsborough* (Oxford, Pergamon Press, 1986).

85 *Belfast Newsletter*, 1 April 1985.

86 See G. McGimpsey, 'The Ulster Unionist Party 1985–1995' (Ph.D. thesis, Queen's University, Belfast, 2000), ch. 4 for retrospective criticism of Molyneaux by prominent Unionists such as Taylor, Empey and Carson. See also McDonald, *Trimble*, pp. 92–3.

87 A. Aughey, *Under siege: Ulster Unionism and the Anglo-Irish Agreement* (London, Hurst & Co., 1989), p. 55. The McGimpsey brothers case which was taken to court in the Republic in 1986 highlighted the issue of articles 2 and 3.

88 See discussion of Agreement in G. Fitzgerald, *All in a life* (Dublin, Gill and Macmillan, 1991), chs 16 and 17.

89 For discussion of the notion of 'coercive consocialionalism' see B. O'Leary, 'The Anglo-Irish Agreement: meanings, explanations, results and a defence', in P. Teague (ed.), *Beyond the rhetoric: politics, the economy and social policy in Northern Ireland* (London, Lawrence and Wishart, 1987). See also comments of Sir David Goodall, 'Hillsborough to Belfast: is it the final lap?', in M. Elliott (ed.), *The long road to peace in Northern Ireland* (Liverpool, Liverpool University Press, 2002).

90 As Molyneaux put it: 'We are going to be delivered, bound and trussed like a turkey ready for the oven, from one nation to another nation'. Quoted in F. Cochrane, *Unionist politics* (Cork, Cork University Press, 1997), p. 28.

91 See quotations from McCusker speech in Cochrane, *Unionist politics*, pp. 28–9.

92 See discussions in Cochrane, *Unionist politics*; Hume, *The Ulster Unionist Party*.

93 See A. Aughey, 'Unionism, conservatism and the Anglo-Irish Agreement', in D. G. Boyce and A. O'Day (eds), *Defenders of the Union* (London, Routledge, 2001).

94 Ibid.; also A. Aughey, 'The character of Ulster Unionism', in P. Shirlow and M. McGovern (eds), *Who are 'the people'? Unionism, Protestantism and Loyalism in Northern Ireland* (London, Pluto Press, 1997); also D. Trimble, 'A Unionist perspective', in C. Townshend (ed.), *Consensus in Ireland* (Oxford, Clarendon, 1988).

95 *Guardian*, 12 February 1987.

96 See coverage in the *Guardian* by correspondent Paul Johnson and in the *Irish Times* by Martin Cowley; also A. Parkinson, 'Bigots in bowler hats? The presentation and reception of the Loyalist case in Great Britain', in Boyce and O'Day (eds), *Defenders of the Union*.

97 *Irish Times*, 8 March 1986.
98 See Wilson, *Ulster*, pp. 199–200.
99 The new Secretary of State, Tom King, who was physically attacked after the Agreement was signed, made efforts to calm Unionist fears and adopted a tougher line in inter-governmental dealings.
100 Cochrane, *Unionist politics*, passim.
101 For this debate see Hume, *The Ulster Unionist Party*, ch. 4; Aughey, *Under siege*, chs 4 and 5.
102 P. Smith, *Why Unionists say no* (Joint Unionist Working Party, n.d.).
103 The group in question, the British and Irish Communist Organisation (BICO), is discussed in Aughey, *Under siege*; see also C. Coulter, 'Direct Rule and the Unionist middle classes', in R. English and G. Walker (eds), *Unionism in modern Ireland* (Basingstoke, Macmillan, 1996).
104 The integration/devolution split seemed roughly to approximate to an east/west split in the Province, and there was a suggestion, short-lived, of the mobilisation around it of the Protestant middle class. See Hume, *The Ulster Unionist Party*, ch. 4; Coulter, 'Direct Rule'.
105 Miller, ironically, was formerly an electoral integrationist in his thinking.
106 *To put right a great wrong* (Ulster Unionist Party, 1987).
107 See comments of Sydney Elliott in *Fortnight*, July/August 1987.
108 B. Clifford, *The Unionist family* (Belfast, Athol Books, 1987).
109 See comments on Aughey's work by John Whyte in his *Interpreting Northern Ireland* (Oxford, Clarendon, 1990), pp. 218–21.
110 Aughey, *Under siege*, p. 178.
111 See the *Guardian*, 12 February 1987; also obituary of McCusker in the *Guardian*, 13 February 1990.
112 There was a parallel to be drawn between the Ulster Clubs and the earlier Vanguard movement. See McDonald, *Trimble*, p. 95.
113 P. O'Malley, *Northern Ireland: questions of nuance* (Belfast, Blackstaff, 1990), p. 37.
114 Ibid. Maginnis and Taylor were spoken of regularly in the late 1980s as possible successors to Molyneaux.
115 See Cochrane, *Unionist politics*, pp. 6–7.
116 See comments of David McKittrick in the *Independent*, 15 November 1989.
117 *Ulster Unionist Information Institute*, 2 (Winter 1988/89).
118 *Ulster Unionist Information Institute*, 3 (Summer 1989).
119 Ibid.
120 See Purdy, *Molyneaux*, ch. 9.
121 For Brooke talks and those of Secretary of State Patrick Mayhew see T. Hennessey, *The Northern Ireland peace process* (Dublin, Gill and Macmillan, 2000), pp. 54–66; Cochrane, *Unionist politics*, pp. 271–84; H. Cox, 'From Hillsborough to Downing Street – and after', in

P. Catterall and S. McDougall (eds), *The Northern Ireland question in British politics* (Basingstoke, Macmillan, 1996).

122 *Ulster Unionist Information*, 5 (Summer 1990).

123 Ibid.

124 Cox, 'From Hillsborough to Downing Street'.

125 McDonald, *Trimble*, pp. 120–1.

126 See Hume, *The Ulster Unionist Party*, p. 130.

127 See G. Walker, *Intimate strangers: political and cultural interaction between Scotland and Ulster in modern times* (Edinburgh, John Donald, 1995), pp. 165–6.

128 Ulster Unionist Party, general election manifesto, April 1992.

129 Ibid.

130 Walker, *Intimate strangers*, pp. 165–8.

131 Ibid.

132 *Unionist Voice*, 14 (October 1994).

133 *Ulster Unionist Information*, 9 (March 1992).

134 See McGimpsey, 'The Ulster Unionist Party', ch. 5; Cochrane, *Unionist politics*, pp. 284–90. The SDLP's plans at the time for the governance of Northern Ireland included a role for Dublin and for the European Union.

135 McGimpsey, 'The Ulster Unionist Party', pp. 264–5.

136 See J. Major, *The autobiography* (London, Harper Collins, 2000), pp. 380–1.

137 See G. Lucy, *Northern Ireland local government election results 1993* (Lurgan, Ulster Society, 1994).

138 See Cox, 'From Hillsborough to Downing Street'; the text of the declaration is in Cochrane, *Unionist politics*, Appendix II.

139 See *Ulster Unionist Information Institute*, 12 (March 1994).

140 See McGimpsey, 'The Ulster Unionist Party', ch. 6 for discussion of the declaration, Molyneaux and the UUP.

141 Ibid., pp. 289–92.

142 See J. Ruane and J. Todd, *The dynamics of conflict in Northern Ireland* (Cambridge, Cambridge University Press, 1996), pp. 295–300; Major, *The autobiography*, pp. 464–70.

143 See discussion in Walker, *Intimate strangers*, ch. 6; also Aughey, 'Unionism, Conservatism'.

144 'A practical approach to problem-solving in Northern Ireland' (UUP, 21 February 1995).

145 'Response to "Frameworks for the future"' (UUP, 10 March 1995).

146 *Guardian*, 13 June 1995.

147 *Guardian*, 10 June 1995.

148 Interview with Roy Bradford, UUP press release, January 1993.

149 Ibid.

150 Ibid.

151 Until a delegation travelled to the USA in 1994, the party under

Molyneaux's leadership largely ignored that country, and Molyneaux's indifference to Europe was in sharp contrast to John Hume.

152 *Unionist Voice*, 14 (October 1994), article by party president Josias Cunningham.
153 Ibid., article by Arlene Kelly.
154 Cochrane, *Unionist politics*, p. 84, fn. 32. The DUP figure was 10 per cent, the SDLP 16 per cent, Sinn Fein 11.5 per cent.
155 Bradford interview, UUP press release, January 1993.
156 Cox, 'From Hillsborough to Downing Street'.
157 See R. Dudley Edwards, *The faithful tribe* (London, Harper Collins, 1999), p. 322.
158 McGimpsey, 'The Ulster Unionist Party', pp. 337–50; McDonald, *Trimble*, pp. 153–7.
159 A. Aughey, 'Ulster Unionist Party leadership election', *Irish Political Studies*, 11 (1996), pp. 160–7.
160 Interview with Gordon Lucy, 24 January 2003. Lucy also believes that Trimble was behind the speech given by Martin Smyth in 1993 about the possibility of the Republican movement plumping un-equivocally for a political path. Trimble was to make frequent reference to Smyth's intervention in the years to come.
161 See articles in *Ulster Review*, 18 (Winter 1995/96).
162 See D. Trimble, *To raise up a new Northern Ireland* (Belfast, Belfast Press, 2001), 'Engaging reality' speech.
163 E. Harris, 'Why Unionists are not understood', in *Selling Unionism* (Belfast, Ulster Young Unionist Council, 1995).
164 See, for example, English and Walker (eds), *Unionism in modern Ireland*.
165 See contributions to *Selling Unionism*.
166 C. Farrington, 'Ulster Unionist political divisions in the late twentieth century', *Irish Political Studies*, 16 (2001), pp. 49–72.
167 See L. O'Dowd, '"New Unionism", British nationalism and the prospects for a negotiated settlement in Northern Ireland', in D. Miller (ed.), *Rethinking Northern Ireland* (London, Longman, 1998). The best collection of 'new Unionist' statements is J. W. Foster (ed.), *The idea of the Union* (Belcouver Press, 1995).
168 N. Porter, *Rethinking Unionism* (Belfast, Blackstaff, 1996). See riposte to Porter by UUP member Esmond Birnie in his *Without profit or prophets* (Belfast, Ulster Review Publications, 1997). See also commentary by John Lloyd, 'These islands', *Prospect*, 44 (September 1999).
169 McDonald, *Trimble*, pp. 122–4.
170 See discussion and critique of Todd's 'two traditions' model in Farrington, 'Ulster Unionist divisions', and R. English, 'The growth of new Unionism', in J. Coakley (ed.), *Changing shades of orange*

and green (Dublin, UCD Press, 2002).

171 McDonald, *Trimble*, p. 162.

172 D. Nesbitt, *Unionism restated* (UUC, 1995).

173 Norman Porter's label for it is 'Cultural Unionism'. See his critique in *Rethinking Unionism*, ch. 2.

174 For the impact of Drumcree on the Unionist community see the various commentaries in S. McKay, *Northern Protestants: an unsettled people* (Belfast, Blackstaff, 2000).

175 *Guardian*, 23 October 1995.

176 The UUP also endangered the life of the government by voting against it on the Scott inquiry. The government won by only one vote.

177 UUP election communication, Forum Election.

178 See D. Morrow, 'Northern Ireland', *Regional and Federal Studies*, 7:3 (1997), pp. 188–96.

179 See G. Walker, 'The Council of the Isles and the Scotland–Northern Ireland relationship', *Scottish Affairs*, 27 (Spring 1999), pp. 108–23.

180 See discussion in Nesbitt, *Unionism restated*.

181 See Foreword to *Unionism restated*.

182 *Unionist* (Spring 1998). This journal was launched by the Unionist information office in London run by David Burnside.

183 See Trimble's article in R. Holmes (ed.), *A vision for the Union* (Belfast, Ulster Young Unionist Council, 1996); also 'Devolution and the Union', in Trimble, *To raise up*.

184 Such concepts are discussed illuminatingly in J. Mitchell, 'Conservatives and the changing meaning of Union', *Regional and Federal Studies*, 6:1 (1996), pp. 30–44; V. Bogdanor, 'Devolution: decentralisation or disintegration?', *Political Quarterly*, 70 (1999), pp. 185–94; E. Meehan, 'The Belfast Agreement and UK devolution', *Parliamentary Affairs*, 52:1 (1999), pp. 19–31.

185 E. Longley, 'What do Protestants want?', *Irish Review*, 20 (Winter/Spring 1997), pp. 104–20.

186 See Trimble's comments on nationalism in 'The Belfast Agreement', in Trimble, *To raise up*.

187 See George Boyce, 'A place apart?', in E. Hughes (ed.), *Culture and politics in Northern Ireland* (Milton Keynes, Open University Press, 1991); H. Kearney, *The British Isles* (Cambridge, Cambridge University Press, 1989).

188 Interview with Gordon Lucy, 24 January 2003. Trimble once remarked to Lucy that he considered himself a more intelligent politician than Faulkner.

189 While Sinn Fein signed up to the Mitchell Principles, an IRA statement referred to the organisation having problems with them. Unionists reacted angrily to what appeared to be the Republican movement having it both ways.

190 Ross, Thompson, Beggs, Forsythe and, more ambiguously, Smyth.
191 See Senator George Mitchell, *Making peace* (London, Heinemann, 1999), p. 110.
192 See McDonald, *Trimble*, pp. 179–82.
193 See Hennessey, *The Northern Ireland peace process*, part 3 – the author seems to have had access to UUP position papers and was associated with the party's talks delegation. See also M. Mowlam, *Momentum* (London, Hodder & Stoughton, 2002); Mitchell, *Making peace*; McDonald, *Trimble*, ch. 6.
194 A level of 60 per cent support in the Assembly was required for key decisions. See commentary on the Agreement in R. Wilford (ed.), *Aspects of the Belfast Agreement* (Oxford, Oxford University Press, 2001).
195 The Government of Ireland Act of 1920 was also repealed, but Trimble argued that this was not of great significance. See P. Bew, 'Analysis', *Parliamentary Brief*, 5:6 (May/June 1998), pp. 32–5.
196 See Hennessey, *The Northern Ireland peace process*, pp. 169–70.
197 For analysis of the Agreement see Wilford (ed.), *Aspects*; J. Ruane and J. Todd (eds), *After the Good Friday Agreement* (Dublin, UCD Press, 1999); special issue of *Parliamentary Brief*, 5:6 (May/June 1998).
198 Henry Patterson, 'No vex please', in *Parliamentary Brief*, 5:6 (May/June 1998), pp. 10–11.
199 See A. Aughey, 'Learning from "the leopard"', in Wilford (ed.), *Aspects*.
200 See 'An immediate assessment', in Trimble, *To raise up*.
201 See 'Being nominated as First Minister', in Trimble, *To raise up* ('partnership administration based on proportionality'); also A. Aughey, 'The 1998 Agreement: Unionist responses', in M. Cox et al., *A farewell to arms?* (Manchester, Manchester University Press, 2000).
202 However, strand three of the Agreement involved a new British–Irish Inter-governmental Conference which anti-Agreement Unionists claimed was a continuation of the Anglo-Irish Agreement arrangements by other means.
203 See Aughey, 'Learning'.
204 Referendums took place North and South. The 'yes' verdict was 71.2 per cent in the North, and 94 per cent (on a turnout of less than 60 per cent) in the South. The South's referendum provided the popular consent required to rewrite articles 2 and 3.
205 The highly publicised image of Trimble and Hume with U2 singer Bono seems to have made a vital impact at a late stage in the campaign.
206 See P. Mitchell, 'Transcending an ethnic party system?', in Wilford (ed.), *Aspects*. It should be noted that the UUP fielded two Catholic

candidates, one of whom, Sir John Gorman, was elected.

207 See 'The President at the Waterfront' and 'Nobel lecture' in Trimble, *To raise up*. Trimble was awarded the Nobel prize along with Hume. His speech on the occasion of receiving it cited various intellectual influences such as Edmund Burke and Karl Popper, and its reference to the people of Northern Ireland being 'no petty people' echoed Yeats. See also discussion in D. Nesbitt, 'Redefining Unionism', in Coakley (ed.), *Changing shades*.

208 *Irish News*, 19 October 1998.

209 See 'Post-Agreement Ireland: North and South', in Trimble, *To raise up*.

210 *Guardian*, 28 October 2000. See also Frank Millar's sketch of delegates in the *Irish Times*, 20 November 1999: 'Teachers and students, baby barristers and baby boomers, farmers, doctors, stockbrokers and insurance salesmen, butchers, housewives and small shopowners'.

211 Quoted in McDonald, *Trimble*, p. 219; see also H. Cox, 'Keeping going: beyond Good Friday', in Elliott (ed.), *The long road*. Cox uses the analogy of the Presbyterian minister and the Kirk session.

212 See F. O'Connor, *Breaking the bonds* (Edinburgh, Mainstream, 2002), pp. 197–8, 202–3; also editorial in *Irish News*, 28 October 2000.

213 See editorial, *Irish News*, 29 May 2000.

214 *Guardian*, 17 April 2000.

215 See Cox, 'Keeping going'.

216 See Dudley Edwards, *Faithful tribe* for a sympathetic appraisal of the Order, and also much comment about the Orange/UUP link in the context of recent political developments.

217 *Belfast Newsletter*, 18 April 2000.

218 *Guardian*, 17 April 2000.

219 *Observer*, 26 March 2000. See also Henry McDonald's piece in the *Observer*, 8 April 2001, in which he argues that Trimble's gesture helped lead to the IRA agreeing to its arms dumps being inspected in May 2000.

220 J. Tongue and J. A. C. Evans, 'Faultlines in Unionism: division and dissent within the Ulster Unionist Council', *Irish Political Studies*, 16 (2001), pp. 111–32. The authors also made the important point that the Order itself was divided over the link to the UUP.

221 Andrew J. Wilson, 'The Billy Boys meet Slick Willy: the Ulster Unionist Party and the American dimension to the Northern Ireland peace process, 1994–9', *Irish Studies in International Affairs*, 11 (2000), pp. 121–36.

222 See R. Miller et al., *Women and political participation in Northern Ireland* (Aldershot, Avebury, 1996).

223 L. Racioppi and K. O'Sullivan See, '"This we will maintain": gender,

ethno-nationalism and the politics of Unionism in Northern Ireland', *Nations and Nationalism*, 7:1 (2001), pp. 93–112.

224 See *Irish Times*, 6 April 2000.

225 *Belfast Newsletter*, 17 February 2001. See Cooper's comments on the Orange connection in *Belfast Newsletter*, 21 October 2002. In February 2003 the executive committee of the UUC voted against breaking the link – see *Belfast Newsletter*, 15 February 2003.

226 See McDonald, *Trimble*, Epilogue.

227 See R. Wilford and R. Wilson, 'Northern Ireland: a bareknuckle ride', in R. Hazell (ed.), *The state and the nations* (London, Imprint Academic, 2000) for a comprehensive account of political developments from the Belfast Agreement to 2000.

228 The DUP, notwithstanding its opposition to the Agreement, also took its seats in the executive.

229 See J. Ruane and J. Todd, 'The politics of transition? Explaining political crises in the implementation of the Belfast Good Friday Agreement', *Political Studies*, 49 (2001), pp. 923–40.

230 The UUP tabled an amendment at Westminster on the Police Service of Northern Ireland. See Wilford and Wilson, 'Northern Ireland'.

231 See profile in *Irish News*, 23 October 2000. Donaldson has a strong background in the Young Unionists, was a former election agent for Enoch Powell and was an assistant of Molyneaux's for several years. He is an evangelical Christian.

232 For discussion of the consocialionalist nature of the Agreement see B. O'Leary, 'The character of the 1998 Agreement: results and prospects', in Wilford (ed.), *Aspects*; Mitchell, 'Transcending an ethnic party system?', in Wilford (ed.), *Aspects*; Cox, 'Keeping going'.

233 See obituaries in the *Guardian*, 11 August 2000, and *Belfast Newsletter*, 11 August 2000.

234 See UUP Member of Assembly Esmond Birnie's later comments in *Belfast Newsletter*, 27 July 2001, regarding the need for genuine 'parity of esteem' between the BIC and the North–South institutions.

235 'As it is', in Trimble, *To raise up*.

236 Attempts have been made to bolster self-confidence at community level through appreciation of history and cultural identity issues. Central to this have been the efforts of the Ulster-Scots movement. Recognition of Ulster-Scots as a minority language was given in the Belfast Agreement. The movement invites comparative consideration with the role of the Ulster-Scottish connection in the cultivation of Ulster distinctiveness and the promotion of the Unionist political project in previous eras. See Chapters 1 and 2 above especially.

237 See Tongue and Evans, 'Faultlines in Unionism'.

238 The Alliance Party agreed to re-designate itself as 'Unionist'. The majority of Unionist members of the Assembly (of all parties) refused to back Trimble. See *Irish Times*, 12 October 2002, Frank Millar

article.

239   *Monitor* (Bulletin of the Constitution Unit), 18 (March 2002).

240   See *Belfast Newsletter*, 14 June 2002 (editorial) for a critical view of proposed UUP/Tory link; *Ulster Review*, 32 (2002) for a more favourable slant.

241   *Observer*, 10 March 2002.

242   See articles by Dennis Kennedy, *Irish Times*, 24 July 2001 and 23 January 2002. Unionists also took note of the reluctance of Southern politicians to accept Sinn Fein in government while the IRA remained armed.

243   See R. Kearney, 'Toward a postnationalist archipelago', *Edinburgh Review*, 103 (2000), pp. 21–34.

244   See Alex Kane's column, *Belfast Newsletter*, 28 September 2002.

245   *Belfast Newsletter*, 14 February 2003.

246   *Irish Times*, 19 April 2003.

247   This was the description of the party in a leaked Irish government memo of the previous year. See Susan McKay in the *Sunday Tribune*, 4 May 2003; Steven King in the *Irish Times*, 21 June 2003.

248   See, for example, *Irish Times*, 14 June 2003; *Belfast Telegraph*, 16 June 2003.

249   *Irish Times*, 25 June 2003.

250   See column in the *Belfast Newsletter*, 28 June 2003.

251   See letter in the *Belfast Newsletter*, 28 June 2003.

CONCLUSION

The political challenge of Irish Nationalism was answered by the organisation of the Ulster Unionist Council and the mobilisation of a distinct community which claimed a corresponding right to self-determination. Both the organisation and the communal claim of right remain central to the Irish question today.

Ulster Unionism took shape as a form of nationalism, notwithstanding its preference to maintain the Union rather than pursue independence.[1] An Ulster national identity developed, ironically, out of the distinctly Irish experience of the Union. It was another way of defining the Irish identity of those in Ireland who set themselves against changes to the nature of the Union established in 1800. This Irish identity had always been a phenomenon shaped by local (Ulster) cultural forces, hence the elision of Irish/Ulster and the heightened manner in which it was associated with British loyalty and allegiance. A political allegiance which, like that of Scotland, may have in other circumstances remained ambiguously related to an emotional and ethnic form of Britishness, instead assumed such characteristics on account of the threat Irish Nationalism was deemed to present. Nevertheless, Ulster Unionists wished for Union on the same terms as those understood by Scotland: as a joint venture rather than a takeover by the largest (English) part. For a long time commentators on the behaviour of Ulster Unionists, past and present, have seen contradictions where they should have seen ambiguities in the wider issue of British identity.

The Irish question's exceptional difficulties were to ensure that the price of Ulster avoiding Dublin rule was the punishing one of political marginalisation within the context of the United Kingdom as it came to be redefined in 1922. In a sense Ulster Unionists essayed their own dislocation from British politics by interpreting

Irish Home Rule as the road out of the Union and opposing Dublin rule at all costs. They were forced to accept Home Rule for themselves, and the fact that they had never desired this was crucial to the manner in which, as a governing party, Ulster Unionists operated it.

Critical assessments of the Ulster Unionist Party in government have to be set beside the many flaws in the working of devolution. The arrangements the party had to accept were designed to meet an entirely different scenario, and proved particularly inadequate in relation to finance. London–Belfast relations thereafter centred on revisions to the financial basis of devolved government. Changes were made in an *ad hoc* manner, and no transparent, formalised or equitable inter-governmental system emerged. If it had, then there may have been a central government check on Unionist populism to the long-term benefit of Northern Ireland and its community relations; and the Province's economy might have been properly treated as a regional part of the wider British whole. The Ulster Unionist Party in such circumstances would have been highly unlikely to have got away with its failure to reform the local government franchise in 1946.

The party's development from the establishment of Northern Ireland reflected the loss of its political influence in Britain and its estrangement from the rest of Ireland; energies focused stultifyingly on the Nationalist foe within. Edna Longley has written of the poet John Hewitt's point about Ulster exemplifying 'the cultural interpenetration' of the British Isles, and she has observed that this could have supplied 'the subtler ideology Unionist paranoia precluded'.[2] The Unionist Party, in its continuing struggle against Irish Nationalism, lost much of its appreciation of the kind of arguments for the Union likely to make a positive impact outside Ulster.

Yet it would be naïve to discount the political pressures applied by various kinds of Irish Nationalist and Republican campaign over the years. Between them, for example, the Anti-Partition League and the IRA fatally reduced Brooke's scope to nudge the party in the more liberal direction favoured by more far-sighted figures such as Brian Maginess. Terence O'Neill was then faced with the formidable challenge of the civil rights movement, whose relationship to the national question was ambiguous enough to ensure the prevalence once more of the politics of tribal honour. O'Neill's failure to retain the confidence of his party, convince Nationalists he was serious about reform, and defuse the Paisleyite threat may in retrospect appear inevitable, yet there remains the impression that his misjudgements and personal failings were instrumental in triggering the crisis which engulfed the Ulster Unionist Party and Northern Ireland.

If the party had become defined by its exercise of albeit limited power, it is notable how resilient it managed to remain throughout Direct Rule, notwithstanding splits, the onslaught of a sustained campaign of violence and the continuing threat of the rival DUP. Along with the SDLP it was central to successive British governments' vain attempts to build a solution around the 'moderate' centre. Even within the context of the inclusive peace process from the mid-1990s the UUP's survival as the main Unionist voice was broadly viewed as vital, and the inseparability of Trimble's leadership with the health of the Belfast Agreement illustrates the point.

Trimble was a product of Vanguard, whose disturbing features should not preclude acknowledgement of its role as a laboratory of ideas and political debate. It was a pro-active influence whose energies were lost to the UUP when it split from the party in 1973; and it should be reiterated how crucial to the UUP's survival and future development was the decision of several leading personalities not to follow William Craig. The party was enabled to continue as a broad church and eventually to reabsorb many defectors. Thus by the mid-1990s it was former Vanguard activists who were in the driving seat, steering the UUP away from the static, prevaricating style of Molyneaux towards full-blown engagement with opponents and realities. To date, this more dynamic approach has held a precarious advantage over the 'know nothingism' of alternative strands of the party and the vapid strategising and empty interventionism of the main rival to Trimble, Jeffrey Donaldson.

The Ulster Unionist Party, at the beginning of the twenty-first century, remains essentially the one-issue organisation of its inception and formative years. As such, there are those within it who feel politically stunted, and yearn for a context in which the national question would cease to exert such a deadening force.[3] There are many blueprints for breaking the circle of this Unionist–Nationalist endgame, and the Belfast Agreement in a convoluted way is one of them, yet there will be no definitive political departure of the kind desired while the community on whom the UUP depends, and out of which it emerged, continues to feel that its identity and very being are gravely threatened.

Over the years the Ulster Unionist Party has indulged in Olym-

Conclusion

pian posturing and displayed elitist pretensions; half a century of unbroken rule has bred certain attitudes. Nevertheless, it would be folly to allow such considerations to obscure the crisis of community confidence on the part of Protestant Ulster which frames the challenges facing its main political voice. A profound and dangerous sense of pessimism and defeatism coexists with the new Unionist politics represented by Trimble, which has moved significantly if tentatively beyond the politics of birthright and the static idea that the Union is their inheritance and their security. Protestant Ulster is a community quite finely balanced between traditional displays of defiance and a pragmatic willingness to take risks for a better future. The time is long overdue to abandon simplistic notions about Ulster Unionist triumphalism or supremacism or homogeneity. The future of the Ulster Unionist Party will turn on its ability to instil confidence in the Protestant community, while being genuinely inclusive and non-sectarian, and on transcending the pessimism which historically has characterised it.

Notes

1 See F. Halliday, *Irish nationalisms in perspective* (Belfast, Democratic Dialogue, 1998).
2 E. Longley, 'John Hewitt, 1907–87', *Fortnight*, September 1987.
3 Interview with Lord Laird of Artigarvan, 21 March 2003.

THE ULSTER UNIONIST COUNCIL

Structure of the Ulster Unionist Council as at 1/1/03

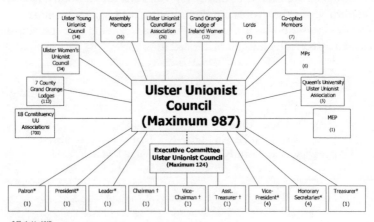

* Elected by UUC
† Elected by Executive Committee

Notes: a) The Executive Committee is indirectly elected although all members are members of the UUC.
b) Some delegates have multiple membership making 987 and 124 theoretical maximum figures.

LEADERSHIP FIGURES: BIOGRAPHICAL DETAILS

Edward Saunderson (1837–1906) was born in County Fermanagh but spent his childhood in Nice, France. He returned to Ireland in 1858 and joined the Royal Irish Fusiliers in 1862, where he rose to the rank of colonel. He was elected as a Liberal MP for Cavan (1865–74) but changed his allegiances to the Conservative Party after Gladstone disestablished the Church of Ireland (he was a prominent lay member of the Synod of the Church of Ireland). He joined the Orange Order in 1882 and became Deputy Grand Master of Ireland in 1884. He was elected MP for North Armagh (1885–1906) and was leader of the parliamentary Unionists (1888–1906) and of the Irish Unionist Alliance (1891–1906). He was made Sheriff of Cavan in 1859 and Lord Lieutenant of Cavan in 1900.

Walter Long (1854–1924) was born in Bath, England, and educated at Harrow and Oxford. He was an MP at Westminster from 1880 to 1921 and held governmental positions for much of that time. He was President of the Board of Agriculture (1895–1900), President of the Local Government Board (1900–05 and 1915–16), Colonial Secretary (1916–19) and First Lord of the Admiralty (1919–21). He had also been Chief Secretary for Ireland (March–December 1905) and was returned as a Conservative for South County Dublin in 1906 (although he lost his English seat in Bristol at the same election). After Saunderson's death in 1906 Long was offered the leadership of the Unionist Party but was never comfortable in the position and when he was returned for the Strand Division in Westminster he relinquished the post. However, he continued to have a prominent role in national politics and chaired the committee on the 1920 Government of Ireland Act.

Edward Carson (1854–1935) was born in Dublin and educated at Portalington School and Trinity College Dublin. He entered the law profession and was called to the bar in 1877. In 1892 he was Solicitor General for Dublin. In 1895 he was made an English QC and in 1900 he was appointed Solicitor General for England. His political career formally began in 1892 when he was elected as a Liberal Unionist MP for the University of Dublin. However, during the debates on the Land Acts of the late nineteenth century he moved into the Tory Party, for which he was briefly considered for the leadership in 1911. In 1910 he was offered and accepted the leadership of the UUP and led the Unionist resistance to Home Rule. During the First World War he was appointed to the British cabinet and was Attorney General (1915–16) and First Lord of the Admiralty (1916–18). In 1918 he successfully stood for election in the Duncairn district of Belfast and in 1921 he resigned from the leadership of the UUP before the establishment of the Northern Ireland government. In May 1921 he accepted judicial office as Lord of Appeal (Lord Carson of Duncairn), a position from which he retired in 1929. He died at Cleve Court, Ramsgate, on 22 October 1935 and was given a state funeral and buried at St Anne's Cathedral, Belfast, on 26 October.

Richard Dawson Bates (1876–1949) was born in Belfast and educated at Coleraine Academical Institution. He was a solicitor by profession and was the first UUC Secretary, a position which he held from 1906 to 1921, during which time he organised the 1912 Covenant. He was a member of the Orange Order and was elected as a Stormont MP for East Belfast (1921–29) and then Victoria (1929–43), and was Minister for Home Affairs (1921–43). He was knighted in 1921 and received a baronetcy in 1937.

James Craig (1871–1940) was the son of a Presbyterian whiskey millionaire. He was educated at Merchiston College, Edinburgh, and left school at 17 to become a stockbroker. However, he left stocks and enlisted in the Royal Irish Rifles when the Boer War broke out. He inherited money when his father died and decided to enter politics. He stood unsuccessfully in North Fermanagh in 1903 but was returned for East Down in 1906. He was elected MP for Mid-Down in 1918 and for County Down from 1921 to 1927. The third Home Rule Bill brought Craig to the fore in the UUP and he was responsible for persuading Carson to become leader of the UUP and for organising the Unionist campaign. He was Grand Master of

County Down Orangemen and Quarter Master General of the 36th Ulster Division (1914–16). He was knighted in 1918 and held positions in the British cabinet as Secretary to the Ministry of Pensions (1919) and Secretary to the Admiralty (1920–21). He became leader of the UUP in February 1921 and First Prime Minister of Northern Ireland in June 1921 and held both positions until his death in 1940. He met with Michael Collins and concluded the Craig–Collins pacts in 1922. He was created Viscount Craigavon in 1937. He was married with three children and is buried in Stormont.

J. M. Andrews (1871–1956) was educated at Royal Belfast Academical Institution and was a company director of the family flax spinning business. He was elected to Stormont from Down (1921–29) and from Mid-Down (1929–53). He was the High Sheriff of Down in 1928 and President of the Belfast Chamber of Commerce in 1936. In 1943 he was made a Freeman of the City of Londonderry. He was a founder member and chairman of the Ulster Unionist Labour Association and was Minister for Labour (1921–37), Minister for Finance (1937–40) and Prime Minister (1940–43). Although he was ousted from government, the Standing Committee of the UUP continued to recognise him as leader until 1946. He was very active in the Orange Order: Grand Master of County Down (1941–54), Grand Master of the Grand Orange Lodge of Ireland (1948–54) and Grand Master of the Imperial Grand Council of the World (1949–54).

Basil Brooke (1888–1973) was born in Colebrook, County Fermanagh, and educated at Pau (in the south of France), Winchester and Sandhurst. He was from an aristocratic family and his background and experiences reflected the wealth and influence that came with land. He served in India from 1908 and during the First World War was awarded the Military Cross and the Croix de Guerre. After the war he returned to farming in Fermanagh, and although he was elected to the Senate in 1921, he resigned in 1922 to become the County Commandant of the Ulster Special Constabulary and active in the Orange Order. He was a member of Fermanagh County Council from 1924 and was returned to Stormont for Lisnaskea in 1929. He was Assistant Whip (1930), Minister of Agriculture (1933–41) and Minister of Commerce and Production (1941–45), a position he continued to hold when he became Prime Minister in 1943. He was given a peerage in 1952 but resigned from the Prime Minister position in 1963 and left parliament in 1967.

Edmund Warnock (1887–1971) was educated at Methodist College Belfast and Trinity College Dublin. He was called to the Irish bar in 1911 and became a KC in 1932. He married Jessie McCleland in 1913 and had three daughters. He served with the Royal Artillery (1914–18) and was a member of the Orange Order. He was returned to Stormont for St Anne's constituency (1938–69) and became Parliamentary Secretary to the Minister of Home Affairs (1939–40), Minister for Home Affairs (1944–49) and Attorney General (1949–56).

Brian Maginnis (1901–67) was educated in Lisburn and at Trinity College Dublin, where he graduated with a LLD in 1922. He was a Barrister King's Inn in 1922, a QC in 1946 and completed his legal career after he resigned from politics to become County Court Judge of Down in 1964. He was a member of the Orange Order and served with Royal Artillery from 1939 to 1941. He was elected Stormont MP for Iveagh (1938–64) and was Under-Secretary to the Ministry of Agriculture (1941–43), Parliamentary Secretary to the Minister of Commerce (1943–45), Minister of Labour and National Insurance (1945–49), Minister of Commerce (1949), Minister of Home Affairs (1949–53), Minister of Finance (1953–56) and Attorney General (1956–64). He represented a strand of liberal Unionism and his departure from the Ministry of Finance was a sign that a more hardline Unionism was eclipsing this strand.

Terence O'Neill, Lord of the Maine (1914–90) was educated at Eton and lived in London and Italy for most of his early life. He was from an aristocratic Anglo-Irish background (he could trace his ancestors back to the Celtic aristocracy). He served in and was a Captain of the Irish Guards in the Second World War. He was elected Stormont MP for Bannside (1946–69), during which time he was Parliamentary Secretary to the Ministry of Health (1948–53), Deputy Speaker (1953–56), Minister of Home Affairs (1956), Finance Minister (1956–63) and Prime Minister (1963–69). In 1965 he met with the Irish Taoiseach Sean Lemass in Stormont, the first meeting between Northern and Southern premiers since Craig and Collins. He died in 1990 in Lymington, Hampshire.

James Dawson Chichester-Clark (1923–2002) was educated at Eton and joined the Irish Guards in 1942 but retired as Major in

1960 to become MP for South Derry, the seat vacated by his grand-mother, Dame Dehra Parker. He was returned unopposed in 1960 and 1965 and beat Bernadette Devlin in 1969. He was Chief Whip of the UUP (1963–69), leader of the Commons (1966) and Minister of Agriculture (1967–69). He resigned over the timing of the pro-posed reforms in April 1969 but became leader of UUP and Prime Minister of Northern Ireland in May 1969 after O'Neill's resigna-tion. He gave an amnesty for those charged of political offences from the previous October (releasing Ian Paisley amongst others) but violence increased and he requested British troops in Northern Ireland in August 1969. During his time in office the USC was phased out and the RUC disarmed. He resigned on 20 March 1971 after he was unable to persuade the British government of the need for security measures and after a campaign for his resignation from Loyalists because of the deteriorating security situation. He was created Lord Moyola in 1971.

Brian Faulkner (1921–77) was born in Helen's Bay, County Down, and was educated at Elm Park School in Armagh and St Columba's College at Rathfarnham, Dublin. He worked in the family textile business and was an active Orangeman (he was a member of Grand Orange Lodge of Ireland) and Young Unionist. British Labour min-ister Hugh Dalton spotted him early as a potential politician and at the time of his election for East Down in 1949 he was the youngest ever MP in Stormont. He became the Chief Whip of the UUP (1956–59), Minister for Home Affairs (1959–63) (active in counter-ing the Border Campaign) and Minister of Commerce (1963–69) in O'Neill's government. He resigned upon the establishment of the Cameron Commission in January 1969 but failed by one vote to replace O'Neill after the latter's resignation and became Minister of Development (1969–71) in Chichester-Clark's government. He eventually became leader of the UUP and last Prime Minister for Northern Ireland from March 1971 to March 1972. During that time he introduced internment in August 1971, protested against the proroguing of Stormont and refused to cooperate with the Com-mission to advise the Secretary of State. He signed the Sunningdale Agreement in December 1973 and became the Chief Executive of the power-sharing Assembly from January to May 1974. In January 1974 he was ejected from the UUP and founded the Unionist Party of Northern Ireland. He retired from politics in 1976 and was cre-ated Lord Faulkner of Downpatrick in January 1977 (he could have had a peerage in 1972). He was killed in a riding accident in March 1977.

William Craig (1924–) was born in Cookstown and was educated at Dungannon Royal School, Larne Grammar School and Queen's University Belfast. He served in the RAF (1943–46) and qualified as a solicitor in 1952. He was a founder of the Queen's University Unionist Association in 1950, a member of the Orange Order and a leading member of the Ulster Young Unionist Council (he was chairman for seven years). He was elected to Stormont as MP for Larne (1960–73) and during that time became government Chief Whip (1962–63), Minister for Home Affairs (1963–64), Minister for Health and Local Government (1964–65) and Minister of Development (1965–66). As Minister for Home Affairs (1966–68) he was responsible for restricting the civil rights march in Duke Street, Derry, in October 1968. He was sacked in 1968 by O'Neill, who said he was an advocate of unilateral declaration of independence. He headed the Ulster Loyalist Association (1969–72). He led the Unionist pressure group Ulster Vanguard, which later converted into a full political party. He was elected to Westminster as MP for East Belfast (1974–79) and joined with Paisley and West to plan the 1974 Loyalist strike. He was elected to the Constitutional Convention from North Antrim (1975–76) but when he advocated a voluntary coalition with the SDLP, he lost support. In 1977 he was appointed to the Council of Europe on the nomination of the British government to report on human rights. In February 1978 the Vanguard Unionist Political Party reverted back to Ulster Vanguard and a pressure group. He lost his Westminster seat by 64 votes in 1979. He remained vocal but failed to take a seat for the Assembly in 1982 and faded out of politics.

Harry West (1917–) was educated at Enniskillen Model School and Portora Royal School. He was a farmer before he entered politics. He was High Sheriff of Fermanagh (1954), President of Ulster Farmers' Union (1955–56) and the Northern Ireland representative on the British Wool Marketing Board (1950–58). He was elected as a UUP MP for Enniskillen (1954–72) and during that time was Parliamentary Secretary to the Ministry of Agriculture (1958) and Minister of Agriculture (1960–67 and 1971–72). He led the West Ulster Unionist Council (1968–71), which was a pressure group defending traditional Unionism and opposing reforms, heavily supported in the west of Northern Ireland, but resigned in 1971 to accept Faulkner's offer of a ministerial portfolio. He did not support Sunningdale and replaced Faulkner as the leader of the UUP (1974–79). He was elected to the Assembly for Fermanagh South Tyrone (1973–74) and to Westminster (February–October 1974) where he was leader of the United Unionist Parliamentary Coalition. He was a member of the Constitutional Convention for Fermanagh South Tyrone (1975–76). During his leadership he led the UUP into the UUUC with Ernest Baird and Paisley but moved away from them after differences over the 1977 strike. He tendered his resignation as leader when he only polled 57,000 first preference votes during the 1979 European election and failed to get elected. In the April 1981 Fermanagh South Tyrone Westminster by-election he lost to Bobby Sands but was active in politics through the remainder of the 1980s through the Charter Group and the Campaign for a Devolved Parliament.

John Taylor, Lord Kilclooney (1937–) was born in Armagh and educated at Royal School Armagh and Queen's University Belfast. He was a partner in an architect and civil engineering business before entering politics and still has a wide array of business interests, particularly in newspapers. He was the youngest ever Stormont MP when he was returned for South Tyrone (1965–72) and during his time at Stormont he was Parliamentary Secretary at Home Affairs (1969–70) and Minister of State, Home Affairs (1970–72). He was elected to the Assembly for Fermanagh South Tyrone (1973–74), to the Convention for North Down (1975–76), to the European Parliament as a UUP MEP (1979–89), to Westminster as MP for Strangford (1983–2001), to Castlereagh Council (1989–97), to the Northern Ireland Forum (1996–98) and to the Northern Ireland Assembly for North Down (1982–86). He is also a member of the Assembly of the Council of Europe (1997–). He was critical of O'Neill's leadership and was later opposed to Sunningdale. He is a member of the Orange Order and took part in Operation USA, a joint UUP–DUP mission to America in 1982. While he was not a member of the 1992–93 talks, he was critical of them but played a crucial role in persuading the UUP to support the 1998 Belfast Agreement. He contested the UUP leadership in 1995 but was beaten by Trimble on the last count and subsequently became Deputy Leader.

Rev. Martin Smyth (1931–) was educated at Methodist College Belfast, Magee College Londonderry and Trinity College Dublin.

He was a Presbyterian minister in Finaghy, Crossgar and North Belfast until 1982 along with his elected posts. He was elected to the Constitutional Convention for South Belfast (1975) and to Westminster for South Belfast (1982–). He has been a high-ranking Orangeman for much of his political career. He was Grand Master of the Orange Order in Ireland (1972–97), Imperial Grand Master of the Orange Order (1974–82), Honorary Past Grand Master of Canada and Honorary Deputy Grand Master of USA, New Zealand and New South Wales. He has been Chairman of the UUC executive (1974–76), Vice-President of the UUC (1974–2001), Honorary Secretary (2000–1) and President (2001–). He has been an advocate of a federal British Isles. He coordinated the UUP talks team during the Brooke–Mayhew talks and has been the party's spokesperson on health and foreign affairs. He was the first Unionist to suggest that Sinn Fein could be included in talks after meeting conditions in the future in 1993. He unsuccessfully stood for the leadership in 1995 and in 2000. He resigned from the position of Grand Master in 1997 after the fall-out from Drumcree (he was heavily criticised for not being present) and has been an anti-Agreement Unionist. He was suspended from the party in June 2003 when he resigned the party whip at Westminster after he disagreed with a number of decisions taken at special meetings of the UUC.

James Molyneaux, Lord Molyneaux of Killead (1920–) was educated at Aldergrove School and joined the RAF (1941–46). He was Honorary Secretary of South Antrim Unionist Association (1964–70), Vice-President of the UUC (1974–79), member of Antrim County Council (1964–73) and whip and secretary of Unionist coalition MPs (March–October 1974). He was beaten by West in the leadership election of 1974 but became leader of the UUP in Westminster (1974–79) and then leader of the UUP (1979–95). He was elected to Westminster for South Antrim (1970–83) and for Lagan Valley (1983–97), and to the Northern Ireland Assembly for South Antrim (1982–86). He has been the Imperial Grand Master of the Orange Order, Sovereign Commonwealth Grand Master of the Royal Black Institution and Honorary Past Grand Master of the Orange Order in Canada. He resigned as a JP (1957–87) in protest at the Anglo-Irish Agreement. He stood down from the leadership on his 75th birthday in 1995 after a stalking horse challenge and announced in 1996 that he would not stand for re-election. He was knighted in 1996 and was granted a life peerage in 1997 as Lord

Molyneaux of Killead. In 1998 he stepped down as Sovereign Grand Master of the Royal Black Institution after over twenty years in post.

Ken Maginnis, Maginnis of Drumglass (1938–) was educated at Royal School Dungannon and Stranmillis College. He is a former school teacher and primary school headmaster. He served in the USC (1958–65) and UDR (1970–81), where he was a Major. He was elected to Westminster for Fermanagh South Tyrone (1983–2001), to the Assembly (1982–86), to the Northern Ireland Forum (1996–98) and to Dungannon Council (1981–93) and (2001–). He was chairman of Dungannon Council in 1991 for six months and has advocated responsibility sharing in Northern Ireland and local government. He has been a Vice-President of the UUC from 1990 to the present and is the security spokesperson. In 1990 he attended the inauguration of Irish President Mary Robinson and the installation of Catholic Primate Archbishop Cahal Daly. He had a key role in strand two of the 1992–93 talks, was a member of the delegation in 1996–98 and is a committed devolutionist. He was the first Unionist to debate publicly with Sinn Fein when he and Gerry Adams appeared on CNN's *Larry King Live Show*. He stood for election as leader in 1995 but was beaten by Trimble. He is a member of the Apprentice Boys of Derry and was given a peerage in 2001.

David Trimble (1944–) was educated at Bangor Grammar and Queen's University Belfast and qualified as a barrister and lectured in law at Queen's (1968–90) (he was called to the bar in 1969). He was elected as a VUPP Convention member for South Belfast (1975–76) and when he supported Craig over his voluntary coalition idea he became deputy leader of VUPP. After the VUPP dissolved in 1978 he joined the UUP. During the 1980s he was associated with the Ulster Clubs and was Honorary Secretary of the UUP executive. He sought but did not receive the UUP nomination for the 1989 European election but did win the nomination and subsequent by-election for Upper Bann in 1990. Until he became leader in 1995 he was spokesperson on legal and home affairs and was in charge of strand three in the Brooke–Mayhew talks and proposed a Council of the Isles. He became prominent after his involvement with the first Drumcree stand-off in 1995. He was elected to the Northern Ireland Forum (1996–98) and the Northern Ireland Assembly (1998–) for Upper Bann. He became First Minister of

Northern Ireland in 1999 and received the Nobel peace prize jointly with John Hume in 1999.

Jeffrey Donaldson (1962–) was educated at Kilkeel High School and Castlereagh College. He qualified with a Financial Planning Certificate from the Chartered Insurance Institute and was a partner in a financial services/estate agency practice (1986–97). He was a member of the UDR, a chairman of the Ulster Young Unionist Council, an election agent for Enoch Powell and a personal assistant to Molyneaux (1984–85). He was elected in a by-election for the 1982–86 Assembly for South Down in 1985. He was elected MP for Lagan Valley in 1997 and to the Northern Ireland Forum (1996–98). He has been an Honorary Secretary of the UUC from 1988 to the present and was an unsuccessful contender for 1989 European nomination. He walked out of the 1998 talks in the final week and has since been critical of the process and the leadership. He was suspended from the party in June 2003 after he lost a motion at a special meeting of the UUC and then resigned the party whip in Westminster.

INDEX

Index

Index

Index

Index

Index

Index